Critical Elections

Critical Elections

British Parties and Voters
in Long-term Perspective

edited by
Geoffrey Evans and Pippa Norris

SAGE Publications
London • Thousand Oaks • New Delhi

SAGE Publications Ltd
6 Bonhill Street
London EC2A 4PU

SAGE Publications Inc.
2455 Teller Road
Thousand Oaks, California 91320

SAGE Publications India Pvt Ltd
32, M-Block Market
Greater Kailash-I
New Delhi 110 048

British Cataloguing in Publication Data

A catalogue record for this book is available from the British Library

ISBN 0-7619-6019-8
ISBN 0-7619-6020-1 (pbk)

Library of Congress catalog card number available

Typeset by Anneset, Weston-super-Mare, Somerset
Printed and bound in Great Britain by Athenaeum Press, Gateshead

Contents

List of Figures

List of Tables

Preface

In common with most large-scale projects this book has incurred many debts – intellectual, administrative and financial – upon the way. The British Election Study 1997 was conducted by the Centre for Research into Elections and Social Trends (CREST). CREST is an ESRC Research Centre linking Social and Community Planning Research (SCPR) and Nuffield College, Oxford, in conjunction with Pippa Norris (Harvard University). The 1997 British Election Cross-section Survey was funded by the Economic and Social Research Council (ESRC Grant Number H552/255/003) and the Gatsby Charitable Foundation, one of the Sainsbury Family Charitable Trusts. The survey was directed by Anthony Heath, Roger Jowell, John Curtice and Pippa Norris and it would not have been possible without the help of Geoffrey Evans and Bridget Taylor at Nuffield College, Katarina Thomson, Lindsay Brook and Alison Park at SCPR, and Ann Mair at Strathclyde University. The book also draws on the 1997 Ethnic Minority Survey conducted by CREST with Shamit Saggar (Queen Mary and Westfield College, London) with funding from the ESRC (R000 222 123) and the Commission for Racial Equality. Similarly chapters utilize the 1997 Scottish Election Study conducted by CREST in collaboration with David McCrone (University of Edinburgh) and colleagues, funded by the ESRC (H552/225/004), and the British Representation Study 1997, conducted by Pippa Norris and colleagues, administered by the University of East Anglia, and funded by the Nuffield Foundation. We would also like to thank all the fieldwork interviewers and all the respondents who co-operated with the 1997 survey, and indeed to all the directors of the series of BES studies, one of the longest continuous series of post-election studies available anywhere in the world. Details about the BES series, and in particular the related studies carried out in 1997, are provided in the Technical Appendix.

We would also like to acknowledge the assistance of Mandy Roberts at Nuffield College with preparation of the final manuscript and support from colleagues at the Joan Shorenstein Center on the Press, Politics and Public Policy, Kennedy School of Government. This book is a companion volume to three closely related studies focusing on different aspects of electoral change: *On Message: Communicating the Campaign* by Pippa Norris, John Curtice, David Sanders, Margaret Scammell and Holli Semetko (London: Sage, 1999), *The Scottish Electorate* by Alice Brown, David McCrone, Lindsay Paterson and Paula Surridge (London: Macmillan, 1998) and *New Labour and the Future of the Left* by Anthony

Heath *et al.* (Oxford: Oxford University Press, forthcoming).

Lastly our intellectual debts are many and varied. We would particularly like to acknowledge the support of Jean Blondel, the members of ESRC's Election Study Management Advisory Committee (ESMAC) and all colleagues involved in the consultative process for the design of the 1997 BES. We greatly appreciated the stimulus and critical advice we received from colleagues who attended the book conference in May 1997, the generous hospitality of the Warden and Fellows of Nuffield College, Oxford, and the financial support of Sage Publications. As well as the contributors, the conference included Ron Amman (ESRC), Ole Borre (Aarhus University), David Butler (Exeter College, Oxford), Bruno Cautres (Maison Francaise), Sir David Cox (Nuffield College, Oxford), Stephen Fisher (Nuffield College, Oxford), Ron Johnston (University of Bristol), Richard Johnston (University of British Columbia), Peter Kellner (*The Observer/Evening Standard*), Anthony King (University of Essex), Peter Lynn (SCPR/CREST), Iain McLean (Nuffield College, Oxford), Nelson Polsby (University of California, Berkeley), Byron Shafer (Nuffield College, Oxford), Stephen Struthers (ESRC), Marc Swyngedouw (Leuven), Dafydd Trystan (University of Wales, Aberystwyth), Alan Ware (Worcester College, Oxford) and Richard Wyn Jones (University of Wales, Aberystwyth). We greatly benefited from all the comments and feedback generated by colleagues at the meeting. Lastly the book is dedicated to two remarkable colleagues without whom the BES series would not have existed. Donald E. Stokes pioneered the behavioural study of voting and elections in the USA and, with David Butler, initiated and maintained the BES surveys from 1963 to 1970. Bo Särlvik inherited this mantle, along with colleagues at Essex University, when the BES transferred there for the three general elections from 1974 to 1979. This book is a memorial to their legacy.

November 1998
Harvard University, Cambridge, MA, and Nuffield College, Oxford.

Notes on Contributors

Alice Brown is Professor of Politics at the University of Edinburgh. Her research interests include Scottish politics, women and politics and economic policy. She is co-author with David McCrone and Lindsay Paterson of *Politics and Society in Scotland* (1998) and co-author with David McCrone, Lindsay Paterson and Paula Surridge of *The Scottish Electorate* (1998). She is Co-Director with David McCrone of the Governance of Scotland Forum at the University of Edinburgh; and a member of the Scottish Office cross-party consultative steering group which will report to the Secretary of State for Scotland on the standing orders and procedures for the new Scottish Parliament.

Ian Budge is Professor of Politics at the University of Essex. His books include *Voting and Party Competition* (1977) [with Dennis Farlie]; *Ideology Strategy and Party Change* (1987) [co-edited with David Robertson and Derek Hearl]; *Parties, Policies and Democracy* (1994) [with Hans-Dieter Klingemann and Richard Hofferbert]; and *The New British Politics* (1998) [with Ivor Crewe, David McKay and Ken Newton].

Ivor Crewe is Vice Chancellor and Professor of Government at the University of Essex. He was Co-Director of the British Election Study programme from 1973 to 1981. Recent publications include *The British Electorate 1963–1992* (1995) [with Anthony Fox and Neil Day]; *SDP: The Birth, Life and Death of the Social Democratic Party 1981–1987* (1995) [with Anthony King]; *The New British Politics* (1998) [with Ian Budge, David McKay and Kenneth Newton]; and *Political Communications: Why Labour Won the 1997 Election* (1998) [co-edited with John Bartle and Brian Gosschalk]. His current research interests are the impact of party leader images on the vote and the politics of higher education in Britain.

John Curtice is Deputy Director of CREST, and Professor of Politics and Director of the Social Statistics Laboratory at the University of Strathclyde. His publications include *How Britain Votes* (1985, with Anthony Heath and Roger Jowell); *Understanding Political Change* (1991, with Anthony Heath and others); *Labour's Last Chance?* (1994, co-edited) and *On Message* (1999, with Pippa Norris and others). He has been a co-editor of SCPR's *British Social Attitudes* series since 1994 and is a regular consultant and commentator on electoral matters for the media.

Geoffrey Evans is Faculty Fellow, Nuffield College. He has been a member of the British Election Studies team since 1987 and is a consultant with CREST. He is the author of many articles on electoral behaviour, political sociology and democratization. Other publications include *Understanding Political Change* (1991, with CREST colleagues) and *The End of Class Politics?* (forthcoming). He is currently completing *The Formation of Political Cleavages in Post-Communist Democracies* (with Stephen Whitefield; forthcoming).

David M. Farrell is Senior Jean Monnet Lecturer in European Politics at the University of Manchester. Co-editor of *Party Politics*, his recent books include *Comparing Electoral Systems* (1998) and *Party Discipline and Parliamentary Government* (co-editor, 1999). Dr Farrell has published widely on parties, campaigning and electoral systems.

Mark Franklin is the John R. Reitemeyer Professor of Political Science at Trinity College, Hartford, Connecticut. He was previously Moores Professor at the University of Houston after having spent 20 years at the University of Strathclyde. He is the author of *The Decline of Class Voting in Britain* (1985) and co-author of *Electoral Change* (1992). His recent publications include *Choosing Europe? The European Electorate and National Politics in the Face of Union* (1996) [with Cees van der Eijk and others] and articles about voting in European elections, referendum votes and turnout in national elections around the world.

Anthony Heath is Professor of Sociology at the University of Oxford, Official Fellow of Nuffield College, Oxford, and Co-Director of CREST. His publications include *How Britain Votes* (1985, with Roger Jowell and John Curtice); *Understanding Political Change* (1991, with CREST colleagues); and *Labour's Last Chance*, (1994, co-edited), along with recent articles in journals such as the *American Journal of Sociology*, the *British Journal of Political Science* and the *Journal of the Royal Statistical Society*.

Christina Hughes is a doctoral candidate at the University of Houston. Her main areas of interest are comparative voting behaviour and comparative parties. She plans to write her dissertation about the effects of social cross-pressures on voting behavior using a cross-national analysis in order to control for institutional effects.

David McCrone is Professor of Sociology, and Convener of the Unit for the Study of Government in Scotland. He is also Co-Director, with Alice Brown, of the University of Edinburgh's Governance of Scotland Forum. Recent books include *The Scottish Electorate* (1998); *The Sociology of Nationalism* (1998); *Politics and Society in Scotland* (1998) [with Alice Brown and Lindsay Paterson]; *Scotland – the Brand: The Making of Scottish Heritage* (1995); and *Understanding Scotland: The Sociology of a*

Stateless Nation (1992). He is Co-Director of the ESRC-funded Scottish Election Study 1997. David McCrone is a member of the expert panel on procedures and standing orders for the Scottish Parliament.

Pippa Norris is Associate Director (Research) at the Shorenstein Center on the Press, Politics and Public Policy at the Kennedy School of Government, Harvard University. Recent books include *On Message* (1999, with John Curtice, David Sanders, Margaret Scammell and Holli Semetko); *Critical Citizens* (1999); *Elections and Voting Behaviour* (1998); *Britain Votes 1997* (1997); and *Electoral Change Since 1945* (1997). She was Co-Director of the 1997 British Election Study and co-edits *The Harvard International Journal of Press/Politics*.

Alison Park is a Research Director at Social and Community Planning Research and a co-editor of the *British Social Attitudes Report* series. She worked on the 1997 British Election Study and the 1997 Scottish and Welsh Referendum Studies. Recent publications include 'Thatcher's children?' in the *14th British Social Attitudes Report* (1997, with Anthony Heath); 'Teenagers and their politics' (1995) in the *12th British Social Attitudes Report*; and *Young People, Politics and Citizenship: A Disengaged Generation* (1998, with Roger Jowell).

Lindsay Paterson is Professor of Educational Policy at Edinburgh University. He has published on many aspects of Scottish politics and the sociology of education. His books include *A Diverse Assembly: The Debate on a Scottish Parliament* (1998) and *The Autonomy of Modern Scotland* (1994). He is Vice-Convener of the Unit for the Study of Government in Scotland, and edits its quarterly journal, *Scottish Affairs*.

Clive Payne is Director of the Computing and Research Support Unit, Social Studies Faculty, University of Oxford and a Fellow of Nuffield College, Oxford. He has published widely on statistical modelling in sociology, politics and social policy. He has been a consultant to the BBC on election-night forecasting since 1969. He is co-editor of *Statistics in Society*, a journal of the Royal Statistical Society.

Shamit Saggar is Senior Lecturer in Government at Queen Mary and Westfield College. His books include *Race and Public Policy* (1991); *Race and Politics in Britain* (1992); *Race and British Electoral Politics* (1998); and *Race and Representation* (forthcoming). Dr Saggar was the Director of the 1997 British Ethnic Minority Election Study. He is currently preparing a major intellectual history of racial politics in Britain and the USA.

David Sanders is Professor of Government and Pro-Vice-Chancellor (Research) at the University of Essex. He has recently published articles on electoral forecasting and outcomes in *Political Studies, Electoral Studies, Political Quarterly, Parliamentary Affairs* and numerous edited volumes. He is co-editor of the *British Journal of Political Science*. He is co-author of *On Message* (1999 with Pippa Norris, John Curtice, Margaret Scammell and Holli Semetko).

Paula Surridge is Lecturer in Sociology at the University of Salford. She is currently Co-Director of the 1997 Scottish Election Study and was research assistant on the 1992 study. Her research interests are in political behaviour and stratification. Recent publications include *The Scottish Electorate* (1998) [with Alice Brown, David McCrone and Lindsay Paterson] and, with David McCrone, 'National pride' in Roger Jowell *et al.* (eds.) *British and European Social Attitudes: How Britain Differs.*

Bridget Taylor is a Research Officer in CREST at Nuffield College, Oxford. Her publications include *Scotland and Wales: Nations Again?* (1999 co-edited with Katarina Thompson), *Understanding Change in Social Attitudes* (1996, co-edited with Katarina Thomson) and *Labour's Last Chance?* (1994, co-edited with CREST colleagues).

Katarina Thomson is a Research Director at Social and Community Planning Research and a co-editor of the *British Social Attitudes Report* series. She worked on the 1997 British Election Study and the 1997 Scottish and Welsh Referendum Studies. Recent publications include 'Portraying sex: the limits of tolerance' (1996) and 'How we view violence' (1997) [both with Steven Barnett] in the *13th* and *14th British Social Attitudes Reports*, and *Understanding Change in Social Attitudes* (1996, co-edited with Bridget Taylor).

Paul Webb is a Senior Lecturer in Government at Brunel University and a former Visiting Fellow in Social Sciences at Curtin University in Western Australia. The review editor of *Party Politics*, he is the author of *Trade Unions and the British Electorate* (1992) as well as numerous articles and chapters on British and European parties. He is currently writing a book on British political parties for Sage Publications and editing a comparative volume on parties in democratic societies for Oxford University Press.

Introduction: Understanding Electoral Change

Pippa Norris and Geoffrey Evans

As Tony Blair passed cheering crowds to enter Downing Street on 2 May 1997, accompanied by his wife and young children, many believed that Britain had experienced an election which inaugurated a new political era. Given the size of the Labour landslide in seats, and the sharp reversal in Conservative fortunes after 18 years in power, the 1997 election produced a decisive break in the pattern of parliamentary politics which had dominated Britain under successive Conservative administrations since 1979. The central questions this book addresses is *whether, in what respects and by how much, the 1997 election differs from its predecessors*. If we look critically at the evidence beyond the impression derived from the popular headlines, were there actually new patterns of party competition? New issue alignments? New social alignments? And was the overall outcome the result of a 'critical' realignment representing a decisive watershed in the established pattern of party competition in Britain?

This issue is important, not just for explaining the outcome of this particular election, and the reasons for Labour's victory, but also for understanding the general dynamics of electoral change. The common view that May 1st was critical has been heavily coloured by Labour's return to power after so many years in the wilderness and by the massive landslide of seats. The popular assumption, reflecting democratic theory, is that such a decisive change must rest on the decision of the electorate finally to 'throw the rascals out' due to the government's record on sleaze, their management of the economy and splits over Europe. Many also commonly believe that voters were responding positively to Labour's electoral strategy and ideological appeal. But so far few have looked beyond the outcome to examine the attitudes and values of the electorate and thereby test these assumptions on a systematic basis. To consider these issues this Introduction lays out alternative interpretations of the outcome, describes the core conceptual framework and outlines the plan of the book.

Interpreting the 1997 Election

The Critical Elections Thesis

As the scale of Labour's victory became apparent on election night, Anthony King captured the mood by describing the outcome as equivalent to an asteroid hitting the planet (Cathcart 1997). The headlines concurred, describing the results as a 'Landslide' (*Daily Express* and *The Daily Telegraph*), a 'Massacre' (*Daily Mail*) or 'Buried: The Worst Tory Defeat This Century' (*Evening Standard*). 'Everything has changed', claimed *The Independent*. Commentators commonly argued that the 1997 election represents one of the great political landmarks of the century (Pimlott 1997). In the early hours of the morning after the election, in the heady atmosphere of the South Bank victory rally, Tony Blair made exuberant claims before party workers that a new (metaphorical) dawn had broken:

> Today, on the eve of this new millennium, the British people have ushered in this new era of politics, and the great thing about it is that we have won support in this election from all walks of life, from all classes of people, from every single corner of our country. We are now today the People's Party (Cathcart 1997).

From this perspective, therefore, the 1997 election represents a critical realignment in the established pattern of British party politics, as demonstrated by the succession of historic records toppled and overturned. The clearest evidence rests on Labour's landslide of seats (see Table I.1). The Labour Party, which had not won a general election since October 1974, was returned with almost two-thirds of the House of Commons, 419 MPs (including the Speaker), their highest number ever. The Blair government won a parliamentary majority of 179 seats, the largest for any administration since Baldwin's 1935 coalition and the biggest in Labour history. Labour gained 145 seats, its best sweep since 1945. In total 266 new MPs flooded into the corridors of Westminster including record numbers of women members. Labour not only strengthened its grip in Scotland and

TABLE I.1 *The change in UK seats, 1992–97*

	Actual seats 1992	Notional seats 1992	Gains	Losses	Seats 1 May 1997	Seats 1997
Lab*	271	273	146	0	419	63.6
Con	336	343	0	178	165	25.0
Lib Dem	20	18	30	2	46	7.0
SNP	3	3	3	0	6	.9
PC	4	4	0	0	4	.6
N. Ireland	17	18	4	4	18	2.7
Independent	0	0	1	0	1	.2
Total	651	659	184	184	659	100.0
Overall maj.	Con 21	Con 27			Lab 179	

Note: *Including the Speaker.
Source: Norris (1997c).

Wales but it also re-established itself across large stretches of southern England.

After 18 years in power, the Conservatives experienced an electoral rout. The Conservative Party lost a quarter of its 1992 vote, a third of its Cabinet and over half its seats (178). The Conservative share of the UK vote fell from 41.9% to 30.7%, their worst result since modern party politics began in 1832. As William Hague acknowledged, 'The Conservative party was not merely defeated. It was humiliated'. Reduced to an English rural rump, the Conservatives were obliterated for the first time in Scotland, as well as winning no seats in Wales and most major cities outside London including Sheffield, Bristol and Manchester. Reduced to 165 MPs, the Conservatives had their lowest tally since 1906. The overall Conservative–Labour swing of 10.3% across Britain was the largest since 1945 (see Figure I.1). To regain a bare overall majority in the next election the Conservatives would need a swing more than twice the size of that achieved by Mrs Thatcher in 1979. Labour were not the only ones to benefit from the Conservative demise: the number of Liberal Democrats more than doubled to 46 MPs, representing their best parliamentary result since 1929 (for more details see Norris 1997c).

The Conservative Party was not just defeated badly at the polls, it was left with a deeply damaged organizational machine. Eighteen months later the party was estimated to be saddled with debts to the tune of £11 million, forcing party managers to cut staff at Smith Square by a fifth and to close eight regional offices. One of the first priorities which William Hague implemented was a reorganization of the party structure and an attempt to staunch the demoralized and shrinking membership, estimated to be reduced from 1,000,000 in 1987 down to 400,000 at the time of the

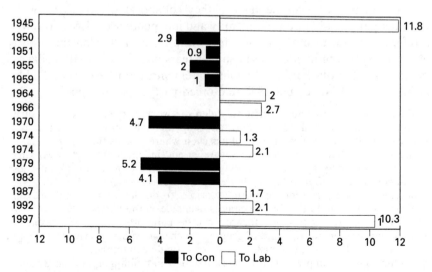

FIGURE I.1   UK *vote, 1945–97: the 'Butler swing'*

1997 election, before plummeting to 300,000 eighteen months later (see Chapter 3). Moreover the Conservative base in local government was also low; after the May 1996 local elections the party was left with only 4,400 councillors, well behind the Liberal Democrats (5,100) and Labour (11,000). In contrast, in May 1979, when Mrs Thatcher first won power, there were 12,143 Conservative local councillors up and down the land.

During the first years of the new Blair administration there is evidence that British party politics continued to realign on the centre-left, with closure of the gap between Labour and the Liberal Democrats. Discussion of parliamentary co-operation, an informal pact or even a Lib–Lab merger was strengthened by appointment of five Liberal Democrats on the Cabinet subcommittee on the Constitution and by the selection of Lord Jenkins to chair the Electoral Reform Commission. Both parties worked closely together with the Joint Consultative Committee on much legislation especially a radical series of government initiatives on constitutional reform, one of the issues closest to the Liberal Democrat agenda. This included devolution for Scotland and Wales, the creation of a directly elected mayor and assembly for London, plans to reform the Lords and the introduction of a Freedom of Information Act, as well as a new constitutional settlement for Northern Ireland. The future party order will be shaped by electoral reform: the additional member system (AMS) for the Scottish Parliament and the Welsh Assembly, closed regional lists for the European elections, the supplementary vote for the mayor and AMS for the assembly in London and, if implemented, by the introduction of the alternative vote for Westminster (http://www.officialdocuments.co.uk/document/cm40/4090/annex-a.htm).

Party conferences in 1998 debated how far these parties could, and should, work together. The Liberal Democrats expressed concern that, like a mouse in bed with an elephant, if they collaborated too closely with Blair the party could lose their identity and independence. Moves towards a referendum on electoral reform for Westminster, following the report of the Jenkins commission, raised similar fears about cross-party collaboration in the Labour Party. But a joint statement by Tony Blair and Paddy Ashdown on 11 November 1998 reinforced party co-operation:

> We believe it is now appropriate to widen the work of the Joint Consultative Committee. This will be an important step in challenging the destructive tribalism that can afflict British politics even where parties find themselves in agreement. Of course we are two sovereign and independent parties working together where we agree and opposing each other where we do not. Our parties will continue to offer different choices to the British people in the ballot box whenever the appropriate opportunity arises. To do otherwise would weaken British politics and diminish the choices available to the voters.
>
> We are confident this step forward can deepen co-operation and result in widening support for the kind of progressive change which we wish to see and to which we believe the British people are strongly committed.
>
> Our aims are simply stated. To work together in building a modern Britain. To create a new, more constructive and rational culture for our national politics.

To ensure the ascendancy of progressive politics in Britain, against a Conservative Party which seems determined to travel further and further to the Right. And to continue the reshaping of British politics for the next century.

The vision implied by the leaders seemed to be nothing less than a new party order at Westminster, persisting for more than one term of office, defined by legislative co-operation on the centre-left and the long-term marginalization of the Conservatives on the right.

Other evidence comes from opinion polls during the early stages of the Labour government where the continued weakness of the Conservative Party, and in contrast the lengthy Labour 'honeymoon', reinforces the popular notion of a decisive shift in party fortunes. Without any major upsets in the early stages, New Labour not only maintained but even increased their support. Polls for MORI reported that average approval for Tony Blair during his first year in office was 67%, well above the average rating during the same period (54%) for occupants of No. 10 since the war. In contrast, William Hague's ratings were among the lowest for any Tory party leader since opinion polls began, on a par with those for Michael Foot. From 1997 to 1998 satisfaction with the government's performance also easily surpassed many of their predecessors at the equivalent stage of office (Atkinson and Mortimore 1998). On 1 May 1997 the Conservatives received 31.4% of the popular vote in Britain, their lowest level since 1832, but five months later Gallup polls reported that Tory support had dropped even further to 22%. By October 1998 Conservative popularity had edged up to 30% and they trailed far behind Labour. The length and size of the Blair honeymoon broke modern records. In contrast, a year after the 1945 Labour landslide the polls suggested that the Conservatives were almost neck and neck. After the Labour victory in 1966 the Tories were comfortably in the lead within a year. Similar patterns are evident in most election cycles. Of course polls can change rapidly. A sudden recession, or unexpected external events, can damage government popularity. But nevertheless faced with these figures, little wonder that many observers, even Mrs Thatcher, believed that there was no chance of Conservatives winning the next election, allowing Labour to consolidate its position in power for at least two terms. William Hague faces a mountain to climb before re-entering the portals of No. 10; he requires a swing of at least 8% to wipe out the Labour lead and a vast swing of 11.6% to achieve a bare parliamentary majority of one seat (Norris 1997: 23).

Sceptical Challenges

Yet after the initial excitement about the new government faded a more sceptical and cautious view emerged to challenge the popular wisdom. A substantial victory for one party, even a landslide which lays the groundwork for more than one term in office, does not in itself constitute the basis for a new party order. There have been many previous false dawns when observers have proclaimed that an election represented a realigned party system, only to find the restoration of the status quo ante in subsequent contests. In the mid-1970s it became fashionable to claim that Britain was becoming a 'multiparty system' (Drucker 1989). The death of the Labour Party was often forecast prematurely in previous studies asking *Can Labour Win?* (Harrop and Shaw 1989) or *Can the Tories Lose?* (Smyth 1991), or even whether Britain was *Turning Japanese?* with the Conservatives permanently in power (Margetts and Smyth 1993). Journalists often make political headlines appear brighter, newer and more exciting than is actually the case. The Blair government hopes to consolidate its grip on power over successive elections. But if we focus on the electorate rather than Parliament, the results of the 1997 election are less dramatic. The more cautious interpretation suggests that 1997 showed considerable continuity with established patterns of party politics among voters. In this view, 1997 represented a secular evolution in party support, following an incremental series of steps in previous elections, but not a critical realignment.

As shown in Table I.2, popular support for Labour and Liberal Democrat was far from record-breaking. Granted, Labour increased their share of the UK vote by 8.9% while Conservative support fell by 11.2%. Nevertheless Labour's share of the UK vote (43.2%) was almost identical to when they lost in 1970 (43.1%), and far less than their peak in 1966 (48.0%) (see Figure I.2). Overall, 13.5 million people voted Labour, fewer than voted Conservative in 1987 or 1992. Due to the more efficient distribution of their support, the Liberal Democrats gained seats despite their share of the vote subsiding from 17.9% to 16.8%, representing a steady erosion in their support for the third successive general election. Moreover during the campaign it was hard to discern signs of enthusiasm in the electorate: compared with 1992, 2.3 million fewer people cast ballot papers. Turnout fell to 71.5%, its lowest point since 1935. Many partici-

TABLE I.2   *The share of the UK vote, 1992–97 (%)*

	1992 UK	1997 UK	Change UK	1997 GB	Standard deviation of GB mean
Con	41.9	30.7	–11.2	31.4	12.20
Lab	34.4	43.3	8.9	44.4	17.90
Lib Dem	17.8	16.8	–1.0	17.2	10.90
SNP	1.8	2.0	.2	2.0	7.60
PC	.5	.5	.0	.5	4.20
Other	3.5	6.8	3.3	4.4	3.70
Turnout	77.7	71.5	–6.2	71.6	5.56
Butler swing				–10.3	

Source: Norris (1997c).

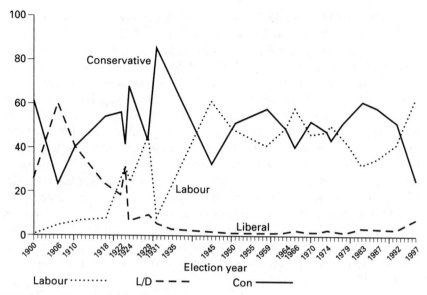

FIGURE I.2   *Seats won at UK general elections,* 1900–97 (%)

pants remarked that the campaign, as opposed to its aftermath, felt dull and predictable.

The dramatic landslide of seats was largely the result of the strong bias against the Conservatives in the British electoral system in the last election. Even with an equal share of the 1997 vote, Labour would still have been 87 seats ahead of the Conservatives. Labour's 43.3% of the UK vote turned into 63.6% of parliamentary seats: a votes:seats ratio of 1.46. The size of the winner's bonus, and the penalty for the main party in second place, were larger than any since the war. This disproportionality was produced by several factors: the geographic distribution of party support; the winner's bonus awarded by the first-past-the-post system; the effects of tactical voting; and continuing disparities in the size of British constituency electorates (Curtice and Steed 1997; Dunleavy and Margetts 1997; Norris 1997).

The more sceptical view therefore emphasizes considerable continuity in the electorate. For commentators such as Butler and Kavanagh (1997), it is too early to say whether 1997 represents a realigning election in which Labour becomes the 'normal' party of government. The Conservatives face a mountain to climb to return to government. Nevertheless, as with previous cycles of party popularity, we might expect the strong anti-Conservative sentiments to pass with time and for Labour's honeymoon to be eroded in the mid-term period (Rose 1997). In a dealigned electorate, sharp swings in support towards one party are possible but equally strong countersurges in subsequent contests remain equally likely.

We therefore set out to examine the evidence for these alternative interpretations of the 1997 election and its consequences for the British party system. Other books have already described the campaigns in the 1997 election (Butler and Kavanagh 1997; Jones 1997; King 1997; Crewe *et al.* 1998) and a companion study has analysed the role of the media in this process (Norris *et al.* 1999). Previous studies have analysed constituency results and the NOP/BBC exit poll (Curtice and Steed 1997; Norris and Gavin 1997). But in order to understand whether the 1997 election was as distinctive as many assume, representing a critical break with the past, we need to be able to compare voting behaviour in long-term historical perspective. This book draws on the rich legacy of more than three decades of data in the British Election Studies (BES), one of the longest time-series survey of voting behaviour in the world. This series of studies have been carried out after each general election since 1964 among a representative cross-sectional sample survey of the electorate in Great Britain (see the Technical Appendix for details). This unique resource allows us to understand voting behaviour in Britain utilizing the series of ten post-election cross-sectional surveys of the electorate from 1964 to 1997.

The Conceptual Framework

As a first step we need to clarify the core concepts and alternative interpretations of secular trends and critical elections which the book explores. We often refer fairly loosely to 'landslide' or 'watershed' elections, but here we need to nail down our common terms. The core focus is upon how far the 1997 election represents a critical discontinuity in the 'party order', understood to refer to the durable structure of party competition in government and the electorate. Party politics are in a state of constant flux, following the fortunes of the latest opinion poll or parliamentary division, but the party order represents the relatively enduring features of British politics which persist across successive elections. Party systems involve patterned, stable and predictable interactions in the competition for seats and votes.

The concept of critical elections has a long pedigree, particularly in American political science which has conventionally divided the party order into distinct eras. The theory of critical elections originated with V.O. Key (1955) and the extensive literature generated by this work has considered the most appropriate conceptual framework, debated the historical periodization of party systems and argued about alternative accounts of realignment, particularly in the USA (Campbell *et al.* 1966; Burnham 1970; Sundquist 1973; Clubb *et al.* 1990). This books develops and expands the traditional framework to classify elections into the categories outlined schematically in Figure I.3.

These categories differ in terms of the magnitude, durability and direction of change and its consequences for party government. Classifying recent elections, without the benefit of hindsight, is often

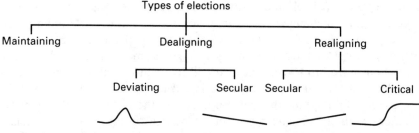

FIGURE I.3   *Analytical typology of elections*

highly problematic. As Chapter 4 points out, in the early 1980s, with the country in deep recession and unemployment soaring, few would have predicted that Conservative government would continue uninterrupted for 18 years. In the past there have been many false dawns of realignments as new parties like the SDP or Greens have temporarily surged at the polls only to fall back in subsequent contests. In the aftermath of the 1992 election many thought Conservatism was invincible (Margetts and Smyth 1993). As with any predictions, we can only provide cautious interpretations of the current political landscape which may, or may not, be borne out by subsequent events. Psephology is far more like a provisional medical diagnosis based on exploratory surgery than the laws of physics. We will only know the full extent of the change in electoral behaviour which occurred in 1997 after subsequent contests either consolidate or reverse the alterations. Nevertheless we can carefully assemble the available evidence to see whether 1997 seems to share some of the characteristics of critical elections in the past, in Britain and elsewhere. In the Introduction we reserve an agnostic position, since each of these models provides plausible hypotheses which can be tested further in subsequent chapters. We give our overall interpretation and summarize the overall evidence in the book's conclusion.

Maintaining Elections

In the classification adopted by this book the essential difference is that maintaining elections reflect the status quo: there are no strong issues, events or major shifts in party policy to deflect voters from their habitual electoral preferences. Each party mobilizes its 'normal base' of support. This concept requires splitting the actual vote cast for a party into two parts: a 'normal' or baseline vote to be expected from a group, based on their behaviour over successive elections in the past, and the current deviation from that norm, due to the immediate circumstances of the specific election. This relies upon the traditional 'Michigan' model, exemplified in Britain by Butler and Stokes (1974), whereby most voters are perceived to be psychologically glued for long periods of time, perhaps for their lifetime, to parties through stable party and social alignments. Maintaining elections are characterized by electoral flux, but not flow, as a few voters shift back and forth between parties leaving the balance of power largely unchanged. In maintaining elections the underlying party order persists largely unaltered so they rarely produce much parliamentary turnover, let alone changes of government. The psychological party bonds are reinforced and overlaid by institutional anchors, such as the electoral system. Many contests in earlier decades were commonly regarded as falling into this category, such as the 1955 and 1959 general elections, with class anchoring voters to parties via the process of socialization, although in an era of dealignment we would expect fewer elections to fit this type.

Clearly at parliamentary level, the sheer size of Labour's landslide, the extent of the Conservative defeat and the rise to power of the new Blair government make it implausible to claim that the 1997 election represented a maintaining contest at Westminster. Nevertheless if the evidence points to considerable continuity in the underlying social and ideological basis of voting behaviour, for example in terms of voting patterns in Scotland, then the 1997 election may legitimately still be regarded as a maintaining election among the electorate in this region (see Chapter 12).

Dealigning Elections

In contrast, under conditions of dealignment the social psychological bonds linking parties and voters loosen. The party order may persist but it becomes destabilized, less predictable and more fluid. Two main subtypes of dealignment can be distinguished, based on the pace and durability of electoral change.

In *deviating elections* particular personalities, issues or events produce a temporary sharp reversal in the 'normal' share of the vote for major parties. Deviating contests are characterized by negative protests against the government, which cause dissatisfied voters to defect temporarily to minor parties, only to return home in subsequent contests. Second-order contests often fall into this category, such as local elections, by-elections and European elections. The model of change can be understood as one of 'impulse-decay' (Carmines and Stimson 1989), or 'trendless fluctuations', where a temporary shift in one election is not maintained in subsequent contests, leaving no permanent imprint on the party system.

During the early 1980s the strong surge of support for the Social Democratic–Liberal Alliance in by-elections, and their record levels of popularity in opinion polls, can be regarded as a short-term deviation in the usual pattern of centre party support (Norris 1990; Crewe and King 1995). The performance of the National Front in the early 1970s or the Green's record vote in the 1989 European elections can similarly be seen as deviating elections, since in contrast to their European counterparts these parties failed to sustain this level of support over successive contests. Flash parties, which suddenly rocket upwards for one election but splutter and fold in subsequent contests, like support for Perot in 1992, have been evident since the mid-1970s in many countries (Ware 1996). The majoritarian electoral system at Westminster acts as a major barrier to such breakthroughs, with a relatively high electoral threshold for minor parties whose support is not spatially concentrated. For the new pattern of party politics to survive there has to be continuity in the issues that evoked the pattern, otherwise the change will prove highly transient. But if the primary factors leading to new parties persist, for example if rising concern about the environment fuels continuing support for the Greens among the younger generation, then the more likely it becomes that socialization processes will reinforce the new pattern.

The 1997 election can be most plausibly regarded as a deviating election if the outcome is interpreted primarily as an expression of negative protest against the 18 years of Conservative rule, prompted by the pervasive problems of sexual and financial sleaze, internal leadership splits and the sense of economic mismanagement which afflicted the Major administration after the 'Black Wednesday' ERM debacle. As one Conservative strategist, Daniel Finkelstein (1998), encapsulated the perceived reasons for Tory failure within Smith Square: 'Rightly or wrongly, they [the public] saw us as arrogant, smug, sleazy, weak, incompetent and divided.' In this sense, as a temporary protest vote, we might expect that dissatisfaction would weaken Conservative support without necessarily strengthening the positive attraction towards Labour on a long-term basis. Others like Tony King (1998: 197) concluded that the Conservatives lost so heavily because of their economic mismanagement, broken promises and because voters no longer trusted them to maintain Britain's social fabric. King argued that disaffection with the government was probably more important than any overwhelming enthusiasm for the Labour Party. If 1997 was 'time for a change' against the Conservative administration then eventually, given the regular swing of the pendulum, we might expect that subsequent elections will prove 'time for a change' against the Labour government. In the words of David Sanders (1997: 73): 'The danger for new Labour is encapsulated in the phrase "easy come, easy go".'

Secular Dealignment

While deviating elections represent a short, sharp shock, a closely related type of contest involves *secular dealignment*, meaning a long-term, incremental and cumulative progressive weakening in party-voter bonds. We would expect more elections today to fall into this pattern if we accept that the process of class dealignment has gradually eroded the structural links anchoring voters to parties in successive elections since the early 1970s, as argued by Särlvik and Crewe (1983), Franklin (1985) and Rose and McAllister (1990). Butler and Stokes (1974) suggest that in the early 1960s most voters were stable in their voting choices due to enduring party loyalties which framed attitudes towards party leaders, policy issues and party images. This stability was the product of a cohesive socialization process which reinforced party alignments within the family, work group and social milieu. Class provided the predominant anchoring mechanism in the electorate reflecting the main cleavage in British party politics, although other social divisions like religion, gender, housing tenure and centre-periphery cleavages left a faint imprint on voting behaviour. Theories of dealignment suggest that from the late 1960s onwards the social psychological bonds of partisan and class identities gradually weakened so that short-term factors became more influential in voting choice.

If the 1997 election provides another step along the continuing path of partisan and social dealignment, then the series of Labour gains over successive elections since 1983 can be understood as contingent phenomena. With a rootless electorate, large swings towards the Conservatives or Labour in any one election can be expected to be replaced, in due course, with equally large swings against them. At the individual level, if voters are politically semi-detached, we would expect to find evidence over successive elections leading up to 1997 of considerable electoral flux, progressive erosion of party loyalties and secular class dealignment. A dealigned electorate increases the importance of contingent factors during the long and short campaign, examined in a companion study (Norris *et al.* 1999), including evaluations of the government's record, the rival attractions of Blair, Major and Ashdown, news headlines about Conservative splits over Europe and sleaze, and campaign debates about issues like taxes and pensions. The defining feature of all dealigning elections is weakening social and psychological bonds between voters and parties, but with secular dealignment the erosion is steady and incremental over a series of contests, whereas with deviating elections the change is more sudden, dramatic and sharp.

Secular Realignments

Alternatively secular realignments are elections characterized by an evolutionary and cumulative *strengthening* in party support over a series of elections. For V.O. Key, the American party system maintained a stable equilibrium for long periods of time: over successive elections the pattern of voting by different regions, counties and social groups was largely predictable. But the party system could change due to secular realignment which produced a gradual shift in the electorate over successive elections, with the more or less continuous creation of new party-voter alignments and the decay of the old (Key 1959). This is a familiar model which gives primacy to broad sociodemographic developments, such as generational turnover in the electorate and migrational movements or socioeconomic trends which gradually produce new generations exposed to different experiences from their parents. Much attention in voting studies has focused on understanding long-term secular trends in postindustrial societies, including the growth of new social cleavages and the process of generational value change which may glacially transform the electorate (Heath *et al.* 1985, 1991; Inglehart 1990, 1997). The secular realignment model produces an incremental, durable and persistent strengthening in the long-term contours of party support.

If 1997 falls into this category, then we would expect to find that Labour's victory rested on trends which gradually developed in an incremental process of recovery in successive elections since 1983. If the outcome can legitimately be regarded as the result of secular realignment then 1997 was 'one more heave' in Labour's efforts to develop a new coalitional base. Such an interpretation would rest on broadened Labour support among non-traditional constituencies for the party, such as among women or younger voters, due to the process of value change in the British electorate. In this regard the outcome would reflect the positive appeal of new Labour's strategy and image, built up under successive leaders, rather than simply a negative rejection of the Major government or contingent support for Tony Blair's leadership.

Critical Elections

Lastly, *critical* elections are defined as *those exceptional contests which produce abrupt, significant and durable realignments in the electorate with major consequences for the long-term party order*. Critical elections have significant consequences, not just for a single administration but also for the dominant policy agenda of successive governments. In this sense the pendulum of party competition ratchets decisively in a new direction. While every contest sees some electoral flux back and forth between parties, lasting transformations of the party order rarely occur. Critical elections are characterized by three inter-related features:

1) Realignments in the *ideological* basis of party competition.
2) Realignments in the *social* basis of party support.
3) Realignments in the *partisan* loyalties of voters.

Ideological realignment involves major changes in the programmatic basis of party competition, for example if new cross-cutting issues and events arise which deeply divide parties and the electorate, or if parties shift rapidly or 'leapfrog' over each other across the ideological spectrum, or if new parties become established in Parliament. *Social realignment* concerns major shifts in the traditional coalitional basis of party support based on structural cleavages such as those of class, gender, race and region. If Labour's strategic appeals have broken party ties with the working class and trade unions, but also forged lasting and persistent links with new social groups, then this would count towards social realignment. Lastly, if these shifts consolidate, we would expect to see realignments in the *partisan loyalties* of voters. Significant change across not one but all three levels provides convincing evidence for a durable and deep-rooted alteration in the party order which is likely to persist for more than one term of office.

V.O. Key (1955: 4) identified critical elections as those '... in which more or less profound readjustments occur in the relations of power within the community, and in which new and durable electoral groupings are formed'. These exceptional contests represent sudden and large breaks in the established social and ideological basis of party competition, with enduring consequences for government and for the public policy agenda. Critical elections move the party system from equilibrium to a new level and then the new level stabilizes and consolidates. The classic exemplar is the 1928–32 New Deal coalition assembled by Roosevelt, returning Democrats in the White House for a quarter century and still evident in faded form today, forging a diverse alliance of conservative, southern Dixiecrats with northern blacks, rust-belt unionized blue-collar workers with mid-western small farmers, and urban Italian and Irish émigrés with liberal Jews (Burnham 1970). The deep economic recession created new political divisions and cross-cutting issue cleavages which subsequently consolidated around fundamentally different visions of the role of government in society. Most elections display secular trends; these remain the norm, but in exceptional circumstances party systems occasionally experience more decisive and abrupt discontinuity.

Borrowing from the natural sciences, the model of change in critical elections is one of punctured equilibrium (Krasner 1993). The party order is maintained for successive elections, due to a process of dynamic equilibrium, before experiencing an external 'shock' which produces a critical break, then settling back into a new period of stasis. The pattern of change is less linear than stepped. Governing parties seek to maintain the status quo, and institutional structures like electoral systems, which reinforce the existing party system, cannot easily be reformed.

Powerful illustrations of this model elsewhere includes regional polarization among Canadian parties following the electoral annihilation of the Progressive Conservatives in 1993; the breakdown of the long-dominant Italian Christian Democrats in 1994 after the end of the Cold War; and the dramatic fragmentation of the two-party system in New Zealand following electoral reform. Other historical examples include the dominance of Gaullism in the Fifth French Republic after 1958, the revival of SDP fortunes in Germany after 1965 and the fragmentation of Danish parties in 1973. In Britain, the 1924 and 1945 contests are widely acknowledged to be watersheds where the party order changed, and changed decisively. These shifts in party fortunes may be the net result of an accumulation of incremental steps, but at the same time certain contests can be regarded as decisive or 'critical' elections, which symbolize a definitive turning point in the established pattern of party politics. The period before, and after, these contests can be regarded, rightly, as distinct eras. The difference between critical and secular realignments relates to the magnitude of the initial step and to its causes. Catalysts for critical realignment include institutional, ideological and social change.

Institutional accounts, which were somewhat neglected in the early

American literature, emphasize the importance of the electoral context for maintaining party systems. Changes to the established rules of the game, such as moving from a majoritarian to a mixed-member electoral system, alter the choices confronting citizens and parties. The mobilization of new voters, notably the tripling in the size of the electorate following the enfranchisement of new working class and older women in 1918, exemplifies such changes (Wald 1983). More modest alterations during the last quarter century include the extension of the franchise to 18–20-year-olds in 1968, the growth in the number of Liberal candidates and the altered tactical situation in many constituencies (Heath *et al.* 1991; Evans *et al.* 1998). The introduction of AMS electoral systems for the Scottish Parliament and the Welsh Assembly are expected to have a major impact on the party order in these regions. New constitutional arrangements have dramatically realigned Northern Ireland parties, with the peace settlement cross-cutting the old Catholic–Protestant cleavage. In May 1997, although the formal rules did not change, the workings of the British electoral system altered with major consequences for the outcome. As mentioned earlier, the overwhelming Labour landslide of seats was largely the result of the strong bias against the Conservatives in the British electoral system. The size of the seats bonus for the party in first place, and the penalty for the main party in second place, were larger than any since the war. Chapter 7 discusses the reasons for this disproportionality and assesses its consequences.

Ideological change provides an alternative catalyst. Accounts of critical elections commonly stress the emergence of new, salient polarizing issues which cross-cut traditional ideological divisions, breaking up and reassembling the familiar landscape of party competition. As V.O. Key (1959: 198) noted, 'Only events with widespread and powerful impact or issues touching deep emotions produce abrupt changes.' Major international wars, widespread ethnic conflict or deep recessions are believed to have the capacity to transform the normal basis of support for the major parties or to allow new parties to gain momentum. In the USA, heated conflict over racial equality and civil rights after 1948 deeply split liberal and conservative Democrats, contributing to Republican resurgence in the South after 1948. In Belgium linguistic cleavages fragmented the party system in the 1970s, in Germany changing value priorities and the rise of environmental concern fuelled the growth of the Greens in the early 1980s (Dalton 1994), while in France racialism and divisions over ethnic minorities encouraged support for le Pen's National Front (Kitschelt 1995). As discussed in Chapter 12, in recent decades nationalism and constitutional issues have transformed party competition in Scotland; a durable realignment in the early 1970s produced a four-party system in marked contrast to England. In the 1997 British election the closure of the traditional left–right gap was dramatic. As Chapter 1 demonstrates, Labour's shift to the centre of the ideological spectrum, flanked by the Conservatives to the right and the Liberal Democrats to the left, transformed the familiar postwar landscape of party politics at Westminster. The impact of traditional left–right issues for Labour support also declined (Chapter 10). This may have led to the rise of Europe as a polarizing and cross-cutting issue on the political agenda, which split the old patterns of left and right in British party politics and clearly deeply divided the Conservative Parliamentary Party. We therefore need to explore the consequences of these ideological changes for the electorate.

Lastly *social* change may occasionally act as catalysts for critical elections, although by their nature demographic factors normally function to produce secular rather than critical realignments. Nevertheless in some circumstances we can identify certain elections where social groups switched partisan allegiances in a shift which subsequently consolidated and persisted in subsequent elections. Exemplars would include the emergence of the modern gender gap in the 1980 election in the USA, and a major change in the basis of the Democratic coalition with significant consequences for subsequent races at every level of government, for patterns of party identification and for the predominant policy agenda.

The literature remains divided about many central features of critical elections and realignment theory. In the USA, disputes continue to revolve around the conceptual framework and the most appropriate historical periodization of the party system, particularly after 1932 (Shafer 1991). For Burnham (1970) and Sundquist (1983) the American party system changed at roughly 30-year intervals, first in 1792, then around 1828, 1860, 1896 and 1932. Yet Bartels (1998) argues that American elections since 1868 show a complex mix of large, medium and small effects rather than a few great peaks separated by broad plateaux reflecting political stasis. For Carmines and Stimson (1989: 21–3) more detailed analysis of each 'critical' election reveals a multiple number of movements before and after, so that the very notion of 'critical' events becomes muddied. Since many central features of realignment theory remain unresolved, some scholars, in frustration, have argued that we should abandon the idea of critical elections altogether, or seriously limit the use of the concept (Shafer 1991). Yet others like Nardulli (1995) have suggested, as we do, that we need to modify, develop and refine the original concept of critical realignment, to provide a more accurate and nuanced account of electoral change.

Therefore in analysing the 1997 election in long-term perspective certain common themes will run through all chapters. In particular, can the election best be understood as one which *maintained* familiar social and ideological patterns of voting in the electorate? Can it be seen as evidence of social and partisan *dealignment* in the British electorate, either a sharp deviating contest or another step along the road of secular dealignment? Can it be viewed as *secular realignment*, with an incremental strengthening of Labour support based on a series of steps which gradually accumulated over successive elections since 1983? Or can 1997 legitimately be regarded as a *'critical' realignment*, as some claimed after the event? We started this book with an agnostic view about the most appropriate interpretation and, after working through the evidence provided by our collaborators, we draw together our conclusions in the final chapter. In considering these questions we are seeking to understand the specific reasons for Labour's victory in 1997, but more generally we are aiming to gain theoretical insights into the capacity of parties and the electorate to change.

Plan of the Book

New Patterns of Party Competition?

To explore these issues this book falls into three sections. Part I focuses on changes in the party system. Scholars conventionally draw a distinction between three distinct levels of analysis: parties-in-the-electorate, parties-as-mass-organizations and parties-in-government (Katz and Mair 1994). The relationship between these different levels may vary. On the one hand, these components may be only loosely connected: party competition may change at one level (for example, a weakening of party identification among the electorate) without necessarily influencing others (for example, the structure of party organizations or the strength of party discipline in Parliament). Alternatively, these levels may be intimately connected: hence Labour's shift centre-left on economic issues may have altered their party image, thereby drawing many more middle-class professionals into the party membership, and perhaps altering the party's traditional working-class base of voting support. In the long term we would expect to find significant interaction between different components.

In Chapter 1, *Ian Budge* explores the pattern of competition among parties-in-government based on content analysis of the party manifestos since 1945. Through systematically comparing official party programmes in the postwar period this chapter considers whether the changes in Labour's manifesto represent a gradual, incremental shift to the centre-left since 1983, or whether the 1997 manifesto can be seen as a radical break with the past. The study concludes that there is some evidence that 1997 was, indeed, distinct from past patterns. In particular, the 1997 Labour Party manifesto represented the most right-wing position they have adopted since the war. Most importantly, in shifting centre-right, Labour actually leapfrogged over the Liberal Democrats, only the second time this has happened since 1945. Under Blair, flanked by the Conservatives on the right and the Liberal Democrats on the left, Labour became the party in the centre of party competition on the traditional economic issues which have always provided the basic left–right division in British politics, as well as on the 'social conservatism' issues. This produced new patterns of competition in party policies, yet the chapter concludes that, based on past patterns, this may not prove a durable change and Labour may drift back towards the left in due course.

Are shifts in official party policy found in the attitudes of MPs? Chapter 2, by *Pippa Norris*, goes on to explore changes in the culture of parliamentary parties. In particular, given that the official policy in the Labour Party shifted towards centre, do Labour politicians reflect this change? This chapter draws on the surveys of over 1,000 politicians in the 1992 and 1997 general elections. The study demonstrates that the parliamentary Labour Party did move towards the centre on many of the classic economic issues, such as on the debate over nationalization v. privatization, and also became more socially conservative. By the time of the 1997 election on the economic issues Labour was close to the median British voter while Conservative politicians were furthest apart. One reason for this is that Conservatives were less accurate than Labour in estimating the position of their voters. Politicians assumed that the public was more right wing than was actually the case. The chapter concludes that the change in the Labour Party may well persist and even be reinforced in subsequent elections, since younger politicians proved significantly more right wing than the older generation.

Chapter 3, by *Paul Webb* and *David Farrell*, explores whether party members have experienced a similar transformation. Conservative Party membership plummeted during the last Parliament from an estimated 780,000 in 1992 to under 350,000 in 1997, falling below Labour for the first time this century (Pinto-Duschinsky 1998). In contrast the same period has seen a remarkable revival of Labour's grassroots party membership, up from 280,000 in 1992 to 405,000 by the time of the 1997 election. These changes in membership have potential implications for party funds, local campaign strength and the pool of candidates available to fight local, regional and general elections. But have they altered the composition of parties, such as the ideology of party members? And has there been a change in the political attitudes and values of party members, reflecting changes in official party policies? To examine these issues this chapter analyses data on party members from the British Election Studies, 1964–97. Webb and Farrell conclude that by 1997 Labour Party members had moved away from the traditional left on issues such as public ownership and the redistribution of wealth. Labour members also became the most pro-European party during this period. In short, there is a convincing body of evidence that the shifts in party competition produced by Labour's move towards the centre from 1992 to 1997 represent more than just packaging and presentation, and instead penetrated to the hearts and minds of the parliamentary and grassroots party.

Critical elections require more than just a shift among élites and some of the most important evidence for a durable change concerns party loyalties among the electorate. In Chapter 4, *Ivor Crewe* and *Katarina Thomson* consider the evidence for patterns of partisan dealignment (representing a loosening of partisan bonds between voters and all parties) or whether there is any indication of partisan realignment in Labour Party support in the last election. Crewe and Thomson found that the 1997 election saw the most dramatic redistribution of party identification since 1964, with a strong shift towards Labour. Moreover this movement was based on positive attraction towards the new party, not merely a negative protest against the Conservative government. The chapter concludes that the 1997 election has some but not all of the characteristics of a realigning election, which offers the Labour government an exceptional opportunity to capture a new generation of semi-detached but favourably inclined young voters.

New Social Alignments?

The evidence for change in competition among parties-in-the-electorate is less well established. Parties may well alter in government and as organizations, but whether the electorate perceives these changes, and whether this perception influences voting behaviour, remains to be established. Subsequent sections go on to consider whether shifts in parliamentary parties have trickled downwards to produce new social and issue alignments among the electorate. If parties change their strategic appeals do voters respond? How far has Labour's shift centre-left altered established patterns of voting behaviour in terms of class, ethnic minorities, major regions and among women? Who participated in the election, and did turnout decline among particular groups in the electorate?

One common claim is that Labour has become a catch-all party in its appeal to different socioeconomic groups. To examine this thesis Chapter 5, by *Geoffrey Evans, Anthony Heath* and *Clive Payne*, summarizes traditional structural theories of social cleavages and then traces the evidence for class dealignment in Britain since 1964. The chapter concludes that class voting in the 1997 election was the lowest it has ever been in the series of BES surveys. The pattern over time in the class–vote relationship is one of a stepped secular decline, with peaks and troughs around a falling level. The chapter considers how far this pattern can be explained by party competition around left-right issues, and whether Labour's movement towards the centre from 1992–97 weakened their appeal to the traditional working class.

Another potentially important cleavage in British politics, although one where we have little systematic evidence in previous studies, concerns race. Chapter 6, by *Shamit Saggar* and *Anthony Heath*, examines the composition of the ethnic minority community and the pattern of party support from 1974 to 1997. The chapter concludes that ethnic minority voters have backed Labour in overwhelming numbers, and this pattern is relatively insulated from short-term trends. In line with past trends, in the 1997 general election four out of five ethnic minority voters supported Labour. Yet the pattern was not wholly uniform, since within the ethnic minority community Asian Indians gave higher than average support to the Conservatives. Heath and Saggar conclude that irrespective of party strategy in Britain during the last quarter century there has been a stable pattern of voter-party alignments by race, rather than any evidence of dealignment or realignment. Although class alignments have weakened, Labour can still count on overwhelming support from ethnic minorities.

Chapter 7, by *John Curtice* and *Alison Park*, summarizes long-term trends in regional voting patterns. The 1997 election was marked by two major changes in the geography of party support. Labour's vote rose, and the Conservatives' vote fell, rather more in the south than north. The evidence points to dealignment in the regional cleavage since the north–south divide peaked in 1987. Moreover in 1997 there was a higher incidence of 'tactical voting' in constituencies which the Conservatives were defending, as voters switched to whichever Labour or Liberal Democrat was best able to defeat the Conservative incumbent. Curtice and Park consider alternative interpretations of these patterns, arguing that the strategies adopted by the parties, and Labour's move to occupy the ideological centre-ground, are the primary explanation. Both these factors had important consequences for the outcome in seats, producing an electoral system in 1997 strongly biased against the Conservative Party.

In Chapter 8, *Pippa Norris* examines patterns in the gender gap in Britain since the war to see whether Labour's strategic appeals to women managed to close their traditional disadvantage among this group. The study found a gradual long-term convergence in the overall size of the gender gap in Britain, indicating gender dealignment. The chapter considers alternative explanations for this pattern based on secular trends in generational turnover, structural explanations and cultural accounts. The chapter concludes that generational differences proved critical: older women remain slightly more Conservative than older men but the pattern was reversed among the younger generation. As a result secular trends of generational replacement seem likely to produce a gradual long-term shift of women towards the Labour Party in future decades.

A final area in which new social alignments may be occurring is considered by *Anthony Heath* and *Bridget Taylor* in Chapter 9, which explores the issues of turnout and abstention. The 1997 election was characterized by the lowest level of turnout since 1935. Many commentators are concerned that certain sectors of the electorate are failing to participate, with implications for the legitimacy of Parliament. Turnout was especially low in safe Labour seats, often in the inner city, and many young people appeared to be particularly apathetic. This chapter looks at trends in turnout to explain who is abstaining, why and whether we have seen long-term changes in the social characteristics of non-voters. Heath and Taylor conclude that the closeness of the 'horse-race' is the major explanation for fluctuations in turnout over time, so that it was the widespread assumption of a comfortable Labour victory in 1997 which produced the fall in participation.

New Issue Alignments?

The first section of the book monitored how far the parliamentary parties moved to the centre-ground in competition over the social and economic agenda. Labour not only tried to move to the middle but they also attempted to redefine the terms of engagement. As Philip Gould (1998: 6) expressed the strategy, 'We wanted to remake the political map by establishing new dividing lines, new prisms through which politics was perceived. Not tax and spend, but save and invest; not private versus public, but partnership between the two'. The question addressed by the last section of the book is how far voters were aware of changes in official party policy, and how far this influenced voting behaviour. In terms of issue alignments, were voters still mainly divided by the postwar economic and social policy cleavages such as taxes and spending, or did 'new' issue cleavages become more salient including those involving national identity such as Europe and devolution? How important were issues in accounting for Labour's victory? And, lastly, how do we assess the outcome?

In Chapter 10, *David Sanders* considers long-term trends in public opinion on the major left–right cleavages concerning the economy and welfare state, and the importance of political ideology for electoral behaviour. Did Labour's catch-all strategy reduce the relevance of ideology for voting choice? Sanders establishes that in 1997 ideology did have far less influence over the electoral decisions of Labour voters than in any previous election since the BES series started in 1964, a development which can plausibly be attributed to Blair's move towards the centre-ground of British politics. At the same time Sanders found that ideological considerations influenced Conservative voting support more in 1997, probably because their vote was condensed to its core.

What of controversial 'new' issues? During the last decade the Conservative Party in Parliament has become deeply divided over Britain's position in the European Union, in particular entry into the European Monetary Union. In a critical election we would expect to see the rise of more controversial issues on the public agenda, and this seems like one of the most plausible candidates. The end of the Cold War meant that, unlike in 1983 and 1987, British defence policy was 'the dog which did not bark' in the election. Debate about Britain's role in Europe received extensive attention in the news media during the long and short campaign (Norris 1997). But did the heated debate about Europe within the parliamentary élite resonate with the public? Did the parliamentary division between Eurosceptics and Europhiles represent a new issue cleavage among the electorate? Chapter 11, by *Geoffrey Evans* considers long-term trends in public opinion towards Europe (where we have a consistent series of items in the BES), the perceived position of the parties on this issue, and assesses the influence of attitudes towards Europe on voting behaviour in the 1997 election.

Constitutional issues may also represent a new issue cleavage between the Conservative government, who favoured maintaining the status quo in Scotland, and all the opposition parties who had shifted into the reform camp in different degrees. In Chapter 12, *Paula Surridge*, *Alice Brown*, *David McCrone* and *Lindsay Paterson* consider long-term trends in attitudes towards constitutional reform in Scotland, analyse how far public opinion can be seen as similar to, or different from, the situation in the mid-1970s and consider the impact of this issue on voting behaviour in 1997. The study concludes that far from representing a 'new' cleavage in Scottish politics, the pattern of public opinion and voting behaviour showed considerable continuity with the past. Although the Conservative MPs were wiped out of Scotland, this was due to the electoral system rather than critical changes in the electorate.

In Chapter 13, *Mark Franklin* and *Christina Hughes* outline a theory of the responsive public, develop an overview of the structure of attitudes in the British electorate, and analyse how the components of voting behaviour have changed in recent decades. The chapter concludes that the issue space of British politics has altered by expanding in terms of 'new' politics compared with the 'old' left–right cleavage.

Finally, the conclusion by *Pippa Norris* and *Geoffrey Evans* draws together the primary findings from these chapters to reflect on their implications for the main themes developed in the book. The conclusion considers the pattern of critical elections in twentieth-century British politics and analyses whether there are plausible grounds and a convincing body of evidence to believe that 1997 can be regarded as a critical election which symbolizes a decisive watershed in British party politics or whether it is more legitimate to regard this contest as the result of secular realignment over a series of elections.

PART I

NEW PATTERNS OF PARTY COMPETITION?

1   Party Policy and Ideology: Reversing the 1950s?

Ian Budge

How 'new' is 'New Labour'? This question is crucial to assessments of the 1997 election. If the party has truly transformed itself then the policy choices put before electors have changed quite radically – precipitating long-term shifts in support and justifying diagnoses of the election as 'critical'. If, on the other hand, the party has simply made a temporary strategic adjustment and will gradually drift back to its old positions over the next decade, then perhaps the 1997 election has to be seen simply as 'deviating'.

The Evidence of the Manifestos

As the Introduction has suggested, three conditions mark out an election as critical:

1) Realignment in the social basis of party support.
2) Realignment in the partisan loyalties of electors.
3) Realignment in the ideological and programmatic basis of party competition.

These conditions are interlinked in the sense that change in one will feed through to the others. If a party starts attracting a new type of supporter (1), leaders may well alter their policies to appeal to them (3), thus precipitating a change in partisan loyalties (2). Conversely parties may initiate the process by altering their policies first (3), thus attracting new social groupings (1) and augmenting their partisan support (2).

This chapter, based on a comparison of the parties' public policy stands in 1997 with what they have said in previous elections, concentrates on condition (3) – ideological and policy change. How far such public shifts have been reflected in the individual attitudes of MPs, members and voters is the concern of three following chapters of Part I. Part II traces out the effects this may have had on social support, while Part III examines how far party policy shifts have been reflected among electors.

An assessment of official policy can be based on the party manifesto or election programme. As is well known, the manifesto takes the shape of a glossy booklet, launched by the leader and other party representatives at a press conference at the beginning of the election, and made available to the public in bookshops (it was also available, in 1997, on the Internet). Manifestos are not widely read by the British public. Their importance is that they are read by the political and media élite and reported intensively in newspapers, TV and radio. Thus their textual emphases set the tone and themes of campaign discussion.

The document does, therefore, represent the way party leaders, after lengthy consideration, want to present themselves to the public. There if anywhere we ought to be able to identify sharp breaks and discontinuities with the past and check the idea that 'New Labour' positions are not those of 'Old Labour'. Incidentally, as the manifesto is the only document regularly issued as an official, all-party statement of policy, it also helps in tracking the evolution of underlying ideology – a point we shall come back to below, as it is vital to the assessment of the 'new' element in Labour as opposed to the 'old'.

Of course the other parties issue manifestos too, in exactly the same way as Labour. Common influences can be seen in the glossy format of all three: prominent cover photographs of the leader and texts edited into snappy sections with headings suitable as sound-bites. We cannot judge what Labour was up to without seeing what Liberals and Conservatives were saying – though the media did not identify radical changes in their policies as they did with Labour.

To see if Labour radically changed position in 1997 we have also to compare what it said in this election with what it said in the past – not just in 1992 but in the whole series of postwar elections. Are its 1997 positions unprecedented or do they find clear parallels in the 1960s and 1970s under Wilson – or even further back, as the title of this chapter suggests?

Analysing a whole series of texts and judging precisely what they tell us about party ideology is a difficult task. Fortunately the British manifestos, along with others from about 30 other democracies, have been coded into a form which makes long time series more manageable, by subjecting them to statistical analysis. The coding focuses on party policy emphases, for 1945–97 inclusive. Categories, developed by the Manifesto Research Group of the European Consortium for Political Research, evolved from members' reading of party documents in each country and their grouping of references into major themes and policy areas. This comprehensive listing of politically relevant policy areas is given in Table 1.1.

For the analysis, each sentence of each document was counted under one, and only one, of these categories. The resulting numerical distribution

TABLE 1.1 *Major policy areas in election manifestos, 1945–97*

101	Foreign special relationships: positive
102	Foreign special relationships: negative
103	Decolonization
104	Military: positive
105	Military: negative
106	Peace
107	Internationalism: positive
108	European Community: positive
109	Internationalism: negative
110	European Community: negative
201	Freedom and domestic human rights
202	Democracy
203	Constitutionalism: positive
204	Constitutionalism: negative
301	Decentralization
302	Centralization
303	Government efficiency
304	Government corruption
305	Government effectiveness and authority
401	Free enterprise
402	Incentives
403	Regulation of capitalism
404	Economic planning
405	Corporatism
406	Protectionism: positive
407	Protectionism: negative
408	Economic goals
409	Keynesian demand management
410	Productivity
411	Technology and infrastructure
412	Controlled economy
413	Nationalization
414	Economic orthodoxy
415	Marxist analysis
416	Anti-growth economy
501	Environmental protection
502	Arts, sports, leisure, media
503	Social justice
504	Social services expansion
505	Social services limitation
506	Education expansion
507	Education limitation
601	National way of life: positive
602	National way of life: negative
603	Traditional morality: positive
604	Traditional morality: negative
605	Law and order
606	National effort and social harmony
607	Multiculturalism: positive
608	Multiculturalism: negative
701	Labour groups: positive
702	Labour groups: negative
703	Agriculture
704	Middle-class and professional groups
705	Minority groups
706	Non-economic demographic groups

of sentences was then percentaged out of the total number of sentences in order to standardize for the varying lengths of the documents. (A comprehensive description of these procedures is given in Budge *et al.* 1987: 15–38, 417–71.)

This set of simple and directly interpretable percentages thus gives us the opportunity to compare each of the 1997 manifestos with the others – and not only with each other but with their predecessors in earlier elections as well. We can track the parties' policy movements, in terms of topics they endorse, in a directly graphical form (Figure 1.1, below). And we can see in detail what particular policy shifts have brought about general convergence or divergence in left-right terms.

Quantitative analysis of these key texts thus gives us an enormously powerful tool with which to judge precisely whether there is anything new in Labour policy positions: and if so, what is it? It thus provides direct evidence, at least in terms of leadership appeals (condition 3), for judging whether the 1997 election was deviating or critical. (For more on this general approach to the analysis of elections through texts, see Robertson 1976; Budge and Farlie 1977; Budge *et al.* 1987.)

Left–Right Movement of the Parties

Tony Blair and his followers were commonly credited with 'seizing the centre-ground' in their pursuit of 'Middle England' in 1997. Moving to the centre implies that there is actually a centre, differentiated from the extremes of 'left' and 'right' along a one-dimensional policy continuum (Figure 1.1). Though this is a bold assumption there are good grounds for making it. Media and party debates do tend in the course of an election to simplify policy alternatives into one over-riding choice between 'left' and 'right'. In 1997, for example, 'more of the same' under Major and the Conservatives – privatization, centralization, social conservatism, sound economic management – was contrasted with the constitutional and legal reforms, social concern (and sound economic management!) promised by Blair and New Labour.

This kind of left–right contrast is not new. One can argue indeed that it has dominated party confrontation throughout the postwar – and even prewar – era. Because of this it can also be traced throughout the post-war manifestos. The only question is how to measure it. Previous research across a number of countries has identified a number of policy stands and emphases as classically 'left wing' and another set as characteristically right wing (Klingemann *et al.* 1994: 38–41). By adding all the percentages of sentences in 'left' categories and subtracting the total from the sum of percentages in 'right' categories, we can create a unified scale going from +100% (all sentences in a manifesto are 'right wing'), to –100% (all sentences in a manifesto are 'left wing') (Table 1.2). More details about the creation of this scale are given in the Appendix at the end of the

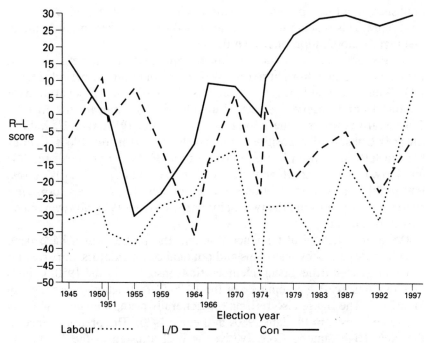

FIGURE 1.1   *British parties' ideological movement on a left–right scale, 1945–97*

chapter. It should be noted here, however, that it is a simple additive measure which sums and subtracts percentages of sentences devoted to certain policies, and is *not* based on factor scores.

Of course, no manifesto makes exclusively 'left' and 'right' wing references – many sentences do not fall under either type, and those that do are mixed in character. However, we can trace the relative leanings of manifestos towards 'left' and 'right', and hence of the party which

TABLE 1.2   *The left–right coding scale*

Codings of manifesto sentences		
Right emphases (sum of %s for)		Left emphases (sum of %s for)
Pro-military		Decolonization
Freedom, human rights		Anti-military
Constitutionalism		Peace
Effective authority		Internationalism
Free enterprise		Democracy
Economic incentives		Regulate capitalism
Anti-protectionism	Minus	Economic planning
Economic orthodoxy		Pro-protectionism
Social services limitation		Controlled economy
National way of life		Nationalization
Traditional morality		Social services expansion
Law and order		Education expansion
Social harmony		Pro-labour

Source: Comparative Manifestos Project Klingemann *et al.* 1994: 40.

published them in a particular election year, by estimating the combined final score. This is generally in the range –40 to +30, reflecting the general ideological moderation of British parties.

On the basis of these calculations we can trace the movement of all British parties, in 'left–right' terms, over the whole postwar period (Figure 1.1). What the graph reveals overall is the initial sharp separation of Labour from Conservatives and Liberals in 1945: movements first by Conservatives towards the Labour position in the 1950s, then by Labour towards Conservative positions (but much less so) in the 1960s. Labour headed leftwards again in the 1970s up to 1983, then rightwards in 1987 and leftwards in 1992. Meanwhile the Conservatives moved fairly consistently rightwards from 1959 onwards. From 1964 the Liberals took up a centre position between the two major parties – from 1974, however, much closer to Labour.

These are ideological tendencies among the parties which have been broadly recognized by historians and political commentators. In particular the emergence of the 'Social Democratic Consensus' in the 1950s chimes in with Conservative acceptance of the 1945–51 restructuring, as shown in Figure 1.1. The figure also reflects the generally acknowledged fracturing of the consensus in the late 1960s and early 1970s. The predominance of the New Right among Conservatives is well attested in the 1980s. The figure helps to fill in details of the parties' ideological progression. But its broad conformity to accepted historical interpretations helps confirm its general validity.

Overall Party Positions in the 1997 Election

The really fascinating question is what the manifesto analysis shows for 1997 in terms of 'left–right' movement. Here there is, from one point of view, a marked change. Labour moves sharply rightwards from 1992 and *for the first time in postwar history shows a preponderance of right-wing positions over left-wing ones* (+8). The Liberals shadow Labour's move but their stance remains more consistent with their positions of the 1970s and 1980s – a left-leaning balance of –6. The Conservatives remain broadly where they were throughout the 1980s at +30 – still relatively far from Labour in a rightward direction.

Labour's move to the centre-right confirms the overwhelming perception that it had moderated its traditional policies for the 1997 election. Indeed the evidence may have a certain value in correcting the more exaggerated depictions of this move. In particular, Labour were far from whole-heartedly endorsing Thatcherite positions. A fair amount of 'clear blue water' still separated the Conservative position from their own. Nevertheless compared with the Liberal Democrats, Labour moved rightwards and 'leapfrogged' over them for only the second time in the postwar period. In relative terms, *Labour became the most centrist party.*

Looking over the postwar period as a whole, the closest parallel to the 1997 position of Labour and the Conservatives is 1955. But the moves of that year are reversed. Then the Conservatives came close to Labour's positions on welfare and government intervention, implicitly accepting the reforms of the 1945–51 Attlee governments as *un fait accompli* which they promised not to reverse. In 1997 Labour moved closer to the Conservatives by accepting the reforms of the 1979–90 Thatcher governments. In both 1955 and 1997 the party which had carried through the restructuring maintained its fairly extreme ideological position – perhaps in the belief that its victory in the ideological debate was enough to ensure electoral victory. If this was so it proved fallacious on both occasions, when the more adaptable challenger gained the plurality.

What does this tell us about the likely course of future events? Will 1997 be an ideologically deviating election or 'critical' in marking the start of a sustained ideological convergence between Labour and Conservatives – perhaps even the 'end of ideology' in the sense of classical 'left–right' differences at any rate being eliminated?

If we believe in the parallel with 1955 – or even review the whole pattern of postwar party movements – we would be wise to reject any such apocalyptic interpretation of the last election. In historical perspective it seems more like business as usual. Having failed to make a breakthrough with a leftwards shift in 1992 (the 'War of Jennifer's Ear'), Labour tried out a rightward shift in 1997, as in 1987. Having lost in that year, however, it made its change stronger and more marked – following the Conservative precedent of 1955.

Their change of policy did not prevent the Conservatives moving steadily rightwards in the elections subsequent to 1955, however. Indeed they hardly stopped until they reached the extreme Thatcherite positions of the 1980s. Labour's socially orientated stances such as 'welfare to work' – and even more its increasingly interventionist and pro-welfare rhetoric in the year after it took office – provide evidence of a shift back to more traditional positions. Having demonstrated that the country is safe in their hands they can, like the Conservatives earlier, begin a cautious trek back to their ideological home.

1997 in Comparative Perspective

Judgements on this point can be reinforced by comparisons with other elections, both in Britain and abroad. The clearest case of a critical election in postwar history is the 1945 general election, where Labour's landslide victory changed the whole face of later politics. Unfortunately we do not have exactly comparable information with which to chart ideological changes between 1935 and 1945 – prewar manifestos have been coded slightly differently so our measures are also slightly different.

What evidence we do have shows that Labour had a very left-wing position in 1935 and moved quite substantially to the right in 1945. As its earlier position had been so very far to the left, however, this still gave it a clearly Leftist position in 1945 (see Figure 1.1). As the Conservatives had also moved slightly rightwards between 1935 and 1945, this still left a considerable policy gap between the parties (Budge and Farlie 1977: 425).

In this last respect 1997 resembles 1945. In 1997, however, Labour took up a centre-right position which shows no parallel with the solidly leftist position of 1945. On balance it seems likely that Labour appealed to electors in 1945 because it offered a radical alternative to prewar policies rather than that it had watered down this alternative somewhat since 1935. From this point of view the important thing about 1997 would be the continuing gap between Labour and Conservatives (see also Chapter 2, Table 2.2), rather than Labour's own move to the right.

A comparison with critical elections abroad may also cast light on 1997 in Britain. The most dramatic example of policy change is the famous renunciation of Marxism by the German Social Democrats at their Bad Godesburg conference of 1959. This was credited with improving their electoral performance throughout the 1960s until it eventually surpassed that of the rival Christian Democrats in 1972. In the mean time their growing electoral strength had secured a government coalition with the Christians in 1966 and the Free Democrats in 1969, ending their exclusion from government since the end of the war.

Arguably all the 1960s elections were critical for the German parties. Figure 1.2 describes their left–right movements over the period. The rightward shift of the SPD (Social Democrats) is quite marked from 1957 through to 1965. By 1969 and 1972, however – the year of their greatest

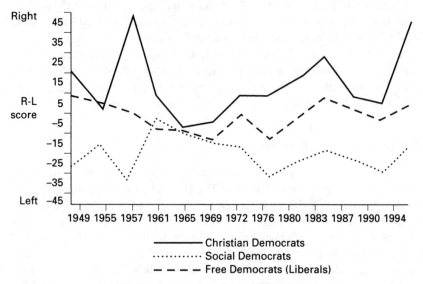

FIGURE 1.2 *German parties' ideological movement on a left–right scale, 1949–94*

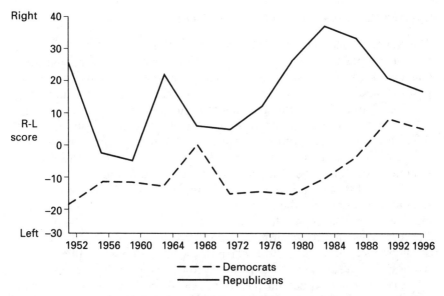

FIGURE 1.2   US *parties' ideological movement on a left–right scale,* 1952–96

electoral success – they had moved left again. By 1983 they had returned as far left as they had been in 1953, before Bad Godesburg. This seems to indicate that parties have a tendency to drift back to their ideological home however much they may move from it in light of particular electoral considerations.

A more immediate influence on Tony Blair's 1997 strategy may, however, have been his transatlantic exemplar Bill Clinton, whose dramatic shift to the right in 1992 was credited with outflanking the Republicans and securing the Presidency for the Democrats after 20 years of Republican near-hegemony. Figure 1.3 (constructed in the same way as the two previous ones on the basis of the policy 'platforms' issued by the parties) shows how Clinton made a quite dramatic move to the right in 1992 from a Democratic position that had been solidly left-leaning over the postwar period. This resembles Labour's shift in 1997 better than either the 'Bad Godesburg' switch or Labour's movements in 1945. Reinforcing the similarity is the fact that the Republicans were so far to the right that there was still a considerable difference between the parties, despite Clinton's move to right-centre. Little changed in the 1996 election, where both parties were some but not much more left.

Few people, however, have claimed that 1992 was a critical election, despite Democratic change and success. The similarity of Clinton's move to Blair's might make us look at the British 1997 election too as a strategic victory but not a critical change. It also strengthens the conjecture that New Labour, like the New Democrats, will gradually drift back to its natural ideological roots as circumstances permit – in terms at least of the broad overall position it takes.

Specific Party Positions in the 1997 Election

This general conclusion can, however, be usefully fleshed out by asking how the parties stood on particular issues in the election. Looking at these enables us to ask what particular policy changes affected the Labour position, and how these corresponded to or contrasted with other party positions. This is all the more relevant as some quite important policy areas – Europe, for instance – do not enter into the calculation of 'left–right' differences. As party attitudes towards the EU were an important topic of debate in the election, this could alter our judgements both of where Labour stood and of its tendency to change in the future.

Table 1.3 lists the 'top ten' issues in the 1997 manifestos, in terms of sentences counted into the separate categories specified in Table 1.1. The most striking feature of the table is the extent to which Labour and Conservatives emphasize broadly the same range of issues – contrary to usual practice (Table 1.4). Both parties concentrate on government effectiveness in preference to all other topics – possibly because the Conservatives had to defend themselves on sleaze and corruption, while Labour were emphasizing their own credentials to govern. To some extent this also spills over into the 'economic goals' of prosperity and stable growth and the emphasis on technology. All parties stressed law and order to a considerable extent – the Conservatives, reflecting Michael Howard's initiatives as Home Secretary, more than others.

Picking up on opposition issues the Conservatives emphasized the regulation of markets to prevent abuses – but balanced this with references

TABLE 1.3   *'Top ten' issues for major British parties, 1997*

Policy areas	% of sentences in manifesto		
	Conservative	Liberal Democrat	Labour
Government effectiveness and authority	13.4		11.3
Law and order	9.9	5.8	6.9
Economic goals	8.0	5.5	5.8
Regulation of capitalism	5.4		
Technology and infrastructure	5.1	4.5	6.5
Incentives	4.7		
Non-economic groups	4.0	4.8	4.0
Decentralization: positive	4.0	4.5	5.4
European Union: negative	3.9		
European Union: positive		4.5	3.4
Social services expansion		9.5	6.4
Social justice		6.5	5.4
Education expansion	3.4	5.8	3.9
Environmental protection		8.0	

Notes: The entries in the table are percentages of sentences in each party manifesto devoted to the policy areas listed down the side. Percentages are given only for the leading ten issues in each manifesto. Where these do not coincide no entry is given for the party(ies) for which they do not come in the top ten.
Source: Comparative Manifestos Project.

TABLE 1.4 *'Top ten' issues for major British parties, 1945–83*

Issue	Conservative	Labour
Peace		3.2
Internationalism: positive	3.2	3.8
Government efficiency	3.0	
Free enterprise	3.0	
Incentives	3.5	
Economic planning		3.4
Specific economic goals	4.0	3.1
Technology and infrastructure	2.9	
Controlled economy		3.0
Nationalization		3.8
Economic orthodoxy	2.9	
Social justice		5.2
Social services expansion	5.0	7.3
Education expansion	3.4	3.2
Law and order	2.9	
Labour groups		3.0

Notes: The entries are the average percentage of sentences over each major party's manifestos for all elections from 1945 to 1983 inclusive. Percentages are reported only for the ten issues which received most coverage by each party over this period. These can be compared with the leading topics emphasized in the 1997 election in Table 1.3.
Source: Comparative Manifestos Project.

to incentives, lacking in the other manifestos. They even devoted some attention to decentralization, though not in the form of the devolution plans which formed a substantial plank in opposition platforms.

Europe divided Conservatives, with mainly negative references to the EU, from Labour, with mainly positive ones. However, in both cases it was far from the leading topic; Liberals, on the other hand, reaffirmed their traditional support for the European project. Dividing the two main parties more sharply were Labour's commitments to social services expansion and social justice. 'Education, education, education' was relatively little emphasized on either side.

It is the Liberal Democrats who really stand out as distinct. More strongly engaged than Labour on all social matters – their leading emphasis was on the need to extend the social services – they also made the environment their second strongest concern. Their social emphases account for their overall leftward position (–6) in Figure 1.1 – which may have induced Labour supporters to vote for them strategically in key constituencies (Evans *et al.* 1998).

Shifting Postwar Emphases

To get a historical perspective on Conservative and Labour emphases in 1997 we can compare them with average coverage for the period 1945–83 inclusive, reflecting the emphases of 'old Labour' (pre-Kinnock) and, substantially, of 'old Conservatives' (pre-Thatcher).

Here we see a more traditional pattern of contrasts between the parties, mirrored by the fact that they only average four out of ten 'top issues' in common, as compared to seven out of ten in 1997 (Table 1.3). Reflecting changed times, party divisions before 1983 focused more on the general international scene than on Europe. Traditional battle lines were drawn on direct forms of government intervention like nationalization and planning as opposed to incentives, free enterprise and economic orthodoxy. A continuing difference, reflected also in 1997, is Labour's heavier stress on social justice and social services. Support for working-class groups like trade unions has now almost totally disappeared from Labour discourse, in favour of non-economic groups like women.

Change in Major Issues

Focusing on the major underlying issues we can examine graphically how emphases have changed over the whole postwar period up to 1997. We cannot graph all the 57 areas distinguished in Table 1.1 but we can group them into the broader categories shown in the left-hand side of Table 1.5. These groupings cover the broader traditional and contemporary differences between the parties so they are quite adequate for tracing out generally where change is taking place and where there is continuity with the earlier postwar period.

Of course, even the grouped topics in the table are still 20 in number. We cannot illustrate change in all of them. Selection is aided, however, by various features which render some of the graphs less interesting:

- Some topics attract fairly limited attention except for the odd election (not 1997). These are references to labour and agricultural groups, military expenditures and alliances, and opposition to the establishment.
- Other topics never separate out the parties much, such as productivity and technology – a fairly non-controversial topic. Democracy and freedom figure here – all parties are agreed on these – and indeed education
- Government efficiency was heavily stressed under Mrs Thatcher and, in 1992, as a distinctive feature of Conservatism. Its de-emphasis in 1997 echoes its neglect in earlier periods and does not need to be traced in detail.
- Emphases on 'social justice' generally move in harmony with those on social services expansion so need not be examined separately.

This leaves us with three areas which are taken up in later chapters – Europe (Chapter 11), decentralization (Chapters 7 and 12) and groups, ethnic minorities and women, examined in Chapters 6 and 8, respectively. We can analyse what the parties have said about these topics to see if they are indeed promoting policy changes which touch off a response in the electorate. Change in this sense would indeed mark out 1997 as a critical election.

There are <u>five other policy areas</u> where change is apparent in 1997. They show either a new convergence between parties or continuing and emerging differences. The first four – <u>support for capitalist economics,</u> <u>state intervention, social conservatism and social service expansion</u> –

TABLE 1.5 *Combination of full policy-coding categories into 20 groupings*

New category		Old categories
State intervention	403	Regulation of capitalism
	404	Economic planning
	406	Protectionism: positive
	412	Controlled economy
	413	Nationalization
Quality of life	501	Environmental protection
	502	Art, sport, leisure and media
Peace and co-operation	103	Decolonization
	105	Military: negative
	106	Peace
	107	Internationalism: positive
Anti-establishment views	204	Constitutionalism: negative
	304	Government corruption
	602	National way of life: negative
	604	Traditional morality: negative
Capitalist economics	401	Free enterprise
	402	Incentives
	407	Protectionism: negative
	414	Economic orthodoxy
	505	Social services limitation
Social conservatism	203	Constitutionalism: positive
	305	Government effectiveness and authority
	601	National way of life: positive
	603	Traditional morality: positive
	605	Law and order
	606	National effort, social harmony
Productivity and technology	410	Productivity
	411	Technology and infrastructure

Detailed coding categories retained intact

	104	Military: positive
	108	European Community: positive
	110	European Community: negative
	201	Freedom and domestic human rights
	202	Democracy
	301	Decentralization: positive
	303	Government efficiency
	503	Social justice
	504	Social services expansion
	506	Education: expansion
	701	Labour groups: positive
	702	Labour groups: negative
	703	Agriculture and farmers
	704	Middle class and professional
	705	Minority groups
	706	Non-economic demographic groups

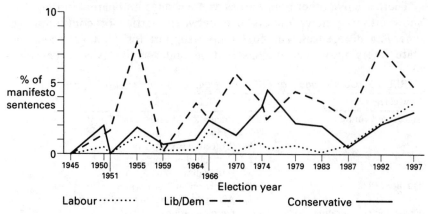

FIGURE 1.4   *Party programmatic emphasis on 'Europe': positive, 1945–97*

relate to the traditional 'left–right' differences already summarized in Figure 1.1. The fifth bears on 'new politics' – the 'quality of life' question emphasized by the Liberals.

Taking up the first group of topics bearing explicitly on Chapters 6–8 and 11 and 12, Figures 1.4–1.8 show trends in party positions on Europe, decentralization and minorities. 'Europe' in fact has two charts, tracing out positive references to the EU (Figure 1.4) and negative ones (Figure 1.5).

Consistently positive reactions are made by the Liberals, overtaken only by the Conservatives in 1974. Labour support for the European project is a phenomenon of the 1990s. As Figure 1.5 reveals, previous Labour emphases have been predominantly hostile, peaking in 1974 and 1979. On the whole the Conservatives refrained from hostile comment until their volte-face of 1997. Clearly the major parties' European positions show sharp changes in 1997, even if they are not their major issues. This forms

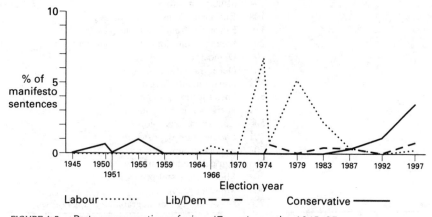

FIGURE 1.5   *Party programmatic emphasis on 'Europe': negative, 1945–97*

a background to Chapter 11's discussion of electoral reactions.

Decentralization was another topic which received attention in 1997, in light of the general discussion over devolution in Scotland and Wales (and of course, London). Figure 1.6 shows that Labour's support in 1997 was not unprecedented – it was in fact substantially exceeded by the attention they gave to the topic (in a different form, of course) in 1970. The Conservatives were also substantially supportive at that time. The Liberals have been most consistent of all the parties in advocating it. Seen against this background decentralization does not seem as new an issue as 'Europe' in the last election. With all parties' acceptance of the regional reforms it has now presumably been taken out of politics.

Minority groups (see Chapters 6 and 8) hardly entered the 1997 election so far as manifestos were concerned. As Figure 1.7 shows, the parties only gave much attention to them in relation to immigration and equal rights in the late 1950s and early 1970s. In 1997 Labour may have been so sure of ethnic voting support that it felt no need to rally it through rhetoric. In regard to gender the unprecedented 'Women's Slate' may have been felt enough to underpin Labour's credentials. Whatever the reason no party took up their cause at this level in 1997.

Turning to the second group of issues in which we have manifesto evidence – those linked to traditional left–right differences – support for pure capitalist economics (Figure 1.8) appears as an area where Conservatives have modified their stand since the heyday of Thatcherism and come closer (not too close) to the Labour position. On state intervention (Figure 1.9) they have actually surpassed Labour in their enthusiasm, for only the second time in the postwar period. Here we perhaps have an example of 'New Conservatism' rather than of 'New Labour'.

FIGURE 1.6   *Party programmatic emphasis on decentralization, 1945–97*

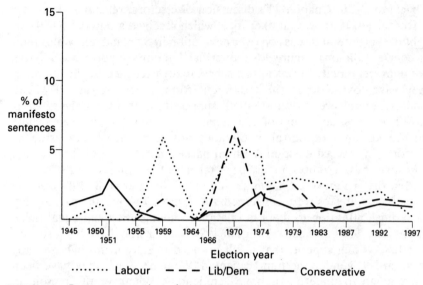

FIGURE 1.7   *Party programmatic emphasis on minority groups (women, ethnic), 1945–97*

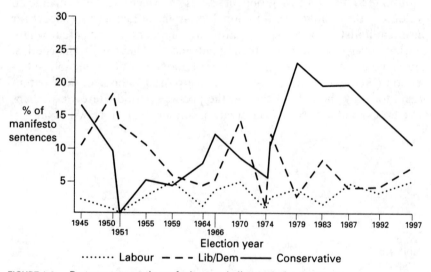

FIGURE 1.8   *Party programmatic emphasis on capitalist economics, 1945–97*

Where Labour and Conservatives have both boosted their engagement, to a dramatic extent, is in the area of social conservatism (Figure 1.10). This includes their leading issues of Table 1.3 – government authority and law and order – so it is no surprise that emphases have gone up. This is the policy area which more than anything else accounts for Labour's rightward shift in 1997.

The heavily moralizing tone of the new government in action, and its strong stances on authority and traditional morality in drugs and work, indicate that this area is quite congenial to a powerful section of the New Labour leadership, including Tony Blair. Such emphases also seem generally popular. So one could expect this stance to continue into subsequent elections, and to be an element of New Conservatism under Hague as well as of New Labour under Blair. Attitudes towards state intervention are much more likely to produce future leftward shifts than social conservatism, which may even demand more intervention in defence of its preferred values.

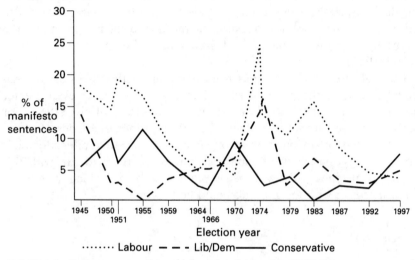

FIGURE 1.9   *Party programmatic emphasis on state intervention, 1945–97*

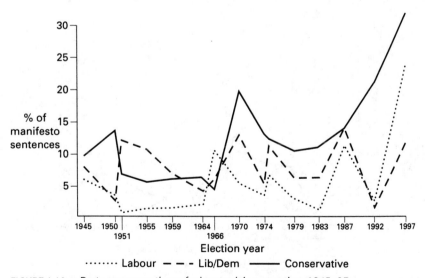

FIGURE 1.10   *Party programmatic emphasis on social conservatism, 1945–97*

Where traditional differences still remain is in support of the social services (Figure 1.11). This is, of course, a traditional 'left–right' difference. However, it is a less consistent one than might be thought. With Conservative acceptance of the 'social democratic consensus' in the 1950s they have on occasion favoured expansion more than Labour. This might be a natural stance for an opposition party critical of government priorities to take during the next few years – which would contribute to blurring major party differences in the next general election.

Economics rather than society thus seem likely to be the battleground for the two major parties in the next election. Both, however, may try to seize on the 'new politics' question of the quality of life, including the environment, on which the Liberals have chiefly distinguished themselves (Figure 1.12).

General attention to this has been going up. With increasing international threats to the natural order, this may well come to even greater popular prominence. It would be an attractive issue as it gives the major parties a cause without tying them into old positions. The Conservatives' uncritical support of business in office, and the negative effects of their privatizations, may, however, make it harder for them to run with this cause. If it does, this will be another policy on which a Labour *rapprochement* with the Liberals could be based.

Conclusions

Most assessments of elections base themselves on only half the evidence – on how voters reacted to parties rather than what the parties themselves were doing. The proper analytic question to ask is how electors reacted

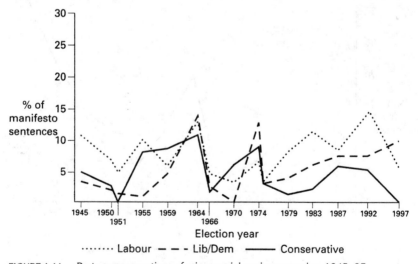

FIGURE 1.11 *Party programmatic emphasis on social services expansion, 1945–97*

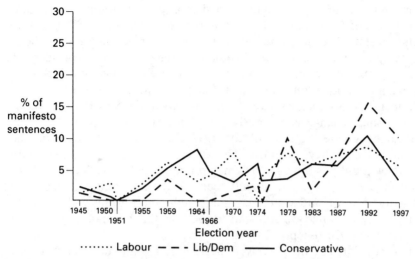

FIGURE 1.12   *Party programmatic emphasis on quality of life, 1945–97*

to the cues parties were sending out, rather than trying to infer indirectly, from electors' responses, what these cues were in the first place.

This imbalance results in large part from a bias in the evidence about elections which is usually examined. Analyses base themselves on survey evidence from the typical large-scale election study, or from polls and macroeconomic data put together to form a time series. From such a perspective political influences usually enter to fill the gaps left by a purely economic explanation. We have a 'Blair' or 'New Labour' effect, for example, because the improving economy does not produce the expected Conservative revival from 1994 onwards.

Analysing the written texts by which leaders try to appeal to voters through the media provides direct evidence on what parties try to do. This provides independent evidence on what the party appeal actually was. With regard to voting reactions it enables us to ask the more interesting question of how voters responded to a particular campaign strategy rather than trying to infer from their responses what the nature of the strategy was in the first place.

What our direct textual analysis of manifestos demonstrates is that at the level of strategy – at any rate for two out of the three national parties involved – 1997 was a maintaining rather than a deviating or critical election. The Conservatives kept, broadly speaking, their Thatcherite right-wing posture, even though they modified some of the individual emphases which go to make this up. The Liberal Democrats held their centre-left position.

It was Labour which deviated – but only from their leftward shift of position in 1992. This had clearly not worked, even in terms of making them credible runners-up after 13 years of Conservative rule. The alternative was to go to the right – to demonstrate that they were safe, dependable and attractive. This had already been tried in 1987, with very limited results. The only alternative was to go further, and more whole-heartedly, along the same road. The new strategy worked, to considerable effect. As the continuing commitment to welfare demonstrates it did not involve a total abandonment of Old Labour positions, however.

In light of our comparisons Labour certainly looks New but not wholly so. And some change is obviously going on in the other parties as well. Indeed the greatest effects of the 1997 election may well be on the Conservative policy position. The electoral losses associated with maintaining old positions in 1997 may prompt a radical rethink for 2002. After the election we have already seen this development with regard to party organization and structure. Undoubtedly the reforms will spread to policy as well, though we still wait to see how far they can go in face of an entrenched Eurosceptical right.

In particular, as the perceived need grows, state intervention may receive more emphasis on the New Labour agenda, while positive refer-ences to capitalist economics may drop away. Ultimately, we are likely to see a slow drift of all the parties towards the left. Labour will probably also begin to pick up on the 'new left' issue of environmentalism. From this perspective 1997 looks more like a deviating election than a critical one – part of the continuing series of party adaptations to changing circumstances mapped out in Figure 1.1 and marked most obviously by the Conservative endorsement of the social democratic consensus in 1955, which Labour in 1997 reversed.

Appendix: The Creation of a Left-Right Scale from Manifesto Emphases

In their analysis of European voting behaviour over the last century, Bartolini and Mair (1990) have pointed out the only universal political division between parties is the left-right one. This conclusion receives support from the factor analyses of election programmes in 20 postwar democracies reported in Budge *et al.* (1987) where the leading dimension in practically all of them was left-right. The factor solutions for each country produced three or four other less important dimen-sions, usually peculiar to that country. A complete specification of national politics thus has to take several dimensions into account. To locate national politics in their general setting however, a one-dimensional, Left-Right analysis is not only sufficient but necessary – in the sense that it is the only dimension not bounded by national idiosyncrasies.

Building on these results a later comparative investigation of election programmes (manifestos) constructed the simple additive scale whose construction is summarized in Table 1.2 (Laver and Budge 1992: 25–30). Essentially the method there was to group the emphases on government intervention, welfare and peace, which left-wing parties put together to make the basis of their appeal, and to contrast these with the emphases on freedom, traditional morality and military alliances which right-wing parties put together. Other issues were examined comparatively to see whether they consistently loaded on the resulting scale. Any that did were added to it. Factor analysis of the programmatic data was also done to see if any second dimension emerged consistently across all countries. None did, leaving the left–right scale used in this chapter the only generalizeable one which enables positions estimated for British parties to be compared across time and across countries – as is done in this chapter.

Although validated by factor analyses, as well as its 'fit' to accepted historical interpretations of British and other national politics, the left–right scale used here is not based on factor scores, which vary sharply with the cases taken into analysis. Instead it is based on simple addition and subtraction of percentages, as described in Table 2.1 and the text. For more detail on its construction see Laver and Budge (1992: 25–30) and Klingemann *et al.* (1994: 38–41).

2 New Politicians? Changes in Party Competition at Westminster

Pippa Norris

The classification used in this book suggests that elections fall into a number of distinct types and each of these can be applied to the level of parliamentary élites as well as to the electorate. In *maintaining* elections there is minimal change in the established pattern of party competition in Parliament, with politicians displaying considerable continuity over time. In *deviating* elections, in a model of 'impulse-decay', there is a temporary shift in the pattern of parliamentary politics and the balance of power in government which fails to maintain itself in subsequent contests. *Secular* realignments among politicians are characterized by a long-term and gradual evolution of parliamentary culture, for example with the gradual decline of working-class MPs and their replacement by middle-class professionals, or with the gradual entry of the baby-boom generation of MPs with different values from their predecessors. In contrast in *critical* elections there is a decisive or 'stepped' break with the past pattern of parliamentary politics – for example if many of the massive influx of New Labour MPs, including many women who entered Westminster in 1997, share a distinctive 'Blairite' agenda. In the US Congress certain mid-term elections – such as the 1974 post-Watergate and the 1994 'Gingrich revolution' – brought in an influx of new members with a radically different agenda from their predecessors. Critical elections are characterized by sharp realignments in the ideological basis of parliamentary parties with consequences, not just for a single administration, but also for the dominant policy agenda of successive governments.

This chapter examines three issues which throw light on critical election theory: first, to establish baseline trends, did the culture and ideology of the Parliamentary Labour Party change decisively, as many assume, from 1992 to 1997? Secondly, what were the consequences of this shift for competition among all major British parties in the 1997 election and, in particular, as a result of this change did Labour politicians move closer than Conservatives to the position of the median British voter? Lastly, does this change at Westminster represent an enduring shift, indicating a critical realignment in party competition? Cohort analysis of generation differences among politicians provides insights into the future of British party politics.

Theoretical Framework

There are many reasons to believe that the attitudes and values of the Parliamentary Labour Party may have changed decisively in recent years. The revival of New Labour since its nadir in 1983 has been well documented in the literature. Under Kinnock, Smith and Blair, Labour modernized the party structure, expanded grassroots membership, regenerated the party image, revised the rhetoric and rewrote the official party platform to replace traditional socialist doctrine with more market-orientated policies (Seyd and Whiteley 1992; Smith and Spear 1992; Rentoul 1995; Sopel 1995; Mandelson and Liddle 1996; Shaw 1994, 1996; Anderson and Mann 1997). The previous chapter has documented Labour's move towards the centre in terms of official party policy. If the 'old politics' division between Labour and the Conservatives over the role of the state in the economy has faded, perhaps Britain may be experiencing the emergence of a new party cleavage around the issue of constitutional reform (*Scottish Affairs* 1998). In the heady aftermath of Blair's sweeping election victory, the conventional view claimed that the Labour party had been turned upside-down: 'By the time the Labour Party was elected to government in May 1997 it had a new constitution, new policies, new internal structure, and a new image' (Seyd 1997: 49). But did it have new politicians? If the changes in official policy were forced by the Labour leadership upon a recalcitrant party, as some suggest, then we might expect to find many backbenchers adhering to traditional socialist principles. On the other hand if 1997 saw the election of a Parliamentary Labour Party which rejected its traditional socialist heritage, embraced the market economy and moved towards the Liberal Democrats on constitutional reform, this represents an important indicator in favour of the critical election thesis. To summarize our conclusions, evidence presented in the first part of this chapter will demonstrate that shifts in official Labour Party policy did indeed reflect backbench attitudes.

This leads to the second issue: what were the implications of changes in Parliament for party competition and for the choices facing voters in the 1997 election? The relative positions of all British parties were altered by Labour's movement towards the centre of the British political landscape, notably the way that Labour's official policies 'leapfrogged' over the Liberal Democrats on the left on many issues. The most common explanation why Labour moved centre-right was the attempt to gain votes. Downsian theory assumes that catch-all parties try to gain popularity and maximize support by moving strategically to the centre of the ideological spectrum. But the success of such an electoralist strategy depends upon the ability of politicians to identify the median position of voters with a fair degree of accuracy. If politicians believe that most voters are further to the left or right than is actually the case then, like a blind man in a shooting gallery, any strategic attempts to gain votes may miss their target. The key question to examine here is whether ideological shifts brought different parties closer towards, or further away, from the actual position of voters. The chapter will demonstrate that on the fundamental economic issues Conservative politicians positioned themselves furthest away from their own voters. One reason for this was that Conservative politicians believed mistakenly that Conservative voters were more right wing on economic issues than was actually the case. This conclusion can throw light on the broader conse-quences of strategic changes for Labour's victory, as well as providing new insights into Downsian theories of electoral competition.

Lastly, if there is solid evidence that New Labour politicians have moved centre-right, does this represent a durable realignment? Of course at present, in the early stages of the Blair administration, it is far too early to be certain. Events like the onset of a deep global economic recession, the outbreak of major international conflict, changes in party leadership, unexpected mid-term defeats or major reforms to the electoral system, could all potentially alter the basis of party competition in subsequent general elections. Chapter 1 suggests that, as in the past, eventually Labour will start to drift left again. One way to analyse the persistence of any change in party competition is to examine the ideological differences between political generations. Socialization theory suggests that political attitudes and values are acquired in early youth and reinforced through a lifetime learning process. Committed politicians are particularly likely to hold well formed, deeply rooted and ideologically structured convic-tions. We demonstrate that younger politicians are more centre-right than older members which suggests that the ideological changes evident in recent years may well be maintained, or even reinforced, in subsequent decades.

To explore these issues we can draw on evidence about the attitudes and values of more than 1,000 politicians in each election (including MPs and parliamentary candidates) based on two surveys. The 1997 British Representation Study (BRS) was a major national survey of parlia-mentary candidates and MPs from all major parties standing in the 1997 British general election. In mid-summer 1996, well before publication of the official manifestos, the BRS-1997 sent a mail survey to 1,628 candi-dates selected by the main British parties (Conservative, Labour, Liberal Democrat, SNP, Plaid Cymru and Green). In total 999 politicians replied, representing a response rate of 61.4%. The survey includes 272 MPs elected into the May 1997 Parliament (or 43% of all British MPs), distributed as a representative cross-section by party (for details see the Technical Appendix at the end of the book and www.ksg.harvard.edu/people/pnorris). The results can be compared with a similar survey, the 1992 British Candidate Study, involving 1,658 politi-cians in the previous election (Norris and Lovenduski 1995). Attitudes among the politicians can be compared with the electorate using the 1997 British Election Study (BES).

Ideological change was monitored by a series of measures. 'Socialist–*laissez-faire*' and 'libertarian–authoritarian' value scales were based on a dozen items with a five-point agree/disagree format, used in the BES and found to form consistent and reliable value scales (Heath *et al.* 1994). The socialist–*laissez-faire* scale tapped the values of equality, collectivism and government intervention. The libertarian–authoritarian items tapped the classic values of tolerance and freedom of expression.

Issue scales, included for the first time in the 1997 BRS, asked politicians to identify their position on six key issues dividing the parties, replicated from the 1997 BES. The 11-point scales measured left–right self-placement, the trade-off between inflation versus unemployment, taxation versus public spending, nationalization versus privatization, integration within the European Union and gender equality. The surveys also included seven standard items established in a long BES time-series measuring attitudes towards public policies, such as spending on the NHS and regulation of trade unions, as well as five items tapping support for constitutional reform. For comparison over time the first section focuses on the attitudes of Labour MPs in 1992 and 1997. Subsequent sections compare the position of politicians and voters from all major British parties in the 1997 election.

Changes within the Culture of the Labour Party, 1992–97

The first question is whether Labour politicians abandoned their traditional socialist principles and policies in 1997. The conventional wisdom in popular commentary suggests a clear dividing line between 'New Labour' (perhaps best personified in members such as Barbara Follett, Harriet Harman and Stephen Twigg) and 'Old Labour' (exemplified possibly by those such as Ken Livingstone, Audrey Wise and Diane Abbott). Nevertheless, beyond a rather vague and oversimple popular distinction between 'Old' and 'New', or 'modernizers' and 'traditionalists' (Heffernan and Marqusee 1992), and analysis of backbench rebellions in previous parliaments (Cowley and Norton 1996), little systematic evidence exists about the contemporary culture of the Parliamentary Labour Party and its critical fault-lines.

Moreover the conventional wisdom about 'New' Labour is open to challenge. Sceptics suggest that the Labour leadership has failed to change the basic ideological commitments of died-in-the-wool Labour backbenchers. This view was echoed during the 1997 election in the Conservative campaign 'New Labour, Old Danger', as well as in coverage in newspapers such as the *Daily Mail* which tried to emphasize that underneath 'New Labour' there remained a hidden 'Old Labour' cadre, the *bête rouge*. Further support for this view came from the elections of left-wingers to the NEC in October 1998. Therefore, is there systematic evidence that the Parliamentary Labour Party did move towards the centre-ground of British politics from 1992 to 1997, in their attitudes as well as in official policy?

Table 2.1 compares support for socialist–*laissez-faire* values among Labour MPs in 1992 and 1997. The results confirm falling endorsement for classic 'Old Politics' articles of faith on three out of six indicators. The principle of state ownership of major public services was supported in 1992 by almost three-quarters of the parliamentary party (70%) but by under half (48%) in 1997. The Parliamentary Labour Party also became significantly less hostile towards private enterprise as the best way to solve Britain's economic problems. Moreover the proportion of Labour MPs who believed that it was the government's responsibility to provide jobs fell from two-thirds to one-half. On two out of the remaining three items there was a modest shift towards the centre but, given the limited number of cases, this proved statistically insignificant. The distribution of support across all the items suggest that the sympathies of the Parliamentary Labour Party remain broadly on the left, but the 1992–97 period saw an important shift towards abandoning Keynesianism and embracing the market economy.

Further evidence of change is provided by attitudes towards a range of social and foreign policy issues which have commonly divided the major parties along the left–right spectrum, including funding of the National Health Service, equal opportunities for women and minorities, and unilateral nuclear disarmament. If we compare the culture of the Parliamentary Labour Party measured in 1992 and 1997, the results provide additional indications of the erosion of the old left (see Table 2.2). By 1997 Labour MPs were significantly less supportive of increased government spending on the NHS, and fewer endorsed cutting defence expenditure, equal opportunities for women and unilateral disarmament.

Contrary to postmaterialist theory (Inglehart 1997), the decline in support for the Old Left politics of state intervention was not accompanied by growing endorsement for New Left values among the Parliamentary Labour Party (see Table 2.3). Instead on most indicators Labour moved away from social liberalism towards a more populist stance, reflecting the findings in Chapter 1 of a parallel increase in social conservatism in official Labour Party policy. From 1992 to 1997 significantly more Labour MPs endorsed censorship to uphold moral standards, while fewer expressed tolerance of political rights for anti-democratic parties. Many more Labour MPs agreed that 'young people today don't have enough respect for traditional values', echoing some of the leadership rhetoric defending traditional family values, responsibility and discipline. The only exception proved to be greater tolerance of homosexuality. This comparison of the Parliamentary Labour Party in 1992 and 1997, as monitored in successive surveys, suggests that the development of New Labour represents more than superficial presentation and packaging. The evidence indicates, if not a wholesale conversion, at least a significant revision of the core values of traditional socialism within the parliamentary party. Support for the 'Old Politics' of Keynesian economic management has declined while there was no countervailing move

TABLE 2.1   *Labour MPs' support for socialist-laissez-faire values, 1992–97*

	1992	1997	Changes	Significance
Ordinary working people get their fair share of the nation's wealth				
Agree strongly	7	6	–1	
Agree	2	1	–2	
Neither	0	0	0	
Disagree	21	31	10	
Disagree strongly	70	63	–8	
There is one law for the rich and one for the poor				
Agree strongly	58	51	–7	
Agree	33	42	9	
Neither	5	2	-3	
Disagree	4	4	0	
Disagree strongly	1	2	2	
There's no need for strong trade unions . . .				
Agree strongly	4	3	0	
Agree	4	5	2	
Neither	2	1	–1	
Disagree	20	21	2	
Disagree strongly	72	69	–2	
Private enterprise is the best way to solve Britain's economic problems				**
Agree strongly	2	2	0	
Agree	4	13	8	
Neither	8	37	20	
Disagree	42	28	–13	
Disagree strongly	33	20	–13	
Major public services should be in state ownership				**
Agree strongly	29	18	–11	
Agree	41	30	–11	
Neither	20	31	11	
Disagree	6	20	14	
Disagree strongly	2	1	0	
It's the government's responsibility to provide jobs . . .				*
Agree strongly	14	11	–3	
Agree	51	39	–12	
Neither	21	28	6	
Disagree	11	22	11	
Disagree strongly	1	1	0	
n.	135	173		
% Parliamentary Labour Party	50	41		

Note: The significance of the mean difference between groups was tested using ANOVA: $p = >.05$; ** = >.01.
Sources: British Candidate Study, 1992; British Representation Study, 1997.

towards the 'New Politics' libertarian and postmaterialist agenda.

If the old cleavage has faded, there is some evidence that a new division in party politics may have arisen around constitutional issues. One of the most important developments in the early stages of the new Blair administration has been the focus on constitutional change. Early legislation on issues such as devolution for Scotland and Wales, the constitutional settlement for Northern Ireland and electoral reform may represent the defining issue of the new government, the equivalent of privatization for Mrs Thatcher. We lack evidence to compare how attitudes towards these issues have changed in the Labour Party since 1992 but we can compare the relative position of politicians in 1997. The BRS included five items tapping responses towards a range of proposals for constitutional reform, including public funding of political parties; establishing a written constitution; replacing the House of Lords with an elected Second Chamber; introducing proportional representation for British elections; and holding a referendum on electoral reform. These items were designed to measure the general attitudes of politicians towards reform, rather than support for specific proposals contained in party manifestos (Norris 1998).

Labour MPs strongly supported the reform agenda, with nearly all favouring a new Second Chamber replacing the Lords, public funding of parties and the establishment of a written constitution, and the majority supporting a referendum on electoral reform (see Table 2.4). Only the introduction of PR found Labour MPs evenly split for and against. The other striking finding of this analysis is how far constitutional reform deeply divides Conservatives from other politicians. In the past it was often assumed that the left–right economic cleavage on issues such as privatization and government spending represented the basic and most enduring cleavage in British party politics, one which polarized in the early 1980s under Thatcherism. During the postwar period the manifestos of the major parties shared a broad consensus on most constitutional issues. As Chapter 1 shows, based on the content analysis of their manifestos the major parties became more divided on these issues in the early 1970s, due to Labour's shift towards devolution, but differences remained much smaller than the cleavage over the economy (see Norris 1997: 151–77). Yet in terms of MPs' attitudes, a gulf has opened on these issues between the Conservatives, who opt for preserving the status quo, and other politicians in the reform camp.

The Consequences for Party Competition

What were the consequences of Labour's move towards the centre for party competition at Westminster and for the choices facing voters in the 1997 election? To explore this we can start by comparing the relative distance or proximity of politicians in each party on the socialist–*laissez-faire* and the libertarian–authoritarian scales. The results in Table 2.5

TABLE 2.2   *Labour MPs' attitudes towards policy issues, 1992–97*

	1992	1997	Change	Significance
Government should put more money into the NHS				**
Definitely should	96	65	–31	
Probably should	4	33	30	
Doesn't matter either way		1	1	
Probably shouldn't		1	1	
Definitely shouldn't				
Government should introduce stricter laws to regulate unions				
Definitely should	1	0	–1	
Probably should	1	1	0	
Doesn't matter either way	2	4	1	
Probably shouldn't	17	15	–2	
Definitely shouldn't	78	81	3	
Government should spend less on defence				*
Definitely should	54	32	–22	
Probably should	34	48	14	
Doesn't matter either way	1	6	5	
Probably shouldn't	9	12	3	
Definitely shouldn't	2	2	–1	
Attempts to give equal opportunities to women				**
Gone much too far	0	0	0	
Gone too far	1	0	–1	
About right	4	14	10	
Not gone far enough	45	60	14	
Not gone nearly far enough	50	25	–26	
Attempts to give equal opportunities to blacks/Asians				
Gone much too far	0	0	0	
Gone too far	0	1	1	
About right	2	15	3	
Not gone far enough	42	50	8	
Not gone nearly far enough	46	35	–11	
Availability of abortion on the NHS				
Gone much too far	2	1	–1	
Gone too far	5	5	–1	
About right	42	63	21	
Not gone far enough	39	25	–14	
Not gone nearly far enough	10	6	–5	
Opinion on nuclear weapons				*
Britain should keep own nuclear weapons	1	8	8	
Britain should keep nuclear weapons as part of NATO	55	55	1	
Britain should have nothing to do with nuclear weapons	42	37	–5	
n	135	173		
% Parliamentary Labour Party	50	41		

Note: The significance of the mean difference between groups was tested using ANOVA.
p = >.05; ** = >.01
Sources: British Candidate Study, 1992; British Representation Study, 1997.

TABLE 2.3   *Labour MPs' support for libertarian–authoritarian values, 1992–97*

	1992	1997	Change	Significance
Young people today don't have enough				
respect for traditional values				**
Agree strongly	1	4	3	
Agree	7	19	12	
Neither	33	41	8	
Disagree	43	31	−12	
Disagree strongly	13	5	−8	
Censorship . . . is necessary to uphold				
moral standards				**
Agree strongly	1	5	4	
Agree	16	31	15	
Neither	14	23	9	
Disagree	47	33	−14	
Disagree strongly	21	8	−13	
People should be allowed to organize				
protest meetings. . .				
Agree strongly	79	70	−9	
Agree	20	29	10	
Neither	1	1	0	
Disagree	1	−1	−2	
Disagree strongly	0	0	0	
Homosexual relations are always wrong				**
Agree strongly	3	1	−2	
Agree	2	3	1	
Neither	9	6	−3	
Disagree	32	28	−4	
Disagree strongly	54	63	9	
People . . . should be tolerant of those who				
lead unconventional lives				
Agree strongly	43	39	−3	
Agree	49	53	4	
Neither	7	7	0	
Disagree	2	−2	−4	
Disagree strongly	0	1	1	
Political parties which wish to overthrow				
democracy should be allowed to stand for				
election				
Agree strongly	10	8	−2	
Agree	44	31	−13	
Neither	6	12	6	
Disagree	28	27	−2	
Disagree strongly	10	23	13	
n	135	173		
% of the Parliamentary Labour Party	50	41		

Note: The significance of the mean difference between groups was tested using ANOVA: $p = >.05$; ** $= >.01$.
Sources: British Candidate Study, 1992; British Representation Study, 1997.

TABLE 2.4   MPs' support for constitutional reform, 1997

% Support	Con	Lab	Lib/Dem	Nat	All
Replace Lords with elected chamber	2	95	100	100	**76**
Written constitution	9	85	100	80	**71**
Public funding parties	16	87	94	80	**72**
Introduce PR	11	49	100	100	**48**
Referendum electoral reform	7	68	77	40	**56**

Note: 'Do you think the government should, or should not, do each of the following things, or doesn't it matter either way?

　　Establish a written constitution
　　Replace the House of Lords with an elected second chamber
　　Introduce proportional representation for British elections
　　Hold a referendum on electoral reform
　　Provide public funding of political parties.'

% 'definitely' or 'probably' should.
Source: British Representation Study, 1997.

demonstrate a dramatic ideological convergence across parties during the 1992–97 period. The pattern reveals a modest but significant Conservative move towards the centre, with all the other parties shifting centre-right producing a closure of the party cleavage. If not 'the end of ideology' at least this confirms the reduction of these particular dimensions in British politics. During this period the general process of value change can best be described as a glacial change of emphasis, not an ideological conversion on the road to No 10. Nevertheless greater agreement between Tony Blair and Paddy Ashdown, and parliamentary co-operation between their

TABLE 2.5   Ideological change among politicians, 1992–97

	1992	n	1997	n	Change	Significance
Socialist–*laissez-faire* scale						
Conservative	23.5	343	20.6	288	–2.9	**
Labour	13.8	391	19.7	327	+5.9	**
Liberal Democrat	17.8	300	19.9	284	+2.1	**
SNP	14.1	59	18.6	41	+4.5	**
PC	15.2	19	18.8	22	+3.6	**
Green	15.7	134	19.4	23	+3.7	**
Liberal–authoritarian scale						
Conservative	16.8	343	15.6	287	–1.2	*
Labour	11.9	391	17.1	327	+5.2	**
Liberal Democrat	12.8	313	16.5	284	+3.7	**
SNP	12.9	58	16.5	41	+3.6	*
PC	13.3	17	16.5	22	+3.2	
Green	11.8	136	15.4	23	+3.6	

Notes: The socialist–*laissez faire* scale is composed of items listed in Table 2.1. The libertarian–authoritarian scale is composed of items listed in Table 2.3. The scales run from low (left) to high (right). The significance of the difference in group means is tested using ANOVA: * = $p < .05$; ** = $p < .01$.
Sources: The British Candidate Study, 1992; British Representation Study, 1997.

parties, reflects growing ideological convergence among their backbenchers.

So far we have compared the relative position of different parliamentary parties. But given these changes, one important issue for understanding the outcome of the election is how far this moved politicians closer to, or further way from, their core groups of voters. Downsian theory assumes that electoralist parties will move to the centre of the political spectrum in the pursuit of votes. But a successful strategy requires that politicians can identify where the centre lies. To examine this we can compare how politicians and voters placed themselves on the six major issue scales available in 1997. The BRS asked politicians to use the scales (such as jobs v. prices and taxes v. spending) to identify their own position and also to estimate the position of their own party's voters. In the same way the BES asked voters to identify their own position and to place the parties on these scales. All the scales range from left (1) to right (11) (except for the left–right 10-point scale). Combining these data sets allows us to compare the actual position of voters (how they rated themselves) with the actual position of politicians.

As a results of mapping the (self-assigned) position of *voters* and politicians across the left–right ideological scale, in Figure 2.1, *voters were more tightly clustered in the centre of the spectrum while politicians were more dispersed to left and right.* A similar pattern was found in 1992 with politicians more extreme than voters (Norris 1994). Most importantly, the figure also reveals that in the 1997 election the *average Labour politician was closer to the median British voter than the average Conservative politician.*

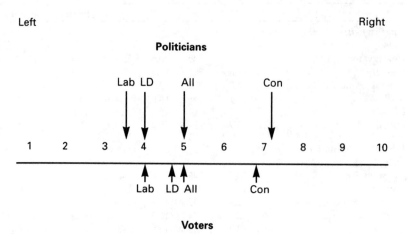

FIGURE 2.1   *Left–right ideological position of politicians and voters,* 1997

Note: 'In politics people sometimes talk of left and right. Using the following scale, where 1 means left and 10 means right, where would you place yourself . . .'
Sources: British Representation Study, 1997, including all MPs and parliamentary candidates (n = 999); British Election Study 1997.

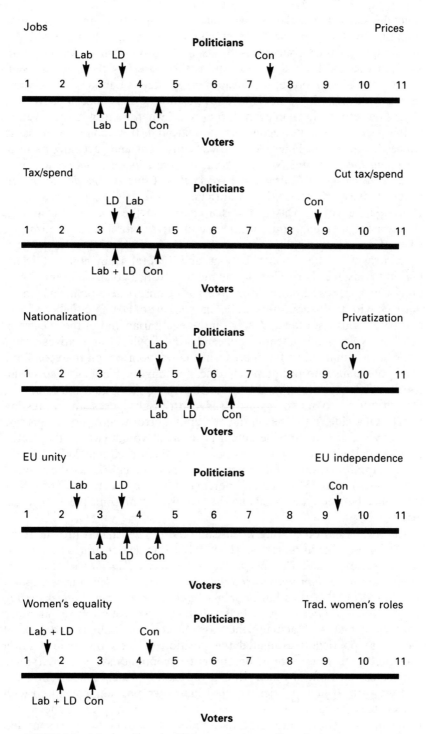

FIGURE 2.2 *Actual position of politicians and voters on the major issues*

If in the early 1980s Labour was out of touch with mainstream public opinion, by the time of the last election they closely reflected the prevailing ethos. Of course this, by itself, is not enough to win elections as otherwise the Liberal Democrats, as the closest to the median voter, would have been in power for decades. Nevertheless Labour's shift centre-right placed them in an advantageous position to maximize support.

This pattern is shown in even starker relief when we turn to the position of the parties in the key economic battleground. If we compare the issue scales the results in Figure 2.2 show a consistent and revealing pattern: *across all the economic issues Labour and the Liberal Democratic politicians were closer to Conservative voters than Conservative politicians*. In other words, Conservative politicians were furthest away from Conservative voters. This gap was a chasm on the issue of taxation v. government spending, and on the issue of privatization v. nationalization, where Conservative politicians were well to the right of their supporters. In contrast, on these issues Labour and Liberal Democrat politicians placed themselves fairly close to the median British voter (see Table 2.6a). Only Europe proved more distinctive, with Conservative politicians more in touch with their supporters, while on the issue of gender equality parties and voters clustered fairly closely on the egalitarian end of the spectrum.

What explains this phenomenon and why should Conservatives politicians have remained so far apart from their supporters on the economy? If all politicians shift positions strategically along the ideological spectrum to maximize their vote, as Downsian theory suggests, then the failure of Conservatives to move towards the centre-right poses an interesting puzzle. One clue to this lies in the perceptual error of how politicians saw voters. We can compare the actual position of voters (where they rated themselves) with how politicians perceived them (in Table 2.6b). We can also compare the actual position of politicians (how they rated themselves) with how voters perceived them (in Table 2.6c). The difference between the actual and the perceived represents the 'perceptual error'.

The results show a strikingly consistent pattern which may provide some important insights into party strategy. Table 2.6b demonstrates that across all the scales except Europe *politicians believed that the electorate was more right wing than voters actually were in practice*. This misperception was found in all parties but *the perceptual error was far stronger among Conservative politicians*, who believed their own voters were far more right wing than was actually the case. In contrast Labour and Liberal Democrat politicians estimated the position of their own voters fairly accurately. In other words, on the core economic issues Conservative politicians were out of touch with the attitudes of their supporters.

If we turn to how politicians rated their own position, compared with how voters perceived them, we see a mirror image. Again the actual position of Labour and Liberal Democrat politicians corresponded remarkably well with how most voters perceived them – the size of the

TABLE 2.6a Actual position of politicians and voters on the issue scales, 1997

	Actual position of voters (i)				Actual position of politician (ii)				Difference (i–ii)			
	Con	LDem	Lab	All	Con	LDem	Lab	All	Con	LDem	Lab	All
Left-right	6.8	4.9	4.0	5.0	7.3	4.0	3.4	4.7	0.5	−0.9	−0.6	−0.3
Jobs v. prices	4.4	3.6	3.1	3.6	7.4	3.4	2.4	4.0	3.0	−0.2	−0.7	0.9
Tax v. spend	4.4	3.3	3.3	3.7	8.9	3.4	3.7	5.0	4.5	0.1	0.4	1.3
Privatization	6.3	5.2	4.7	5.3	9.9	5.4	4.7	6.4	3.6	0.2	0.0	1.1
EU	7.8	6.0	6.0	6.6	9.2	2.5	3.5	5.0	1.4	−3.5	−2.5	−1.6
Women's role	2.6	2.0	2.0	2.3	4.1	1.5	1.3	2.2	1.5	−0.5	−0.7	−0.1

Notes: The scales run from left (low) to right (high). All the scales are 11 point except for the left-right scale which is 10 point. The figures represent the mean position on the scales. The 'actual' position is the self-placement on the scales by voters and by politicians.
Source: British Representation Study, 1997, including all MPs and parliamentary candidates (n = 999); British Election Study, 1997.

TABLE 2.6b   *How politicians saw voters*, 1997

	Actual position of voters (i)				How politicians saw their own voters (ii)				Perceptual error (i–ii)			
	Con	LDem	Lab	All	Con	LDem	Lab	All	Con	LDem	Lab	All
Left-right	6.8	4.9	4.0	5.0	7.2	5.0	4.6	5.4	0.4	0.1	0.6	0.4
Jobs v. prices	4.4	3.6	3.1	3.6	6.9	4.5	3.5	4.7	2.5	0.9	0.4	1.1
Tax v. spend	4.4	3.3	3.3	3.7	8.1	4.5	4.9	5.6	3.7	1.2	1.6	1.9
Privatization	6.3	5.2	4.7	5.3	8.4	5.5	5.3	6.2	2.1	0.3	0.6	0.9
EU	7.8	6.0	6.0	6.6	9.3	4.9	5.7	6.4	1.5	-1.1	-0.3	-0.2
Women's role	2.6	2.0	2.0	2.3	5.3	3.0	3.0	3.8	2.7	1.0	1.4	1.5

Notes: The scales run from left (low) to right (high). All the scales are 11 point except for the left-right scale which is 10 point. The figures represent the mean position on the scales. The 'actual' position is the self-placement by voters. The 'perceived' position is the estimated position of their own party voters by politicians. The 'perceptual error' is the difference between 'actual' and 'perceived'.

Source: British Representation Study, 1997, including all MPs and parliamentary candidates (*n* = 999); British Election Study, 1997.

TABLE 2.6c *How voters saw politicians*, 1997

	Actual position of politician			How voters saw parties			Perceptual error (i–ii)		
	Con	LDem	Lab	Con	LDem	Lab	Con	LDem	Lab
Left-right	7.3	4.0	3.4	7.4	5.0	4.5	0.1	1.0	1.1
Jobs v. prices	7.4	3.4	2.4	5.4	3.8	3.0	-2.0	0.4	-0.6
Tax v. spend	8.9	3.4	3.7	6.0	3.2	3.4	-2.9	-0.2	-0.3
Privatization	9.9	5.4	4.7	7.4	5.2	4.6	-2.5	-0.2	-0.1
EU	9.2	2.5	3.5	6.8	4.7	4.8	-2.4	2.2	1.3
Women's Role	4.1	1.5	1.3	3.5	2.7	2.4	-0.6	1.2	1.1

Note: The scales run from left (low) to right (high). All the scales are 11 point except for the left-right scale which is 10 point. The figures represent the mean position on the scales. The 'actual' position is the self-placement by politicians. The 'perceived' position is the estimated position of parties by their own voters. The 'perceptual error' is the difference between 'actual' and 'perceived'.
Source: British Representation Study, 1997, including all MPs and parliamentary candidates (*n* = 999); British Election Study 1997.

perceptual errors are extremely low on all issues except the EU. But again the perceptual errors concerning the Conservatives were larger than for other parties, with Conservative voters believing that Tory politicians were more moderate than they actually were in practice. What this pattern strongly suggests is a self-reinforcing projection which was particularly marked in the Conservative Party, as voters and politicians tended to perceive each other as closer to their own attitudes and values than was actually the case. This analysis carries some important implications for Downsian theories of party competition. Downs assumes that electoralist parties attempt to gain popularity by moving to the centre of the ideological spectrum. But any effective party strategy to maximize support requires politicians to identify public opinion accurately. The results of this analysis suggest that the Conservatives were more mistaken in their perception of their supporters than politicians in other parties. We can only speculate at this stage about the causes of this intriguing phenomenon. This perceptual error may have been due to the Conservative government having been in power for 18 years, which may have made Conservative politicians increasingly ideologically dogmatic and out of touch with grassroots support. Labour's long climb back to power, such as the 'Labour Listens' strategy, may have made their electoral antenna more sensitive to the nuances of public opinion. Perhaps the demonstrable electoral success of Thatcherism encouraged all politicians to assume that public opinion was more right wing than was actually the case. Whatever the reason, this perceptual error probably encouraged Conservatives politicians to advocate more right wing policies than Conservative voters' actually supported.

A Critical Realignment in Party Competition?

Given the pattern of political ideology which we have established, the remaining puzzle is whether the change in the Labour Party culture seems likely to represent an enduring realignment. One way to explore this is to use cohort analysis to examine the pattern of attitudes and values. If younger politicians prove more centre-right than older colleagues, this suggests that the process of generational replacement will eventually consolidate and even reinforce this change. In every parliament some new members enter Westminster and other MPs depart through retirement, ill-health or defeat. Incumbency turnover is usually fairly substantial from one parliament to the next but the 1997 election was remarkable (see Table 2.7). Combining all the sources of replacement, controlling for the length of each parliament, the standard rate of turnover is about 52 MPs per year, or about 8% per annum. Out of 651 MPs elected in 1992, 17 left through ill-health, death or retirement at by-elections and 117 retired at the 1997 general election. Of those who remained, 132 were defeated on 1 May 1997, leaving only 410 incumbent MPs (63%) who returned

TABLE 2.7   Turnover in the House of Commons 1929–97

	MPs (total HoC)	MPs leave at BE	MPs retire at GE	MPs seeking re-elec	MPs defeat at GE	MPs total re-elec	% of those seeking re-elec	Re-elected as % House members	MPs (total new)	% MPs (New)	Months of Parlt	Standard annual turnover
1929/31	615	36	42	573	225	348	.61	50.7	303	49.3	28	130
1931/35	615	62	68	547	85	462	.84	65.0	215	35.0	47	55
1935/45	615	219	129	486	173	313	.64	15.3	521	84.7	113	55
1945/50	640	52	60	580	70	510	.88	71.6	182	28.4	52	42
1950/51	625	16	29	596	25	571	.96	88.8	70	11.2	19	44
1951/55	630	48	42	588	19	569	.97	82.7	109	17.3	42	31
1955/59	630	52	66	564	33	531	.94	76.0	151	24.0	51	36
1959/64	630	62	60	570	61	509	.89	71.0	183	29.0	59	37
1964/66	630	13	38	592	51	541	.91	83.8	102	16.2	17	72
1966/70	630	38	78	552	77	475	.86	69.4	193	30.6	49	47
1970/74 Feb	635	30	70	565	53	512	.91	75.9	153	24.1	43	43
1974/74 Oct	635	1	14	621	30	591	.95	92.9	45	7.1	6	90
1974/79	635	30	61	574	65	509	.89	75.4	156	24.6	53	35
1979/83	650	20	77	573	63	510	.89	75.4	160	24.6	48	40
1983/87	650	16	87	563	41	522	.93	77.8	144	22.2	47	37
1987/92	651	23	85	566	60	506	.89	74.2	168	25.8	57	35
1992/97	659	17	117	525	132	393	.75	59.6	266	40.4	60	53
Total	10,775	735	1,123	9,652	1,263	8,389			3,121			883
Mean	634	43	66	568	74	493	.87	70.9	184	29.1	47	52

Source: Calculated from successive volumes of The Times Guide to the House of Commons 1929–97.

TABLE 2.8 *Left–right position of politicians by age,* 1997

Age group	Con	Lib/Dem	Lab	All
Under 35	7.56	4.12	3.43	5.44
36–45	7.52	4.06	3.52	4.66
46–55	7.11	4.03	3.24	4.38
Over 56	6.59	3.86	3.26	4.46
All	7.34	4.04	3.38	4.75
n	280	323	319	913

Note: 'In politics people sometimes talk of left and right. Using the following scale, where 1 means left and 10 means right, where would you place yourself . . .' All politicians includes MPs and parliamentary candidates in the 1997 election.
Source: British Representation Study, 1997 (*n* = 913).

unscathed. The 1997 general election therefore brought 249 new members into the corridors of Westminster, the highest parliamentary turnover since 1945. This process usually brings in a younger generation of MPs. The average age of the new Labour MP who first entered in 1997 was 44, including five in their thirties, while the average incumbent Labour MP was 53 years old. If this process gradually alters the dominant culture within the parliamentary élite, then we would expect to find significant differences in attitudes and values between younger and older generations of politicians.

To examine this issue we can analyse responses to the issue scales in the BRS-1997, described earlier, which asked politicians to identify their own position on the left–right scale. We will compare the attitudes of all politicians (including parliamentary candidates), not just elected MPs, since this provides a more reliable analysis of party culture based on a larger sample of cases. The results in Table 2.8 show a striking and consistent pattern: across all parties the younger politicians (under 35) proved more right wing than their older counterparts. This age difference was particularly marked among the Conservatives, with a one-point difference on a 10-point scale, but a similar pattern was evident among Liberal Democrats and Labour politicians. If these patterns represent persistent and durable generational differences, in the long term the process of incumbency turnover is likely to move British parliamentary politics gradually further to the right in future. Similar patterns were evident on the other issue scales, such as the trade-off between jobs v. prices, where again the pattern showed that the younger generation of MPs were consistently to the right within each party (Table 2.9).

To examine this pattern more systematically, and the relative influence of age and cohort of entry, the position of all MPs elected in 1997 was compared across the full range of the ten-issue scales used earlier. All scales were consistently recoded so that higher scores represented the more 'right-wing' response. A series of ordinary least squared regression models were used to analyse the impact of age and cohort of entry on these values, controlling for party. The age of politicians was entered first,

TABLE 2.9   *Position of politicians on jobs v. prices by age, 1997*

Age group	Con	Lib/Dem	Lab	All
Under 35	8.06	3.86	2.81	5.36
36–45	7.17	3.90	2.46	3.89
46–55	7.12	3.04	2.10	3.35
Over 56	5.93	2.69	2.06	3.44
All	7.37	3.41	2.36	4.04
n	247	273	318	913

Note: 'Some people feel that getting people back to work should be the government's top priority. These people would put themselves in box 1. Other people feel that getting prices down should be the government's top priority. These people would put themselves in box 11. Other people have views somewhere in-between . . . Where would you place your view?' All politicians includes MPs and parliamentary candidates in the 1997 election.

given the logic of the classic 'funnel of causality' which suggests that age can affect entry into Parliament, but not *vice versa*. Cohort of entry into Westminster was then entered as a dummy variable (coding first entry into the Commons in 1997 as 1 and any earlier year of entry as 0) .

The results of the models (in Table 2.10) demonstrate that, as expected, party proves to be the strongest and most significant predictor of political values across all scales. But after controlling for party, the age of members proved to be significant on four out of five 'old politics' value scales. As noted earlier, younger members proved significantly more right wing on socialist–*laissez-faire* values, as well as on the issue scales of national-ization v. privatization, jobs v. prices, and taxes v. spending. In contrast across these scales, after controlling for age, the entry of the 1997 cohort of MPs proved insignificant. In terms of the New Politics scales, neither

TABLE 2.10   *Age and cohort effects on value scales: all 1997 MPs*

Value scales	Party	Age	1997 cohort	Adjusted R^2
Old politics scales				
Socialist–*laissez-faire*	.77**	.12**	.01	.60
Nationalize v. privatize	.75**	.10*	−.05	.58
Left-right self-position	.69**	.04	.03	.47
Jobs v. prices	.66**	.12*	−.01	.44
Taxes v. spending	.65**	.15**	−.04	.44
New politics scales				
Libertarian–authoritarian	.35**	−.04	.02	.58
European Union	.60**	.04	.03	.35
Women's rights	.58**	−.08	−.06	.36
Postmaterialism	.49**	−.07	.02	.24

Note: The models use ordinary least-squared regression analysis and the figures represent standardized beta coefficients; ** = p <.01; *= p <.05.
See the Appendix to this book for scale items.
Age = year of birth.
1997 cohort: MPs elected for the first time in 1997 = (1); incumbent MP = (0).
Party = coded Lab (1), Lib/Dem (2), Con (3).
Source: British Representation Study, 1997, including only MPs elected in 1997 (*n* = 277).

age nor cohort proved to be statistically significant. What the overall pattern suggests is that the secular process of generational turnover promises to have a long-term influence upon the culture of Parliament, moving party politicians gradually towards the right. This process proved more important than the entry of a new cohort of Blairite MPs *per se* in 1997: it was the age of New Labour members, rather than their recruitment under Blair's leadership, which proved most significant in transforming the parliamentary culture of the New Labour Party.

The Implications for Party Politics

This chapter aimed to see whether the 1997 election represented a critical break with the past in Parliament, especially for the Labour Party. The evidence we have assembled suggests that, contrary to the sceptical view, the values of the Parliamentary Labour Party did change from 1992 to 1997, particularly on many of the traditional touchstones of socialist faith. The shifts in official Labour Party policy documented in Chapter 1 reflect the attitudes and values of backbench Labour MPs. While Labour politicians have not 'leapfrogged over' the Liberal Democrats, the rush to occupy the middle ground has produced far greater ideological convergence among these parliamentary parties. On most indicators, even more than in 1992 (Norris 1994), the map of British party politics is one with Labour and the Liberal Democrat politicians clustered fairly closely in the centre-left while the Conservatives occupy a lonely but distinctive position on the right.

The main reason for this development, we suggest, lies in the process of generational replacement as older members retire and younger MPs take their place. Generational turnover is usually a slow process: in every parliament some older members retire from office – due to age, ill-health, career changes or death, as well as being defeated at elections – and younger members fill their shoes. The 1997 election saw the highest number of retiring MPs (117) in any election since 1945. The dramatic landslide of seats in 1997 accelerated this process, bringing 249 new MPs into Westminster representing more than one-third of the Commons. The massive influx of new members has produced a new middle-of-the-road cohort of Blairite MPs in 1997, replacing left-wing members elected earlier. Our interpretation of this development suggests that it was the younger *age* of the new Labour MPs which produced the major shift rightwards, not their *cohort of entry per se.*

This interpretation carries a number of important implications. First, despite some well publicized internal party conflict about certain issues, nevertheless the centrist shift within official Labour Party policy is fully consistent with the values of the new politicians. Therefore at least in the first term the parliamentary party seems likely to prove relatively cohesive under Blair's leadership, rather than riven by the sort of internal party schisms suffered by Michael Foot in the early 1980s or by John Major in the early 1990s. In broader terms, what this analysis also suggests is that parliamentary élites have considerable capacity to change as older representatives leave the House and younger members gradually fill their place on the backbenches. This process is critical for the capacity of parliamentary parties to evolve over time.

Theoretically this process also provides important insights into the theory of critical elections. The argument which we have provided suggests that in many regards, as a result of the 1997 general election, the new House does represent a decisive break with the past pattern of party competition. Most obviously, more than one-third of the membership is new and that, in itself, brought fresh blood into parliament. In all parties we found that the younger generation of MPs is consistently more right wing than older politicians. This suggests that the changes in party competition are likely to prove durable, producing a stepped break with the past, since many new MPs can expect to be re-elected to Westminster for careers spanning 20 or 30 years. The generational attitudes we have documented indicate that, if they reflect enduring cultural changes, British party politics may well shift further towards the right in future elections. If the Conservatives want to learn the lessons of Labour success these are that, under Blair's leadership, the party changed its public image, revised its doctrine and platform, but also brought in an influx of younger politicians. The pattern of generational change produced by the 1997 landslide may well have important implications for British politics long after the Blair government is ended.

3 Party Members and Ideological Change

Paul Webb and David M. Farrell

The central purpose of this chapter is to consider how far there are signs of critical realignment among major party memberships. The Introduction suggested that a critical election can be understood as one which produces 'significant and durable realignments in the mass basis of party support with major consequences for the long-term balance of party competition'. As such, a critical election involves enduring realignments both at the level of the electorate (in terms of partisan loyalties, issue attitudes and patterns of social support) and within the parties themselves (in terms of ideology and policy). In particular, the focus of this chapter is on how far programmatic shifts identifiable in party manifestos (Chapter 1), which resonate within parliamentary parties (Chapter 2), are also evident among rank-and-file party memberships.

Why should this matter from the perspective of critical elections theory? It is easiest to answer such a question with some hypothetical examples. Thus, should we discover that the sharp movement towards a centre-left position in New Labour's manifesto revealed by Ian Budge in Chapter 1 was consistently replicated among party members, this would strengthen the likelihood that the 1997 election represented a critical departure from long-term patterns of party competition. Similarly, evidence that Conservative Party divisions over Europe extended beyond the parliamentary party would point to the probability of continuing intraparty turmoil over the issue, in turn suggesting the basis for possible future breakaways and/or realignments. On the other hand, evidence to the contrary would tend to suggest that change in 1997 was essentially shallow and transient, amounting at most, perhaps, to a deviating rather than a critical election.

A secondary purpose of this chapter is to consider the question of how far British political parties in the late 1990s have come to approximate ideal-type organizations of electoral contestation. In order to become effective electoral competitors, party leaders need to be able to rely on the support of their followers, both in terms of political beliefs and activist commitment. To put it slightly differently, members carry both benefits and costs for an electorally motivated leadership (Scarrow 1996). In particular, such a leadership will regard the membership as a resource of continuing significance in the battle for votes, but this benefit must be set against the potential costs of a membership which may not whole-heartedly endorse the policy package which the leadership wishes to set before the electorate. These costs spring from the widespread perception, shared by many academics, journalists and politicians alike, that grassroots members are inclined to see themselves as keepers of the flame of ideological purity.

Of particular note in this respect is John May's well-known 'law of curvi-linear disparity', premised on the notion that, while leaders are driven by vote-maximizing imperatives, activists are motivated by purposive incen-tives such as the desire to influence party policy or candidate selection; thus, while leaders can be expected to seek out policy positions which approximate those of the median voter as nearly as possible, members could be more concerned to maintain ideologically 'pure' (which is to say radical) positions (May 1973). This scenario creates the obvious prospect of intraparty tension and difficulties of party management.

The problem of curvilinear disparity can be seen as particularly taxing in the light of party transformation, especially for left-wing parties. These parties were credited by Duverger (1954) with having 'invented' the mass party, and they consequently faced greater difficulties than right-of-centre parties in reducing their 'ideological baggage'. Social democratic and labour parties were founded primarily as agents of social integration and group representation for the newly enfranchised masses during the era in which west European politics was democratized. During this time they devised and pursued ideological programmes which were driven by social group interests, and they sought to capture the loyal political support of these groups, perhaps even to 'encapsulate' them in a network of inter-connected social, economic and political organizations (Wellhofer 1979). In terms of British electoral analysis, this translated into the well-known epithet of the 'two-class, two-party' system of competition, which captured the notion of a process of political conflict dominated by major parties and a single social fault-line; the 'democratic translation of the class struggle', indeed (Lipset 1960).

But for over 30 years commentators have been suggesting the trans-formation of western political parties away from the classic mass party model into something inherently less concerned with the functions of mass integration or the articulation of specific social group interests. Major parties, at least since Otto Kirchheimer (1966), have generally been regarded as motivated primarily by vote-winning and office-seeking goals, a change which requires, *inter alia*, the downgrading of narrow group ties and softening of class ideologies in favour of broadly aggregative program-matic appeals. This conception of party change lies at the heart of Kirchheimer's own model of the 'catch-all' party, but is equally central to later conceptions which have added further layers of analysis, such as Angelo Panebianco's 'electoral-professional' party (1988) and Katz and Mair's 'cartel party' (1995).

In the light of this, it is legitimate to ask whether party members have been problematic for the major party leaderships in contemporary Britain. We can shed some light on this by examining the changing attitudinal profiles of party members. Thus, in a perfectly formulated party of electoral contestation, be it catch-all or electoral-professional, we might envisage a membership which adopted a cohesive ideological location close to that of the party leadership, which in turn would be as close as possible to that of the median voter. This would certainly smooth the task of party management and afford the leadership maximum scope for strategic flexibility in establishing an effective electoral appeal. Of course, it may be that, as May suggests, such a scenario is implausible and that tensions are likely to persist, but this remains a matter for empirical investigation.

To summarize, therefore, the analysis which ensues engages with five[1] specific questions, all of which cast light on the themes outlined above:

1) Did the major party memberships display particularly acute ideological shifts from 1992 to 1997? If so, such changes might indicate the possibility of critical realignment.

2) How far are party members attitudinally cohesive? A sudden or exceptional decline in attitudinal cohesion might indicate the onset of ideological tensions too great to be contained within a party; cross-party realignments or breakaways become more serious prospects at such times. Moreover, intraparty cohesion can be important for votes; many commentators, both inside and outside the party, suggested that the Conservatives performed poorly in the 1997 election precisely because they failed to convince British voters that they constituted a cohesive and unified party. The internal group cohesion of party members can be measured by the standard deviation around the group mean on attitudinal scales.

3) Do the major parties in Britain continue to harbour ideological difference at grassroots level? In a literal account of the party transformation model, we might expect – given the predominantly centripetal two-party pattern of competition which Britain exemplifies – that the ideological differences between major party members would melt away. Is this in fact true, or do contemporary British parties still display ideological distinctiveness among their members? To examine this, we analyse the mean positions of major party members over time on attitudinal scales to measure the degree of ideological polarization between major party members.

4) How extreme are party members? In particular, have party members come closer to 'ordinary voters' over time, as a model of electoralist party transformation might imply? 'Extremism' is always a relative term, of course, and in this case we examine the differences in mean attitudinal positions of party members and voters.

5) How disperate are the attitudes of party members from party voters

in general? Here we offer a limited test of May's Law; while we cannot directly compare the beliefs of leaders and members, it is legitimate to assume that the perfect electoralist party would be one in which members were not significantly more radical than non-members who vote for the same party, and we test this by comparing the mean attitudinal positions of these groups.

The Fall and Rise of Party Members in Britain

Before engaging in our analysis, it is useful to set it in historical and intellectual context. There has been a revival of interest in recent years in the role and electoral significance of party members. The last two or three decades have seen fundamental changes in the way parties run their organizations, with clear evidence of an internal power shift from the 'organizational' towards their 'parliamentary' face (Katz and Mair 1994). This seems to confirm a conviction, which has been widely held since Otto Kirchheimer (1966), that modern political parties have transformed themselves into catch-all electoral phenomena. Central to this understanding was the premise that the 'mass' party was undergoing a process of secular decline. The causes of this transformation were held to be multifarious, but one of the main results seemed straightforwardly apparent – a dying out of the 'party member' as a breed. The argument is simple, and has been widely rehearsed: the gist is that parties apparently have less need for members, because alternative resources more suitable to the electoral goals of the party and to the contemporary social and technological circumstances under which they operate, are available to them (see, for instance, Epstein 1967; Panebianco 1988; Farrell 1996). Indeed, in certain respects this line of argument was already implicit in British psephology in the late 1950s (Butler and Rose 1960). If the explanation seems compelling so too does some of the basic evidence. In most other west European countries, although not all, the number of party members has declined in recent decades (Katz *et al.* 1992; Widfeldt 1995).

Table 3.1 summarizes the trends in British party membership for each election since 1964. In 1964, 9.4% of all registered voters were members of the three main political parties. By the time of the 1997 general election this proportion had plummeted to less than 2%. Even when we allow something for the vagaries of membership statistics, and indeed for the growth of nationalist and flash parties (not reported in Table 3.1), the downward trend is undeniable. Moreover, it seems unlikely that the impressive resurgence of Constituency Labour Party (CLP) membership after Tony Blair's election as party leader in 1994 heralds the onset of a new and enduring trajectory of revival; despite the euphoria surrounding New Labour's electoral victory of May 1997, by the following year the membership numbers dipped from their temporary highpoint of 405,000 to 385,000 (MacAskill 1998).

TABLE 3.1   *British party membership, 1964–97*

	Labour	Conservative	Liberals [1]
1964	830,116	2,150,000	278,690
1966	775,693	2,150,000	234,345
1970	680,191	2,150,000	234,345
1974	691,889	1,500,000	190,000
1979	666,091	1,350,000	145,000
1983	295,344	1,200,000	145,258
1987	288,829	1,000,000	137,500
1992	279,530	500,000	100,000
1997	405,000[2]	400,000	100,000

Notes: 1) Liberals, SDP and Liberal Democrats; 2) Kavanagh (1997) claims that Labour's individual membership figure reached 420,000 by the time of the 1997 general election, though this is denied by the party's Assistant General Secretary, David Gardner (correspondence with authors).
Sources: Labour Party NEC *Annual Reports*; Conservative National Union; Liberal Democrats' Information Office; Norris and Gavin (1997).

Despite this, there has been a renascent interest in the continuing importance of party members. Membership drives are the order of the day: indeed, for Labour, the first signs of renewed initiatives along such lines were evident under Neil Kinnock, though they were hardly resounding successes (Webb 1994: 115–16). Under Blair recruitment drives have apparently been far more successful, and even subsequent to the 1997 election victory, Deputy Leader John Prescott declared the ambition of further increasing Labour's mass membership; to foster this, a senior-level 'healthy party' taskforce was established to draw up proposals for keeping members happy and active. Seemingly in an attempt to mirror the successes of New Labour, William Hague launched a membership drive as well as an ambitious plan to overhaul the Conservative Party's creaky organizational structure; this initiative rests in part on the inducement of new participatory incentives for the members, especially in the area of the leadership election (Conservative Party 1997). The revival of academic interest in the parties' rank-and-file has been led by surveys of major party members in Britain (Seyd and Whiteley 1992; Whiteley *et al.* 1994; Whiteley and Seyd 1998), work which has found an echo in surveys of the Liberal Democrats by John Curtice and his colleagues, and of the Greens by Wolfgang Rüdig *et al.* Also prominent in this revival has been the British Candidate Study of 1992, directed by Pippa Norris and Joni Lovenduski (1995); the work of Susan Scarrow (1996) on party members in Britain and Germany; and the spate of related research on the electoral impact of local party campaigning by David Denver and Gordon Hands (1992, 1997b), and by Ron Johnston, Charles Pattie and their colleagues (1995). The major parties have become once more convinced of the importance of the individual membership base (Whiteley and Seyd 1998: 4). Of particular relevance to this chapter is the work by Whiteley and Seyd on the influx of new members into the Labour Party after Tony Blair's election to the leadership. Contrary to some media speculation, they contend that these New Labour recruits are neither more middle class nor more affluent than 'Old Labour' members, though they do appear to be less active, less left wing and a little more authoritarian in their beliefs. But where do such developments leave Labour's membership in long-term perspective?

Ideological Change among Party Members

A useful basis on which to build our understanding of party members' attitudinal trends is provided by referring to the most commonly cited 'synoptic' issue indicator of class values, which is the question of nationalization of industry (Heath *et al.* 1985: 132; Norris 1997: 164–5). This has been one of the classic indicators of left–right conflict in postwar British party politics. Figure 3.1 plots the mean position of the various groups of party members and voters that we shall be examining for each of the possible BES samples since 1964. Though offering a very limited insight into the changing ideological hue of the major party memberships in Britain since the 1960s, it is immediately apparent that there is indeed something quite distinct about the 1997 Labour sample; the shift to the right (that is, in

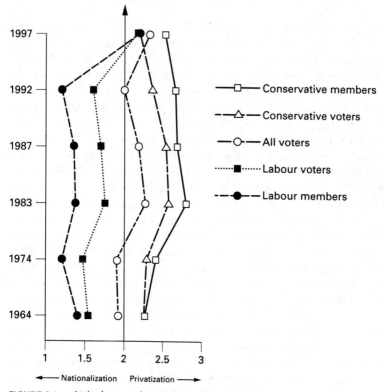

FIGURE 3.1   *Attitudes towards nationalization and privatization, 1964–97*

TABLE 3.2 *Major party members' attitudes on nationalization, 1964–97*

Year	Con	n	Lab	n	Polarization index	p
1964	2.2	120	1.4	37	0.8	.000
1974 (O)	2.4	102	1.2	29	1.2	.000
1983	2.8	153	1.4	47	1.4	.000
1987	2.7	139	1.4	42	1.3	.000
1992	2.6	308	1.2	498	1.4	.000
1997	2.5	46	2.2	43	0.3	.063

Notes: Ideological positions are group means for an attitudinal scale coded as follows: 1 = would prefer to see more industries nationalized; 2 = would prefer things to stay as they are; 3 = would prefer to see more industries privatized.

The polarization index is calculated by subtracting Labour members' mean position on the scale from Conservative members' mean score. *p* denotes the statistical significance of differences in group means; specifically, these are (2-tailed) independent samples *T*-test significance levels (i.e. reporting the probability of the null hypothesis that the Labour and Conservative samples are taken from a population in which they have identical means).

The 1992 figures are based on the party membership sample generated by the British Candidate Survey (BCS) rather than the BES of 1992; this is necessitated by the non-inclusion of a party membership variable in the BES of 1992.

Sources: BES, 1964–97; BCS, 1992.

favour of privatization) within this group represents a quite unprecedented lurch in the time series (see Table 3.2 for confirmation), and it plainly points to a widespread degree of acceptance at grassroots level of the leadership's reform of Clause 4 of the party constitution in 1995. This implies that the public ownership issue will probably henceforward cease to be one of the main points of distinction between the major party memberships (indeed, their attitudes are no longer statistically distinct at the 10% level).

This, in turn, implies the need to look beyond this issue if we are to gain a broader understanding of attitudinal change, and trends across a number of other indicators are reported in Tables 3.3a and 3.3b. Relatively few comparable items can be found over time in the BES series (not, at least, in the data sets which also permit us to distinguish party members), but we are able to consider evidence relating to four other class (or 'left-right') values items and three items relating to the cross-cutting dimension of moral traditionalism (or libertarianism–authoritarianism). Indeed, it has become increasingly common for political scientists investigating patterns of electoral behaviour and party competition in western democracies to offer analysis in terms of these two ideological dimensions in recent years (see, for instance, Heath *et al.* 1994a). We are, unfortunately, limited by these variables to data gathered in October 1974, 1987, 1992 and 1997, but this 24-year period takes in some notable swings in electoral behaviour and party fortunes. The evidence from these indicators is somewhat mixed; certainly, it would be an exaggeration to claim that Labour members moved as sharply to the right on each and every one of these items as

TABLE 3.3a   *Party members' attitudes, 1974–97: socialism–laissez-faire indicators*

Issue	Party	Year	Strongly agree	Agree	Doesn't matter	Disagree	Strongly disagree	PDI
Government should spend to alleviate poverty?	Con	1974 (O)	35	36	9	9	10	52
		1987	23	52	8	15	2	57
		1992	21	49	9	11	10	50
		1997	34	39	2	17	8	47
	Lab	1974 (O)	71	29	—	—	—	100
		1987	87	11	—	2	—	96
		1992	89	10	1	—	—	98
		1997	71	23	2	4	—	89
Government should take action to redistribute income and wealth?	Con	1974 (O)	1	16	13	35	34	−52
		1987	—	18	14	50	18	−49
		1992	7	18	20	36	20	−32
		1997	4	21	21	43	11	−28
	Lab	1974 (O)	52	28	10	3	7	69
		1987	37	48	11	4	—	80
		1992	75	22	2	0.2	0.4	96
		1997	36	32	14	18	—	50
Government should increase spending on the NHS?	Con	1974 (O)	41.9	32.4	8.6	8.6	5.7	60
		1987	22.9	50.0	6.3	14.6	2.8	56
		1992	25.4	43.6	10.1	16.0	4.9	48
		1997	50.0	37.0	13.0	—	—	87
	Lab	1974 (O)	58.6	34.5	6.9	—	—	93
		1987	93.6	6.4	—	—	—	100
		1992	95.1	4.5	—	0.2	0.2	99
		1997	88.0	12.0	—	—	—	100
Government should legislate to give workers more say?	Con	1974 (O)	2.9	35.9	8.7	26.2	26.2	−14
		1987	19.7	52.1	8.5	13.4	6.3	52
		1992	—	—	—	—	—	—
		1997	22.7	47.7	2.3	22.7	4.6	43
	Lab	1974 (O)	46.4	32.1	7.1	10.7	3.6	64
		1987	63.8	25.5	—	8.5	2.1	79
		1992	—	—	—	—	—	—
		1997	38.8	46.9	6.1	6.1	2.0	78

Notes: PDI is the 'percentage difference index' which is calculated by the formula: (% who strongly agree + % who agree) − (% who strongly disagree + % who disagree).
Sources: BES, 1964–97; BCS, 1992.

they did on the question of public ownership in 1997, though a similar jump is evident with respect to the key question of redistribution. More modest shifts to the right or in the direction of authority (as measured by the percentage difference index reported in the final column of the table) are apparent on most other issues, while Conservative members tended to move somewhat to the left (especially on NHS funding) between 1992 and 1997.

Reference to individual survey items provides some insights, but the more reliable way of summarizing ideological movements through time and across a variety of dimensions of belief is via the construction and analysis of multi-item attitudinal scales. Table 3.4 reports developments from 1974–97 in terms of scales constructed largely from the individual items discussed in Tables 3.2, 3.3a and 3.3b.[2] In addition to multi-item

TABLE 3.3b *Party members' attitudes, 1974–97: liberty–authority indicators*

Issue	Party	Year	Too far	About right	Not far enough	PDI
Availability of abortion	Con	1974 (O)	53.6	38.1	8.2	45.5
has gone ...?		1987	36.3	58.7	5.0	31.3
		1992	27.8	61.7	10.5	17.3
		1997	32.5	62.5	5.0	27.5
	Lab	1974 (O)	42.3	34.6	23.0	19.3
		1987	26.1	56.5	17.4	8.7
		1992	11.7	49.4	38.9	−27.2
		1997	21.7	65.2	13.0	8.7
Attempts to ensure	Con	1974 (O)	22.0	51.0	27.0	−5.0
sexual equality have		1987	8.5	56.3	35.2	−26.7
gone ...?		1992	10.0	61.9	28.1	−18.1
		1997	19.6	58.7	21.7	−2.1
	Lab	1974 (O)	10.3	34.5	55.2	−44.9
		1987	2.1	21.3	76.6	−74.5
		1992	2.2	14.1	83.7	−81.5
		1997	2.0	46.9	51.1	−49.1
Attempts to ensure	Con	1974 (O)	32.7	41.8	25.5	7.2
racial equality have		1987	32.4	52.1	15.5	16.9
gone ...?		1992	27.1	60.5	12.4	14.7
		1997	35.6	46.7	17.7	17.9
	Lab	1974 (O)	13.8	41.4	44.8	−3.1
		1987	10.6	29.8	59.6	−49.0
		1992	5.0	23.5	71.5	−66.5
		1997	14.0	26.0	60.0	−46.0

Notes: PDI is calculated by the formula: (% too far − % not far enough).
Sources: BES, 1964–97; BCS, 1992.

scales for the two ideological dimensions already discussed, we have attempted to take some account of what has become an issue of obvious significance in recent British politics, that of European integration. In this respect, however, we are only able to examine a single item, which is comparable across the 1987 and 1997 (but not 1974 or 1992) data sets. What does the analysis of three-dimensional ideological change among party member's reveal?

Table 3.4 confirms that, while Conservative members have shifted their ideological ground fairly gradually on the whole (for instance, a little to the right on class values (LR) in the 1980s, then somewhat to the left in the 1990s), Labour's members appear to have been more volatile. After moving fairly sharply left between 1987 and 1992, they then lurched even more dramatically to the right between 1992 and 1997. What is more, they displayed a similar pattern, first towards liberty, then towards authority, on the social traditionalism scale (LA), while Conservative members display rather muted changes across the period as a whole in these terms. Indeed, if one compares changes in party member group means on these scales from one election to the next in the decade from 1987, the only shift achieving statistical significance for the Tories is that on the left–right

TABLE 3.4   *Attitudinal change and polarization among major party members, 1974–97*

Scale	Year	Con	n	Lab	n	Polarization index	p
Left–right	1974 (O)	2.00	91	1.25	28	0.75	.000
	1987	2.05	122	1.22	41	0.83	.000
	1992	1.85	222	1.08	419	0.77	.000
	1997	1.85	45	1.36	47	0.49	.000
Libertarian–authoritarian	1974 (O)	2.16	91	1.92	28	0.24	.016
	1987	2.05	118	1.71	46	0.34	.000
	1992	2.04	291	1.41	489	0.63	.000
	1997	2.08	41	1.84	45	0.24	.000
EC	1974 (O)	—	—	—	—	—	—
	1987	1.38	143	1.72	47	–0.34	.033
	1992	—	—	—	—	—	—
	1997	1.69	46	1.34	50	0.35	.048

Notes: 'Left–right' denotes the class-values attitudinal scale, running from 1 (furthest left) to 3 (furthest right). 'Libertarian–authoritarian' denotes the moral traditionalism scale, running from 1 (libertarian/progressive) to 3 (authoritarian/traditional). 'EC' denotes the European integration scale running from 1 (Britain should remain a member of the European Community/Union) to 3 (Britain should withdraw). A comparable European integration indicator is not available in the 1974 or 1992 data sets. See the Appendix to this chapter for full details of scale construction. *n* denotes the number of cases on which the scale mean is calculated. Polarization measures are calculated by subtracting the mean score of Labour members on the various scales from the mean score of Conservative members. *p* denotes the significance level of the polarization in group means. Significance levels are derived from *T*–statistics tests.
Sources: BES, 1964–97; BCS, 1992.

scale between 1987 and 1992, while all of Labour's movements are significant.[3] While the European integration indicator is a simpler single-item scale, it shows an interesting and plausible pattern of attitudinal change in the decade after 1987, in that the major party memberships followed their leaderships in swapping positions on Europe; that is, by 1997 Labour had replaced the Conservatives as the more 'pro-European' party.[4]

This then, provides some *prima facie* support for the critical election hypothesis; something clearly did alter quite profoundly in the overall ideological stance of Labour Party members between the general elections of 1992 and 1997. It is hard to resist the conclusion that the massive influx of new members who joined the party after Tony Blair's election to the leadership must go some way towards accounting for this, though Whiteley and Seyd (1998: 20) suggest this is not the whole story; they make it quite clear that there have also been important shifts in the outlook of those who joined the party prior to 1994. So far, so good, then, for the critical election thesis, but this only addresses the first of our two tests of critical realignment among party members; the other requires us to monitor changes in attitudinal cohesion. In particular, the context of the period suggests that we should focus on Conservative members' attitudes towards Europe.

Table 3.5 reports the standard deviations around the mean attitudinal scale scores of major party members. The lower the standard deviation, the more cohesive we may assume the party memberships to be. With

TABLE 3.5   *The attitudinal cohesion of party members, 1974–97*

Election	Scale	Conservative	n	Labour	n	Mean
Oct. 1974	Left–right	0.40	91	0.28	28	0.34
	Libertarian–authoritarian	0.30	91	0.45	26	0.38
	EC	—	—	—	—	
	Mean 'A'	0.35		0.37		
1987	Left–right	0.33	122	0.22	41	0.28
	Libertarian–authoritarian	0.24	118	0.36	46	0.30
	EC	0.77	143	0.97	47	0.87
	Mean 'A'	0.29		0.29		
	Mean 'B'	0.45		0.52		
1992	Left–right	0.34	222	0.15	419	0.25
	Libertarian–authoritarian	0.40	291	0.40	489	0.40
	EC	—	—	—	—	
	Mean 'A'	0.37		0.28		
1997	Left–right	0.38	45	0.23	47	0.31
	Libertarian–authoritarian	0.27	41	0.29	45	0.28
	EC	0.93	46	0.67	44	0.80
	Mean 'A'	0.33		0.26		
	Mean 'B'	0.53		0.40		

Note: All figures are standard deviations. 'Mean A' refers to the mean standard deviation on the left–right and libertarian–authoritarian scales for each group of party members. 'Mean B' refers to the mean standard deviation on the left–right, Libertarian–authoritarian and EC scales for each group of party members.
Sources: BES, 1964–97; BCS, 1992.

respect to the left–right and libertarian-authoritarian scales, there is little of real note to comment upon; Labour members became somewhat more cohesive with respect to the left–right scale in 1992, but then became a little more diverse again in 1997. This point may contain a muted warning to Labour's strategists; while their CLP members may have become less radical than a decade previously, they may well also be more variegated now. This, perhaps, is the inevitable cost of the influx of Blair's army of new post-1994 recruits. Conservative members have altered little in terms of their cohesion on class values; the memberships of both parties have tended to fluctuate in terms of moral traditionalism. As expected, however, the question of European integration (EC) presents a quite different picture. At each of the time-points for which we have data, members of both parties prove notably less cohesive on this dimension than on the other two. Moreover, as we also expected, the Conservatives became much more diverse in their views on the issue over the course of the decade after 1987. When checked against other variables relating to the EU in the 1997 data set, however, it becomes clear that Labour has little cause to feel overly sanguine about its own position. Thus, an 11-point integration scale reveals that the difference between the two groups of party memberships is not so great; while the Labour members generate a standard deviation of 3.47 the Conservatives are only a little higher at 3.61. Similarly, the parties share almost identical standard deviations (though around rather different means) on the question of EMU (0.79 as against 0.81), while, surprisingly perhaps, Labour members actually appear far more split than the Conservatives in response to the question of whether Britain should withdraw from the EU in the long term (1.34 as against 0.81). Nevertheless, there can be little doubt that the history of intraparty conflict over Europe which has beset the Conservative Parliamentary Party since the late 1980s has been reflected in the attitudes of ordinary party members. To this extent, our findings remain consistent with the critical election thesis.

Party Members: Polarization, Extremism and Disparity

The analysis so far meets the primary purpose of this chapter, and though we cannot claim to have uncovered incontrovertible evidence that 1997 was indeed a critical election at the level of membership change, our findings are suggestive. We now turn to the second issue: how far does long-term change in members' attitudes conform to a model of electoralist party transformation?

The first test to investigate this relates to the degree of attitudinal polarization between major party members, something we can gauge by returning to Tables 3.2 and 3.4. The former of these unquestionably reveals that the attitudinal gulf between Labour and Conservative members on this issue was smaller in 1997 than at any time since British Election Surveys started in the 1960s. The gap between the two groups of party members on the issue of public ownership (as measured by the polarization index) suggests that the 1983 and 1992 elections provided the points of maximum attitudinal divergence. By 1997, however, the gap had shrunk so much (thanks to Labour's shift) that the difference between the two groups of party members was no longer statistically significant at the 5% level. This, indeed, fits well with most accounts, both academic and journalistic, of recent British party programmatic developments (see, for instance, Topf 1994: 164; Norris 1994, 1996: 158; and Chapter 1 of this volume).

This suggests that the first of our hypotheses, that of depolarization at the level of grassroots party members, is indeed borne out, but the analysis so far is certainly not conclusive. In the first place, it might be contended that ideological convergence between the major parties has been not so much a linear trend over time as the (temporary?) result of a long-term pattern of trendless fluctuation. Thus, Labour and Conservative members may be ideologically closer in the 1990s than in the 1980s, but then they were in the 1960s too. It is impossible to tell if attitudes will repolarize at some time in the future, and we would not wish to suggest that the convergence witnessed in the 1990s is an irreversible phenomenon. Nevertheless, the 1964 sample was gathered at virtually the same time that Kirchheimer was writing his influential account of the rise of the catch-all party, and yet membership polarization appears to have been substantially greater in 1964 than in 1997, at least according to our analysis of the nationalization issue. Thus, even if ideological differences between major party memberships do fluctuate, the current period of convergence appears to be unprecedented.

Table 3.4 provides a broader view of ideological change in the multi-item attitudinal scales. The most obvious feature of this table is that it exactly confirms the impression of recent ideological convergence between major party memberships, which we have already encountered in Table 3.2, at least in respect of class values. Once again, we find that the gap between Conservatives and Constituency Labour Party members is substantially reduced in the course of the decade after 1987, though it is equally plain that, once account is taken of issues other than public ownership, the party differences remain statistically significant. What is more, Table 3.4 suggests (unlike Table 3.2) that this ideological convergence is not dependent on the changing nature of one or the other of the party samples – both Tories and Labour members have apparently shifted towards each other since 1987 (though especially the latter). Ideological distinctions between Labour and Conservative Party members have generally been far less pronounced with respect to moral traditionalism, though once again they have remained significant throughout the period covered by our analysis. Major-party polarization is lower on the European question, though differences are significant at the 5% level. In short, contemporary major British parties still harbour, and most probably stimulate, distinctive ideological profiles at grassroots level, though not, on the whole, to the extent they did in the past.

The convergence of major party members' ideological stances means that they are closer to each other and also to the centre of gravity within

TABLE 3.6   *The extremism of party members, 1974–97*

Scale	Election	Electorate mean	n	Mean difference between Con members and all other voters	p	Mean difference between Lab members and all other voters	p
LR	1974 (O)	1.60	1782	−0.40	.000	0.35	.000
	1987	1.65	3205	−0.40	.000	0.43	.000
	1992	1.58	3092	−0.27	.000	0.50	.000
	1997	1.50	2447	−0.35	.000	0.14	.000
LA	1974 (O)	2.06	1850	−0.10	.006	0.14	.131
	1987	1.99	2970	−0.06	.021	0.28	.000
	1992	1.91	2787	−0.13	.000	0.50	.000
	1997	2.00	2223	−0.08	.057	0.16	.000
EC	1974 (O)	—	—	—	—	—	—
	1987	1.64	3572	0.26	.000	−0.08	.540
	1992	—	—	—	—	—	—
	1997	1.74	2614	0.05	.716	0.40	.001

Notes: 'Electorate mean' is the mean score on the respective attitudinal scales for all voters in the sample who are neither members of the Conservative Party nor the Labour Party. *p* reports the statistical significance of the attitudinal differences between party members and other voters (based on *T*-tests).
Sources: BES, 1964–97; BCS, 1992.

the electorate as whole, especially in terms of the highly salient class values dimension. To this extent, it is less appropriate to describe party members in the 1990s as 'extreme' than it might have been in previous decades. Table 3.6 examines the mean differences on the attitudinal scales between members and the electorate as a whole. Both Conservative and Labour members were closer to the electorate's overall mean for class values in 1997 than in either 1974 or 1987. Interestingly (as we might expect), the party whose members were closest to the grand mean on this scale won the election in each case (Labour in October 1974 and 1997, the Conservatives in 1987 and 1992). Note, however, that by 1997 Labour members had become most distinctive with respect to the relatively progressive and pro-European attitudes they display on the other two (and probably electorally less salient) ideological dimensions; certainly, they are further from the bulk of voters than Conservative members in this regard. By contrast, Conservative members stand out most from ordinary voters in terms of their right-of-centre class values. Even so, in terms of both class values and traditionalism, 1987 is confirmed as the high tide of CLP radicalism; fascinatingly, the clearest sense of membership 'extremism' in the 1990s emanates from the enthusiastic pro-European inclinations of Labour's members.

From the point of view of our ideal type of a party of electoral contestation, the evidence so far is persuasive; both sets of major party members in Britain appear to be as ideologically moderate in the 1990s as they have been at any time over the past quarter of a century (at least in respect of the electorally salient class values dimension), which implies that the parties' electoral strategists have been able to follow the dictates of Downsian competitive logic in pursuing the median voter. However, there must be more to the story than this. May's 'law of curvilinear disparity' suggests that, notwithstanding the efforts of party leaders, members are likely to remain significantly more radical than non-members in the electorate, even those sympathetic enough to vote for the party. Moreover, it is important to be aware that our analysis thus far has been based on the comparison of mean scores on the various attitudinal indicators we have devised; while undoubtedly useful, mean scores alone can of course obscure patterns of considerable variation within groups, and we have already noted that attitudinal cohesion can vary quite considerably across time, and that it remains highly problematic in respect of the European question. May's Law has often been characterized as especially relevant to the Labour Party given the grip which the radicals within the party's activist base were said to have gained over the traditionally moderate PLP leadership in the 1980s, to the party's electoral cost (Kogan and Kogan 1982). As a consequence, leaders since Neil Kinnock have sought to undermine the influence of these CLP radicals in a number of ways, not least through the instigation of new recruitment drives. From this perspective the point of these has been to flood the local parties with an influx of new members who are more 'representative' of the 'ordinary' voter, and thus to dilute the influence of the radicals. The dramatic success of the party in attracting new membership recruits since Tony Blair was elected leader in 1994 clearly points to the possibility that such a strategy has worked; indeed, the evidence we have reviewed so far is entirely consistent with such a possibility. Nevertheless, whatever the truth behind this question, there remains the possibility that, notwithstanding the influx of new 'Blairite' recruits, a more radical component of 'old Labour' radicals is still part of the membership brew; this in turn holds out the prospect of renewed internal opposition to the leadership's policies, especially if Labour in power begins to encounter problems of effective policy development and implementation. We can gain some insight into these matters by considering how disparate the members are and have been from the party's other supporters in the electorate.

In general terms, the gap between party members and voters diminished considerably in the 1990s. Indeed, for neither party is there any statistically significant ideological disparity remaining (at the 5% level) on the class values scale,[5] nor, for the Conservatives, is there on either the traditionalism or European dimensions. This need not necessarily be good news for the electoralist party manager, however, since the erosion of such

TABLE 3.7 *Ideological disparities between party members and voters, 1974–97*

Scale	Election	Members	*n*	Voters	*n*	Member–voter difference	*p*
Conservatives							
LR	1974 (O)	2.00	91	1.83	518	0.17	.000
	1987	2.05	122	1.89	1135	0.16	.000
	1992	1.85	222	1.82	1144	0.03	.206
	1997	1.86	45	1.76	559	0.10	.063
LA	1974 (O)	2.16	91	2.12	527	0.04	.262
	1987	2.05	118	2.04	1068	0.01	.600
	1992	2.04	291	1.94	1046	0.10	.000
	1997	2.08	41	2.07	506	0.01	.728
EC	1974 (O)	—	—	—	—	—	—
	1987	1.38	143	1.50	1259	–0.12	.100
	1992	—	—	—	—	—	—
	1997	1.69	46	1.84	585	–0.16	.299
Labour							
LR	1974 (O)	1.24	28	1.37	639	–0.13	.021
	1987	1.22	41	1.38	852	–0.16	.000
	1992	1.08	419	1.34	940	–0.26	.000
	1997	1.35	41	1.37	951	–0.02	.639
LA	1974 (O)	1.92	26	2.03	666	–0.11	.224
	1987	1.71	46	1.95	789	–0.24	.000
	1992	1.41	489	1.89	847	–0.48	.000
	1997	1.86	39	1.96	860	–0.10	.029
EC	1974 (O)	—	—	—	—	—	—
	1987	1.72	47	1.85	943	–0.13	.394
	1992	—	—	—	—	—	—
	1997	1.26	44	1.63	1016	–0.16	.001

Notes: The 'party voters' groups include those who voted for the party in question who were not also members of that party. Final column figures are *T*–test significance levels.
Sources: BES, 1964–97; BCS, 1992.

differences may simply signify that those who vote for the party have become (nearly) as radical as those who actually join it; if neither group is especially close to the median voter this is unlikely to help the party enhance its electoral performance. Such a scenario is certainly not far-fetched in the case of an organization like the contemporary Conservative Party, given the severe beating it took at the polls in 1997; conceivably, it is precisely because centrist voters deserted the party that its remaining supporters might be expected to be relatively ideological devotees. However, it is unlikely that such a development could provide a full explanation of the diminishing intrastrata attitudinal disparities among Conservatives given what we have already seen of the dwindling extremism of Conservative members in most respects. Indeed, examination of Table 3.7 shows that the shrinking gulf between party members and other Conservative voters on the class values scale owes more to the deradicalization of the former (from 2.05 to 1.86 between 1987 and 1997) than to the radicalization of the latter (who shifted from 1.89 to 1.76 in net terms).

For Labour, it appears that both members and voters (though especially the former) moved in a somewhat left-libertarian direction in the early 1990s before shifting closer to the centre-ground in 1997. On the question of Europe, however, both members and voters became notably more positive in the decade following the 1987 election, especially the former. Indeed, these figures suggest that this dimension of political belief may now be becoming the one which most distinguishes Labour members from other citizens; not only are they clearly more radical than the electorate in general on Europe, but they are significantly more so than other Labour voters too (Table 3.7). Thus, we may conclude that significant disparities between members and supporters in the electorate appear to have eroded to the point of virtual insignificance in the 1990s, except in so far as CLP members are significantly more libertarian and pro-European than Labour voters at large.

Conclusions

Our evidence suggests that the 1997 election, seen in long-term perspective, may have represented a point of critical realignment in the predominant pattern of party competition in Britain. This is shown in the unprecedented swing to the ideological centre-ground of Labour Party members, due in part to the influx of new recruits after Tony Blair's accession to the leadership. Assuming that it is the long-term aim of the New Labour leadership to catalyse an enduring realignment of party–voter links, the news that the party's rank-and-file members seem prepared to follow the Blairite lead in 1997 appears highly significant. It is also possible that the changes in membership attitudes over Europe portend some kind of long-term shift in patterns of party competition and electoral realignment, a point strengthened by the relatively low levels of attitudinal cohesion which both sets of party members (but especially the Conservatives) display on this dimension.

In addition, we have seen that 1997 appears to represent a point as close to that of the ideal model of electoral contestation as major party strategists and managers could realistically hope for, and certainly as close as this country has experienced in recent memory. This is evident in the minimization of two aspects of internal party life which are crucial to the prospects of any electorally motivated organization: the extremism of party members in relation to the electorate as a whole (at least on the class values dimension which has been so salient in British politics); and the degree of ideological disparity between members and non-member supporters in the electorate. In addition, the catch-all model seems to have been fully borne out at the systemic levels by the consequent pattern of ideological convergence between major party members. All these developments might seem to bespeak a state of affairs in which the major parties have become purely electoralist organizations lacking any distinctive ideological profiles at grassroots level. So is that it? Is British party politics simply and nakedly a matter of vote-winning and office-seeking, with the members to be regarded as a nothing more than a useful but deferential resource in the business of garnering votes at the local level? Few who observe the everyday conflicts between and within parties would concur in such a conclusion. There are two points in particular which serve as important caveats against those who would be tempted to conclude that British party politics has arrived at an enduring equilibrium of unalloyed electoralism.

First, historical context is largely ignored in our analysis, and new contexts may well serve to revivify the ideological edge of party conflict at future elections, producing future repolarization and the re-emergence of internal ideological disparities between different party strata. For instance, our evidence seems consistent with the notion that the influx of Blairite members into the Labour Party has heavily moderated the overall ideological profile of the membership and eroded intrastrata disparities since 1994. But what if such members melt away at the first (or even second) sign of disappointment with the Blair government in practice? We have already noted a partial reversal of Labour's recruitment successes over the winter of 1997–98, and research suggests that the Blairite members are generally less active than CLP members of longer standing. There must be some grounds for doubt, therefore, about the depth of commitment of these new members to the party cause. This in turn implies that their moderating influence on the overall attitudinal profile of Labour's membership may yet dwindle.

Secondly, our analysis of the attitudinal cohesion of party memberships suggests that major party leaders would be most unwise to assume that grassroots members are overwhelmingly of precisely the same ideological hue as themselves or less committed supporters within the electorate.

Again, given a change of political context, it is not hard to imagine the re-emergence of intraparty discord both between and within different party strata. This is as much a warning to the Labour government as it is to William Hague's opposition which carries the obvious burden of potential and actual disharmony over the question of European integration; its first year in office provided Tony Blair's government with a number of examples of internal dissent and criticism of the leadership across a range of policy issues. All this means that, while it is undeniable that the 1997 election appears to represent some kind of a summit of catch-all or electoral-professional party development in so far as membership attitudes became as 'tame' as the leaderships could possibly have desired, nothing is for ever; issues, agendas and circumstances are constantly in flux, and the memberships simply cannot be taken for granted.

Notes

1. Note that the measures employed in addressing questions 2–5 owe much to the research design devised by Pippa Norris (1994).
2. Note that, since the question on workers' rights is not included in the BCS 1992, it has been excluded from the LR scale. See the Appendix to this chapter for full details of the construction of these attitudinal scales.
3. Based on single sample *T*-statistic significance tests comparing the differences in group means.
4. This finding is supported by reference to a further European indicator which is, unfortunately, only available in the 1997 BES; on a scale running from 1 (respondent would like to see the UK completely integrated within the EU) to 11 (respondent wishes to see national independence maintained at all costs) the Labour Party members in the sample ($n = 50$) averaged a score of 4.1 while their Tory counterparts averaged 7.4 ($n = 46$).
5. This bears out findings of previous research by Norris (1995: 41).

Appendix: The Attitudinal Scales

Most of the chapters examining aspects of long-term change in this volume have had to confront the problem of identifying comparable and relevant attitudinal variables across a reasonable number of British Election Surveys; in addition, in this chapter we have been further constrained by the fact that these surveys have not always incorporated the party membership variable. However, we have managed to select a number of relevant items included in several BES data sets and in the British Candidate Survey (BCS) 1992; the latter is important in so far as it includes a party membership sample, whereas the BES 1992 does not. It is particularly interesting to include 1992 in our time series since this permits us, if only on the basis of circumstantial evidence, to draw inferences about the impact of 'New Labour' members who joined the party some time after the election held that year. Thus, while our non-member sample for 1992 is drawn from the BES, the membership sample is drawn from the BCS.

Bearing in mind these various constraints, we have been able to create an additive 'left–right' scale (LR) based on four items and a libertarian–authoritarian scale (LA) based on three items. With respect to the former, these include

TABLE 3.A   *Factor analyses*

	Oct 1974		1987		1992 (BES)		1992 (BES)		1997	
	Fac1	Fac2	Fac1	Fac2	Fac1	Fac2	Fac1	Fac2	Fac1	Fac2
Nationalization	.62	.01	.68	-.04	.81	.26	.65	-.05	.59	.04
Poverty	.67	.13	.68	.17	.81	.13	.69	.17	.68	.14
NHS	.44	.29	.69	.12	.81	.17	.72	.12	.69	-.01
Redistribution	.80	.00	.74	.01	.84	.19	.75	-.05	.72	.01
Abortion	-.02	.65	-.14	.57	.53	.53	-.10	.49	-.12	.55
Sex equality	.13	.62	.20	.70	.51	.58	.18	.74	.21	.75
Race equality	.11	.65	.17	.70	.04	.89	.11	.73	.11	.74
Eigenvalue	1.9	1.1	2.2	1.2	3.9	0.9	2.2	1.3	2.0	1.3
% variance explained	27.4	15.8	31.5	17.2	55.3	13.0	30.7	17.9	29.0	18.5

Notes: Factor 1: class values (left-right dimension); factor 2: social traditionalism (libertarian–authoritarian dimension). All factor loadings are varimax rotated.
Sources: It was necessary to use two data sets gathered in 1992 in order to obtain samples of both members and voters; the British Candidate Survey (BCS) provided us with the sample of party members, while the British Election Survey (BES) furnished the voter sample.

questions about the desirability of government action to counter poverty ('poverty'), the funding of the National Health Service ('NHS'), the redistribution of income and wealth ('redistribution') and the public ownership of industry ('nationalization'). With respect to the latter scale, our three items were suggested by a reading of Norris (1997: 169) and consist of attitudes towards the availability of abortion on the NHS ('abortion'), the pursuit of equality between the genders ('sex equality') and action to achieve racial equality ('race equality'). All item responses have been coded so that left-wing or progressive/libertarian responses are consistently valued '1' while right-wing or traditionalist/authoritarian responses are always coded '3'.

To check the presumed validity of these items as scale components, they have been subjected to factor analyses. The results reported in Table 3.A confirm in a very straightforward manner that the seven items do, in the case of each of the surveys in question (October 1974, 1987, 1992 and 1997), break down into just two factors; moreover, without exception they divide in precisely the way we hypothesized, with the proposed class ('left-right') values loading most strongly on to factor 1 and the proposed traditionalism ('libertarian–authoritarian') values loading on to factor 2. The four class values items have been combined into a simple additive scale, while the three traditionalism items have been similarly combined into a separate scale. After dividing by the number of items in each scale we are left with a class values scale running from 1 (left) to 3 (right) and a

TABLE 3.B   *Cronbach alpha reliability coefficients for scales*

	Class values (LR)	Traditionalism (LA)
October 1974	.54 (*n* = 1,941)	.35 (*n* = 2,031)
1987	.64 (*n* = 3,406)	.38 (*n* = 3,173)
1992 (BCS)	.86 (*n* = 641)	.65 (*n* = 780)
1992 (BES)	.63 (*n* = 3,161)	.37 (*n* = 2,851)
1997	.53 (*n* = 2,557)	.44 (*n* = 2,322)

traditionalism scale ranging from 1 (progressive/libertarian) to 3 (tradition-alist/authoritarian). Reliability tests for these scales are reported in Table 3.B Cronbach alpha coefficients). The EC scale on European integration is a far simpler affair. There is only one item relating to the issue of Europe which is common to the 1987 and 1997 BES questionnaires: a comparable indicator appears neither in the BES of October 1974, nor the BCS of 1992, which is why attitude towards Europe is not reported for these years. In 1987 and 1997, however, respondents were asked if they felt Britain should stay in or withdraw from the EC/EU, and we have coded responses so that 1 represents the former position while 3 represents the latter ('don't knows' were coded 2).

4 Party Loyalties: Dealignment or Realignment?

Ivor Crewe and Katarina Thomson

> There are times, perhaps once every thirty years, when there is a sea-change in politics. It then does not matter what you say or what you do. There is a shift in what the public wants and what the public approves of. I suspect there is now such a sea-change – and it is for Mrs. Thatcher (James Callaghan, quoted in Donoughue 1987: 191).

An emphatic election result usually produces the instant verdict that it was a 'critical' election, the moment in history that the old party system made way for the new. The 1997 election is no exception. The media contain countless references to the inevitability of Labour winning a second term, and probably a third, and thus being in power for at least a decade (e.g. Cowling 1998). Usually the pundits turn out to be wrong. Debility and division in government and disillusion on the doorsteps can reverse election landslides in a remarkably short time. The left's past election triumphs have been particularly short-lived. The 1906 Liberal landslide (128 seat majority, 6.0% vote lead) was followed by a hung Parliament in the two elections held four years later; Labour's massive majority of 146 in 1945 (8.4% lead in the vote) crumbled to an unsustainable 5 in 1950 and was overturned in 1951; Harold Wilson's two-stage advance to a majority of 102 in 1966 (6% lead in vote) was wiped out four years later. Twelve months into the last Parliament academics were contributing to debates about the onset of Conservative hegemony and one-party democracy in Britain (King 1992; Margetts and Smyth 1994).

Occasionally, however, the commentators turn out to be right. The warning tremors in the preceding Parliament culminate in an electoral earthquake that permanently alters the party political landscape. The election registers an underlying and enduring change of outlook among voters, a fresh political agenda and a shift in the terms of public debate, which the incoming government exploits in its favour (sometimes abetted by the Opposition) for years to come. In retrospect the 1979 election was one such occasion, as James Callaghan understood.

Will 1997 turn out to be the New Labour equivalent of 1979 or an old Labour repeat of 1966? Will it come to be regarded as a critical 'realigning' election or a one-off 'deviating' election from Conservative hegemony?

These questions are, of course, impossible to answer. The assessment depends on unknowable future events – on the new government's performance, on Conservative reaction to defeat, on global economic forces and geopolitical events beyond the government's control. Who in 1981 – the year of three million unemployed, a savagely deflationary budget and the emergence of the SDP – foresaw 16 more years of Conservative power? That does not make the question about 1997 entirely pointless. We can explore how far the 1997 election resembles what in hindsight were realigning elections of the past in Britain or elsewhere. The closeness or lack of resemblance at least enables us to judge the prospects of the Blair government fashioning a realignment of the party system if it has the skill, will and luck.

The Classical Model of Partisan Realignment

To move beyond mere guesswork, a serious analysis of a party system's prospects needs to base itself on a model of partisan realignment – general propositions about their cause, timing, direction and scale – derived from the analysis of past realignments. Most of the modelling has been done in the USA (Key 1955, 1959; Clubb and Allen 1971; Sundquist 1973; Burnham 1970, 1975) and is heavily influenced by the three 'classical' instances of realignment in 1852–56, 1896 and 1932, and the fuzzier case of 1964–72. The model therefore reflects the particular circumstances of US elections – for example, a directly elected chief executive, split-level elections, the two-party system, the registration of party support, 'independent' party identifiers – but can be adapted to British conditions.

Details vary, but generally realignments are depicted as going through three stages: a prior dealigning phase; a 'critical' realigning election, or perhaps series of elections; followed by a stable period of consolidation (for a more detailed account, see the Introduction). Two crucial concepts are 'dealignment' and 'realignment'. By dealignment is meant a weakening of partisan loyalty to one or both major parties. Evidence of dealignment from a party would include, for example, a weakening in its supporters' identification and constancy or a drop in its nominal and active membership. For the party in office it would include an exceptionally sharp fall in its vote at the various mid-term elections (local, European and parliamentary by-elections); for the main Opposition party, it would include a failure to improve on its previous general election performance at mid-term elections. By realignment is meant an enduring change in the normal level of electoral support for one or both main parties, accompanied by a shift in the social and ideological basis of party support. This change might affect the balance of support between one major party and the other (without necessarily implying a reversal), or between the two parties combined and one or more minor parties, or elements of both. Evidence for a realignment would be based on long-term *levels* of party identification or on voting at a series of elections (not only general elections) or support in regular opinion polls – and on their social and ideological correlates.

The Contrasting Characteristics of Deviating and Realigning Elections

In the American literature the identification of realigning and deviating elections has been based on the pattern of relationships between party identification and the vote, and on trends in these relationships over time. No single critical test can determine decisively the status of a very recent election, but pairs of contrasting propositions, based on the classical model of realignment, can be formulated which, when tested against the evidence, enable us to judge the 1997 election's potential as a realigning election. These propositions, in the form of the contrasting characteristics that one would expect of the two types of election, are set out in Table 4.1. We shall examine each in turn.

The Distribution of Party Identification in 1997

Table 4.2 sets out the changing distribution of party identification from 1964 (the first election at which party identification was measured) to 1997.[1] In a 'deviating' election the underlying distribution of party

TABLE 4.1   *Characteristics of 'deviating' and 'critical' elections*

Characteristic	'Deviating' election	Critical election
Distribution of party identification	Minor or no change	Major change
Shift in distribution of party identification compared with shift in vote	Small	Large
Weakening of party identification in electorate as a whole	Small	Large
Overall change in strength of identification	Minor or none	Major
Among Conservatives	Some weakening	Substantial weakening
Among Labour	Some strengthening	Some weakening
Vote defections from Conservative identification	Sharp increase especially among weak identifiers	Little change
Cohort analysis of change in distribution of party identification	No differences across cohorts	Bigger changes in younger cohorts
Negative/positive motivations of vote	Shift against Conservatives more significant than shift in favour of Labour	Shift against Conservatives less significant than shift in favour of Labour
Balance of positive and negative identification	Negative identification grows	Polarized identification grows
Perceived significance of election	Minor	Major

TABLE 4.2   *Trends in party identification, 1964–97 (%)*

	1964	1966[1]	1970	1974F	1974O[2]	1979	1983	1987	1992	1997
None	4	5	6	4	4	6	5	5	5	7
Conservative	40	38	41	38	36	41	40	42	45	30
Labour	44	47	45	43	42	39	33	33	33	46
LibDem/Liberal/SDP	12	10	8	14	15	12	19	18	13	13
Other	0	1	1	2	3	1	2	2	3	4
Weighted (*n*)	1,828	2,082	1,885	2,462	2,365	1,893	3,955	3,826	2,855	2,677

Notes: (1) 1966: a small number of people who had already given a 'narrow' party ID were also asked the follow-up, thus giving them different 'narrow' and 'broad' party IDs. In these cases, we have used the narrow party ID so as to make the data comparable with other years. (2) Oct 1974: as for 1966.

loyalties is stable but the government is defeated by a temporary protest of dissatisfied voters. If 1997 was a deviating election one would therefore expect any redistribution from Conservative to Labour to be modest and much more muted than the net shift in the national vote between the two parties. If, however, 1997 was a realigning election one would expect a much more significant redistribution, which confirmed a durable change that originated years earlier and was of a similar scale to the change in vote. Either the change in party identification preceded and caused the change in vote, or both party identification and vote were simultaneously changed by the same 'converting' factor.

The redistribution of party identification in 1997 was far and away the most dramatic of any election since 1964. The proportion of Conservative identifiers fell from 45 to 30% and the proportion of Labour identifiers increased from 33 to 46%. At 30% the level of Conservative identification was markedly lower than in any election since 1964, its previously lowest level being 36% in October 1974. At 46% Labour identification was restored to its level in the Wilson years of 1964–70, having remained stuck at 33% from 1983 to 1992. The change in the balance of two-party identi-fication (from a 12-point Conservative lead in 1992 to a 16-point Labour lead in 1997) was by far the sharpest since 1964. Labour has emphatically replaced the Conservatives as the 'natural majority' party. At first glance, therefore, the figures point to a realigning election.

A second glance at Table 4.2, however, raises serious doubts about such an interpretation. It shows that the redistribution of party identification almost always shadows the redistribution of the vote at the same election. (The exceptions, possibly due to sampling error, are 1987 and 1992.) When the Conservative (or Labour) share of the vote increased the Conservative (or Labour) level of identification rose; when its share of the vote decreased, the level of identification fell. The close tracking of changes in vote and party identification prompts acute suspicions about the validity of the standard questions about party identification. Do they measure long-term party attachments or are they, for many respondents, simply an alternatively phrased question about their immediate voting preferences? Does the very distinction between party identification and vote have any meaning for most voters?

In the 1960s Butler and Stokes (1969) noted that vote-switching was more often accompanied by a parallel switch of party identification in Britain than in the USA, and Holmberg (1994) has found the same for Canada, Sweden and The Netherlands (see also Thomassen, 1994).[2] Johnston and Pattie's series of analyses (1996, 1997a, 1997b) of the annual British Household Panel Study has revealed the instability of the strength and direction of party identification of the same respondents over as short a period as a year, even though the party identification questions are intended to measure long-term loyalties. Brynin and Sanders' analysis (1993) of the magnitude of monthly variations in response to the standard party identification question led them to conclude that 'it is highly debatable as to whether these responses can be regarded as reflecting electors' enduring affective attachments to particular political parties'. The conscious distinction in the minds of voters between an enduring party identification and an immediate voting preference may be a peculiarly American phenomenon, brought about by electoral arrangements such as multiple-level elections and party registration which find no parallel in Britain. We have to recognize, therefore, that the particularly sharp redistribution of party identification in 1997 *might* be largely an artifact of the exceptional net change in the Conservative and Labour vote in 1997 and signify nothing more than measurement error.

Table 4.3 offers one crumb of comfort. It answers the following question: in those elections which swung to Labour what proportion of those who switched to a Labour vote but had neither voted nor identified with Labour in the previous election also changed identification to Labour?[3] It shows that a majority of such Labour recruits switched to a Labour identification at the same time; but the proportion was lower in 1997 (59%) than in either February 1974 (83%), October 1974 (68%) or 1987 (67%) although higher than in 1992 (54%). The percentage bases are small and the pattern is not pronounced but the table does suggest that the measure of party identification was no more dependent on voting preferences in 1997 than previously, even though the progressive weakening of partisanship by 1997 (see below) might have been expected to lead in that direction. Unfortunately the problem of measuring party identification can only be resolved by a separate panel study, which experiments with different question designs on split samples, and must be set aside in this chapter.[4]

TABLE 4.3 *Non-Labour identifiers at first election who switched to Labour vote at second election, 1964–97 (%)*

	1964–66	1970–Feb 1974	F1974–O1974	1983–87	1987–92	1992–97
Switched ID to Labour	61	83	68	67	54	59
ID stayed non-Labour	39	17	32	33	46	41
Total	100	100	100	100	100	100
(*n*)	(41)	(24)	(22)	(12)	(69)	(101)

Source: BES panels.

A second reason for believing that the sharp redistribution of party identification in 1997 was not mere measurement error is that it occurred in the first half of the 1992–97 Parliament, well in advance of when the electorate needed to decide how to vote. As Table 4.4 shows, the proportion of a panel established in 1992 (and annually recontacted subsequently) who identified with the Conservatives fell from 45% in 1992 to 36% in 1997 (immediately before the election) while the proportion identifying with Labour rose from 33 to 41%. The loss of Conservative identifiers occurred entirely between 1992 and 1994, after which the level of identification remained stable. The growth of Labour identifiers was not quite a mirror image. It took a year longer, with an additional boost in 1994–95 after Tony Blair's election as Labour leader, but was complete two years before the 1997 election. The weakening of identification among Conservative partisans followed a similar pattern except for a slight recovery in April 1997, when the election campaign was in full swing and mobilized latent loyalties. The rock-solid stability of partisanship from 1995 onwards offers an instructive contrast to the 1959–64 period when the ratio of Labour to Conservative identifiers narrowed appreciably in the final year (Crewe *et al.* 1995: 47)

One further difference between 1997 and earlier elections hints at its potentially realigning character. At previous elections that have overturned the government the net shift in party identification has been smaller than the net shift in the vote (see Table 4.5). For example, in 1970 the net shift in the Conservative and Labour vote was 9.5 percentage points while the net shift in party identification was only 5 percentage points. More people voted Conservative than Labour (by a 3.3% margin) but more people identified with Labour than with the Conservatives (by a 4% margin) – the mark of a classic 'deviating' election. In February 1974 the Conservative vote plummeted by 9 percentage points but Conservative identification slipped by only 3 percentage points; similarly the Labour vote fell by 6 points but Labour identification by only 2 points.

TABLE 4.4 *Party identification, 1992–97 (%)*

	1992	1994	1995	1996	1997
Conservative	45	35	35	36	36
% Very/fairly strong[1]	*0.73*	*0.57*	*0.57*	*0.58*	*0.72*
Labour	33	39	42	41	41
% Very/fairly strong	*0.70*	*0.69*	*0.71*	*0.73*	*0.83*
Lib-Dem	13	18	16	15	16
% Very/fairly strong	*0.54*	*0.39*	*0.44*	*0.47*	*0.63*
Other	3	4	3	3	3
None	5	4	4	4	4
Total[2]	100	100	100	100	100
(Weighted *n*)	(2,855)	(1,859)	(1,625)	(1,372)	(1,391)

Notes: (1) i.e. the proportion of each party's identifiers who expressed a 'very' or 'fairly' strong identification. (2) Columns do not always sum to exactly 100, due to rounding. *Source:* BES, 1992–97, panel (BEPS). There was only a postal survey in 1993.

TABLE 4.5 *Change in the Conservative and Labour share of the vote and party identification,* 1966–97

	Conservative share of		Labour share of		Con and Lab combined swing in	
	The vote	Party ID	The vote	Party ID	The vote	Party ID
1966	−2	−3	+4	+4	6	6
1970	+5	+3	−5	−3	10	6
Feb 1974	−7	−3	−6	−1	13	5
1979	+8	+5	−2	−3	11	8
1983	−1	−1	−10	−6	11	7
1997	−11	−14	+9	+12	20	26

Source: BES cross-section surveys, 1966–97.

In 1979 the swing back in the Conservative vote (8 percentage points) exceeded the growth of Conservative identification (5 points) and in 1983 the collapse of Labour support was more marked in its vote (down 9 points) than in its level of identification (down 6 points). The 1997 election was different: the Conservative level of identification (down 15 points) fell by even more than the Conservative share of the vote (down 11 points) while the Labour level of identification (up 13 points) rose by even more than the Labour share of the vote (9 points). For the first time since measurements were taken a major reversal of party support in an election has been matched by an equally major reversal of underlying party loyalties. The election tremors of the past have left the foundations of the party system more or less intact; but the tremors of 1992–95 cracked the foundations and led to the earthquake of 1997.

But the foundations have anyway been wearing away over the past 30 years. An irregular but unremitting weakening of partisanship in the electorate – 'partisan dealignment' – was first identified by Crewe *et al.* (1977) in the late 1970s, who showed that it was partly a short-term reaction to the successive failures of Wilson's Labour administration of 1966–70 and Heath's Conservative administration of 1970–74 but was underpinned by two parallel trends – a weakening of class-based voting and a growing ideological gulf between the Labour Party and its working-class base. As Figure 4.1 shows, partisan dealignment has continued unremittingly since. Without exception each election has recorded a slightly weaker attachment in the electorate to the parties than in the previous election. The most notable weakening occurred at the two elections which ushered in long-lasting changes in the shape of the party system – February 1974 and 1979 – and in 1997. The cumulative effect over the whole period amounts to a pronounced change in the partisan character of the electorate. In 1964 and 1966 fully 44% described themselves as 'very strong' party identifiers (almost all Conservative or Labour) and only 18% said that they were 'not very strong' identifiers or identified with no party at all. In 1997 the proportions were almost exactly reversed: only 16% declared themselves to be 'very strong identifiers' while 42% acknowledged having a weak identification or none. Over the

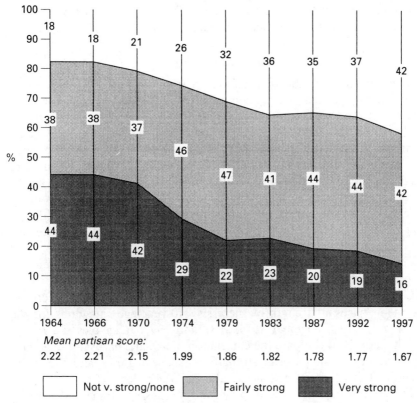

FIGURE 4.1   *Strength of identification,* 1964–97
Source: BES

three decades the electorate has moved from committed partisanship to semi-detached preferences. The conditions for a realigning election have steadily become more favourable.

A measure of dealignment is a precondition for any realignment of the party system. The weaker the electorate's loyalties the more volatile its voting decisions and the greater the opportunity for a new or reconstituted party to capture support that was hitherto beyond its reach. (For a warning against assuming an automatic link, however, see Heath and McDonald 1988.) If the contraction or weakening of partisanship is confined to only one of the major parties, that party is vulnerable to a sudden relegation to permanent minority status, or at least long-lasting opposition. If the contraction or weakening applies simultaneously to both major parties, the party system is open to the permanent breakthrough of new or previously small parties to major status. The connection between dealignment and realignment is illustrated by the change occurring among 18–24-year-olds, whose partisanship was weaker than that of any other age group in both 1992 and 1997: it registered by far the largest shift in party identification from Conservative to Labour.[5] In 1997 Labour trounced the Conservatives in the important battle for the allegiance of new electors.

Age/Cohort Analysis of Dealignment, 1966–97

The unremitting erosion of partisanship from 1964 to 1997 could be a generational (or 'cohort') phenomenon or a 'period' phenomenon, or a mixture of the two. It could be explained by the entry into the electorate in the 1960s and 1970s of one or a succession of cohorts of very weak partisans (the result itself, of course, of the politics of the time). The partisanship of the electorate overall will have weakened as older and more partisan generations died out – so long as there was no reversion to strong partisanship among the incoming 'Thatcher' cohorts of the 1980s or an acceleration of the normal strengthening of partisanship with age during that politically divided and strident period. Alternatively the progressive dealignment of the three decades could be explained by long-term and deep political and social forces, which have gradually loosened the emotional attachment of voter to party across all generations and ages.

Light is shed by the age and cohort analysis of Table 4.6, which sets out the mean partisan strength of successive 10-year age categories for the elections of 1966, October 1974, 1987 and 1997. It enables the reader simultaneously to compare the correlation of age and partisanship at each election, the mean partisan strength of age categories and the mean partisan strength of cohorts, across the three decades.

The columns in the table display the relationship of age and partisan strength at each election. In the standard account of the lifetime evolution of partisanship, people's sense of identification with a party strengthens as they age, particularly as they mature through their late twenties and thirties. The columns in Table 4.6 confirm for each election that, with few exceptions, the older the voter the stronger their partisanship; thus in 1997 mean partisan strength varied from 1.72 among 18–24-year-olds to 2.00

TABLE 4.6 *Age and cohort analysis of mean partisan strength, 1966–97*

Age	1966	Oct 1974	1987	1997	1966–97 (age category)	(cohort)
Under 25	2.08	1.85	1.63	1.72	–0.36	
25–34	2.19	1.91	1.75	1.65	–0.54	
35–44	2.32	2.00	1.85	1.79	–0.53	
45–54	2.31	2.02	1.95	1.77	–0.54	
55–64	2.41	2.02	2.02	1.83	–0.56	–0.36
65–74	2.48	2.30	2.14	2.01	–0.47	–0.31
75+	2.60	2.38	2.11	2.00	–0.60	–0.30
Difference:						
Under 25–75+	0.52	0.53	0.48	0.28		

Note: Limited to Conservative, Labour and Liberal (Democrat) party identifiers.
Source: BES cross-sections. See also Crewe *et al.* (1995: 48–51).

among the 65 plus. If dealignment were a generational phenomenon, attributable to the exceptionally weak partisanship of younger cohorts, the gap in partisan strength between youngest and oldest age groups would increase over time. In fact the gap in partisan strength narrows rather than widens between 1966 and 1997, partly because the youngest cohort in 1997 was more partisan than its predecessor in 1987 (and 1992).

The rows in the table measure the change over 30 years in the mean partisan strength of the same age categories. They show that partisan strength is weaker in all categories in 1997 than 1966 – as one might have expected from the marked dealignment of the electorate as a whole over this period. For example, the mean partisan strength of the under 25s fell from 2.08 in 1966 to 1.72 in 1997; and that of the over 74s from 2.60 to 2.00. Thus the under 25s in 1966 were stronger partisans than the over 74s in 1997. A generational dealignment would reveal itself in a steeper fall in the middle of the age range than the ends, whereas a period dealignment would reveal itself in similar falls across all age categories – which is what the data show.

The diagonals in the table allow the reader to trace the changes (with a little imprecision) in the partisan strength of different 1966 cohorts across the three decades to 1997. For example, the 25–34-year age group in 1966 was (roughly) 35–44 in October 1974, 45–54 in 1987 and 55–64 in 1997; the 35–44-year age group in 1966 was 65–74 by 1997; and so forth. In a generational dealignment the partisanship of new cohorts would strengthen as they matured, on a lower but parallel slope to that of predecessor cohorts. In a period of dealignment, the natural deepening of party attachments among those maturing through their thirties and forties would be retarded, compared with previous generations, by countervailing forces. Table 4.6 shows that period effects were so much more powerful than normal maturation effects that the 25–34-year-old generation in 1966 (the Labour-leaning young generation of the Wilson years) grew steadily less attached to parties as they aged, even in Labour's *annus mirabilis* of 1997: in 1966 their mean partisan strength was 2.19; in 1997 it had fallen to 1.83. The same pattern applies to the 35–44 and 45–54-year-old cohorts of 1966.

The uninterrupted dissolution of partisanship over the past three decades suggests that powerful and lasting forces are eroding the social and ideological bases of voters' loyalties to party, even if the trend is retarded or accelerated at particular points by political events. Trends are never irreversible; but the British electorate is likely to remain relatively feeble in its partisanship over the medium term. This provides the new Labour government with the opportunity to harden the overwhelming but soft Labour partisanship of young voters into a New Labour generation; but those same voters are open to conversion to another party if the government is perceived to fail.

The opportunity open to the Blair government to rebuild Labour partisanship is underlined by Table 4.7, which replicates the age/cohort analysis

TABLE 4.7   *Age and cohort analysis of mean partisan strength: Labour identifiers, 1966–97*

Age	1966	Oct 1974	1987	1997	1966–97 (age category)	(cohort)
Under 25	2.04	1.97	1.68	1.76	–0.28	
25–34	2.19	1.99	1.84	1.71	–0.48	
35–44	2.33	2.11	1.88	1.91	–0.42	
45–54	2.38	2.17	2.02	1.91	–0.47	
55–64	2.56	2.31	2.09	1.92	–0.64	–0.27
65–74	2.58	2.45	2.24	2.19	–0.39	–0.14
75+	2.58	2.51	2.15	2.21	–0.37	–0.17
Difference:						
Under 25–75+	0.54	0.54	0.47	0.47		

Source: BES cross–sections. See also Crewe *et al.* (1995: 48–51).

of the 1966–97 period for Labour identifiers only. As expected, it shows that the partisan strength of each age group of Labour identifiers was markedly lower in 1997 than in 1966 (see the changes across the rows) and that generational cohorts weakened in their Labour partisanship as they aged through the three decades (see the changes along the diagonals).[6] However, comparison between 1987 and 1997 does point to a revival of partisan strength in recent years. The under-25 cohort – very largely first-time voters – were marginally stronger partisans (with a mean score of 1.76) than their counterparts in 1987 (1.68). Moreover, the three youngest cohorts in 1987 have each strengthened their Labour partisanship over the most recent decade, in contrast to the pattern of weakening found among their counterparts in the 1970s and 1980s. In 1997 the allegiance of the younger generations of Labour sympathizers was much more precarious than in the previous landslide of 1966; but at least the long-term trend of partisan weakening went into reverse.

Strength of Conservative and Labour Partisanship

A further particle of support for the thesis that 1997 is a potentially realigning election is provided by Tables 4.9 and 4.10 (below), which compare the strength of Conservative and Labour identification, respectively, in 1997 with 1992 and with earlier elections won by Labour. Had 1997 been a deviating election one would have expected sharply increased vote defection rates from a stable bloc of Conservative party identifiers, that is, who had diminished only slightly in number and in strength of partisanship. Table 4.8 reveals a very different picture. Vote defection rates in 1997 among categories of Conservative identifier did rise compared with 1992 but were similar to those in previous elections at which the Conservatives have been defeated (although slightly higher overall). The marked change was the sharp rise in the proportion of 'not very strong' identifiers and equally sharp fall in the proportion of 'very strong' identifiers, despite the significant shrinkage in the size of the Conservative bloc. This contradicts what one might have expected, for it would be natural

TABLE 4.8 *Conservative partisan identification and vote defection, 1964–97 (%)*

	1964	1966	Oct 1974	1992	1997
Very strong	47	47	26	21	14
% Vote defection	*3%*	*2%*	*4%*	*1%*	*2%*
Fairly strong	40	38	51	50	48
% Vote defection	*6%*	*7%*	*11%*	*7%*	*12%*
Not very strong	13	15	23	29	38
% Vote defection	*20%*	*27%*	*27%*	*20%*	*25%*
Total	100	100	100	100	100
(*n*)	(716)	(692)	(838)	(1,265)	(1,057)
Mean strength[1]	2.35	2.32	2.04	1.91	1.75
% of electorate who are Conservative identifiers[2]	40	38	36	45	30
% Vote defection	*6%*	*7%*	*12%*	*9%*	*15%*
'Very strong' identifiers	19	18	9	10	4
'Very'/'fairly' strong identifiers	35	32	28	32	16

Notes: (1) 'Very strong' = 3; 'Fairly strong' = 2; 'Not very strong' = 1.
(2) i.e. Conservative identifiers as % of all respondents, including non-identifiers and d/k/ refusers.
Source: BES cross-section surveys. See also Crewe *et al.* (1995: 47).

to assume that a contraction of Conservative identifiers would involve the dropping away of the least committed, leaving a smaller but more steadfast group. Comparison between 1997 and the previous Labour landslide of 1966 is instructive. In 1966, 38% of the electorate were Conservative identifiers (only a fraction below the mean proportion for the whole of the 1964–92 period) and the overwhelming majority (85%) were 'very' or 'fairly' strong identifiers. By this measure the bloc of committed partisan Conservatives constituted one-third (32%) of the electorate – of sufficient size to provide a platform for rapid recovery. In October 1974 that bloc was a little smaller (27%) but still sizeable. But in 1997 only 30% gave themselves a Conservative identification and of these a much diminished proportion (62%) were 'very' or 'fairly' strong identifiers: committed partisans had therefore diminished to under a fifth (18%), and steadfast party loyalists – the 'very strong' identifiers – to a mere 4%, a very low base from which to restore electoral fortunes in a single Parliament.

The dwindling Conservative base of partisan loyalists has not been matched by a commensurate expansion of Labour's base – despite the one-third increase in the proportion of Labour identifiers between 1992 and 1997. For, as Table 4.9 shows, the partisanship of Labour identifiers was marginally weaker in 1997 than in 1992 and markedly weaker than in 1974 or 1964–66. The slight weakening between 1992 and 1997 reflects the substantial entry of new recruits into the ranks of Labour identifiers and is unsurprising: one would expect them to call themselves 'not very strong' identifiers. Once again, the telling comparison is with 1964–66. Then the bloc of committed Labour partisans comprised about 40% of the electorate (38% in 1964, 42% in 1966); now, even though the Labour

TABLE 4.9 *Strength of Labour partisan identification,* 1964–97 (%)

	1964	1966	Oct 1974	1992	1997
Very strong	50	48	35	25	22
Fairly strong	37	40	46	45	46
Not very strong	13	12	19	31	32
Total	100	100	100	100	100
(*n*)	(772)	(889)	(972)	(928)	(1,623)
Mean strength	2.37	2.36	2.16	1.94	1.91
% of electorate who are Labour identifiers	43	47	41	33	45
'Very strong' identifiers	22	23	14	9	10
'Very/fairly strong' identifiers	37	41	33	23	32

Source and Notes: See Table 4.8.

share of the vote is almost identical to that of 1964, the bloc of committed Labour partisans, at 31%, is much smaller. Moreover, the number of 'very strong' Labour identifiers in the electorate – the unwavering loyalists – has halved between these two landmark elections, from 23% in 1966 to only 10% in 1997. The onward march of dealignment offers the present Labour government the prize of a realigned party system if it successfully exploits its political opportunities; but it presents the risk of rapid and deep declines if it fails.

Negative and Positive Feelings towards Parties

A supplementary approach to the question of whether the 1997 election shows the characteristics of a deviating or realigning election is to ask whether the balance of motives of those who switched to a Labour vote was negative or positive. A deviating election is a protest election: the party in government repels more than the Opposition party attracts and its regular supporters abandon it – but temporarily – as a result. By contrast, in a realigning election the switchers to the winning party are not simply refugees, but converts. Answers to a question asked in each of the 1987, 1992 and 1997 British Election Studies throw some light on the matter. Respondents were asked to say whether they felt 'strongly in favour', 'in favour', 'neither in favour nor against', 'against' or 'strongly against' each of the main parties. Table 4.10 scores the answers from +2 to –2 for each party and sets out the average change in the feelings of the 1987–92 and 1992–97 panels among all respondents, stable Labour and non-Labour voters, and Labour recruits. Two features stand out. First, in 1992, when the swing from Conservative to Labour was only 2.0%, there was no change of feeling towards the Conservatives in the electorate as a whole and a very modest movement in favour of Labour. In 1997, when the swing was 10.0%, shifts in feelings about both parties were, not surprisingly, much sharper: the Conservatives' mean score fell by 0.59 points, but

TABLE 4.10 *Changes in feelings towards Conservative and Labour parties*

	1987–92 Changes in feelings towards		1992–97 Changes in feeling towards	
	Con	Lab	Con	Lab
All	0.00	+0.18	–0.59	+0.76
Stable Labour	+0.08	+0.70	–0.26	+0.24
Stable non–Labour	0.00	+0.16	–0.61	+0.92
Labour recruits	–0.51	+1.14	–1.22	+1.58

Note: Entries are the difference in the means between each election, not the mean of the differences.
Source: BES, 1987–92, panel; BES, 1992–97, panel.

Labour's mean score by even more: +0.76 points. Secondly, among Labour's recruits shifts in attitudes towards the two parties were much stronger in both directions: the average score for the Conservatives deteriorated by a substantial 1.22 but the average score for Labour improved by an even more remarkable 1.58. In other words, voters switched to Labour in such exceptional numbers because they were simultaneously turned off by the Conservatives and turned on by Labour; but the turn-on was stronger. The Labour vote in 1997 was a positive vote.

An alternative analysis of the data makes the same point from a different perspective. We have categorized respondents according to their combination of feelings towards the Conservative and Labour Parties in the three elections of 1987, 1992 and 1997. 'Polarized' Conservatives are those who simultaneously felt positive about the Conservatives and negative about Labour. They can be regarded as the bulwark of reliable Conservative support. 'Positive' Conservatives, by contrast, were not negative about Labour: they were neutral or even 'in favour' but always less positive than they were towards the Conservatives: Labour could seduce them. 'Anti-Labour' respondents felt neutral or even negative towards the Conservatives but even more negative towards Labour: they are more vulnerable to third-party attack. 'Polarized' Labour, 'positive' Labour and 'anti-Conservative' respondents were defined equivalently. The three 'neutral' categories of respondents were positive, neutral or negative about both parties at once.

A deviating election is characterized by an increment of negative feelings towards the party in office even though the underlying distribution of support for the parties remains the same. It should be characterized by a modest decline in the number of polarized Conservatives and a commensurate increase of polarized Labour respondents and anti-Conservatives (and perhaps negative neutrals). A realigning election is characterized by a sharp reversal of feelings towards the two main parties, which reconfigures the bases of party support. We would therefore expect a significant growth of 'polarized' and 'positive' Labour and a clear decline in the number of 'polarized' Conservatives. Table 4.11 shows that in these terms the 1997 election bore a closer resemblance to a realigning than deviating election. The number of anti-Conservatives (and negative

TABLE 4.11   *Negative, positive and polarized partisanship,*[1] 1987–97

	1987	1992	1997
Polarized Conservatives	38	37	11
Positive Conservatives	7	8	11
Anti-Labour	8	6	2
Polarized Labour	24	26	41
Positive Labour	7	7	14
Anti-Conservative	5	4	6
Positive neutral	1	1	2
Neutral negative	6	8	13
Neutral	2	2	1
Total[2]	100%	100%	100%

Notes: (1) For an explanation of the construction of the categories, see p. 77.
(2) Totals do not sum exactly to 100% due to rounding.
Source: BES cross-sections 1987, 1992, 1997.

neutrals) barely changed from 1992. But the reversal in the proportions of polarized Conservatives and polarized Labour supporters was very sharp. In 1992 (and 1987) polarized Conservatives outnumbered polarized Labour supporters by about three to two. By 1997 the proportion of polarised Labour supporters had risen from 26% to 41% while the number of polarized Conservatives had plummeted from 37% to a mere 11%: thus polarized Labour supporters outnumbered polarized Conservatives by almost four to one. The profile of joint feelings towards the two major parties depicted in Table 4.11 places Labour in an even more dominant position than the distribution of party identification implies. Whether the Labour Party can consolidate that new dominance into a lasting hegemony remains an open question.

The Significance of the Election for Voters

Not least of the indicators of a 'critical' election are that voters regard it as such. The classical critical elections of the USA were accompanied by heightened conflict and excitement, a surge in turnout and a sense of significance on the part of ordinary voters as well as commentators (Sundquist 1973). A deviating election, by contrast, is more likely to be a low-key affair in which temporarily disillusioned supporters of the governing party quietly abstain or defect, allowing the Opposition to win by default. The fall in turnout to its lowest level (71.4%) since 1935 suggests that the British electorate did not regard the election as particularly critical. However, the overall proportion claiming that they 'cared a good deal which party won the 1997 election' was, at 76%, virtually identical to that for the three preceding elections and higher than that for the last Labour landslide, in 1966 (72%) (Crewe *et al.* 1995: 166). Moreover, the result mattered particularly deeply to Labour supporters: the 85% of Labour identifiers who 'cared a good deal' was the highest proportion for any election going back to 1964 when the BES first asked the question.[7]

TABLE 4.12 *Party difference index among vote switchers, 1964–97*

		Perceived party difference index	% perceiving 'a good deal' of difference
1964–66	Conservative defectors	1.88	34
1964–66	Labour recruits	1.93	34
1974–79	Labour defectors	2.07	33
1974–79	Conservative recruits	2.30	47
1992–97	Conservative defectors	1.90	19
1992–97	Labour recruits	2.20	39

Note: The question was 'Considering everything the Conservative and Labour parties (1966: "stand for") would you say there is a good deal of difference between them?' (1966: 'between the parties' some differences or not much difference?). Responses were scored 3 for 'a good deal', 2 for 'some' and 1 for 'not much' and the index is the mean.
Source: BES panels, 1964–66, 1974–79, 1992–97.

The fact that Labour sympathizers cared intensely about the outcome in 1997 does not by itself make the election a critical one. It might signify no more than a profound relief that the election had 'thrown the rascals out', which would be consistent with a deviating election. To regard the 1997 election as critical, voters would also need to believe that the result would make a significant difference to the direction of government. A heightened sense among voters of substantial philosophical and policy differences between the two parties contending for government would mark the 1997 election out as potentially 'critical'. Yet the opposite was the case: the proportion perceiving 'a great deal of difference' between the Conservative and Labour parties was a modest 34%, considerably smaller than in Labour's landslide year of 1966, when it was 44%, or than in the critical election of 1979 (48%); indeed, it was the lowest for any election year other than – just – 1970 (33%). The sense that little divided the two parties was particularly marked among the under 35s, the age group whose vote swung most sharply to Labour.[8] As Table 4.12 shows, the two key groups of vote switchers (deserters from the government party and recruits to the Opposition party) held a much weaker sense of party difference in 1997 than in the last realigning election, that of 1979, although the proportion of Labour recruits in 1997 with a strong sense of party difference was higher than in 1966, the year of the last Labour landslide. The distinctive feature of 1997 is the very low proportion of Conservative defectors (19%, about half the proportion in 1966) who saw 'a good deal' of difference between the two parties. It is easier to switch parties when they anyway appear to have moved close together – but also easy to return 'home' at the following election. New Labour's conspicuous shift to the centre-right, which produced the ideological convergence between the two parties in voters' eyes, succeeded in converting a crucial increment of Conservatives; but the price was lower turnout (paralleling the dip in turnout in 1970), weaker party identification and the potential for an equally strong flow back to the Conservatives if Labour's competence in government becomes discredited.

The 1997 Election in Perspective: A Comparison with 1979 and 1966

The preceding analysis has focused exclusively on the distinctive features of the electorate's partisanship in the 1997 election. The significance of these features can only be assessed in the wider context of the political developments that led up to the election and by comparison with earlier postwar periods which culminated in a decisive election result. How closely does the 1992–97 period match the characteristics of a classical realigning era? Which does it resemble more, the 1974–79 period, which culminated in the critical election that heralded the Thatcher decades of the 1980s and 1990s; or the 1959–66 period, which led to the emphatic but, as it turned out, deviating election of 1966 and its immediate reversal by 1970?

Interpretations of the historical evidence differ (Clubb and Allen 1971; Andersen 1979), but there is a broad consensus that critical elections are antedated by a period of dealignment, which in the past has been marked by:

- the emergence of new, intense, 'cross-cutting' issues which create new divisions within the organizations and among the supporters of one or both parties;
- a growing psychological detachment from one or both established parties on the part of the electorate;
- growing disenchantment with the wider political order; and
- the emergence of new parties that threaten one or both of the main parties.

Other features are often listed – for example, falling turnout and spiralling electoral volatility – but these can all be subsumed under the four main characteristics listed above.

These features of the dealigning era culminate in a realigning election, dominated by new cross-cutting conflicts, 'in which the depth and intensity of electoral involvement are high, in which more or less profound readjustments occur in the relations of power within the community, and in which new and durable electoral groupings are formed' (Key 1955: 4).

The 1974–79 period displayed many of the characteristics of a dealigning period and the 1979 election bore considerable resemblance to a critical election. New or revived national conflicts over trade union rights, incomes policies and British membership of the EEC divided the Labour Party at all levels. Immigration issues were an emotive divider of opinion among ordinary Labour supporters in England; nationalism had a similar impact in Scotland. All these issues – as well as the damaging image of division – widened the gulf between the Labour Party and its natural supporters and undermined Labour partisanship (Crewe *et al.* 1977; Crewe 1981). Electoral support for Labour in opinion polls, by-elections and local elections plumbed record depths in the mid-1970s.

Small parties – the nationalists in Scotland and Wales and the National Front in England – benefited at Labour's expense. The strikes during the 'Winter of Discontent' both reflected and reinforced disenchantment with established procedures of conflict resolution. The 1979 election recorded the largest net shift in votes between the two major parties since Labour's massive victory of 1945. The incoming Conservative government ushered in 'profound readjustments in the relations of power' between state and organized interests, management and labour, central and local government; transformed the terms and agenda of political debate; and, assisted by a deeply divided Labour Party, consolidated its electoral grip for 18 years.

However, emphatic defeat of the government at an election does not always mark a realigning point in the evolution of the party system. The 1964 election offers an instructive contrast with 1979. Labour overturned a Conservative majority of 100 and ended 13 years of Conservative government. At the time the election was widely regarded as a watershed between the old and new politics, as the anti-Establishment triumph of 'modern' over 'traditional' values and a meritocratic over a privileged élite (Butler and King 1965: 300; Pimlott 1992: 323). But this interpretation was a superficial analysis of the flimsiest cultural trends. In retrospect there was no significant change to the party system. It is true that support for the Conservatives had declined in mid-Parliament to unusually low levels for the postwar period, but it recovered in the final year before the election. The Liberal challenge at by-elections and local elections in 1962–63 faded away. The net shift in votes that converted a Conservative majority of 100 into a Labour majority of 5 was very modest: a 3.2 percentage point drop in the Conservative vote; a mere 0.3 percentage point rise in the Labour vote. Labour consolidated its slim victory in 1966 only to lose office four years later. There were no new cross-cutting issues or divisions and the underlying loyalties and values of the electorate barely changed. The 1964 and 1966 results reflected the short-lived response of voters to the short-term failures of the 1959–64 Conservative administration and to the relatively reassuring performance of the 1964–66 Labour government. Voters decided to throw the rascals out and, in 1964 and 1966, give the new rascals a fair chance. The two elections resembled 'deviating' rather than 'realigning' elections.

Does 1997 look more like 1979 or 1964? There is a good *prima facie* case for depicting 1997 as a potentially realigning election. Certainly the period 1992–97 bears many of the hallmarks of the first, dealigning, stage of a classical realignment – much more so than the 1959–64 period – as the following shows.

New Cross-Cutting Issues

New, emotive, cross-cutting 'position' issues such as slavery, federal intervention in the economy, Vietnam and desegregation triggered realigning elections in the USA. No precise equivalent emerged in the Britain of 1997. No issue deeply divided both parties, provoked breakaway factions, dominated the election and redistributed voters between the parties. But 'Europe', symbolized by the issue of a single currency, deeply divided the Conservative Party from the Cabinet downwards, not only throughout the 1992–97 Parliament but also during the election campaign itself. As Chapter 11 shows, the issue became more salient among voters as the 1990s progressed, reversed its relationship to party choice and appears to have exerted an independent, albeit limited effect, on the vote. It also led to the creation of a new nationwide party on the right, the Referendum Party. Although the new party inflicted only modest damage on the Conservatives (Curtice and Steed 1997), the image of division and weak leadership arising from the backbench rebellions and defections, from Cabinet factionalism, from sniping by Mrs Thatcher and ex-ministers and from challenges to the leadership was a significant contributor to the Conservatives' loss of support (Curtice 1997; Kellner 1997).[9]

British elections normally turn on 'valence' rather than 'position' issues (Stokes 1966), on party performance (prospective as well as actual and reputational), not party position. The functional equivalent of a new cross-cutting position issue is a major shift in voters' association of the parties with a significant dimension of government performance. Voters' perceptions of the comparative prospective performance of the Conservative and Labour Parties in different domains of government tend to be stable over the long term. For decades voters have considered Labour to be the 'better' party for jobs, pensions and the National Health Service and the Conservatives the better party for defence and law and order. In the 1992–97 period these perceptions changed in Labour's favour, but most sharply of all for the domain with most impact of all on the vote, the management of the economy. From the 1950s onwards the Conservatives were consistently seen as the more capable of running the economy, whatever the state of the economy and even when Labour won elections, as in 1964. Shortly after Britain's scrambled departure from the Exchange Rate Mechanism in September 1992, the Conservatives lost that reputation and failed to recover it as the economy steadily improved up to 1997. Aided by its own changes of economic policy Labour had become, in the eyes of the electorate, the party of good economic management. (For the figures, see Crewe 1996: 429; King 1997: 188–9.)

Partisan Dealignment

The haemorrhaging of Conservative support in 1992–97 was unprecedented by postwar, and probably twentieth-century, standards – in its duration as well as depth. The steep decline in the level and strength of Conservative Party identification between 1992 and 1994 was described earlier. In addition, the Conservatives lost every by-election they defended, by swings that broke postwar records. The accumulation of annual local election losses left the party with fewer councillors than the Liberal Democrats and control of only a dozen councils by 1996. In the monthly opinion polls it trailed behind Labour by more than 15 percentage points for the four years from May 1993 to April 1997 (and by more than 20 percentage points from December 1993 to December 1996). A new and notable feature of these years, compared with preceding mid-term slumps in Conservative support, was that after Blair's election as leader in 1995, Labour rather than the Liberal Democrats benefited, by recruiting from both the Conservatives and Liberal Democrats, except where the Liberal Democrats were evidently better placed to defeat the sitting Conservative.

Wider Political Disenchantment

The outward signs of a deeper alienation from the party system and parliamentary politics were not as prominent as in 1974–79. There was noticeably little political violence or direct action or support for causes adopting such methods (outside Northern Ireland, of course). However, measures of confidence and trust in the political system revealed a sharp decline to historically low levels in the 1992–97 Parliament (Curtice and Jowell 1997) despite economic growth – the result, probably, of the unremitting allegations of greed and sleaze that afflicted the Conservative government. From 1992 onwards turnout has drifted down in local elections, after 20 years of stability (Rallings and Thrasher 1997: Table 4.2), and also declined to historically low levels in by-elections (Crewe 1997: 251).[10] As we have already noted, at the 1997 general election turnout fell to its lowest level for over half a century, despite an exceptionally long, media-saturated, campaign and a relatively young register. As Chapter 9 suggests, the main explanation is probably the new ideological convergence of the two major parties.

The Emergence of New Parties

No new parties comparable to the periodic third-party candidates of American presidential elections broke into the British party system in 1992–97. Nor was there a parallel to the SNP revival in Scotland in 1970–74 or the SDP breakaway and alliance with the Liberals in 1981–83. Sir James Goldsmith's Referendum Party was a single-issue party without a countrywide organization, which secured a mere 2.6% of the vote. However, one might reasonably ask whether 'New Labour' should count as a new party, given the speed and thoroughness with which its new leadership jettisoned or even reversed articles of ideological faith, including Clause IV. As Chapter 2 shows, Labour's manifesto shifted so sharply to the right that, for the first time since the war, the party positioned itself on the right rather than left of the ideological spectrum. Moreover, over the 1992–97 period the deep-rooted popular reputation of the Conservatives as united, moderate and well led and of Labour as divided, extreme and weakly led was comprehensively reversed.[11]

Thus the years 1992–97 bear many resemblances to a dealigning era, as much as in 1974–79, and more than in 1959–64. They prepared the ground for a realigning election; but, it needs to be added, they also laid the ground for a 'deviating' election in a party system which, it might transpire, will not change in a lasting way. The typical foundation of realignment in the party system is a new cross-cutting cleavage organized around an issue of enduring and symbolic significance to the electorate. Nothing so clear-cut occurred in 1992–97. While some of the factors in the Conservative collapse may persist for many years (e.g. divisions over Europe) others have disappeared (John Major's leadership) or will soon fade in people's memories (e.g. sleaze). The permanence of Labour's new image, for example as the party of sound economic management, remains to be tested.

Conclusions: Prospects for Consolidation and Realignment

This chapter has sought to show that the 1997 election has some but not all of the characteristics of a realigning election. It offers the Labour Party an exceptional opportunity to convert the demoralized refugees from the Conservative party and capture a new generation of semi-detached but favourably inclined young voters. After over 20 months in office the Labour government has succeeded in maintaining, probably increasing, its general election level of support. Until 1997 all new incoming governments in the postwar period saw their popularity slip after a few months' 'honeymoon'. The exception is the current government. Its lead over the Conservatives in the monthly opinion polls has averaged 29% during the first year and was 26% in January 1999 – comfortably in excess of the already substantial 13% margin it secured at the election. No previous postwar government, new or continuing, has managed to improve on its general election success, let alone do so in such a spectacular way. Exceptionally low turnout makes comparisons suspect, but the 1998 local election results broadly confirmed Labour's consolidation of its 1997 general election position and the absence of Conservative recovery. Although Labour's estimated share of the national vote (39%) fell below its general election level (45%), and a long way behind its support in the opinion polls, its performance was the best for any new incoming government in local elections since 1946. Moreover, both the opinion polls and the local elections provide growing evidence that Labour has been particularly successful in consolidating its new-found 1997 support in the salariat and business classes – a sign that a social class realignment in Labour's favour is a possibility.[12]

Nonetheless, it is difficult to discern the new cross-cutting issues and the emerging interests and identities that might convert Labour's new support into an enduring redistribution of firm, or at least hardening, party loyalties. The 1992–97 dealignment is the product of ideological convergence (as Schmidt and Holmberg (1995) show is common elsewhere), not the cross-pressures on voters that arise when new issue cleavages diverge from the old. Labour succeeded electorally by downplaying the distinctive ideas and interests it represented, not by emphasizing them. It won on the battleground of performance, not policy. For the present, Labour's commanding advantage over the Conservatives in popular support almost certainly owes more to a buoyant economy, the absence of conspicuous policy failure and a divided Conservative Party. These are all short-term assets. They provide some time, but not a lot, for New Labour to turn the prospect of realignment into reality.

Notes

1. This Chapter has adopted the standard convention of including as party identifiers those respondents who, having answered 'none' or 'don't know' to the party identification question (*'Generally speaking, do you consider yourself Conservative, Labour, Liberal or what?'*) offer a party in response to the supplementary question *'Do you generally think of yourself as a little closer to one of the parties than the others?'*

2. Butler and Stokes (1974: 42) showed that 75% of British respondents were stable in both their voting patterns and party identification between 1963 and 1966; but of those who changed their vote, 61% switched their party identification in tandem. Between 1992 and 1997 the proportion with a stable vote and party identification was lower (65%) but the proportion of vote changers who also switched party identification was almost identical, at 60%.

3. 'Switchers to Labour' exclude non-voters and the non-registered at the previous election.

4. Two studies, using the split sample design of the 1992 British Election Study, have concluded that the *ordering* of the party identification and vote questions in the questionnaire makes very little difference (see Heath and Pierce 1992; McAllister and Wattenberg 1995).

5. A 'swing' of 24% compared with 14% for the whole electorate.

6. One cannot strictly speak of the same cohort over time. The table contains comparisons of independent cross-sectional samples. Moreover, a small proportion of Labour identifiers have been converts from a decade earlier or defectors a decade later.

7. The figures for previous elections won by Labour are: 72% in 1964, 79% in 1966, 70% in February 1974 and 73% in October 1974. The historically high proportion who 'cared a good deal' was particularly marked among 'not very strong' identifiers. Note that the question was not asked in 1979 (the only election since 1964 when it was omitted).

8. In previous elections the perceived degree of difference between the two parties has not varied by age (except for the under 25s who consistently see less difference than others do). In 1997 age mattered: the proportion seeing 'a good deal' of difference was 25% among the under 35s, 35% among the 35–64-year-olds and 44% among those aged 65 and over.

9. Some suggest that constitutional reform was a new cross-cutting issue in 1997. However, outside Scotland, the issue was salient only to the political

classes and failed to engage ordinary voters. Moreover, with the exception of electoral reform, which divides the Labour Party, it reinforced rather than cut across the Conservative–Labour cleavage.

10. In 1983–87 by-election turnout averaged 63.4%, down 9.6 points compared with turnout in the same seats in the previous general election. In 1987–92 it averaged 57.5% (down 16.9 points) and after 1992 it ebbed down further to a mere 53.0% (down 23.6 points). This was not an artifact of the concentration of by-elections in low-turnout seats.

11. For example, the BEPS panel study recorded the following shift of party image among the same panel of respondents between 1992 and 1997:

Image of Conservative Party % perceiving party as:	1992	1997	Change
Moderate (rather than extreme)	65	51	–14
United (rather than divided)	70	4	–66
Capable of strong government (rather than not capable)	86	19	–67

Image of Labour Party % perceiving party as:	1992	1997	Change
Moderate (rather than extreme)	65	83	+18
United (rather than divided)	31	92	+61
Capable of strong government (rather than not capable)	40	92	+52

12. For example, in MORI's aggregated polls for the final quarter of 1997 the swing from Conservative to Labour was 13% in the AB social classes, compared to 8.5% in the DE class and 11% overall (MORI 1998: 6). Conservative and Labour support among owner-managers of independent, medium-sized businesses changed from 69 to 7% at the 1997 general election to 53–20% in November 1997 – a 'swing' of 14.5%. (see MORI: 1998: 5). In London, where Labour did well in the middle-class outer suburbs, May 1998 opinion polls by ICM and NOP showed Labour's lead to be as large in the middle-class as in the working class.

PART II

NEW SOCIAL ALIGNMENTS?

---

5   Class: Labour as a Catch-All Party?

Geoffrey Evans, Anthony Heath and Clive Payne

The significance of the class cleavage for British politics is a long-established topic of controversy. Much debate has surrounded the nature and explanation of the relationship over time between class and party support. In the 1950s and 1960s it was generally agreed that class was 'pre-eminent among the factors used to explain party allegiance in Britain' (Butler and Stokes 1974; see also Lipset 1960; Pulzer 1968). Since then a new orthodoxy has proclaimed that class has lost its ability to condition electoral behaviour in Britain, so heralding the possibility of new lines of division reflecting other sources of conflict which can, in turn, be expected to alter the structure of political competition – exactly the sort of change that is central to the idea of critical election theory.

Certainly, if the nature of class voting in 1997 differs substantially from that in previous elections it would provide important evidence for the critical election thesis. Labour's move to the centre in recent years on the issues that have traditionally divided the classes has put this question into sharp focus. The first part of this book has demonstrated how 'New' Labour would now appear to have followed several other west European left-wing parties down the road to centrist social democracy (Koelble 1992; Kitschelt 1994). The momentum for this shift comes from four consecutive election defeats but its deeper origins lie in the changing shape of the social structure which makes a parliamentary majority derived from a working-class base far less likely than it would have been only 20 years previously. Far from being the representative of an interest group – the working class – this transformation recasts Labour potentially as a 'catch-all' party.[1]

The validity of this interpretation rests, however, not only on the provision of empirical evidence of changes in class voting but on the plausibility of how any such changes are explained. Explanations of the class basis to partisanship in western party systems have tended to fall into one of two camps: those that privilege social structural factors and those that emphasize the political. The former highlights the primacy of changes in the class system itself: it can be considered a 'bottom-up' approach to the structuring of political divisions. The latter, by contrast, argues that class partisanship derives from the strategies of parties themselves, or from the changing character of political institutions: it can be characterized as 'top-down' in nature.[2]

The bottom-up approach to explaining political change has been very popular and has taken various forms: rising living standards and the spread of affluence, the changing gender composition of class positions (Kitschelt 1994), the growth of alternative social bases of interests that cross-cut class position (Dunleavy and Husbands 1985), the expansion of mass higher education, the decline of traditional communities and increased social mobility may have undermined class solidarity and led to more privatized, individualistic and instrumental voters (Franklin 1985; Rose and McAllister 1986). Sometimes it is also argued that these issue preferences reflect the growth of new political values resulting from the increased security and affluence of the postwar era (Lipset 1981: 503–21; Inglehart 1990). Despite their differences, these approaches all share the assumption that glacial transformations in social structure, or in the economic experiences of classes, are the source of changes in the relationship between party and class.

The top-down, political explanation for the strength of class voting has also been advanced by a number of scholars. Sartori (1969) argues that the salience of any one factor, including class, is an effect of the willingness of organizations such as parties to politicize it. As he puts it: 'Class conditions are only a facilitating condition. To put it bluntly, it is not the "objective" class (class conditions) that creates the party, but the party that creates the "subjective" class (class consciousness)' (Sartori 1969: 84). In a similar vein, Przeworski (1985: 100–1) has claimed that 'the thesis of this study is that individual voting behaviour is an effect of the activities of political parties. More precisely, the relative salience of class as a determinant of voting behaviour is a cumulative consequence of strategies pursued by political parties of the left'. Without this party strategy, class is much less strongly associated with vote.[3] Party positions therefore create class allegiances.

So on the one hand, the social structural account would hold that any decline in class voting would need to be explained by reference to some changing characteristics of class or class experience. We would therefore expect class dealignment to be gradual, as is social change itself. On the other hand, the political account would appeal to the strategies of parties or élites, independently of changing class experience. Changes in class voting might therefore be swift and discontinuous in their patterning. Specifically, if the extent of class–party polarization is a reflection of the degree to which parties differentiate themselves on class-related issues, Labour's moderation of its policy platform since 1983 (see Chapter 1) should produce a clear *convergence* in class voting – and over a relatively short space of time. Labour should now be perceived as occupying a position near the centre-ground in terms of the key left-right issues in British politics. The power of left-right attitudes to predict party support should have declined (as shown in Chapter 10) and this would, in turn, have implications for the social basis of party support. Labour should have increased its support disproportionately among the middle class, thus reducing the level of class voting.[4]

In this chapter we do not examine social structural explanations of changes in class voting in any detail as we have devoted a variety of publications over the years to assessing these arguments (see Heath *et al.* 1985, 1991; Evans *et al.* 1996b). Rather, we are mainly concerned with modelling the explicitly *political* explanations of changes in the class/vote relation. In particular, we shall examine evidence that trends in class voting can be understood in relation to changes in the *parties' ideological positions*.

The Pattern of Change, 1964–97

First we examine the evidence on the changing association between class and vote over time. In what sense has there been class dealignment? Has it taken the form of a gradual and continuous secular decline, as implied by the sociological thesis? Or have the changes been more of a discontinuous form that might be related to political factors? In particular, does 1997 represent a critical break?

As in our previous analyses we use the Goldthorpe–Heath (1992) class schema rather than the conventional manual/non-manual dichotomy.[5] The seven-class version of this schema distinguishes between the upper and lower service class (jointly, the salariat); routine non-manual workers; the petty bourgeoisie; foremen and technicians; and skilled, semi- and unskilled manual workers (jointly, the working class). We include all three main party groupings in our measure of vote.[6]

Because of the well documented limitations in other approaches to modelling voting in a multiparty context (Manza *et al.* 1995; Goldthorpe 1996; Whitten and Palmer 1996; Evans 1999a) we use log-linear models to estimate the class–vote relation.[7] These models distinguish the association between class and vote from other changes that are taking place, namely the changing sizes of classes and the changing overall shares of the vote going to the three main party groupings. A further advantage of using a log-linear approach is that it does not require the dependent variable (in this case, party voted for) to be dichotomized or ordered.[8] Recent advances in the development of these techniques also allow the specification of models that can summarize complex patterns of odds ratios and partition odds ratios into substantively relevant comparisons in ways that were unavailable to earlier studies that employed these techniques.

The basic pattern over time of changes in the relationship between class

TABLE 5.1 *Class by party vote for British elections, 1964–97 (%)*

Election	Base n	Party	Higher service	Lower service	Routine non-manual	Petty bourgeoisie	Foremen & technicians	Skilled working class	Unskilled working class
1964	1,359	Con	**65**	**61**	**59**	**74**	37	25	26
		Lab	18	20	26	15	**48**	**70**	**66**
		Lib	17	19	15	11	15	5	8
1966	1,413	Con	**66**	**56**	**49**	**67**	35	22	25
		Lab	19	29	41	20	**61**	**73**	**70**
		Lib	15	15	10	13	4	5	5
1970	1,303	Con	**66**	**60**	**51**	**69**	39	33	32
		Lab	22	32	40	20	**56**	**63**	**61**
		Lib	12	8	9	11	5	4	7
1974 Feb	1,858	Con	**59**	**51**	**45**	**68**	39	23	24
		Lab	17	26	29	18	39	**59**	**61**
		Lib	24	23	26	14	22	18	15
1974 Oct	1,746	Con	**57**	**47**	**44**	**70**	35	20	22
		Lab	17	30	32	13	**52**	**62**	**65**
		Lib	26	23	24	17	13	18	13
1979	1,410	Con	**61**	**61**	**52**	**77**	44	28	34
		Lab	24	19	32	13	**45**	**58**	**53**
		Lib	15	20	16	10	11	14	13
1983	2,877	Con	**60**	**53**	**53**	**71**	**44**	33	29
		Lab	8	16	20	12	28	**47**	**49**
		Lib/SDP	32	31	27	17	28	20	22
1987	2,860	Con	**63**	**50**	**51**	**64**	**39**	31	31
		Lab	11	19	26	16	37	**48**	**48**
		Lib/SDP	26	31	23	20	24	21	21
1992	2,131	Con	**66**	**50**	**54**	**66**	41	37	28
		Lab	16	21	30	17	**45**	**50**	**60**
		Lib Dem	18	29	16	17	14	13	12
1997	1,822	Con	**44**	37	33	**43**	21	14	18
		Lab	34	**42**	**49**	40	**62**	**67**	**69**
		Lib Dem	22	21	18	17	17	19	13
Change 1992–97		Con	*–22*	*–13*	*–21*	*–23*	*–20*	*–23*	*–10*
		Lab	*+18*	*+21*	*+19*	*+23*	*+17*	*+17*	*+9*
		Lib Dem	*+4*	*–8*	*–2*	*0*	*+3*	*+6*	*+1*

membership and voting across all the British Election Surveys is shown in Table 5.1. The most striking finding is that in 1997 the proportion of the middle class (classes I, II, III and IV) voting Labour is far higher than at any previous point in the BES series. Conversely, the proportion of the middle class voting Conservative is far lower than in any previous general election. Yet we need to note that support for the Conservatives is also at its lowest point among the working class (classes V, VI and VII), which indicates that there was an across-the-board move away from the Conservatives between 1992 and 1997 rather than a change in class basis of preference for the party. Interestingly, though, although levels of Labour voting were high among the working class they were no higher than in the 1960s, which indicates there has been some decline since that time in the relative propensity of the working classes to vote Labour compared with the middle classes. The proportion of Labour voters found in the middle class is now closer to the levels found in the working class.

The change during the last three decades has been dramatic. In 1964 Harold Wilson swept into power based on the support of two-thirds or more of the skilled and unskilled working class. A similar level of support among these groups was evident for Tony Blair in 1997. But in 1997, in contrast to 1964, Labour support from all the middle-class groups more than doubled. In 1964, the higher salariat, for example, divided 65% Conservative to 18% Labour, a sharp gap, with the remainder voting Liberal. In comparison in 1997 this class split far more evenly 44% Conservative to 34% Labour.

Looking at such figures can at best be suggestive. To assess whether 1997 represents a change in class voting alignments we need to test the pattern of change systematically over the full ten election studies at our disposal. We can then see if 1997 signalled a substantial break, or whether it fits with a more general pattern of electoral fluctuation. For this purpose in Table 5.2 we fit a set of log-linear models to the class by party by election table. We begin by fitting a 'constant class voting' or 'no trends' model for all ten elections between 1964 and 1997. This model implies that the association between party and class does not vary with election. In other words, the odds ratios for each class/party combination are set to be constant across elections. An inspection of the standardized residuals from this model shows that the 'no trends' model is a poor fit in only 11 of the 210 cells so that 97% of cases are classified accurately. Nevertheless,

TABLE 5.2 *Basic models for class by party by election, 1964–97*

Model	Description	Deviance	Df
1	No trends	166.21	108
2	UNIDIFF	117.78**	99
3	Working class, Labour, election	121.01**	99
4	UNIDIFF linear trend	150.86**	107

Note: Significance levels: ** = <0.01.
Source: BES, 1964–97.

the model has a deviance of 166.21 with 108 degrees of freedom indicating that in terms of overall statistical significance it does not fit well. On this basis we reject the hypothesis that there have been no changes in the class/party relation across elections and examine the pattern of change over time.

To estimate change over time we use the UNIDIFF model we have employed previously (Heath *et al.* 1995; Evans *et al.* 1996b). The UNIDIFF parameter summarizes changes in all the odds ratios between classes and parties across elections. It is a global test of the tightness of the link between all social classes and all three parties. This avoids the problems of selectivity that can occur with more specific indices.

The UNIDIFF model essentially fits an extra parameter for each election which measures the extent to which all the class/party odds ratios either move towards one (i.e. a lower class–party association) or away from one (an increased class–party association) as we go from election to election. The model gives a significant improvement in fit over the 'no trends' model (Table 5.2, model 2). The UNIDIFF parameters are given (in their multiplicative or odds form) in Table 5.3. The first election (1964) is taken as a reference category. Thus the parameter for the next election in 1966 shows that on average the class–party odds ratios have been reduced by a factor of 0.85, showing a reduction in the overall class–party association. The UNIDIFF parameters are plotted in Figure 5.1; they show a generally declining trend from the highest point in 1964 to the lowest in 1997 with some fluctuations in-between.

In addition, however, we fit a further model, which partitions the three-way interaction term between party, class and election by estimating changes in the relationship between the Labour Party versus other parties and the working class (Classes V, VI and VII) versus other classes. This model specifies that the association between the Labour Party and the working-class changes (in unspecified directions) as we move from election to election (*pari passu*, within the non-working class, Classes

TABLE 5.3 UNIDIFF *parameters and odds ratios for British elections, 1964–97*

Election	UNIDIFF parameter	Fitted odds ratios[1]
1964	1.00	13.1
1966	0.85	10.0
1970	0.63	6.2
1974F	0.78	8.1
1974O	0.86	9.5
1979	0.67	6.7
1983	0.84	9.0
1987	0.71	7.0
1992	0.74	7.9
1997	0.59	5.5

Note: (1) Fitted service/working-class odds ratios for Con/Lab from model 3 in Table 5.2.
Source: BES, 1964–97.

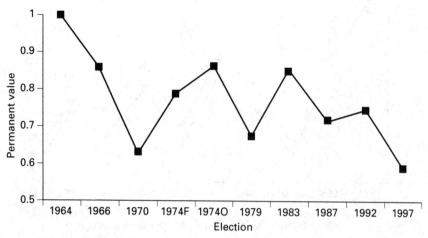

FIGURE 5.1   UNIDIFF *parameters by election*

I–IV). If the model fits well we can inspect the pattern of fitted odds ratios which shows whether the association between the working class and the parties strengthens or weakens as we move from election to election. This approach is closer in spirit to standard two-class/two-party indices such as those devised by Alford (1963) or Thomsen (1987). The advantage of this approach over these simpler indices is that it controls for the changing composition of the working and middle classes over time. In odds ratio terms, all odds ratios involving subclasses within the working class and the Labour Party versus other parties will remain constant over elections, and similarly for the non-working class. But odds ratios involving a subclass from the working class and a subclass from the non-working class will differ between elections.

Table 5.2 (model 3) shows that fitting this term improves the fit of the model considerably. This tells us that much of the over-time variation in the class–vote relation in Britain results from the changing relationship between the working class and the Labour Party – a characteristic of the British electoral system that we have observed in previous analyses (Evans *et al.* 1991).

Figures 5.1 and 5.2 thus present two different summaries of the changing pattern of class voting since 1964. It can be seen from Figure 5.2 that the fitted odds ratios for the links between working class versus service class and Labour versus other party voting closely follows the trend for the UNIDIFF parameter. In combination, these suggest that despite its global character, the UNIDIFF parameter does not differ from the key class–vote relationship – that between the working class and the Labour Party – that has traditionally been of most substantive interest in considerations of British politics.

These analyses allow us to conclude that, however measured, *there has*

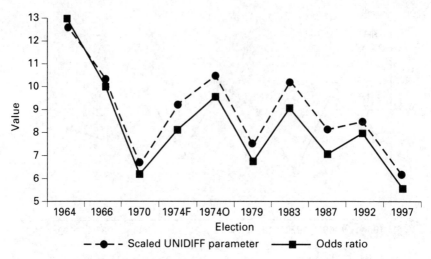

FIGURE 5.2   *Scaled UNIDIFF parameter and fitted service/working-class Con/Lab odds ratio by election*

been both trendless fluctuation and a decline in class voting between 1964 and 1997. A linear trend for the UNIDIFF parameter fits reasonably well (see Table 5.2, model 4), but there is still strong evidence of considerable short-term movement both up and down, rather than a glacial fall. This makes us sceptical of the sociological explanation of class dealignment. How then might we explain this politically?

Changing Party Positions on Left-Right Ideology and Class Voting

One such explanation concerns ideological changes at the élite level, more specifically the strategic move to the centre of the ideological spectrum by a vote-seeking Labour Party. To examine this thesis we need evidence of shifts in the ideological position of the Labour Party. Chapter 1 by Ian Budge provides exactly that sort of information. We can use his detailed measures of changes in manifesto positions over the years to try to account for the decline over time in class voting. Figure 5.3 shows the plot of UNIDIFF parameter and levels of polarization between the Labour and Conservative Parties on the dimension of left-right ideology described in Chapter 1. Figure 5.4 provides the same plot for Labour's position on this dimension.

When taken in conjunction Figures 5.3 and 5.4 point to a relatively clear pattern of relationship between ideological positions and extent of class voting *after* the 1960s, a pattern which is most evident from 1979 onwards. The picture obtained from Figure 5.4 – which maps the Labour Party's position alone – is perhaps clearest: as Labour moves to the centre, the class voting parameter declines. But even Figure 5.3 shows a clear enough image: 1970 and 1997 anchor the bottom left with low levels of both class voting and party polarization and all other years except the two 1960s surveys stretch to the top right.

The difference between the elections in the 1960s and later is also indicated by formal tests of the statistical significance of the observed linkage between ideological polarization and levels of class voting. These tests were undertaken by fitting a set of log-multiplicative models (see Firth 1998) which allows us to investigate whether the UNIDIFF parameter for each election, interpreted as an overall index of the class–party association for that election, is linearly related to parties' ideological positions as measured by party manifesto scores.[9] Thus we can test whether the overall level of class–party association declines as Labour

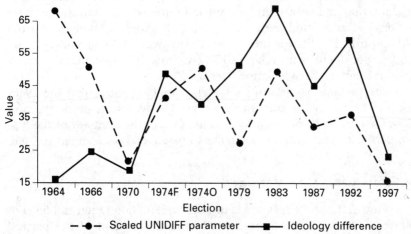

FIGURE 5.3   *Scaled* UNIDIFF *parameter and Con–Lab ideology scale difference by election*

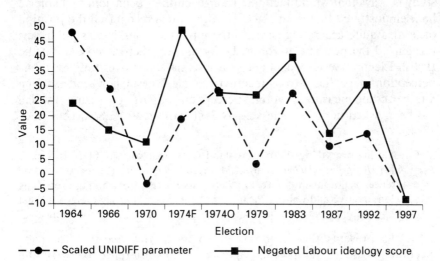

FIGURE 5.4   *Scaled* UNIDIFF *parameter and negated Labour ideology score ('left-wingness') by election*

TABLE 5.4 *Log-multiplicative models for class by party by election*

Model	Description	Elections 1964–67 deviance	df	Elections 1970–97 deviance	df
1	No trends (baseline)	166.2	108	122.6	84
2	Con–Lab ideology scale difference	164.9	107	106.5**	83
3	Labour ideology scale score	148.3**	107	101.4**	83
4	Voter view of Con–Lab difference	164.4	107	118.6*	83

Note: Significance levels: * = <0.05; ** = <0.01.
Source: BES, 1964–97.

(or the Conservatives) moves towards a more centrist position. As it is apparent that the 1960s do not seem to follow the pattern of later elections, we also fitted these models to only those elections held from 1970 onwards. The fits for these models are given in Table 5.4. Over the whole period there is no relationship, but from 1970 onwards there is a significant pattern of association.

As with previous studies of class voting, we have found that the 1960s appear to be somewhat different. We consider why this might be the case below. First however we need to examine further the accuracy of the link from parties to voters that this manifesto-based analysis assumes to hold.

Are Voters Getting the Message?

The notion that parties seek votes through redefinition requires a level of analysis at the level of voters as well as in the content of the parties' manifestos. Do the voters perceive the changes identified in the manifesto study in ways that would facilitate changes in their behaviour? Chapter 2 has demonstrated that in the 1997 election voters recognized the position of parties quite accurately across different issue scales, just as politicians recognized the position of voters. Unfortunately, there is no data in the British Election Series which allows a systematic test over time of public perceptions of parties across the left-right scale. We can, however, examine a rather crude measure of voters' perceptions of party polarization which has been asked in more or less equivalent form in all BES surveys since 1964:

> Considering everything the parties stand for, would you say there is a good (1964–1970)/great (1974) deal of difference between the parties, some difference, or not much difference? *Later modified to*: Considering everything the Conservative and Labour Parties stand for, would you say there is a great deal of difference between them, some difference, or not much difference?

Table 5.5 presents the responses of voters to this question for each election. Figure 5.5 graphs this data with the difference between the Labour and Conservative parties in left-right manifesto positions.

TABLE 5.5   *Perceptions of party difference, 1964–97*

Responses		Elections									
	1964	1966	1970	1974F	1974O	1979	1983	1987	1992	1997
A good deal	46	42	32	33	39	46	82	84	55	33
Some	23	26	27	30	30	29	10	11	31	42
Not much	26	28	37	35	30	22	6	4	12	23
Don't know	4	3	3	2	1	2	1	1	2	2
n	(1,733)	(1,834)	(1,828)	(2,443)	(2,361)	(1,871)	(3,952)	(3,822)	(2,851)	(2,730)

Note: See text for question wording.
Source: BES, 1964–97.

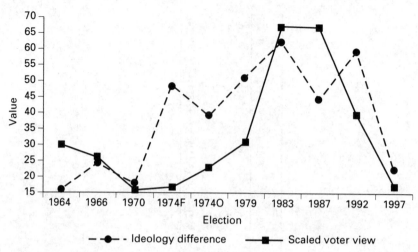

FIGURE 5.5   *Con–Lab ideology scale difference and scaled voter view of Con–Lab difference by election*

On the whole these figures show that even with this crude and variable measure there is evidence that people are aware of the major differences between the main parties, such as those which occurred in the 1980s and the subsequent convergence in 1992 and 1997 which returned the level of perceived marked difference to that in 1970. Unsurprisingly, the variations in party positions picked up in the manifesto study are not fully captured, but with the exception of February 1974 – which was of course called in rather special circumstances – the two trends, one derived from manifesto content analysis and BES respondents' answers to a simple question on party differences, are very similar. We can conclude therefore that levels of ideological polarization between the main parties are noticed by the electorate and, hence, given the intimate link between left-right ideology and the interests of different classes, can provide a plausible account of over-time variation in levels of class voting.

Why were the 1960s Different?

Despite the relationship between ideological polarization and class voting observed from 1970 onwards, we are still left with the conundrum of why this pattern was not observed in the 1960s. Various interpretations of this finding are possible. First it may be the case that there were real 'once-for-all' sociological or political differences between the 1960s and early 1970s and the subsequent period. For example, the franchise was reduced to 18 in 1969, and it may be that young voters do not vote on class lines to the same extent that older voters do.

Alternatively, it may be that the early election studies differ procedurally from the later studies. For example, there was a greater degree of clustering of the 1960s samples (only 80 sampling points being used compared with 250 in the 1983 and 1987 surveys).[10] This would tend to produce larger design effects and hence larger confidence intervals. In addition, data collection and coding procedures appear to be somewhat different.

Also, of course, it is possible that there has been a real change in voters' class-based responsiveness to parties' ideological signals during this period – perhaps because of a change in levels of issue attentiveness and hence issue voting (although some analyses of change up to 1987 have not found this to be the case: see Heath *et al.* 1991). The lack of class–vote responsiveness to party programmes in the 1960s and early 1970s might reflect the effects of postwar consensus – but this would not explain why class voting went up and down so markedly during this period. However, if the ideological polarization between parties in the 1970s and onwards sensitized voters to their interests it may in turn have increased the impact of issues and ideology on electoral outcomes. This does not of course imply the necessary decline of structural bases of party support – class position, like other social characteristics, continues to influence voters' perceptions of their interests and hence their position on issues and ideological spectrums. None the less, the mechanism linking social structure to voting is more instrumental and less a reflection of unquestioning loyalty – a change that was identified among certain types of working-class voters as far back as the 1960s (Goldthorpe *et al.* 1968). So the nature of class support for parties may well have changed as issue voting has become more prevalent, and parties' policy programmes may well have become more significant influences on their electoral fortunes than they once were.

Conclusions

We have seen that changes in class voting do not follow a smooth pattern of secular decline consistent with 'sociological' trends of a relatively irreversible nature. Moreover, after the 1960s the level of class voting observed in the electorate closely parallels the extent of the main parties' ideological polarization. Given that voter perceptions of party difference tend to follow the pattern of polarization in parties' manifestos, we can conclude that there is *prima facie* evidence that party positions influence the electorate's perceptions and, through this, the over-time variation in the voting behaviour of the different social classes.[11]

With respect to the questions that motivate this book, we must conclude that the association between class voting and ideological polarization observed from the 1970s onwards would suggest that political processes are capable of generating changes in patterns of voting behaviour over relatively short periods of time. True, these changes are of rather limited magnitude – and to claim that 1997 was a critical change in patterns of class voting would be implausible. But the dip in class voting to its lowest level in 1997 is certainly consistent with Labour's recent move to the centre, shown in other chapters in this book and in the data on manifesto positions modelled here. Given the relationship that appears to have emerged after the 1960s, it is possible that by continuing to compete for the middle (class) ground Labour can further weaken the pattern of class–vote allegiance in future elections also. The same consequence might well follow from the Conservatives' opposition to European monetary union (see Chapter 11), so although 1997 saw only a small class dealignment it could herald more far-reaching changes in coming contests. This depends on party strategies, however, and, as we know from research into the actual policy responses of west European parties over time, these do not always follow any simple pattern. If the major parties in Britain move closer together on the left–right spectrum in subsequent elections, crafting strategic appeals to all groups in society, then we might expect to find further evidence of class dealigment. On the other hand if Labour drifts back towards the left, as Budge suggests in Chapter 1, and the Conservatives maintain their position or shift further towards the right, perhaps in an attempt to maintain 'clear blue water', then class voting may strengthen again. The future strength of class voting therefore depends more upon party strategy and electoral appeals than upon secular trends in society.

Notes

1. The term 'catch-all' was first advocated by Kirchheimer (1966) in his analysis of a similar transformation of the German Social Democratic Party as far back as the late 1950s and 1960s.

2. It should be acknowledged of course that in some circumstances the two explanations do not necessarily present stark alternatives: as Kitschelt (1994) among others has emphasized, there is probably a process of mutual inter- action. Parties, with shrinking support bases, evolve strategies to expand their constituencies, or they fade from contention. None the less, even when they complement each other, these differing elements of political change tend to occur at different time points (see Chapter 14): the process of party strategy change is complex and there is often a delay in the response; parties often do not know how to mobilize new groups of voters effectively, or voters may not be paying much attention to party efforts.

3. In our earlier work we have also highlighted the importance of two political factors – the determination of the Liberal Party (in all its electoral incar- nations) to contest all seats and changes in the law defining electoral partic- ipation in 1969 to include 18–20-year-olds – in explaining much of the apparent decline in class alignment (Heath *et al.* 1991) and the deleterious effects of party incumbency on support among the party's core classes, particularly on working-class support for Labour (Evans *et al.* 1991).

4. A further possibility is that there have been changes in the class basis of *abstention*. If the British parties converge on a centre-right position we could see the pattern observed in the USA, where the convergence to the centre of the two main contenders has been accompanied by increasing class differ-

ences in turnout, as the working and underclasses have stopped voting (Weakliem and Heath 1999). Abstention is one response to being left stranded on the left by the party most likely to represent your interests. Of course, if Labour has moved nearer to the working classes' ideological position then we should not expect a fall in working-class turnout to occur – see Chapter 9.

5. The use of a dichotomy of manual and non-manual workers to represent social class does not allow theoretically important effects of variations in class position within the manual and non-manual categories to be measured. So, for example, own-account manual workers are less likely to vote Labour than other manual workers. An increase in the relative number of own-account workers within the manual 'class' would be expected to reduce Labour support within the class of manual workers as a whole. This would not however mean that there had been a change in the tendency of working-class people to support Labour – only that there had been a relative increase in the size of a category of manual workers who have consistently been less supportive of Labour.

6. Because of the very small numbers in the surveys, we exclude voters for the SNP, Plaid Cymru and other small parties.

7. In the case of the two-class, two-party model, for example, the unstandardized regression coefficient and the Alford index are formally equivalent and suffer from the same drawbacks. Just as OLS regression gives reasonably accurate estimates when the dependent variable is relatively unskewed, so the Alford index is a reasonable approximation when votes are divided more or less evenly between the two main parties. However, as the distribution becomes more skewed, the use of either of these measures becomes more problematic. In effect, 'floor' and 'ceiling' effects come into operation thus limiting the value which the index can reach. Thus as a party's votes decline in number (that is, as the dependent variable becomes more skewed), it becomes mathematically impossible for either the Alford index or OLS coefficients to remain constant.

8. As we have noted often before, measures based on the correlation coefficient confuse these three associations and also require the recoding of a multiparty reality into contrasts between two parties, or between one party and the rest, or to assume a fixed ordering of the parties.

9. As these models cannot yet be fitted using standard statistical software, we had to write special GLIM macros for this purpose. For help in doing so we are indebted to David Firth.

10. Interestingly, another survey conducted in the 1960s showed a lower level of class voting than that reported in the two British Election Surveys (Miller *et al.* 1986).

11. It should be noted that in this analysis we have focused on the traditional question of whether there has been class–party dealignment – a question that is clearly pertinent to the debate over Labour's move to the ideological centre of British politics – but have not estimated the extent to which changes in class–party voting have occurred within the same general level of overall class voting. However, research that has examined the question of over-time realignment has found little evidence of such changes (Weakliem 1991; Goldthorpe 1999; Weakliem and Heath 1999).

6 Race: Towards a Multicultural Electorate?

Shamit Saggar and Anthony Heath

In recent years, it has been possible to identify a conventional view of the role played by ethnic minorities[1] in Britain's electoral process. This view held that the ethnic minority population, totalling around one-twentieth of the general population, remained relatively weak and politically isolated on the British electoral landscape. The reasoning was largely based on a combination of demographic analysis (there are too-few-to-matter, it was said) and constituency-level analysis (where sizeable concentrations exist they tend to be in overwhelmingly safe seats). In addition, it was thought that the minority community's historic electoral allegiance to the Labour Party could, over the long term, only serve to weaken its political leverage by encouraging Labour to take such support for granted. In any case, the idea that race constituted a major electoral cleavage in its own right was open to some doubt (Welch and Studlar 1985). Finally, the argument also noted that, by and large, there remained serious registration and turnout deficits among the minority population that only added to the weaknesses caused by a disproportionately young age profile. The upshot was that the chances of substantial electoral influence were discounted in a political system that contained precious few prizes (Crewe 1983). This in turn had obvious downbeat implications for the politics of patronage and spoils where the potential electoral muscle of minorities was thought to count only at the margins (Layton-Henry and Studlar 1985).

The forces of electoral geography were seen as another major flaw since minorities and minority interests were often tacitly written off by Labour and Conservative strategists as a result of their scarce presence in genuinely marginal constituencies and wards. A decade ago, one commentator even wrote of the political interests of the ethnic minority voter effectively 'slipping between the cracks' of a competitive two-party system (Messina 1989). The conventional understanding, in other words, required little embellishment and pronounced loudly on the effects of the British electoral process upon the representation of discrete, putatively unpopular minorities.

Interestingly, something of a counterperspective to this dominant position has emerged, partly based on a dramatically different reading of similar evidence. Most importantly, this school, which can be dubbed the 'ethnicity counts' viewpoint, suggests that the conventional understanding overlooks the most pressing evidence of all, namely the *potential* of ethnic-based political outlook and voting. Thus, large-scale loyalty to one of the major parties is interpreted in terms of a common ethnic tie running through many minority communities. Where these ethnic ties are interrupted, distorted or over-ridden by other bonds or sources of common interest, these are seen to be evidence of the underlying possibilities of not merely ethnic-based electoral mobilization but also of ethnic-driven strategies for political and policy influence. In other words, this viewpoint is not dissuaded by the structural and other limitations of the Britain political system. At its heart there is an ethnically related theorization of political attitudes and behaviour. This school thus emphasizes race as the source of a new electoral cleavage and, significantly, suggests that it might develop into a growing basis of alignment in British politics.

This chapter is concerned with developing this debate a stage further by examining recent empirical evidence about the political attitudes and voting behaviour of ethnic minorities in comparison with their white counterparts. Its first task is to readdress the empirical building blocks of the conventional view (i.e. party support, political engagement and political attitudes). One central bone of contention here has been the degree to which ethnic commonness has over-ridden social class in shaping political outlook and action. If the influence of factors such as class, age and education is outstripped by ethnicity, then, this chapter argues, ethnicity continues to be a major political cleavage in British electoral behaviour. Members of the ethnic minorities cannot therefore be adequately described as integrated fully into the sources of political difference found in the white population. The theoretical ramifications of such a characterization are far-reaching and not easily dismissed.

A second task of this chapter is to look again at ethnic minority electoral participation and its part in moulding party strategy. We should remember that the conventional viewpoint saw the whole question of minority politics as of fairly marginal concern to party strategists. The wonder lay, if anything, in accounting for the fact that parties had been bothered at all in courting minority voters, members and donors. What has driven the efforts to attract a group that has persistently remained amongst the most loyal of Labour's constituencies, to say nothing of its status as one of the least popular groups in the eyes of the white electorate?

However, by viewing the electorate in terms that are dealigned from traditional group-party lines, it is possible to argue that party strategy, especially that of the Conservatives, has been gradually reorientated to a 'new politics' in which cross-class coalitions can be built and sustained. In any case, the 'ethnicity counts' school has observed that subtle but important variations exist in the structure of opinion and patterns of behaviour within the minority electorate. In particular, fairly significant

Asian–black variations can be tracked that reveal the motives of party efforts to mobilize at least segments of the minority electorate. Sections of the Asian electorate, it is widely thought, stand out as relatively fertile territory for non-Labour campaigns. The acid test here is to assess whether, and to what degree, such ethnic campaigns have succeeded. The evidence suggests they have not succeeded in any marked way, but one sometimes-hidden by-product has been to make each of the two main parties more reliant on certain groups of minority voters than others. At first glance, therefore, party strategy in this field has been something of a puzzle on the political map. However, a closer look reveals that selective cherry picking has been going on and will be, most probably, the way forward in loosening Labour's grip.

The third job of this chapter is to tackle the question of ethnic minority political integration and the role of the 1997 general election in this context. What this means in practice is to look at aspects of similarity and difference both *between* white and ethnic minority electorates and *within* the ethnic minorities. It is clear that very large variations exist in comparing whites alongside minorities. Variations are also apparent among different minority communities and this starts to take on a repetitive pattern if specific groups are singled out (ethnic Indians being the prime example).

Electoral Engagement

Basic questions of electoral engagement cannot be overlooked in studying modern British politics and the involvement of ethnic minorities in elective politics is a theme that requires close attention for two reasons. First, taking part in the electoral process, and exerting political leverage through the democratic decision-making process, is presumed to be a useful marker for involvement in mainstream society. Consequently, different levels of mainstream electoral participation among different ethnic groups may be taken as proxy indicators of wider integration patterns. If groups shun participation in mainstream schooling, housing and other areas, we can surmise that electoral involvement is likely to follow a similar pattern, according to this argument. Secondly, the under-lying reputation of liberal democracy can be at stake in assessing the breadth of involvement of all groups within society. Democratic processes and institutions can be harmed in the longer run, it is feared, if large pockets of the would-be electorate remain aloof from participative norms. This argument, to be sure, developed into something of a received wisdom on the question of threatened black abstention in the months preceding the 1997 election. Moreover, if their non-participation cannot be accounted for in social class or circumstantial terms, one obvious worry is that democratic institutions such as political parties are at fault. At the very least, parties and politicians cannot make unfettered claims about the quality of the democratic system.

It is necessary to introduce some basic qualifications first. The most pressing is to isolate the degree to which legal citizenship defines other rights, including voting rights. In the wake of large-scale postwar immigration, the UK tended to grant and recognize voting rights on rather more generous terms than in many countries across continental Europe and indeed elsewhere. Immigration from New Commonwealth sources was usually associated with the enjoyment of full political rights by the immigrant newcomers at or shortly after the point of entry. This legacy has meant that examination of the electoral participation of ethnic minority groups does not involve any prior assumptions as to whether these groups are likely to enjoy political rights or not. This is something of a vexed question in countries such as Germany and Italy but largely irrelevant in Britain.

The rates of British citizenship found across different groups contain a high degree of variance, with black Africans exhibiting the highest level of non-British citizenship in 1997 (Table 6.1).[2] This group tends to comprise large numbers of students, graduate trainees and other essentially temporary residents, few of whom would be expected to wish to relinquish citizenship of their country of origin. Asian Indians and Pakistanis, together with their black Caribbean counterparts, all have rather similar levels of British citizenship (around 9 in 10). All three groups have their origins in labour migration – and to a lesser degree political refuge – dating from the 1950s to the 1970s. Asian Bangladeshis stands out, only three-quarters of whom are British citizens, a fact that reflects their more recent immigration history and the dilemmas associated with a naturalization log-jam. Finally, dual citizenship appears to be a significant option in the case of all minority groups except Asian Indians. This might be due to a much earlier immigrant history, thereby ensuring that many among this group are today relatively distant from

TABLE 6.1 *Citizenship by ethnic group,* 1997 (%)

	White	Indian	Pakistani	Bangladeshi	Black-African	Black-Caribbean	Misc.	
Are you a British citizen?								
Yes, British citizen	97.1	85.9	82.6	77.0	50.0	92.0	80.9	
No, citizen of (an)other country	2.3	13.7	14.0	14.8	42.9	5.0	18.1	
Both countries	0.6	0.4	3.3	8.2	7.1	3.0	1.1	
Total (*n*)	2,481	284	121	61	70	100	94	(3,211)
Total (%)	100	100	100	100	100	100	100	

Notes: Excludes Scotland. Includes respondents not on the electoral register.
Source: BES, 1997, merged file (weighted data).

their (or their parents') Indian national origins. Furthermore, rapidly falling rates of dual citizenship might be associated with higher economic standing, educational attainment and general security, areas where this group has led other minorities in recent years (Robinson 1990). Additionally, dual citizenship is not permitted by the Indian state for Indian citizens.

Individuals holding requisite citizenship need to be registered to vote. In the past it has been suggested that ethnic minority registration might have been subdued because of factors such as newness, language difficulties, general alienation, racial harassment fears, as well as fears of 'fishing expeditions' by immigration authorities (Anwar 1996). Poor registration rates amongst minorities have been linked to voter disinterest and disillusionment. Little can be done in the short run to tackle the root causes of such alienation, though pressure groups and other campaigners will aim to encourage abstainers on to the register. The work of Operation Black Vote (OBV), jointly established by Charter 88 and the 1990 Trust a year before the 1997 election, is one campaign that stands out. Its central message was to encourage minority voters to place themselves on the register, equipping literally new voters with the basic tools for democratic involvement. Furthermore, OBV's cutting edge was sharpened by its genuinely non-partisan stance, a position, it must be said, increasingly hard to sustain in the heated world of minority politics. It is unlikely that parties will be able to overlook such efforts if they can be shown to raise registration levels. The difficulty lies in assessing OBV's role beyond the participation–voter interest effects of single elections.

Earlier studies of ethnic minority voting have suggested minority registration rates lower than that found among whites ranging from 3 to 24 point deficits (CRE 1984; Anwar 1996). The data in Table 6.2 broadly confirm such a picture in 1997. Among Asian groups there is scant evidence of any such group falling appreciably below the 9 in 10 prevailing level. Asian Indians, once again, lead the minority cohort with rates that match those of whites. Similar figures have been found in earlier local-level studies suggesting that these rates are credible (Le Lohe 1998). Black Africans were dramatically out of line with most ethnic minorities, whilst black Caribbean registration rivalled the very high rates seen among whites and Asian Indians. It would appear that earlier, pre-election claims about significant levels of black Caribbean under-registration were *very* wide of the mark (*The Guardian* 1996).

Turnout data need to be added to the picture, to help us distinguish between casual abstainers (citing *ad hoc* circumstantial factors disrupting an intention to vote), hard-core abstainers (showing no real interest in an election or its outcome) and serial abstainers (those who rarely, if ever, vote). The focus of parties tends to be on trying to get those who, at the margin, are somewhat doubtful about going out to vote. Minority voters can pose very serious challenges in terms of large groups of abstainers thought to be highly unlikely to engage in the democratic process. Language

TABLE 6.2   *Electoral registration by ethnic group, 1997 (%)*

	White	Indian	Pakistani	Bangladeshi	Black-African	Black-Caribbean	Misc.
Is your name on the electoral register?							
Yes	97.0	96.5	88.4	91.7	86.1	95.0	90.6
No	2.7	2.5	11.7	8.3	12.5	4.0	5.3
Don't know	0.2	1.1	0.0	0.0	1.4	1.0	4.2
Total (*n*)	2,480	284	120	60	72	100	95
Total (%)	100	100	100	100	100	100	100

Notes: As Table 6.1.
Source: As Table 6.1.

difficulties can create further obstacles on top of this. Table 6.3 shows the turnout of those respondents whose names were on the electoral register. The image of high-involvement Asian Indians is reflected in the fact that their turnout rate in 1997 exceeded that of whites, and by a margin that is far from negligible. They were almost matched by the Pakistanis while the turnout of the Bangladeshis was not significantly out of line with that of whites. However, a rather different story is told in the case of both black Africans and black Caribbeans: turnout rates dipped far below those of all other ethnic groups suggesting, at the minimum, the existence of a serious mobilization problem. It is difficult to avoid the conclusion that, for some minorities, a serious issue for democratic participation is bound up in these figures.

Taken together, these figures indicate that some identifiable variations exist in the degree to which different ethnic groups are engaged in the

TABLE 6.3   *Turnout by ethnic group, 1997 (%)*

	White	Indian	Pakistani	Bangladeshi	Black-African	Black-Caribbean	Misc.
Did you manage to vote in the general election?							
Yes	80.8	85.4	84.9	80.4	74.2	73.4	71.8
No	19.2	14.6	15.1	19.6	25.8	26.6	28.2
Total (*n*)	2,406	274	106	56	62	94	85
Total (%)	100	100	100	100	100	100	100

Notes: As Table 6.1. Excludes respondents who were not registered.
Source: As Table 6.1.

democratic process. However, the magnitude of some of the intergroup differences is perhaps less than might be thought or predicted. Most minorities share a lot in common with most other minorities in their electoral involvement, contrasting only at the margin with their white counterparts. However, no group falls dramatically short of the underlying minority rate of engagement, though some occasionally remain above. Arguments emphasizing substantial underparticipation among minorities must take care to evaluate these variations accordingly.

Party Preferences

Measurement of the voting patterns of ethnic minorities has taken place at every general election since October 1974. The party loyalties of ethnic minority voters have been overwhelmingly skewed towards Labour according to this evidence. Despite this, there have been a number of organized attempts to lure these voters to parties at the centre and right, often accompanied by academic and practitioner predictions of the long-term inevitability of such drift (Bald 1989).

The claims, counterclaims and evidence have developed a significance of their own for three principal reasons. First, party allegiances arguably make a material difference to the politics of delivering racially explicit and targeted public policy. Labour-supporting minorities (or, rather, some of their leaders) might therefore argue that their endorsement implies that the party is under a special obligation to show itself to be responsive to racially exclusive policy demands and expectations. It should be added that most party managers are probably unwilling to accept the need for such responsiveness, however. Secondly, it is important to know the degree to which familiar ideological, policy and other differences between the parties are reflected in minority voter preferences. Conversely, we need to throw more light on the factors, ethnic or otherwise, that underscore such strong patterns of Labour support among minorities. This is important in assessing the value of ethnically related theories of political thinking and action, mentioned previously. Thirdly, alterations in patterns of party choice, especially if drawn out over long periods, are important because of what these movements suggest about underlying developments in the socioeconomic circumstances of different ethnic groups. If these forces grow in importance over time, the implication might be for greater convergence not only in white-minority party choice but also in terms of the foundations of political difference.

Historic Patterns

Historically, it is no secret that British ethnic minority voters have backed the Labour Party in quite staggering numbers: typically four in five minority voters have backed Labour (Table 6.4). Much of the earlier evidence is based on stand-alone surveys of minorities but nevertheless provides a reasonably reliable indicator of sharply skewed voting allegiances. Two features of this picture stand out. First, the overwhelming bias to Labour is self-evidently out of line with the varying (and usually weak) fortunes of Labour among white voters in this period. Labour's strength among minorities over this period stands in sharp contrast to its poor track record in attracting non-minority voters. Secondly, this bias appears to be relatively insulated from short-term trends. For instance, the rout suffered by Labour in 1983 is not reflected among minority voters. Equally, the gradual rise in Labour's fortunes thereafter (including 1997) is not particularly mirrored in minority support patterns. The upshot of this is that the Labour Party is probably enjoying saturation levels of minority electoral support and has been doing so for many past elections.

The backdrop to 1997 was one in which interest fell, once again, on the likelihood of a Tory or third-party breakthrough among minority voters. Conservative strategists have been active in trying to court minority voters since the 1970s, and there was little that was terribly new in the waging of so-called 'ethnic campaigns' in 1997 (Layton-Henry 1978; Rich 1998). The Tory campaigns, in truth, had produced few results. Nevertheless, the party returned with fresh energy to the challenge a year or so before polling day. The prospects for a genuine Conservative breakthrough, however, remained terribly weak since, as polling day neared, the election was increasingly viewed as a poor year for the Tories. In these circumstances, a breakthrough among any group within the electorate would have been a considerable achievement in itself. On Labour's side, reinforcing its *de facto* monopoly in 1997 implied that Labour allegiances had remained unaffected by pockets of growing prosperity and upward social mobility among sections of the minority electorate (Robinson 1988). So strong had Labour support among minorities become during the 1980s and 1990s, the implication was that it amounted to an instinctive matter of habit.

Party Choice in 1997

There is little doubt that the 1997 election reinforced earlier patterns of ethnic minority voting. Breakthrough claims for the Tories or others can be dismissed from the evidence. Saturation levels of Labour voting, rather

TABLE 6.4 *Party vote among ethnic minorities, 1974–92*

	1974*	1979	1983**	1987	1992**
Labour	81	86	83	72	81
Conservative	9	8	7	18	10
Other party	10	6	10	10	9

Notes: * October 1974 general election; ** Recalculated average of Asian and Afro-Caribbean voting levels.
Source: Adapted from CRC (1975); CRE (1980, 1984); Harris Research Centre, 'Political attitudes among ethnic minorities', unpublished data set JN98746; Ali and Percival (1993).

TABLE 6.5   *Asian and black vote distribution,* 1997 (%)

	Asian	Black	Total (Asian + black)
Conservative	13.6	3.7	11.3
Labour	81.9	94.5	84.8
Liberal Democrat	3.7	1.8	3.2
Other	0.8	0.0	0.6
Total (*n*)	353	109	462
Total (%)	100	100	100

Notes: As Table 6.1. Excludes 'Don't knows' and non-voters.
Source: As Table 6.1.

predictably, were repeated in the 1997 contest. Table 6.5 summarizes the story for Asian and black voters as well as non-white voters a whole.

The message for the Tories is disappointing on two fronts. First, MORI (1997) pre-election data had suggested a more upbeat performance was on the cards and this may have falsely raised morale and expectations (estimated as high as 25%). Secondly, with a very low benchmark legacy from previous elections, the anticipation had grown that Tory non-white support would gradually rise as part of a longer-term, secular trend. Therefore, a hunger had grown for evidence to back this school of thought.

A clear contrast between Asian and black voters is discernible. In the case of the former, Labour voting was very high and entirely in line with the four in five benchmark, whilst exceeding nine in ten among the latter. Furthermore, although the rate of Asian Tory voting remained very low, it was almost four times that found among black voters. Support for the Liberal Democrats was exceptionally low among both Asians and blacks. The hallmarks of Liberal and centre-party progressive positions on race and immigration issues were entirely lost on members of the minority electorate, amounting to a major rebuff to issue-voting models of ethnic minority electoral choice.

Intergroup Comparisons

Further distinctions need to be introduced between minority groups as well as comparisons with white voters in 1997. Table 6.6 sets out some of this detail and reveals several important variations. The appeal of the Labour Party's competitors ranges quite considerably from one ethnic minority group to another. For instance, excepting Asian Indians, Tory voting is desperately poor across all minority groups. This group's rate of Tory support was between two and seven times higher than comparable rates amongst other Asian and black groups. At almost one in six it amounted to more than half that found in Tory-weary white electorate. Arguably, in a generally dismal picture, here is some sign, however limited, of Tory progress. Moreover, such progress is related to what is, after all, the largest single minority group (further bloated, so to speak, by high registration and turnout levels), thereby giving a proportionately larger yield in terms of real voters.

TABLE 6.6 *Vote distribution by ethnic group,* 1997

	White	Indian	Pakistani	Bangladeshi	Black-African	Black-Caribbean	Misc.
Conservative	31.0	17.5	7.1	5.1	2.3	4.5	18.6
Labour	47.0	80.3	85.9	84.6	93.2	93.9	72.9
Liberal Democrat	18.3	2.2	3.5	10.3	4.5	1.5	6.8
Other	3.7	0.0	3.5	0.0	0.0	0.0	1.7
Total (*n*)	1,909	228	85	39	44	66	59
Total (%)	100	100	100	100	100	100	100

Notes: As Table 6.1. Excludes 'Don't knows' and non-voters.
Source: As Table 6.1.

Ethnic Sources of Support

It is exceedingly hard, however strong the effort, to put a credible gloss on non-Labour performance other than to say that 1997 was at least no worse than some earlier elections. This kind of conclusion is based on looking at the distribution of the minority vote in 1997 and observing its overwhelming concentration in one party's hands. A rather different approach can be taken that seeks to examine the ethnic distribution of the minority votes gathered by the parties. As we shall see, this analysis leads to a different insight accompanied by some additional conclusions that may have gone unreported.

Table 6.7 looks at the source of all votes gained by the parties from ethnic minorities in 1997. It highlights a revealing and potentially significant pattern at work. The numerically much larger Asian electorate dwarfs its black counterpart in terms of the reliance upon Asian voters among all the major parties. That is, although some parties get many more minority supporters than others, all parties get the lion's share of their minority support from Asian sources. Demographics alone mean that, across the minority electorate at large, there are three Asian voters for every one black voter, though differential registration and turnout can serve to reinforce this outnumbering effect.

The bias can be even greater when seen at party-specific level. The Conservatives pick up the overwhelming majority of all their minority support from Asian voters (more than nine in ten Tory supporters are Asians, with only a very tiny proportion from the black electorate). In party strategy terms, this means that although the Tories gathered only a tenth of the minority vote in 1997, those few it did attract were almost invariably Asian ones. This is the result of two unrelated factors: first, the greater size of the Asian electorate (already noted) and, secondly, the higher popularity of Tory-voting among Asians relative to that among blacks (14% versus 4%). In the case of Labour, there is another bias at

TABLE 6.7　*Ethnic minority group source of parties' vote, 1997*

	Con	Lab	Lib Dem	Other	Total share of ethnic minority vote
Asian	92.3	73.7	86.7	—	76.4
Black	7.7	26.3	13.3	—	23.6
Total (*n*)	52	392	15	3	462
Total (%)	100	100	100	100	100

Notes: As Table 6.6.
Source: As Table 6.1.

work, namely that of Asian reliance, though rather less dramatic than the Tory profile. In fact, the Asian–black ratio here roughly mirrors the proportions of each respective group within the minority electorate at large. However, given that Labour is slightly more popular among blacks than Asians (about 13 points in all), what appears to be taking place is a reliance upon Asians by Labour which is rather less than might result from even more support from both groups. In other words, despite Labour's strong showing among Asian voters, its relative failure to match its support to that among black voters costs the party in losing – at the margin – a proportionately larger number of Asian voters. This observation could be interpreted on one hand as a warning to Labour (excessive black reliance becoming a trend), or on the other hand as an opportunity (capitalizing even further on its success among Asians will lead to a bigger-than-imagined payoff).

The upshot of this point is that 'ethnic campaign' strategies are often couched in generalized ethnic terms when the reality is that all parties are in fact either holding on to and/or competing for many more Asian voters than any other group. Such reliance has its drawbacks. One danger is that increasingly focused campaign messages might risk edging out interest in – and possibly even the interests of – black minority voters. This possibility may not seem particularly likely in political terms – partly because of efficient internal party lobbies that serve as counterforces – but the rational, competitive basis for it is not hard to spot. Another problem is that cases of very heavily Asian voter reliance (as seen in the Conservative profile) might risk the party being viewed in 'no-go' terms by black voters (Saggar forthcoming). It might, additionally, contain influential activists who in fact wish the party to be seen in such terms, although the underlying purpose of this case is likely to be poorly articulated if not logically flawed. Finally, the more even split in Labour sources (in line with the approximate sizes of the Asian and black electorates) might mask a tendency for gradual Asian-voter depletion. Such depletion might easily go unnoticed for obvious reasons and might also be indirectly reflected in the size and strength of minority group lobbies within the party. This possibility would mean that Labour was becoming increasingly black-voter reliant at the level of voter recruitment and retention but such a pattern would be hidden in the short to medium run by the greater numeric supply of Asian rather than black voters. As such, it would be a recipe for short-term complacency paid for by longer-term difficulties in mobilizing ethnic minority electoral support across the board.

The Influence of Social Class

One key question in understanding the relation between ethnicity and the political parties is to ask whether the traditional cleavages that have divided the white British electorate also divide the ethnic minorities. Class and housing tenure in particular have been the traditional social cleavages that divide Labour from Conservative, while higher education has tended to be a source of support for the Liberal Democrats (albeit more weakly). Do these social factors divide the ethnic minorities, thus giving the Conservatives a potential entry-point among the more advantaged and entrepreneurial groups? Or does ethnicity in a sense over-ride social class, with ethnic minority members voting on the same lines (usually Labour ones) irrespective of their class position?

In Table 6.8 we give an overview of the relationship between class and vote among black and white voters, grouping all our ethnic minority respondents together. We distinguish five social classes – the salariat (composed of professionals, managers and administrators in relatively secure employment); routine non-manual workers (largely women in office work but with little in the way of promotion or career prospects); the petty bourgeoisie, consisting of employers and the self-employed. We finally distinguish between the higher levels of the working class, consisting of foremen, technicians and skilled manual workers, and the lower levels covering semi- and unskilled manual workers. The petty bourgeoisie is of particular interest since it is a class which has been disproportionately favourable to the Conservatives, at least among the white population, and it is also a class where some ethnic minorities (notably Indian and Chinese) have been markedly over-represented. (For a fuller account of the relationship between ethnicity and class position, see Heath and McMahon 1997.)

Given the very small numbers voting for parties other than Labour, we focus solely on Labour voting. As we can see, at all levels of social class, ethnic minority support for Labour is markedly higher than that found in the white population. Thus the lowest level of black and Asian Labour voting is to be found in the salariat, where it is 'only' 76%, whereas the highest level of white Labour voting is to be found in the lower working class, where it manages to climb to 63%. Thus minorities of all social class backgrounds back Labour to a degree that would be unthinkable among even those in Labour's traditional white working-class constituency. In this sense ethnicity clearly dominates class.

However, class seems to divide black and Asian voters in much the same way as it divides whites, with Labour voting being lower both in the

TABLE 6.8   *Ethnicity, social class and Labour voting, 1997*

| | % Voting Labour | | | |
	White		Black and Asian	
Salariat	38	(659)	76	(109)
Routine non-manual	44	(409)	86	(99)
Petty bourgeoisie	31	(172)	78	(46)
Foremen and skilled manual	60	(300)	93	(70)
Semi- and unskilled manual	63	(402)	91	(125)
All	47	(1,942)	85	(448)

Notes: Figures in brackets give the base *n*.
Source: As Table 6.1.

salariat and in the petty bourgeoisie, and being more or less equally high in the upper and lower working class. In this sense, then, the ethnic minority electorate is divided by class in the same way, but not necessarily with the same magnitude, as the white population. The magnitude of the differences is of some interest. If we look at the absolute levels, it is clear that white members of the different social classes differ more substantially from each other than do the black and Asian members: among whites Labour voting ranges from 63% among the lower working class to 31% in the petty bourgeoisie – a range of 32 percentage points; among blacks and Asians the range is a more modest 17 points, only half the size. These absolute differences have a clear interpretation: blacks and Asians in different social classes are more similar to each other in their support for Labour than are whites in the same classes.

However, if we are concerned with the potential for class politics to emerge among the ethnic minorities, it may be illuminating to look at the odds ratios as well as at the absolute differences. The odds ratios tell us about relative class voting, and they take account of floor and ceiling effects: because ethnic minority support for Labour is so high overall, there is relatively little room for class differences to display themselves. Odds ratios, in other words, tell us about the magnitude of relative class voting after allowing for the differences in the overall levels of support for Labour. They may thus give us some clues about the potential for class differences to emerge if overall support for Labour were to decline from its present extraordinarily high level.

What we find is that the class odds ratios for the blacks and Asians are not all that different from those among white voters. For example, comparing Labour voting in the salariat and lower working class, we find an odds ratio of 2.8:1 among the whites but a slightly larger one of 3.2:1 among the blacks and Asians. The odds ratios and the absolute differences thus give us very different perspectives, although both in their own ways are valid ones, on class differences among ethnic minority voters. At present, class differences are (absolutely) smaller although by no means wholly negligible among blacks and Asians, but this is to some extent contingent on their high current levels of support for Labour.

There are also indications that absolute class differences are more marked among those minorities, particularly the Indians, where support for Labour is somewhat lower. In the case of Indians the absolute difference between Labour support in the salariat and lower working class reaches 24 points, approaching the white difference, whereas among the Afro-Caribbeans it is only 12 points. We have to be careful about reading much into these figures, since they are based on very small sample sizes. We also need to remember that ethnic minorities will not be found in a typical cross-section of salaried jobs. It could well be that salaried Afro-Caribbeans are to be found in the 'helping professions' (such as nursing, teaching and social work) rather than in the managerial positions that the majority of the white salariat occupies. In this sense we may not be comparing like with like, but the small sample sizes mean that we cannot pursue this important question further.

What we can do is to explore in somewhat more detail the role of other social cleavages among the ethnic minority population as a whole. To do this, we conduct a multivariate analysis in which our explanatory variables are social class, housing tenure (distinguishing owners, council tenants and other tenures) and educational level (distinguishing degree-level qualifications, intermediate qualifications such as A level and GCSE, and low/no qualifications). Because of the small numbers voting for other parties, we once again focus on Labour voting and therefore use logistic regression. The parameter estimates from a logistic regression can be interpreted as fitted log odds ratios, and they therefore enable us to address questions about relative rather than absolute class voting and so on.

Given the high degree of clustering in our sample of ethnic minority respondents, it is appropriate to use a multilevel model which explicitly takes account of the clustering. We also include a variable (drawn from the census) which measures the level of ethnic minority concentration at the sampling point. This is both of methodological and substantive interest. Methodologically it is important because our booster sample of ethnic minority respondents was drawn from areas which were known to have high concentrations of ethnic minorities living in them. There is therefore a risk that we have a biased sample. By including a control for ethnic minority concentration, we can measure the impact, and if necessary adjust for, any such bias. Substantively, it is also of considerable interest to determine whether ethnic minority concentration has an effect in its own right on support for the Labour Party. Theories of assimilation, for example, might suggest that the voting patterns of ethnic minority members who live in predominantly white neighbourhoods might accord more with those of the white population.

In Table 6.9 we report the results of three logistic regressions. In the first, we look at the impact of class, housing tenure and qualifications, together with ethnic concentration, among the white population of England and Wales. In the second we carry out the same analysis for black and Asian respondents. A comparison of the parameter estimates from these first two regressions enables us to compare in an informal way the impact of social cleavages on Labour support in the two groups, but for a more formal test we must pool the samples of whites and ethnic minorities and introduce specific interaction terms to test whether the impact of, say, housing tenure is the same among blacks and Asians as it is among whites. This is done in the third logistic regression.

The first regression shows a very familiar picture. Relative support for Labour is much the same in the two levels of the working class but then declines in the white-collar classes, and is especially low in the petty bourgeoisie. Council tenants also show the expected higher levels of support relative to owner-occupiers or private tenants while the relationship with education has more of a U-shaped character. Finally, we should note that ethnic concentration has a small, but statistically significant, impact on Labour support even among the white population. It may well be that the measure of ethnic concentration is in fact picking up social disadvantage generally in the area. At any rate, this suggests that some contextual processes may be at work. Moreover, we should note that, even after controlling for ethnic concentration, there is still some significant neighbourhood variation. This merits further investigation.

Turning next to the regression for the black and Asian respondents, we find that the pattern of the class parameters is very similar to that among the white voters. In the case of the salariat and petty bourgeoisie, the

TABLE 6.9   *Logistic multilevel model of Labour voting, 1997*

			Parameter estimates			
	White		Black and Asian		Combined	
Constant	.40	(.19)	1.09	(.78)	.32	(.19)
Ethnic concentration (log)	.023	(.011)	0.36	(.20)	.20	(.08)
Class						
salariat	−0.75	(.17)	−0.70	(.51)	−0.76	(.16)
routine non-manual	−0.52	(.16)	−0.19	(.50)	−0.51	(.16)
petty bourgeoisie	−0.98	(.22)	−1.02	(.54)	−0.98	(.20)
skilled manual	−0.04	(.17)	0.25	(.63)	−0.03	(.17)
semi and unskilled						
(reference)	0		0		0	
Housing tenure						
owner	−0.19	(.16)	0.71	(.42)	−0.17	(.16)
council tenant	0.76	(.22)	1.05	(.60)	0.78	(.20)
other (reference)	0		0		0	
Highest qualification						
degree	0.20	(.19)	−0.97	(.51)	0.17	(.19)
intermediate	−0.29	(.12)	−0.94	(.39)	−0.34	(.11)
none/other (reference)	0		0		0	
Ethnicity					1.10	(.34)
Ethnicity*owner					0.74	(.35)
Ethnicity*degree					−0.82	(.41)
Level 2 variance	0.57	(.11)	0.59	(.36)	0.59	(.11)
n	1,942		448		2,390	

Note: Figures in brackets give the standard errors.
Source: As Table 6.1.

parameters are almost identical, while in the other cases the standard errors suggest that the differences are likely to be well within sampling error. The patterns for tenure and education, however, are rather different. Black and Asian council tenants show the usual pattern of greater relative support for Labour, but owner-occupiers show a surprising pattern with a positive sign rather than the negative sign found in the white regression. Given the large standard errors, we cannot be sure that the parameter estimates for blacks and whites are significantly different from each other, and we shall need to test the difference formally in our third regression. Similarly, the patterns for education are rather different in the first two regressions, but a formal test is again needed.

Finally, it is interesting to note that ethnic concentration seems to have a much larger impact on the black and Asian voters than it does on the whites, although it falls slightly below conventional levels of statistical significance. This result needs to be replicated from other research before any firm conclusions can be drawn, but it does suggest that contextual processes, of the sort suggested by theories of assimilation, may be at work.

We now turn to the third model, in which the white and ethnic minority samples are pooled. In this third model we introduce a new explanatory term representing ethnicity (coded 0 for whites and 1 for blacks and Asians). We also introduce two interaction terms which test whether the effects of owner-occupation and degree qualifications respectively are the same for blacks and Asians as they are for whites.

The first important point to emerge from this third model is that the parameter estimate associated with ethnicity is of broadly similar magnitude to the ones associated with the salariat and the petty bourgeoisie. In others words, the impact of ethnicity on Labour voting (when measured in terms of odds ratios) is of more or less the same magnitude as that of social class.

The two interaction terms then tell us by how much the owner-occupation and degree parameter estimates differ for the white majority and the ethnic minorities. In the case of owner-occupation the interaction term has a value of 0.74, which is over twice its standard error. We therefore conclude that there is a significant difference here. The positive sign indicates that, other things being equal, the ethnic minority owner-occupiers in our sample were more likely to support Labour than were white owners. Among the ethnic minorities, then, home-ownership does not seem to have the usual association with Conservatism that it does among the white majority.

To understand this, we need to recall the operation of the housing market, and the choices made by members of ethnic minorities. These have been studied in a number of classic works, notably those of Rex and Moore (1967), Dahya (1974) and Ballard and Ballard (1977). (Ratcliffe (1997) gives an up-to-date review of ethnic minorities' housing.) Broadly speaking there were processes of discrimination (both overt and institutional) in the availability of finance and the allocation of council housing and private renting, and there were also distinctive ethnic preferences for the purchase of homes in ethnic neighbourhoods. As a result, owner-occupation has not come to be associated with upward mobility and abandonment of traditional community ties in the way that it has among the white working class. This suggests that it is not the mere fact of owner-occupation or the objective interests associated with it that are crucial for political behaviour. Rather, the political implications of ownership depend on the meanings and social relationships associated with housing.

The interaction between ethnicity and degree qualifications is also of borderline significance. At –0.82 the parameter estimate is just twice its standard error. This time, unlike the housing interaction, the sign is negative. This indicates that ethnic minority graduates were less likely to support Labour than would have been expected from the white equation. We need to be cautious in our interpretation of this finding, since it is of borderline statistical significance and will be based on a relatively small number of ethnic minority graduates in our sample. As other research has shown, these may well be people who obtained their qualifications overseas (Owen *et al.* 1997). Since higher education in the countries of origin is very strongly related to social class origins, it may well be that the measure of degree qualifications in the ethnic minority sample is acting as a proxy for advantaged social origins, which in general tend to be associated with support for the Conservatives. Among the white British sample, however, higher education is less strongly linked with social origins than it is in, say, India and is also strongly associated with liberal attitudes (Emler and Frazer forthcoming). As with housing, then, the meaning of the education variable may be somewhat different for the ethnic minority members, particularly those educated overseas, and the white majority.

Party Strategy Calculations

The strategic thinking behind political parties' campaigns towards ethnic minority voters has been the subject of considerable comment over the years (Messina 1998). This has been fuelled partly by the huge lead enjoyed by Labour over its rivals and also by the lack of results for Tory and centre-party efforts over the years. An added factor, though poorly studied, has been the widespread belief that economic and social embour-geoisement among selected minority groups would lead to a decisive breakup of Labour's stranglehold. The Jewish parallel has been cited countlessly to show the potential for rightward drift (Alderman 1983). Labour's commanding position, it has been suggested, would be weakened by factors that were both beyond its control as well as, paradoxically, in its historic nature to promote (Crewe 1983). The evidence does, however, indicate that some substantial signs of class differences are now discernible especially within the most populous minority group, Asian Indians. It is too early to say whether this group is in any way leading a path for other minorities, and it should be stressed that non-Labour, class-driven voting remains weak. Ironically, the single biggest factor behind this is the general absence of non-Labour voting (of whichever class) in sufficiently substantial numbers.

What generalized interpretations for party strategy are to be put on the evidence shown previously in the chapter? Three conclusions stand out. First, whilst ethnic minority support for parties other than Labour remains extremely low, there are some glimmers of hope for the Conservatives. For instance, as previously noted, in an electoral year that proved to be very bad for the Tories among white and minority voters alike, almost 18% of Asian Indians voted for the Conservatives. This is significant, partly because of the numerical leverage that this proportion yields among the single largest minority group, and also because it is so considerably out of line with other minorities. Again, the underlying question remains as to the interpretation to be put on this statistic: whether it reflects the socioeconomic status of Indians, or is reliable evidence of a rapport, even trust, that has grown between sections of this group and the party. Given the scale of Indian middle-class support for the Tories (between a fifth and a quarter), it would seem likely that social class membership itself accounts for the bulk of this group's deviation from the ethnic minority 'norm'. That does not rule out seeing this vote in terms of improving group-party dialogue couched in mutual self-interest terms. Indeed, it would be somewhat surprising if Tory strategists had failed to spot this opportunity. The trick centres on how far politically spun, mutual interest claims are used as, and perceived to be, a suitable gloss on underlying socioeconomic realities.

Secondly, Labour's massive lead in 1997 seems to have been earned without much evidence of active, 'ethnicized' Labour campaigning to attract minority support. What 'ethnic campaign' that could be identified in 1997 was chiefly a Tory affair, with some signs of Liberal Democrat activism (Saggar 1997a). Labour's success therefore was achieved without any real campaign effort and was largely assured months or probably years before the election itself. Indeed, there appear to have been very few ethnic or racial dimensions to this continued success.

Thirdly, Labour's lead in 1997 amounted to a testimony to its determination to hold on to minority voters whilst restricting its policy pledges targeted exclusively at minorities. Critics have complained that this was driven by the fear of establishing too close a relationship with minorities, thus risking an electoral backlash, with the party choosing to adopt a low-profile approach accordingly. In any case, there can be no getting away from the fact that Labour's appeal was deliberately couched in non-race specific terms. Whether it succeeded because or in spite of this effort is highly contentious to say the least. The Tories' pitch meanwhile rested almost entirely on a colourful recital of a cultural, values-based argument, the foundation of which was an alleged natural affinity between so-called Asian values and Conservative values. In sloganized terms this translated as 'Your values are our values and our values are your values'.

Future Prospects

The short-term picture of ethnic minority party preferences and loyalty could not be clearer. A variety of demographic, historic and ideological factors have combined to produce a seemingly unassailable position of dominance for the Labour Party. However, parties themselves are not the only players in shaping minority voters' political outlook. Minority pressure groups and various self-help bodies also have a role to play (Werbner and Anwar 1991). Additionally, the trajectory of past party strategy might not be a reliable guide to future party strategy (Rich 1998: 111). Some interesting hints in this direction can be gleaned from the 1997 election and its aftermath. Two observations are worthy of extended discussion.

First, the 1997 election was the first in which a national pressure group organized to try to boost minority participation. OBV achieved considerable exposure in the months running up to the election. Most importantly, it differed from earlier efforts to raise minority political awareness on two grounds: first, because it was genuinely non-partisan (whereas many earlier initiatives were not) and, secondly, because of its preoccupation with basic electoral registration and turnout matters. That said, OBV based its claims about minority electoral leverage on an old and familiar theme, namely the notion of 'ethnic marginals'. In other words, it argued that electoral geography could be made to work for minority voting interests by identifying a list of marginal seats in which minority voters held strategic influence. There was little new in this claim, which was first deployed in a Community Relations Commission report on the October 1974 election (CRC 1975). Others also sought to make similar political capital in 1997 (most notably Zee TV, an independent Asian satellite station). To be sure, it is difficult to measure the real impact of the 'ethnic marginals' strategy. For one thing, the secret ballot ultimately serves as a tight barrier to knowing whether a differential white/minority swing at constituency level resulted in seats changing hands in 1997. Overall, it is far more likely that a pro-Labour swing across the board superseded any specific ethnic minority effect. Moreover, in highlighting possible black abstention, groups such as OBV may have paradoxically reinforced the idea that black electoral muscle was, in truth, rather weaker than had been asserted.

Secondly, the political landscape after 1997 is one in which the long-term rebuilding of Conservative organizational structures has emerged as one of the most pressing concerns for the Opposition. Of course a lot can and has been claimed about the need for a mass and more diverse party membership and the symbolic significance of ethnic minority representatives. It is hard to gauge how far such initiatives in the Conservative Party will go in the longer run (Saggar 1998c). However, it is clear that the post-election environment amounts to a rare occasion in which the party not only finds itself out of office but also deeply diminished in morale and organizational capacity. In this respect the picture resembles the mid-1970s at which time the Conservatives first began a root-and-branch assessment of their appeal towards ethnic minority voters and established specific projects to tackle deficiencies (Behrens and Edmonds 1981).

A new look Tory Party may be a long way off, but the underlying question of its basic attractiveness to different sections of the electorate amounts to a legitimate and far-reaching issue. The party vice-chairman, Archie Norman, has made this issue the subject of several high-profile interventions since the election, many of which have been aimed as much at external commentators as internal activists and factions. It is this factor, above all else, which is most likely (first) to drive substantive reforms, (secondly) change the internal culture of the party and (lastly) project a fresh and credible image to potential minority recruits. Existing analyses of the party's grassroots base and organizational capacity suggest that substantial under-representation of minorities is probably linked to an ageing membership and lingering doubts about the legitimacy of postwar immigration (Whiteley *et al.* 1994). However, added to this is the fact that the collective attitudes of large swathes of the party's membership continue to be shaped by what Wieviorka terms as *infraracism*, the mildest of four levels of racist discourse (Wieviorka 1994). It may be true that One Nation Toryism has, rather against the odds, dominated party affairs on race throughout much of the 1990s. But set against this is substantial evidence of a deep-seated sense of quasi-cultural conflict between many rank-and-file party members on the one hand and an acceptance of the transformation of Britain into a multicultural society on the other (Messina 1998). This is presumably part of a longer-term generational task facing the new leadership of the party. What is certain is that it is a major though problematic factor feeding into ongoing self-assessments of the party's future direction in appealing to ethnic minorities for membership, votes and money.

Conclusion: The Critical Election Thesis Considered

The evidence presented in this chapter shows that there was little that was new in minority voting patterns in 1997. A bold line of continuity ran through these patterns. Labour maintained its virtual monopoly of the allegiances of this group of the electorate. The Tories meanwhile took some comfort from fairly buoyant levels of support from the largest minority group, Asian Indians; however, these levels only compare well against the nadir reached in national levels of Tory support. Ultimately, the biggest influence on party strategies may not be the distribution of minority votes but rather the proportionately larger influence of the Asian electorate over other minority groups. In essence, small changes in a party's rating among Asian voters will yield comparatively large movements across the minority electorate as a whole. In addition, the tight geographic clustering of Asians means that parties may conclude that, on rational vote-maximizing grounds, they have a lot more to gain in wooing this group of voters rather than others. Whether this factor leads to an eclipsing of the interests of other minorities – in campaign terms at least – is probably unlikely in the short term but cannot be ruled out in the longer run. A lot, presumably, will be conditioned by the approach and tactics of activists within the parties themselves, not least during periods of far-reaching structural and organizational renewal, as seen in the Conservative Party since mid-1997.

Furthermore, the political integration question posed at the beginning of this chapter contains elements of change as well as continuity. In assessing the 1997 election, the choice is mainly about emphasizing the latter over the former. Plainly important developments are under way within the minority electorate. If these developments add up to more than several isolated episodes, it might be possible to construct an argument that sees the 1997 contest in sufficiently turning-point terms. However, as the chapter has spelt out, the picture in 1997 was chiefly made up of extensions and reinforcements of established patterns. Ultimately, ethnically related understandings of political thought and behaviour require these existing patterns to follow a path of their own that is different from the white dominant 'norm'. Minority voters in 1997 broadly pursued a similar path to their white counterparts, rather rebuffing the non-conventional school of thought.

Notes

1. The term 'ethnic minority' is used in this chapter to denote people of south Asian, African and Caribbean origin. It is used interchangeably with the term 'minority'. Deployment of these terms as broad, umbrella labels is deliberate in order to signify the wide variety of non-white ethnic groups resident in contemporary Britain. Where greater precision is required in the chapter, as with reference to specific component groups, allowance and departures from this convention are clearly signalled. The reader's attention in drawn in particular to the chapter's delineation of the ethnic minority population into five principal categories: Asian-Indian, Asian-Pakistani, Asian-Bangladeshi, black-African and black-Caribbean. These five groups were isolated in the original research design to represent the significant elements within the ethnic minority population. A further miscellaneous category was included, which allows the analysis to include ethnic minority respondents who did not fall easily into the previous scheme. The research did not extend to southeast Asian, ethnic Chinese and Indo-Chinese groups, though some of these groups might have been picked up under 'Asian other' categories (and therefore included under the miscellaneous heading). No particular political or sociological inference should be drawn from the use of the above convention on terminology.
2. The research in this chapter is based on a specially conducted ethnic

minority booster sample. The project aimed to boost the cases of ethnic minority respondents in the main cross-section study in the BES to a sufficiently reliable level for generalized analysis. A combined data set of 705 cases was achieved drawn from three main sources: 1) ethnic minority respondents who happened to be generated by the main study (106 cases); 2) ethnic minority respondents generated by a large-scale screening exercise in areas of high ethnic minority concentration (405 cases); and 3) ethnic minority respondents generated by next-door screening at some sample points with high ethnic minority concentrations (194 cases). A series of weighting variables were later added to the data set in order to take account of 1) the differing selection probabilities of respondents from the three sample types, and 2) an electoral registration and turnout check based on marked-up electoral registers retained by the Lord Chancellor's Department for a year after the election. The comparative analysis of the main ethnic groups identified in the study was achieved by the creation of a (weighted) single merged file into which main cross-section and booster respondents were placed.

3. The multilevel models reported in Table 6.9 were fitted in Mlwin using the second-order PQL estimation procedure. We are very grateful to Harvey Goldstein and to Min Yang for their help with multilevel modelling.

7 Region: New Labour, New Geography?

John Curtice and Alison Park

Of all the statistics about the 1997 election it is the outcome in seats which gives us most reason to suspect that the election heralded a fundamental change in the structure of party competition. Labour secured its largest tally of seats ever, the Liberal Democrats emerged with more MPs than at any time since 1929, while the Conservatives only just managed to avoid doing even worse than their previous all-time low in 1906. Yet, despite the record swing of 10.3% from Conservative to Labour, none of these outcomes could have been anticipated from the overall movement of votes alone. If every seat had moved in line with the country as a whole, Labour's majority would have been 131 rather than 178, while the Liberal Democrats would have had just 28 seats, not 46 (Curtice and Steed 1997). Evidently the Conservatives' woes were not just a reflection of the steep decline in their overall vote, but also of changes in the way in which the electoral system operated.

Under the single-member plurality system, the number of seats that a party wins depends not just on the proportion of the vote that it secures, but also on how its vote is distributed geographically (Gudgin and Taylor 1979; Curtice and Steed 1986). Analysis of the election results reveals that there were two important changes in the geography of party support in 1997. First, Labour's vote rose and the Conservatives' vote fell rather more in the southern half of the country than in the northern half. As the Conservatives were defending more seats in the south (and given indeed a general tendency irrespective of a constituency's regional location for the Conservative vote to fall more where its vote was previously strong) this inevitably meant that the Conservatives lost rather more seats than they would otherwise have done. Secondly, voters living in constituencies that the Conservatives were defending displayed a tendency to switch to whichever of Labour or the Liberal Democrats were best able locally to defeat the Conservative incumbent. This apparent 'tactical voting' meant that the non-Conservative vote became more concentrated behind a single best placed challenger in each constituency, thereby increasing the chances that the local Conservative would lose.

Together these two patterns ensured that the Conservatives' vote became less effectively distributed across the country while that of both

Labour and the Liberal Democrats became more so. If this were to remain the case in future, the party could find itself with fewer seats than Labour even though it had a higher share of the overall vote (Curtice and Steed 1997; Jenkins 1998). But if we are to conclude that this means that the 1997 election was a 'critical' one, we need to ask whether there is any reason to believe that these changes in the geography of party support might be permanent ones. To address that question we will examine whether the rise in Labour's southern vote and the increase in anti-Conservative tactical voting were associated with any of the traits of a 'critical realignment' as they have been outlined in Chapter 1.

We will argue that there is little evidence of the presence of such traits. Far from representing evidence of a realignment, Labour's relative success in the southern half of the country seems more like the product of a dealignment. The period between the mid-1950s and the mid-1980s had in fact witnessed the emergence of a new regional cleavage, but it was one in which Labour did relatively well in the northern half of the country, not the southern half. Labour's southern success in 1997 thus represented the diminution of a cleavage, not a polarization. Neither was this development a sudden break with the past; rather it was already apparent by the time of the 1992 election. Moreover, the diminution of the regional cleavage occurred despite the fact that the underlying structural factors that had apparently helped to encourage its existence were still in place. To find an explanation for what happened, we will argue, we have to look instead at the strategies adopted by the parties.

Meanwhile, so far as the increased incidence of anti-Conservative tactical voting is concerned, we will argue that this development certainly reflects a change in the nature of party competition in Britain. Many voters have come to see the Liberal Democrats and Labour as relatively close to each other, while the Conservatives are set apart. Moreover, this pattern is new to the 1997 election. But it is not the product of a polarization based on new cleavages, or a growing intensity of partisanship, but rather the opposite. It flows from an increasing feeling that to be a Labour partisan is not incompatible with liking the Liberal Democrats too – and *vice versa*. And as that pattern also appears to be a response to changes in the strategies adopted by political parties rather than a reflection of changes in the structural influences on voters, we cannot presume that this development is a permanent one. Rather, as with the north/south divide, the future of tactical voting in Britain would appear to depend on the behaviour of the parties.

We begin our analysis by looking at what happened to the north/south divide in Conservative and Labour support. What is the history of this divide? How far did it decline in 1997? And what appears to be the explanation for the change? We then turn to the incidence of anti-Conservative tactical voting, again addressing similar questions. We conclude with our observations on what our findings imply for the theory of critical elections.

Regional Variation in Voting Behaviour

In the immediate postwar period, what appeared to be most remarkable about British electoral politics was the uniformity of the outcome across the country. Knowledge of the movement of votes in St Ives often appeared sufficient to anticipate what would happen in Caithness (Butler 1951). Indeed, the 'nationalization' of British politics appeared to be the natural product of 'modernization', as the country came to share a common political life imparted through a national media (Stokes 1968).

Yet in truth, by the second half of the 1950s, Britain was already beginning to diverge politically. At the 1959 election, the swing to the Conservatives from Labour was somewhat higher in the southern half of the country than the North. This inaugurated a process which was to be repeated at almost every subsequent election up to and including 1987 (Curtice and Steed, 1982, 1986). As Table 7.1 shows, in the period between 1955 and 1987, the Conservative share of the vote cast for the Conservatives and Labour combined (the 'two-party' vote) rose by nearly nine percentage points more in the south of England than it did across the country as a whole. In contrast, it rose by nine points less in the north of England. In the Midlands the relative movement in the Conservatives' favour was comparable to that in the south of England. Meanwhile, in Scotland Labour's relative advantage was more than twice what it was in the north of England.

This widening geographical divide was not one that appeared capable of being accounted for by changes in the social composition of the northern and southern halves of Britain. Southern Britain might be growing more rapidly than its northern counterpart but any widening of the social disparities between them was certainly not occurring on the scale implied by Table 7.1. Rather, as Heath *et al.* (1991) argue, during this period region became a new – indeed the only new – cleavage in postwar British politics, becoming particularly important within the working class. Thus, for example, in 1964 there was only a six-point gap between Labour's percentage support in the working class in the south of England and that in the north of England. But by 1987 in contrast, the equivalent gap

TABLE 7.1 *Long-term regional variation in swing*

	South of England	Midlands	North of England	Scotland	Wales
1955–87	+8.9	+5.9	–8.6	–19.1	+0.6
1987–97	–2.6	–2.3	+1.9	+7.4	+2.0

Notes: This table shows difference between the mean two-party swing (defined as the change in the Conservative share of the vote cast for the Conservatives and Labour) in each region and the mean swing across Great Britain as a whole.
South of England: South East (including London) and South West standard regions; Midlands: East Anglia, East Midlands and West Midlands; North of England: Northern region, North West, and Yorkshire & Humberside.
Source: Curtice and Steed (1998).

between those two regions had grown to no less than 29 points.

The increasing regional variation in Conservative and Labour support within each class can be summarized by the index of dissimilarity. In this context, this index is simply the sum of the differences in the proportion of each party's support that comes from each region, divided by two. It thus reflects not only the size of the gap in party support in each region but also the relative size of each region. And as Table 7.2 shows, within the working class this index grew from just nine in 1964 to no less than 31 by 1983 and 1987. Indeed, by the 1980s the regional differences in working-class voting behaviour were greater than those in respect of housing tenure, parent's class or trade union membership. A similar, if less dramatic and straightforward rise also occurred within the salariat.

TABLE 7.2   *Regional differences in each class*

			Index of dissimilarity					
	1964	1970	1974O	1979	1983	1987	1992	1997
Salariat	14	7	4	8	13	21	16	12
Working class	9	13	17	19	31	31	21	25

Source: Heath *et al.* (1991), updated by author.

The evidence of a growing regional cleavage in British politics between the 1950s and the 1980s is therefore clear. Less self-evident, however, are the reasons as to why it occurred. The most commonly offered explanation was an economic one, arguing that the cleavage was a response to the widening economic divide between the north and the south of Britain (Johnston *et al.* 1988; Heath *et al.* 1991, see also Seawright and Curtice 1995). For example, a half-point difference between the north of England and the south of England in their level of unemployment in 1966 had widened to a six-point gap by 1987. As a result it was argued that, thanks to the apparent failure of the market to bring them economic success, people in the north may have come to adopt an ideological position in favour of economic intervention, a position that would incline them towards voting Labour (Curtice 1988).

Changes since 1987

However, as the astute reader will have already noticed from Table 7.1, since 1987 the picture has been somewhat different. At the last two general elections, the swing to the Labour Party has been greater in the southern half of the country than in the north. Altogether, between 1987 and 1997 about a quarter of the gap that opened up over the previous 30 years between the north of England and the south of England was reversed, and over a third of the same gap between the south of England and Scotland. True, at this rate, it would take at least another 20 years before the status quo ante was restored. And between 1992 and 1997 at least much of the decline was associated with a tendency for the Conservative vote to fall most heavily in constituencies where they were previously strongest irrespective of their regional location (Curtice and Steed 1997). But still some of the power of the north/south divide has evidently waned at the last two elections.[1]

Moreover, this pattern of the election results is reflected in our survey data; in Table 7.2 we can see that by 1997 the index of regional dissimilarity was lower amongst both the working class and the salariat than it had been in 1987.[2] True, the pattern is not entirely straightforward. Regional differences within the working class increased somewhat in 1997 after falling heavily in 1992. But thanks in part to the declining size of the working class (see Chapter 5) this still means that if we measure the index of dissimilarity for the 1997 survey sample as a whole rather than separately within each class, at 20 it is not only considerably lower than the equivalent figure for 1987 (28), but is also somewhat lower than that for 1992 (23).

So, we see no sign here of realignment, only of dealignment. Moreover, the evidence predates the 1997 election so not even the dealignment can necessarily be regarded as new rather than part of a longer-term secular process (see Chapter 1). But how do we account for the change? Does it reflect developments in Britain's economic geography, as from earlier arguments we might anticipate to be the case, or is it the result of something else? And what do the answers imply for our understanding of the likely future of the north/south divide?

Economic Explanations

We certainly cannot simply dismiss the possibility that the narrowing of the north/south divide has been brought about by changes in Britain's economic geography. After all some of the difficulties of the recession of the late 1980s and early 1990s, such as the fall in house prices and 'downsizing', proved to be particularly common in the south of England. Thus whereas in 1986 the level of unemployment in the Northern standard region was nearly eight points higher in the South East, by 1994 that gap had narrowed to just three and a half points. Indeed, by the same date unemployment in Scotland had fallen below the UK average for the first time since the Great Depression of the 1930s (Curtice 1996).

So at the time of the 1992 election at least, a closure of the north/south divide was consistent with the argument that the divide was the result of economic circumstances (Curtice and Steed 1992). It was the south that now appeared to be disadvantaged by the operation of the market, not the north. Not only had regional differences in levels of economic optimism clearly narrowed but there was also some suggestion that differences in attitudes towards the market might have become a little less marked (Curtice 1996).

However, the regional economic picture had changed yet again by the time of the 1997 election. By then, the economic recovery was proving to be rather stronger in the south than in the north. For example unemployment as a proportion of the total electorate fell by 1.9% in London in the 15 months before the election compared with 1.3% across the country as a whole. Also house prices rose more rapidly in the South East than in the rest of the country over the same period (Curtice and Steed 1998).

Subjective economic perceptions match the objective picture. As Table 7.3 shows, in 1997 those in the south of England and the Midlands were noticeably more likely than those living further north to say that the general economic situation had got better over the last 12 months. Those living in the south of England were also markedly more optimistic than those in the north of England about recent trends in house prices. And they were also more likely to believe that their region had become more prosperous compared with the rest of the country over the period since the previous general election.

TABLE 7.3   *Subjective economic perceptions by region, 1997*

	South	England Midlands	North	Wales	Scotland
% Saying that Household finances got better in last year	26	26	24	20	21
General economic situation better in last year	47	38	32	22	29
House prices risen in last year	52	40	32	42	58
Region got more prosperous since 92	31	23	20	17	19

Source: BES, 1997.

In short, it is difficult to account for the narrowing of the north/south divide since 1987 simply with reference to economic trends. While there was a clear hiccup in the pattern of relative southern advantage for some of this period, it did not prove to be a continued trend. In the 1997 election, at least, if all that mattered was economics we would have anticipated that once again it was the Conservatives who performed relatively well in the south, and not as proved to be the case, Labour.

Labour's Southern Strategy

It seems then that we have good reason to examine alternative explanations for the narrowing of the north/south divide. But where might we turn? One clear possibility is to look at party strategy. Perhaps what the parties stood for changed in voters' minds in a way that made it more likely that southern voters would back Labour. After all, this was precisely one of the objectives that Labour's modernization strategy was intended to achieve.

One of the key texts in the attempts that were made in the years before the 1997 election to change Labour's image was a Fabian pamphlet penned by the Labour MP, Giles Radice, immediately after Labour's 1992 defeat. Its title was nothing other than *Southern Discomfort* (Radice 1992). Radice accepted that in order to win elections, Labour needed to win back some of the ground that it had lost in the south. The north of England appeared to represent the past, an area of declining industry and falling population, while the south of England, in contrast, was growing both economically and demographically. As Crewe (1987) had already vividly argued, Labour had 'come to represent a declining segment of the working class . . . industrial Scotland and the North . . . while failing to attract the affluent and expanding working class of the new estates and the new service economy of the South'. If Labour remained for ever linked with groups in decline, it would not seem realistic to expect it to be able to win elections again.

But how could Labour possibly win back support in the south of England? For it was here, above all, that the Thatcherite message of economic liberty and opportunity appeared to have most resonance. In short, if Labour were to win back support in the south, it seemed that it would have to abandon some of its socialism. This was, indeed, the strategy urged by Radice. The answer to Labour's 'southern discomfort', he argued, lay in abandoning Clause IV which committed the party to the common ownership of the means of production, shedding the party's image as a high-tax party especially so far as those on middle incomes were concerned, and weakening its association with 'narrow' sectional groups such as the trade unions.

And, of course, in practice Labour took all three of these steps between 1992 and 1997 as part of its 'modernizing' project (see also Chapter 1). Even before 1992 it had reined in its commitments to nationalization and had moved to reduce the manifest influence within the party of the trade unions. But how might this change in the party's ideological positioning have affected the geographical distribution of its support? There are at least three possibilities that we should consider.

How Modernization could Matter

The first two possibilities are based on theories of issue voting. The most straightforward reading of the analyses of Crewe and Radice is that voters in the south were less likely than those living further north to favour nationalization, higher taxation or any other supposedly left-wing proposition, and as a result were also less likely to vote for a party that favoured such aims. Thus if Labour persuaded voters across the country as a whole that it had moved to the centre, it would as a consequence move itself closer to the position of the average southern voter. So, even if voters north and south agreed on the degree of any such perceived shift, it might still result in more voters switching to Labour in the south than in the north.

But we also need to consider a more complex possibility. Perhaps voters in the south had a different view of the Labour Party than voters in the north. For whatever reason (including the possibility that such policies would be more discordant with their own views) perhaps southern voters were more likely to share the belief that Labour was a high-tax left-wing party than were those living further north. Moreover, perhaps they were also particularly likely to notice the changes that Labour made to its policy positions after 1987, not least perhaps because the party itself tried to sell the message to voters in the south that it was now concerned to look after the interests of all of Britain and not just traditional Labour Britain. In other words, rather than perceptions shifting similarly across the whole country, perhaps southern voters took more note of Labour's changed issue positions than did those in the north.

But it may be the case that both these propositions take too narrow a view of the aims and impact of Labour's modernization project. After all, Heath and Jowell (1994) have argued that Labour's policy review under Neil Kinnock had a much more discernible impact on the image that voters had of the Labour Party than it did on their perceptions of the party's detailed policy positions. More recently Evans (forthcoming) has argued that party image is the best predictor of changes in party preference during the first half of the 1992–97 Parliament. Perhaps therefore, what we might find is that what was most transformed by Labour's modernization project amongst southern voters was not Labour's perceived policy positions, but rather its overall image. It is this possibility that constitutes our third potential explanation of how Labour's modernization strategy might have brought about a diminution of the north/south divide.

In each case, however, we will not confine our attention to the 1992–97 period, but look back at the whole decade after 1987. After all, Labour's changes of policy position started well before Tony Blair launched the concept of 'New Labour' in 1994; rather they began under the leadership of Neil Kinnock, most notably with the launch of the 'Policy Review' immediately after Labour's defeat in the 1987–92 Parliament (Seyd 1992). And we have seen that Labour began to make inroads in the south in the 1992 election as well as in 1997. It is thus whether and how Labour's repositioning since 1987 might have helped reduce its 'southern discomfort' that we have to explain, and not just what might have happened between 1992 and 1997.

Issue Voting

Data collected by the British Election Study series enable us to address all three explanations we have posited. So far as those explanations based on theories of issue voting are concerned, we have access to four questions with certain valuable qualities. First, they were asked in each of the 1987, 1992 and 1997 election studies. Secondly, their subject-matter covers some of the issues that were central to Labour's modernization project. And thirdly they give us information not only about where respondents stood on the issue, but also about where they thought each of the main parties stood. Each question comprised a pair of propositions which defined the meaning of the end-points of an 11-point scale. Respondents were then asked to say, first, which point along the scale best described their own views and, then, which point best summarized their view of where each of the parties stood. The four pairs of propositions were as follows:

Jobs and prices Getting people back to work should be the government's main priority *v*. Keeping prices down should be the government's main priority.
Tax and spend Government should put up taxes a lot and spend much more on health and social services *v*. Government should cut taxes a lot and spend much less on health and social services.
Nationalization The government should nationalize many more private companies *v*. The government should sell off many more nationalized industries.
Income equality Government should make much greater effort to make people's incomes more equal *v*. Government should be much less concerned about how equal people's incomes are.

In each case the first of these propositions is given a score of one, and the second a score of eleven. Thus the higher the score on a scale, the more right-wing the answer given.

So, was one of Labour's problems at least that the southern voter was more right wing than his or her northern counterpart? Table 7.4 addresses this question by showing the score of the average voter in each of our regions in 1987 when respondents were asked to say where they stood on the scale. As we might expect from Curtice (1988), there is considerable evidence in support of the proposition. On all four scales the score of the average voter in the south of England and in the Midlands was higher than in the north of England or Scotland. Even so, there is one small surprise. The item on which a north/south divide was least apparent was on taxation and spending, an issue which, as we have seen, featured prominently in Radice's analysis of why Labour was in trouble in the south. The sharpest division between the regions was in fact on income equality, the

TABLE 7.4 *Political attitudes by region,* 1987

| | | Mean scale position | | | |
	South	England Midlands	North	Wales	Scotland
Jobs and prices	3.9	3.5	3.1	3.0	2.9
Tax and spend	4.6	4.6	4.3	3.9	4.3
Nationalization	6.8	6.6	5.9	5.5	5.8
Income equality	5.7	5.0	4.5	3.9	4.3

Source: BES, 1987.

issue which is clearly most central of the four to the debate about socialism and *laissez-faire*.

So a move to the right on Labour's part certainly appears to have had the potential to produce an electoral benefit in the south. But did Labour also have an additional problem in the 1980s, viz. that it was more likely to be believed by southern voters that the party took a left-wing position on these issues? For the most part the answer seems to be no. True, Labour was put slightly further to the left on tax and spend and on nationalization in the south of England than elsewhere, but the results for jobs and prices and income equality do not fit a north/south pattern at all.[3]

Still given what we have already seen in Table 7.4, it is evident that Labour's issue appeal was less strong in the south than in the north. For example, on income equality, no less than two-thirds of voters in the south of England put themselves to the right of the Labour Party (and thus potentially closer to the Conservatives or the Alliance than to Labour) compared with just a half in the north of England. Similarly, on jobs and prices, a half were to the right of the Labour Party in the south of England, compared with just over one-third in the north.[4] If Labour did want to win back votes in the south, a switch to the right did indeed seem to be necessary.

But where was Labour thought to stand ten years later? Was it believed to have moved to the right? And, more importantly for our interest here, can we demonstrate that any such change of perception was of particular benefit to the party in the south? Table 7.5 shows where on average Labour was thought to stand on each of our four issues in 1997 and, in parentheses, how this differed from the position in 1987.

The table clearly indicates that Labour was regarded as significantly further to the right on all four of our measures in 1997 than it was in 1987 (for further analysis of the implications of this shift, see Chapter 10). Labour's modernization project was noticed by the voters. But is there any reason to believe that this brought Labour more benefit in the south than it did in the north? There certainly seems to be some. For, on three of our four items, the perception that Labour had shifted rightwards was greater

TABLE 7.5 *Perception of Labour's position by region, 1997*

	South	England Midlands	North	Wales	Scotland
		Mean scale position (and change since 1987)			
Jobs and prices	3.3	3.4	3.0	3.0	3.0
	(+0.9)	(+1.1)	(+0.7)	(+0.5)	(+0.9)
Tax and spend	3.7	3.9	3.4	3.7	3.6
	(+0.8)	(+0.7)	(+0.3)	(+0.8)	(+0.4)
Nationalization	4.7	4.9	4.7	4.4	4.5
	(+2.0)	(+2.0)	(+1.6)	(+1.3)	(+1.5)
Income equality	3.6	3.6	3.4	3.0	3.4
	(+0.7)	(+0.6)	(+0.5)	(+0.2)	(+0.3)

Source: BES, 1997.

in both the south of England and the Midlands than it was in either the north of England or Scotland. As a result, on three of our four items, voters in the south of England and the Midlands actually placed Labour further to the *right* than did voters in either the north of England or Scotland.

Labour's modernization project seems then to have been peculiarly successful in easing its 'southern discomfort'. Not only did it move its perceived policy position closer to that of the average southern voter, but it was particularly successful in persuading southern voters that it had changed its views. Indeed it appears if anything to have shaped the contours of its appeal so that it matched the regional variation in respondents' own issue positions.

Indeed, the extent to which its perceived issue positions were no longer a particular problem for Labour in the south by 1997 compared with ten years earlier is quite remarkable. On tax and spend, the proportion putting Labour to the left of themselves was, at 35%, exactly the same as in the north of England. On nationalization the gap between the two regions in the proportion putting Labour to the left of themselves was only five points. Indeed, only on income equality was the gap between these two regions greater than ten points.[5]

So, Labour's modernization project did bring the party differential benefit in the south. Whereas in 1987 the party's perceived policy positions were relatively speaking at least out of tune with the beliefs of the average southern voter, by 1997 they were almost as in tune in the south as they were in the north.[6] But this did not happen simply because shifting rightwards brought the party closer to the southern voter. The party also succeeded in communicating an image for itself that was more right wing in the south than in the north.

One other point should also be noted. The change in regional variation in perceptions of the Labour Party was not simply the product of the period between 1992 and 1997. It was already in evidence by 1992. Thus, for example, by 1992, the average voter in the south of England and the Midlands put Labour just over one point further to the right than they did in 1987, whereas in the north of England and Scotland the shift was only just over a half point. Only on tax and spend do Labour's new more centrist credentials in the south appear only to have been obtained since 1992. So 1997 was not a 'critical' change in this respect, but a continuation of what had already come once before.

Party Image

What, then, of our third possible explanation, that Labour's image may have changed? We can look at the answers to three questions that were all asked in each of the last three British Election Surveys and which tap more general impressions of the parties than their policy positions. We asked respondents whether they thought Labour was extreme or moderate, good for all classes or good for one class, and capable or not capable of being a strong government. The latter two images at least have been shown to be strongly correlated with vote-switching between 1992 and 1995 (Evans forthcoming).

In 1987 Labour clearly had a particular image problem in the South. It was less likely to be considered moderate, good for all classes or capable of being a strong government in either the south of England or the Midlands than in the north of England or Scotland. Labour had indeed evidently alienated itself in particular from the southern voter. Yet as Table 7.6 shows, by 1997 the picture had been transformed. Not only was Labour's image far better than it had been ten years earlier, but it was just about as good in the south as it was in the north. Only on whether the party was good for one class or good for all was there still a hint of a north/south divide.[7]

TABLE 7.6 *Labour's image by region, 1997*

% saying party is:	South	England Midlands	North	Wales	Scotland
Moderate	70	72	71	63	73
Good for all classes	67	66	70	77	74
Capable of strong government	82	81	82	85	84

Source: BES, 1997.

But, as we found with perceptions of Labour's issue positions, this change in part predates the 1997 election. Even by 1992, Labour had already been relatively successful in persuading voters in the south of England and the Midlands that it was moderate and capable of strong government. Indeed, so far as moderation is concerned all the closure of the north/south gap had happened by 1992. Labour's improved appeal to southern voters was the product of Neil Kinnock's leadership as well as that of his successors. It certainly was not a sudden change first evident in 1997.

So, overall, Labour's modernization project was particularly successful in overcoming negative perceptions and associations that the southern voter had of the party in the 1980s. But should all the closure of the north/south divide be laid at Labour's door? What about the Conservatives? Do we also have to take on board the possibility that perceptions of them moved in an adverse direction more significantly in the south than in the north?

Perceptions of the Conservatives

There is indeed some evidence to suggest that the closure of the north/south divide may have also owed something to changed perceptions of the Tories as well as of Labour. As Table 7.7 overleaf shows, compared with ten years earlier, the Conservatives were thought by voters in the

TABLE 7.7   *Perception of Conservatives' position by region, 1997*

	South	England Midlands	North	Wales	Scotland
		Mean scale position (and change since 1987)			
Jobs and prices	6.3	6.3	5.9	5.8	6.3
	(+0.0)	(+0.1)	(−0.5)	(−0.9)	(−0.3)
Tax and spend	7.0	7.0	6.6	6.9	7.0
	(−0.1)	(+0.2)	(−0.7)	(−0.5)	(−0.5)
Nationalization	8.0	8.0	7.7	8.1	8.1
	(−1.4)	(−1.1)	(−1.2)	(−1.3)	(−0.9)
Income equality	8.4	8.1	8.0	8.4	8.3
	(−0.1)	(−0.1)	(−0.4)	(−0.5)	(−0.4)

Source: BES, 1987, 1997.

north of England and in Scotland to be a little more left wing on both jobs and prices, tax and spend and income inequality in 1997 than they were in 1987; in contrast there was no such change of perceptions in either the south of England or the Midlands. As a result, by 1997 the party was consistently regarded as more right wing in the south of England and the Midlands than it was in the north of England. In contrast to what we saw in respect of Labour, however, this pattern was mostly the product of the 1992–97 period alone. Even so, it meant that by 1997 the party was more likely to be seen to be further from the centre in just that part of the country where Labour was now more likely to be seen to be closer to the centre.

There is similar evidence in respect of one of our general party image items. Between 1987 and 1997, the decline in the proportion thinking that the Conservative party was 'good for all classes' was rather greater in the south of England and in the Midlands than it was elsewhere, a pattern that was almost wholly the product of the 1992–97 period. However, as Table 7.8 shows, this was not true of the other two items available to us. And overall, and in sharp contrast to Labour's uniform image, the Conservatives' image was still rather better in 1997 in the south than it was further north.

The closure of the north/south divide cannot then simply be accounted

TABLE 7.8   *Conservatives' image by region, 1997*

Say party is:	South	England Midlands	North	Wales	Scotland
		% (and change since 1987)			
Moderate	51	50	44	46	37
	(+9)	(+5)	(+6)	(+17)	(+4)
Good for all classes	27	24	22	18	15
	(−16)	(−14)	(−7)	(−5)	(−9)
Capable of strong government	27	34	24	29	21
	(−67)	(−60)	(−66)	(−62)	(−69)

Source: BES, 1997.

for by the impact of Labour's attempts to rebrand itself. Between 1992 and 1997 at least, there was also some regional variation in reactions to the Conservatives.[8] Why this happened must remain a matter of some speculation. Of course in part it may be that people's perceptions of the Conservatives and Labour are not independent of each other; if voters come to have a more favourable view of Labour they may as a result also start to adopt a more critical attitude towards the Conservatives. If that is so, then even the patterns in Tables 7.10 and 7.11 (below) may be a further reflection of the success of Labour's modernization strategy. But alternatively it may reflect a reaction to the experience of the 1992–97 Conservative government, perhaps because the disappointments of that period had most impact on that part of the country which had been most associated with the alleged successes of the Thatcherite era of the 1980s.

Measuring the Impact of Perceptions

There is then good reason to believe that the closure of the north/south divide in Conservative and Labour support was largely brought about by changes in party strategy, and that these changes had that effect despite the continued existence of economic differences between the two halves of the country. But there is one important gap in our analysis. We have not as yet demonstrated that either the party positions or the images that we have been examining are actually related to voting behaviour. We can hardly claim to have accounted for the decline in the north/south divide unless we can show this is so.

Of course any analysis of the relationship between perceptions of political parties and voting behaviour is potentially bedevilled by the problem of reciprocal causation. Voters may indeed be more inclined to vote Labour because they feel that it is closer to them on the issues of jobs and prices or because they think it is moderate. But equally, they may be more inclined to believe that Labour is close to them on jobs and prices or is a moderate party because they have decided to vote Labour for quite different reasons. In the latter event, their perceptions of the parties may be a consequence of their voting behaviour rather than an explanation.

We cannot wholly overcome this problem using the kinds of cross-sectional surveys being analysed here. However, if our explanation of the decline of the north/south divide is at all correct, we should at least be able to demonstrate one pattern. We should be able to show that once we take into account voters' perceptions, the size of any remaining association between region and voting behaviour should be the same in 1997 as it was in 1987. If this is not the case, and the residual pattern of association is weaker in 1997 than it was in 1987, then our explanation will clearly not have wholly accounted for the north/south decline. On the other hand if this is the case then our explanation must at least be regarded as a highly plausible one.

To examine which of these possibilities is true we can undertake identical logistic analysis of Labour versus Conservative voting in 1987 and in 1997. We first of all introduce into our model both region and a number of other standard demographic variables which previous research has suggested is associated with voting behaviour. We then add measures, based on our scale questions, of which of Conservative or Labour the respondent was closest to on the issues, together with respondents' perceptions of both Labour and the Conservatives on our general image questions. If our account of the decline of the north/south divide is correct we expect to find that whereas the association between region and vote is weaker in 1997 than in 1987 when only the social structural variables are introduced into the model, this is no longer the case once we add the perceptual data to the model.

The model provides substantial support for our interpretation (see Tables 7.9a and 7.9b). Note, first of all, two points. The first is that if we only include social structural variables in the model, the parameter coefficients for region are generally smaller in 1997 than in 1987 albeit still remaining significant; so the results are consistent with our claim that there has been a decline in the association between region and vote independently of the association between vote and other variables. Secondly, with just one exception (that is whether or not the Conservatives are capable of forming a strong government) all our perceptual variables are significantly associated with vote in both years. Indeed, for the most part the coefficients are often very similar in the two years, though it might

TABLE 7.9a *Logistic regression of Labour v. Conservative voting by social structure*

| | Voted Labour v. Conservative | | | |
	1987		1997	
Region				
South of England	−.80	(.10)*	−.67	(.11)*
Midlands	−.70	(.12)*	−.47	(.13)*
North of England	+.11	(.10)	+.03	(.05)
Wales	+1.06	(.19)*	+.70	(.26)*
Social class				
Salariat	−.70	(.12)*	−.64	(.11)*
Lower non–manual	−.06	(.11)	−.12	(.12)
Petty bourgeoisie	−.68	(.17)*	−.42	(.15)*
Foremen, etc.	+.59	(.17)*	+.46	(.19)*
Housing tenure				
Owner occupier	−.54	(.09)*	−.53	(.11)*
Council tenant	+.70	(.11)*	+.80	(.17)*
Education				
Has degree	+1.02	(.21)*	+.73	(.20)*

Note: * Significant at the 5% level. Main cell entries are deviation logistic parameter coefficients (standard errors in brackets). The last category for each variable is omitted. These are area – Scotland; class – working class; tenure – rent other; jobs and prices, etc. – equally close to both; all other variables are dichotomous. Closer to Lab means distance between where respondent put him or herself on the relevant scale and where he or she put Labour less than the distance between him or herself and the Conservatives. Similarly for Closer to Con.
Sources: BES, 1987, 1997.

TABLE 7.9b *Logistic regression of Labour v. Conservative voting by social structure and party image*

	Voted Labour v. Conservative			
	1987		1997	
Region				
South of England	−.75	(.21)*	−.73	(.18)*
Midlands	−.30	(.25)	−.51	(.21)*
North of England	−.18	(.21)	+.27	(.21)
Wales	+.61	(.40)	+.53	(.41)
Social class				
Salariat	−.47	(.26)	−.53	(.17)*
Lower non–manual	−.02	(.24)	−.06	(.19)
Petty bourgeoisie	−.41	(.35)	−.26	(.24)
Foremen, etc.	+.58	(.31)	+.14	(.27)
Housing tenure				
Owner occupier	−.41	(.19)*	−.44	(.17)*
Council tenant	+.96	(.23)*	+.67	(.25)*
Education				
Has degree	+.40	(.54)	+.30	(.35)
Jobs and prices				
Closer to Con	−.83	(.20)*	−.80	(.16)*
Closer to Lab	+.77	(.15)*	+.73	(.13)*
Tax and spend				
Closer to Con	−.73	(.18)*	−.53	(.17)*
Closer to Lab	+.75	(.16)*	+.44	(.14)*
Nationalization				
Closer to Con	−1.05	(.16)*	−.70	(.16)*
Closer to Lab	+1.00	(.16)*	+.41	(.14)*
Income equality				
Closer to Con	−.71	(.18)*	−.79	(.16)*
Closer to Lab	+.55	(.15)*	+.68	(.13)*
Labour moderate	+1.61	(.23)*	+.40	(.22)
Labour good for all classes	+1.10	(.25)*	+1.20	(.27)*
Labour strong government	+1.37	(.23)*	+.1.19	(.27)*
Conservatives moderate	−1.28	(.24)*	−.75	(.20)*
Conservatives good for all classes	−2.25	(.29)*	−2.70	(.23)*
Conservatives strong government	−.45	(.53)	−.19	(.20)

Note: See notes for Table 7.9a.
Source: BES, 1987, 1997.

be noted that tax and spend, nationalization and the moderation of the parties were somewhat less strongly associated with vote in 1997 than in 1987, an indication perhaps that another consequence of Labour's modernization strategy was to reduce the impact of these issues on voting behaviour (see also Chapter 10). But, more importantly for our purposes here, the results are consistent with the presumption which has been implicit throughout our analysis so far that a change in the marginals of these variables is likely to be associated with a change in the relative strength of the Conservatives and Labour.

But what of the association between region and vote once we include our perceptual data in our model? Is it no longer weaker in 1997 than in 1987? Indeed this is precisely what we find. The results are in line with our claim that changes in policy positions and of party images are responsible for the (partial) decline of the north/south divide. Indeed, if anything, we now find the strength of the association between region and vote was slightly stronger in 1997 than it was in 1987. In short, given the changes in the perceptions of the parties that occurred between 1987 and 1997, what has been notable is not how big was the decline in the north/south divide, but rather that it did not decline more.

Indeed, it is not only region of which this finding is true. The same can also be said of the association between class and vote. In other words, our analysis here is consistent with the argument made in Chapter 5 that the decline in the association between class and vote in 1997 is better explained as the product of changes made in the appeals by the parties rather than of some longer-term process of social structural change. If so, this also implies that the decline in the north/south divide should be seen as part of a wider process of dealignment brought about by changes in the behaviour of parties.

We have shown then that the decline in the north/south divide in Conservative and Labour voting in 1997 shows few of the traits of a 'critical' election. It is the product of depolarization and dealignment, not of realignment. And it did not suddenly occur in 1997. But even so we cannot dismiss the possibility that it represents a fundamental long-term change in the structure of party competition. Certainly, if we look at the distribution of party identification rather than vote we find there too that Labour has gained more ground over the last ten years in the south than in the north. Thus within the salariat the regional index of dissimilarity for Conservative and Labour Party identification has fallen from 21 to 12, while within the working class it has fallen from 28 to 25.[9] But whether party identification is sufficiently independent of vote in Britain to enable us to distinguish between a temporary and a permanent change in affiliations is open to doubt (Budge *et al.* 1976). More likely, we should conclude that the implications of our analysis are that the future of the north/south divide is likely to be contingent on the behaviour of the parties rather than determined by the sociology, economics or social psychology of the electorate.

Tactical Voting

We now turn, albeit more briefly, to the second significant change in Britain's electoral geography at the 1997 election (for a more extensive treatment, see Evans *et al.* 1998). This is the apparent increase in the amount of anti-Conservative tactical voting. How do we account for this development. And in particular does it carry any of the traits of a critical realignment?

As with the north/south divide both the election results and survey evidence agree that a change took place in 1997. The evidence from election results is shown in Table 7.10. This table shows the average change between 1992 and 1997 in the percentage of the vote won by the three main parties in five different kinds of constituency. These are as follows:

1) *Lab-Con safe seats* These are seats where Labour were first and the Conservatives second in 1992, but where the Conservatives won at least a third of the vote. This is in effect our control group against which we compare what happened in other situations in order to identify the existence or otherwise of tactical voting. Given both the outcome in these seats in 1992 and the evidence of the opinion polls that Labour was well ahead nationally, there is little reason why people should vote tactically in these seats as the outcome locally did not appear to be in doubt. We exclude those seats where the Conservatives won less than a third of the vote in 1992 because, as noted earlier, Conservative support systematically fell by less than the national average where they were previously weaker (see also Curtice and Steed 1997).

2) *Con-Lab seats* Constituencies where the Conservatives were first and Labour second in 1992. These are seats where voters who were concerned to ensure the defeat of the local Conservative would have reason to support Labour rather than the Liberal Democrats.

3) *Con-LD marginals* Seats where the Conservatives were first and the Liberal Democrats second in 1992, and where the Liberal Democrats were both more than 6% ahead of Labour and less than 30% behind the Conservatives. Here Labour voters had a clear incentive to switch to the Liberal Democrats in order to remove the local Conservative.

4) *Con-LD safe seats* Seats where the Conservatives were first and the Liberal Democrats second in 1992, but where the Liberal Democrats were more than 30% behind the Conservatives. While Labour might not have much apparent chance of winning in these seats, the Liberal Democrats chances did not look very good either, especially given their weak position in the opinion polls. So the incentives to vote tactically in these seats were relatively weak

5) *Three-way marginals* Seats where the Conservatives were first and the Liberal Democrats second in 1992, but where Labour were less than 6% behind the Liberal Democrats and less than 36% behind the

TABLE 7.10 *Tactical voting, 1992–97*

Tactical situation	Change 1992–97 in % voting			
	Con	Lab	LibDem	
Lab seats; Con > 33.3%	−12.6	+ 9.6	− 0.3	(107)
Con/Lab seats	−12.6	+13.0	− 3.0	(181)
Con/Lib Dem; Con lead < 30%	−11.8	+ 6.5	+1.9	(80)
Con/Lib Dem; Con lead > 30%	−13.5	+10.0	− 0.8	(60)
Three–way marginals	−11.6	+10.9	− 2.3	(18)

Source: Aggregate constituency results in Curtice and Steed (1997).

Conservatives. These were in effect 'three-way marginals' where both opposition parties might claim to be best able to defeat the Conservatives, and where voters might find it difficult to know which Opposition party to plump for.

Labour's vote rose most in those seats where it was the unambiguous challenger to the Conservatives, while it was in these seats that the Liberal Democrats fared worst. In contrast the Liberal Democrats' vote rose, against the national trend, in those seats where they started off in a relatively good second position behind the Conservatives, while it is in these very same seats that the Labour tide advanced least. From this we can conclude that where there was a clear incentive to vote tactically, around 2–3% of voters who might have been expected to vote for one of the two main Opposition parties opted instead for the other. And note that this tactical voting was additional to any that happened in 1992.

Meanwhile in the British Election Survey, respondents have been asked the following question after each of the last four elections:

Which one of the reasons on this card comes closest to the main reason you voted for the Party you chose?
I always vote that way.
I thought it was the best party.
I really preferred another Party but it had no chance of winning in this constituency.
Other (Please specify).

Those who say that they 'really preferred another party but it had no chance of winning' are regarded as tactical voters, and in a follow-up question are also asked which party it was they really preferred. Together with the information they give on how they actually voted, this means that we can identify those who switched tactically between Labour and the Liberal Democrats.

Altogether, on this evidence we find that just under 5% of voters switched tactically between Labour and the Liberal Democrats. This compares with just 3.5% who made the same move in 1992 and around 3% in both 1983 and 1987 (Heath *et al.* 1991; Evans 1994; Evans *et al.* 1998). So, the amount of anti-Conservative tactical voting has clearly increased. Moreover, in contrast to the decline in the north/south divide the change is one that primarily occurred in 1997. Here at least it seems possible that 1997 might be regarded as a 'critical' election.

However the increased incidence of anti-Conservative tactical voting would appear to have little to do with notions of realignment. In a realignment we would anticipate that partisanship would become more intense. Regarding oneself as a supporter of one party would be strongly associated with feelings of antipathy towards other parties. Yet previous research on tactical voting has suggested that those who vote tactically are those who, while disliking one party, are relatively indifferent in their feelings towards two others (Heath *et al.* 1991). In other words those who vote tactically are those who have a less exclusive sense of partisanship.

This again proves to be true of anti-Conservative tactical voters in 1997. We asked our respondents to indicate their feelings towards each of the parties on a five-point scale that ranged from 'strongly in favour' to 'strongly against'. And if we look at the average scores given to each of the three main parties by those Liberal Democrat supporters who cast a tactical vote for Labour, we find that the difference in the rating they give to the Liberal Democrats and Labour is just 0.40, whereas amongst Liberal Democrat supporters in general the equivalent gap was 0.91. Meanwhile amongst Labour supporters who voted tactically for the Liberal Democrats, the difference in the scores they gave the two non-Conservative parties was just 0.49, less than half the figure of 1.02 that pertained for Labour supporters in general.

True, anti-Conservative tactical voters are also notable for their dislike of the Conservatives, and to that extent see the party system in polarized terms. But they are less distinctive from other voters in this respect than they are in their indifference between Labour and the Liberal Democrats. Thus, while those Labour supporters who voted tactically for the Conservatives on average gave the Conservatives a score 2.75 lower than they gave Labour, this is only a little higher than the equivalent figure of 2.50 amongst Labour supporters in general.

So, those who cast an anti-Conservative tactical vote in 1997 were notable for the less exclusive nature of their partisanship, and in this respect they were much like those who engaged in the same behaviour at previous elections. So why did the incidence of such voting rise? We find that once again we have to look at the appeals made by the parties. The period between 1992 and 1997 saw Labour and the Liberal Democrats come closer to each other in a number of respects. In 1995 the Liberal Democrats dropped their policy of so-called 'equidistance' between Conservative and Labour, a policy which entailed refusing to declare which of Conservative or Labour they would prefer to work with in the event of a hung Parliament. Instead the party stated that while it would be prepared to work with Labour, it was unwilling to help keep the Conservatives in power. Meanwhile, in moving to the right as part of its 'modernization' strategy Labour inevitably was moving closer to the position of the Liberal Democrats, while in addition Labour came to adopt many proposals for constitutional reform that had long been backed by Liberals and Liberal Democrats. Indeed shortly before election the two parties held talks on constitutional reform under the chairmanship of Robin Cook and Bob Maclennan, and issued a statement indicating areas of constitutional reform to which both parties were committed.

These developments were noticed by voters. After every election since 1974, the British Election Study has asked its respondents whether they felt the Liberal Democrats (and their predecessors) were closer to Labour or closer to the Conservatives. As Table 7.11 shows three times as many people felt that the Liberal Democrats were closer to Labour than they

TABLE 7.11 *Perceived position of Liberals/Liberal Democrats, 1974–97*

| | % saying that party is | | |
	Closer to Con	Closer to Lab	No difference/ don't know
Feb 1974	63	17	20
Oct 1974	59	17	23
1979	43	41	16
1983 – Liberals	47	30	22
– SDP	22	49	28
1987 – Liberals	47	32	22
– SDP	39	35	25
1992	39	33	28
1997	18	57	25

Notes: Figures for 1974 and 1979 are for the Liberal Party. Figures for 1992 and 1997 are for the Liberal Democrats.
Source: BES.

were to the Conservatives. Not even the SDP which was founded by former senior Labour politicians was ever regarded as quite so close to Labour while the Liberals were always thought to be closer to the Conservatives, even in 1979 just a year after the conclusion of the Lib-Lab pact which helped sustain Jim Callaghan's government in office. Equally comparison of all three main parties' perceived issue positions on our scales also reveals a coming together of the perceived positions of Labour and the Liberal Democrats.

In short, never before had Labour and the Liberal Democrats been felt to have so much in common. And as a result, more voters were relatively indifferent in their feelings towards those two parties while at the same time disliking the Conservatives. In 1992, just 9% of voters said they were 'in favour' (either just or 'strongly') of both Labour and the Liberal Democrats while at the same time being against the Conservatives, of whom no less than 19% vote tactically.[10] In 1997, no less than 22% had the same pattern of feelings, of whom the proportion voting tactically, 15%, was actually slightly lower than in 1992. The increase in tactical voting in 1997 is then clearly the result of changes in perceptions of the parties, and not of changes in what induces voters to vote tactically.

Conclusions

The 1997 election saw important changes in the electoral geography of Britain, changes which disadvantaged the Conservatives and helped Labour and the Liberal Democrats, and which potentially had important implications for the structure of party competition. However, they exhibit few of the traits associated with the theory of 'critical realignment'. Rather they were the product of dealignment, that is of a decline in the strength of association between region and voting behaviour and an increased fluidity in switching between Labour and the Liberal Democrats. And so far as the decline of the north/south divide is concerned, the trend was already in train before the 1997 election.

Yet of course dealignment may be as profound in its implications as realignment. And it might matter just as much or even more if it is the result of a long-term secular process rather than a sudden change. The absence of the traits of a 'critical' election does not necessarily tell us that the changes we have analysed are of no long-term consequence for British politics, merely that they do not fit that particular paradigm.

Certainly, if the Conservatives' electoral support were to continue to remain as geographically evenly spread in future as it was in 1997, while voters remained willing to switch tactically between Labour and the Liberal Democrats, the implications for the structure of party competition could be profound. It could mean that the Conservatives would find it difficult to win an overall majority even if they were to win substantially more votes than Labour at a future election (Curtice and Steed 1997). Moreover, this would remain true even if at some point in the future elections were to be held under the so-called 'AV Plus' electoral system proposed by the Independent Commission on Voting Systems (Jenkins 1998).

Our analysis has suggested that the main reason why Britain's electoral geography changed in 1997 was because voters' perceptions of the parties had altered. The new pattern did not arise because the motivations that voters bring to the ballot box have changed. The future of Britain's electoral geography would therefore appear to rest in the parties' hands. If Labour continues to pursue its modernization strategy, avoids giving particular offence to southern voters and continues to maintain good relationships with the Liberal Democrats, the electoral geography of the 1997 election may well be maintained. Our analysis certainly gives them good reason to do so, with the likely consequence that the current electoral system would retain the bias it currently exhibits against the Conservatives. But, on the other hand, may be the Conservatives can renew their appeal to the southern voter and prise the Liberal Democrats away from Labour, learning perhaps from the evidence in Chapter 3 that in 1997 at least the party misperceived the ideological placement of the average voter. In that event, Britain's electoral geography may well undergo another important change, and the bias of the electoral system against the Conservatives might disappear.

There is of course an irony in our story. For while Labour's electoral success may have been accompanied by an attempt to lessen not increase the impact of the north/south cleavage, it was accompanied by a policy platform that gave greater recognition to geographical differences within the UK than ever before. Thus the Labour government has proceeded to implement devolution in Scotland and Wales, to establish a new strategic authority in London and has long-term plans for the creation of regional assemblies in the rest of England. In reaction the Conservative Party is now toying with the possibility of an 'English Parliament'. Geography may have come to matter a little less in voting behaviour in 1997, but the new structures put in place since the election appear to have the potential to make regional differences more salient, and thus an issue that politicians may find it difficult to avoid even if they wish to do so. Britain's regional differences could still matter yet.

Notes

1. Some readers may be surprised to see used here a statistic based on votes cast for Conservative and Labour alone, given that at recent elections around a quarter of the vote has been cast for parties other than these. It should be noted, however, that the north/south cleavage which has developed since the 1950s is one that primarily affects the distribution of support for Conservative and Labour and is not reflected in the pattern of support for other parties. Throughout our analysis of the cleavage in this chapter we thus use measures which focus on the relative strength of those two parties alone in each region.

2. One important implication of the fact that the index of dissimilarity has declined within each class is that the decline in the north/south divide since 1987 is not simply a by-product of the decline in the relationship between class and vote over the same period (see Chapter 5).

3. Interested readers can ascertain details of Labour's perceived position in 1987 by applying the figures in parentheses to the main cell entries in Table 7.5.

4. We secure the same picture if we look at which of Conservative or Labour respondents put themselves closest too. In the south of England, 9% more put themselves closer to the Conservatives than to Labour on income equality, whereas in the north of England 22% more put themselves closer to Labour. On jobs and prices, Labour's lead was 11 points in the south of England, but 26 points in the north.

5. Thus, 61% were closer to Labour than to the Conservatives on tax and spend both in the south of England and the north. On nationalization, only 1% more put themselves closer to Labour in the north of England than in the south. On income equality the equivalent gap was seven points. Note that there is also some evidence that, on nationalization at least, the electorate in the south of England and the Midlands moved further to the left between 1987 and 1997 than did voters in the north of England or Scotland, and thus the narrowing of the regional divide on this issue was not just the result of changes in perceptions of where Labour stood. Indeed, ironically, by 1997 this meant that a north/south divide barely existed in the electorate on either of the two issues, that is tax and spend and nationalization, that lay at the heart of Labour's southern strategy.

6. This conclusion is supported by more formal analysis. For both 1987 and 1997 we undertook a logistic regression of whether the respondent was closer to Labour than the Conservatives or not (measured by the distance between where the respondents placed themselves and where they placed the parties on the relevant scale) against region, class, housing tenure and whether or not the respondent had a degree. In 1997, only on income equality was there a statistically significant association between which of Conservative or Labour the respondent was closer to and region, whereas in 1987 the equivalent association was significant for all four scales.

7. Note that if we undertake a logistic regression of our three image questions against region, social class, housing tenure and whether or not the

respondent had a degree in both 1987 and 1997, we find in each case that while overall there was a significant association between region and image in 1987, this was not so in 1997. Not only does this result confirm our more informal analysis, but indicates that although in fact there was also a weakening of the association between class and image between 1987 and 1997, the change in the association between image and region is not simply the product of changes in the relationship between image and other social structural variables.

8. Given the tendency for Conservative support to fall more heavily in those constituencies where they had previously been strong irrespective of geographical location, we might have anticipated that the Conservatives' image declined most in such constituencies and/or their perceived issue position moved further away from the electorate. For the most part, however, we have been unable to substantiate that hypothesis. Equally, however, our analyses also suggest that this pattern of Conservative performance was not simply the consequence of class dealignment

9. These figures are based on answers to the first only of the two questions used to ascertain a respondent's party identification.

10. Acquiring equivalent figures for 1983 and 1987 is complicated by the fact that respondents were asked separately about their feelings towards the two Alliance parties, the Liberals and the Social Democrats. But, for example, it is clear that the situation in 1987 resembled that of 1992 rather than 1997. Just 4% of voters were 'in favour' of all of Labour, the Liberals and the SDP, while at the same time being against the Conservatives. Even if we adopt a more relaxed criterion and ask how many voters were 'in favour' of Labour and at least one or other of the Liberals and the SDP, while being opposed to the Conservatives, we still only acquire a figure of 9%. As many as 20% of the former group voted tactically, and even amongst the latter tactical voting was as high as 13%.

8   Gender: A Gender-Generation Gap?

Pippa Norris

The conceptual framework in this book classifies maintaining elections as those where patterns of party support display considerable continuity over time. Deviating elections are indicated by trendless fluctuations, or a temporary surge and decline, in long-term alignments. In secular realignments there is a long-term shift which gradually consolidates and changes the familiar landscape of party support. In contrast *critical* elections are characterized by stepped realignments in the electoral basis of party support, with major voting blocs creaking, cracking and reconsolidating like ice floes in the Antarctic. This classification raises important theoretical questions about how far parties can produce realignments by their own efforts – for example by targeting new groups of voters, strategically shifting ideological positions along the left–right spectrum or selecting new leaders – or how far they remain prisoners of social and political forces outside their control (see, for example, the discussion in Kitschelt 1994). If parties make strategic appeals in an election, do voters respond?

To examine this issue this chapter focuses on the politics of the gender gap in postwar Britain. During the 1950s and 1960s the orthodox wisdom was that women tended to be more conservative than men, in their voting choices, partisan loyalties and political attitudes (Durant 1969; Butler and Stokes 1974: 160). Similar patterns were evident in other west European countries (Duverger 1955). Since there are slightly more women than men in the electorate, due to patterns of longevity, this pattern has always proved an advantage for the British Conservatives. Yet Labour, facing a shrinking working-class constituency, has actively attempted in recent years to attract more female support (Hewitt and Mattinson 1987; Perrigo 1996; Lovenduski 1997; Eagle and Lovenduski 1998).[1] Clare Short (1996) has described this as 'a quiet revolution' in the Labour party. In the last election the most dramatic component of this strategy included picking far more female candidates for winnable seats, a policy which helped triple the number of Labour women MPs, from 37 in 1992 to 102 in 1997. The parliamentary face of the Labour Party was transformed with women representing one-quarter of Labour parliamentary backbenchers and one-fifth of the Cabinet, some like Mo Mowlam in high-profile posts. Women have also made inroads at all levels of the party organization. To a lesser extent in the pursuit of women's votes Labour has also attempted to rebrand their party image via campaign communications and packaging, and to a far lesser extent to revise their policy platform (see Figure 1.7 presented earlier). But can parties create the conditions for a *critical* realignment of gender politics in the short term by their own efforts? The central question we address is whether Labour's strategy succeeded in producing a critical realignment of gender politics in the 1997 election or whether there is evidence for secular realignment in the gender gap in Britain. The first section lays out the theoretical framework and then establishes baseline trends in the *size* and *direction* of the gender gap in British elections from 1945 to 1997. The next goes on to consider explanations of women and men's party support in 1997. The conclusion considers the implications of the findings for the future of British party politics and for theories of critical elections.

Theories of Gender Differences in the Electorate

Before we can consider whether the 1997 election broke with the past we need to establish a suitable baseline for historical comparison. The literature provides three plausible hypotheses about the expected direction and size of the British gender gap in the last half century, which can be termed the 'traditional', 'convergence' and 'realignment' perspectives.

The Traditional Orthodoxy of the 1960s and 1970s

When women were enfranchised after the Great War many contemporary observers expected that they would act as a decisive 'swing vote', producing a radical change in party fortunes. In the interwar years women did not vote as a single bloc or homogeneous group, as some feared, but evidence suggests that the Conservatives were slightly more successful in mobilizing women (Tingsten 1937: 42–5; Durant 1949; Ross 1955), as were the Republicans in the USA (Andersen 1996: 65). Women's tendency to lean towards the centre-right, which we can terms the *traditional* gender gap, was confirmed in Duverger's seminal comparison of voting behaviour in Britain, France, Italy and Germany (Duverger 1955). It was subsequently replicated in voting studies during the 1960s and 1970s in other western democracies, including the USA (Campbell *et al.* 1960: 493), Britain (Durant 1969; Butler and Stokes 1974: 160) and western Europe (Inglehart 1977). As a result the literature during these decades conventionally focused on explaining why women voters were more conservative than men due to their religiosity, longevity or class background (see, for example; Lipset 1960: 260; Pulzer 1967: 522; Blondel 1970: 55–6; Rose 1974). Women were often also assumed to be more right wing in their ideological beliefs and partisan identification, although few examined this proposition systematically (Goot and Reid 1984).

The Gender Dealignment Thesis of the 1980s

Yet the gender dealignment perspective, which became common in the 1980s, suggests that political differences between women and men have gradually faded over time, due to increased similarities in lifestyles. This argument is developed in several studies in Britain (Heath *et al.* 1985: 23; Rose and McAllister 1986, 1990: 51; Hayes 1997; Hayes and McAllister 1997; Studlar *et al.* 1998) and in western Europe (de Vaus and McAllister 1989; Jelen *et al.* 1994). When social structural and situational factors are taken into account, like patterns of participation in the paid workforce and in trade unions, it is argued that gender fails to emerge as a significant predictor of voter choice. In Rose and McAllister's words (1990: 51): 'Notwithstanding traditionalist theories of women favouring the Conservatives and feminist theories indicating that women ought to vote Labour, gender has no influence upon voting in Britain today. The reason is straightforward: on matters that are salient to voting men and women tend to share similar political values.'

Theories of Gender Realignment in the 1990s

The more recent literature which developed in the 1990s suggests that the traditional gender gap may have first converged in many countries, and then reversed in some, with women gradually moving to the left of men. Inglehart and Norris (1998) examined the gender gap in almost 60 nations worldwide based on the World Values Surveys, 1981–97. They found that in most advanced industrial societies in the 1980s women tended to be more right wing than men but by the mid-1990s the gender gap had either converged, or women had moved significantly further towards the left than men. In contrast the traditional gender gap, with women more right wing than men, remained more common in postcommunist and developing societies. The *modern* gender gap (with women leaning to the left) has received most extensive attention in the USA. Democratic support for the classic New Deal coalition has steadily eroded among many core constituencies but in contrast during the last two decades the Democrats have made substantial, long-term and consistent inroads among women (see, for example Mueller 1988; Cook and Wilcox 1991; Conover 1994; Seltzer *et al.* 1994). Since 1980 the modern gender gap, with women leaning towards the Democrats while men lean towards the GOP, has been evident in successive presidential, gubernatorial and state-level contests (CAWP). According to the Voter News Service exit poll, for example, in 1998 the majority of women (53%) voted Democrat while the majority of men (54%) voted Republican. This phenomenon has had significant consequences for the policy agenda and for the representation of women in public office. Inglehart and Norris (1998) argue that developments in the USA occurred earlier than in many other comparable democracies, and may therefore be more strongly entrenched, but that by the mid-1990s in most advanced industrial societies the traditional gender gap had disappeared or the modern gender gap had become apparent.

Trends in the Size and Direction of the Gender Gap, 1945–97

How does Britain fit into this picture? The term *gender gap* is a catch-all phrase used to refer to a wide variety of political differences between women and men, whether in terms of voting choice, partisan identification, ideological values or levels of political participation. For consistency in this chapter, unless otherwise noted, the gender gap is defined and measured in terms of the *two-party vote lead*. This is calculated as the difference between the percentage Conservative–Labour lead among women minus the percentage Conservative–Labour lead among men. In 1945, for example, according to Gallup polls (see Table 8.1) women split their vote almost evenly: 43% Conservative to 45% Labour, producing a slim (2 point) Labour lead. In contrast, men divided 51% Labour to 35% Conservative, resulting in a large (16 point) Labour lead. This produced a substantial traditional gender gap of –14 points. For consistency, a negative gap is used throughout to indicate the traditional gap (with women more Conservative than men), while a positive gap denotes the modern gap (with women more Labour). Modest gender differences can also be found in support for the minor parties but this chapter focuses primarily on the two-party vote lead since this is most critical to the outcome for government. To explore trends we use data available from 1945 to 1964 in Gallup election polls and from 1964 to 1997 in the series of British Election Studies. Relying upon two data sources produces problems of strict comparability over time; nevertheless since the items measuring voting intentions are relatively standard the advantages of a longer time-line outweigh the disadvantages.

The results in Table 8.1 and Figure 8.1 show considerable fluctuations in the size of the gender gap over 15 British general elections, rather than a steady linear trend. Nevertheless the long-term pattern confirms the first theme which emerges from this analysis: *Britain has experienced secular dealignment over time in the gender gap*. During the postwar decade women leant strongly towards the Conservatives while men gave greater support to Labour: the size of the gender gap averaged around 14%, peaking in 1951 and 1955. From 1959 to October 1974 this gap tended to shrink to around 8 percentage points. The Conservatives continued to count upon female support to provide a decisive edge in close contests; we can estimate that if Britain had continued with an all-male franchise, all other things being equal, there would have been an unbroken period of Labour government from 1945 to 1979. Yet since 1979 the overall gender gap has been only 3% on average, becoming statistically insignificant in several elections, indicating dealignment in the

TABLE 8.1 *Vote by gender, 1945–97*

| | Con | | Lab | | Lib | | Gender |
	Men	Women	Men	Women	Men	Women	Gap
1945	35	43	51	45	11	12	–14
1950	41	45	46	43	13	12	–7
1951	46	54	51	42	3	4	–17
1955	47	55	51	42	2	3	–17
1959	45	51	48	43	7	6	–11
1964	40	43	47	47	12	10	–4
1966	36	41	54	51	9	8	–8
1970	43	48	48	42	7	8	–11
1974 (F)	37	39	42	40	18	21	–3
1974 (O)	35	37	45	40	16	20	–8
1979	45	49	38	38	15	13	–3
1983	46	45	30	28	23	26	–2
1987	44	44	31	31	24	23	–1
1992	46	48	37	34	17	18	–6
1997	29	31	53	51	18	19	–4
1992–97	–16	–17	16	17	1	1	

Note: The gender gap is calculated as the difference in the Con–Lab lead for women and men.
Source: Gallup polls, 1945–59; BES, 1964–97.

strength of the association between gender and vote choice.

The 1997 election proved consistent with this pattern: although women remained slightly more Conservative than men, the size of the overall gender gap was only 4 percentage points and proved statistically insignificant. Labour's strategic efforts were insufficient to produce a critical

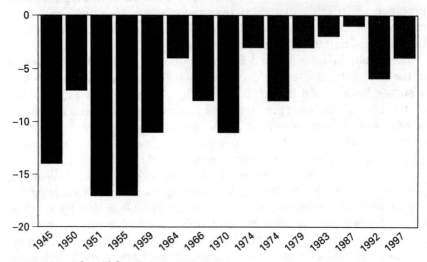

FIGURE 8.1 *The British gender gap*, 1964–97
Source: Gallup polls, 1945–59; BES, 1964–97
Note: See Table 8.1 for measure.

realignment in support among women voters. The traditional Conservative advantage among women has all but disappeared although this cannot be attributed to Labour's recent attempts to win women's votes since the convergence occurred before the mid-1980s.

Certain qualifications need to be added to this picture. The percentage size of the postwar gender gap has often proved relatively modest compared with other social cleavages in the British electorate, such as those by class (see Chapter 5) or by race (see Chapter 6). Nevertheless political differences between women and men have often been electorally important, at least until 1979, for several reasons. First, there is a *demographic gap*. Due to patterns of greater longevity women are the majority of the electorate. As they get older women increasingly outnumber men until, for those aged 85 and over, there are three women to every man (*Social Trends* 1997: 29). In the 1997 election women represented 51.7% of the electorate. While parties may feel that there are few major benefits, and some distinct electoral risks, associated with explicitly targeting groups such as ethnic minorities, or gay and lesbian voters, no party can afford to discount women as one of the largest groups of potential supporters.

Moreover, women's slight edge in the electorate has been magnified by the *turnout gap*. During the postwar decade females were slightly less likely to participate at the ballot box, a pattern found in many western democracies (Christie 1987). Since the 1979 general election, however, women have voted at similar, or even slightly higher, rates than men (see Table 8.2). In the last election 80.1% of women reported voting compared with 76.9% of men, a turnout gap of 3.2% (see Chapter 9). The net result of these differentials is that an estimated 17.7 million women voted in 1997, compared with around 15.8 million men.

Lastly, the spatial distribution of party support is also important politically. The votes of many demographic groups most favourable towards Labour are often concentrated in particular areas, such as ethnic

TABLE 8.2   *Reported turnout by gender, 1964–97*

	Men	Women	Turnout gap
1964	90.9	86.6	−4.3
1966	84.3	82.6	−1.7
1970	81.0	81.0	0.0
1974 (F)	88.8	86.9	−1.9
1974 (O)	85.2	84.8	−0.4
1979	84.4	85.2	0.8
1983	82.5	84.1	1.6
1987	85.5	86.7	1.2
1992	86.4	87.5	1.1
1997	76.9	80.1	3.2

Note: The turnout gap is calculated as the difference in the *reported* turnout for women and men.
Source: BES, 1964–97.

minorities in inner-city London, the north west and the Midlands or the poorer working class clustered in Glasgow, Newcastle and Manchester. In contrast, women and men are dispersed fairly evenly across different types of constituencies, with the exception of certain southern retirement communities where women predominate. As a result even a modest gender gap translates into millions of votes distributed evenly in marginal seats across the country. In recognition of these factors, all parties have actively sought to capture 'the women's vote', although this has often proved elusive (Lovenduski and Norris 1993, 1996).

Theories Explaining the Gender Gap

Why has female conservatism weakened in Britain over the years? One persuasive explanation for gender dealignment and realignment focuses on *generational* changes among women (Inglehart and Norris 1998). In the past sex roles were usually highly differentiated, with women focusing primarily upon the family and child-rearing and men upon bread-winning roles. In contrast, the postwar generation, who gained their formative experiences in the 1960s and 1970s, have been most strongly influenced by the transformation of sex roles, the growth of the women's movement and changes in attitudes towards gender equality which have occurred in recent decades. Value change has produced greater convergence of gender roles in advanced industrial societies, including the norms concerning family structures, child-rearing and sexual mores (Heath and McMahon 1992; Kiernan 1992; Thomson 1995; Inglehart 1990: 177–211; 1997: 267–92). Generational explanations emphasize that formative experiences leave a long-term imprint upon cultural and political values, which then persist for decades.

Structural explanations are also common. The gender gap be modified by female labour-force participation and occupational status (Manza and Brooks 1998). Blondel (1970) argued that women were more Conservative because of their predominance in lower-middle-class occupations, given well established patterns of vertical and horizontal occupational segregation. Yet others suggest that women may be influenced more strongly by their spouses' class position than by their own occupation (Erikson and Goldthorpe 1992; Mills 1994). Rose and McAllister (1990: 50–1) argue that married women at home may be less strongly influenced by their prior occupational class, or by their spouse's class, since they are not exposed to the reinforcing influence of colleagues in the workplace, and they experience more cross-cutting cleavages. Other structural explanations are common. Duverger (1955) argued that the traditional gender gap was based on women's greater *religiosity*, and in the USA other demographic factors have been found influential, notably *marital status* (Plissner 1983) and levels of *education* (Mueller 1988). Lastly, Studlar *et al.* (1988) found that differential patterns of *trade union membership* were important, probably due to the links between the Labour Party and organized labour.

Lastly, *cultural* explanations have also been suggested. Inglehart argues that in advanced industrial societies the growth of postmaterialist values has led to a glacial but steady decline in the class politics of economic and physical security, opening the way for greater priority being given to the values of freedom, self-expression and gender equality (Inglehart 1977, 1990, 1997). This process of value change has had the greatest impact upon the younger generation and the well educated. This pervasive cultural shift, it is argued, has increased the salience of issues such as reproductive choice, sexual harassment in the workplace and equal opportunities. If this process has influenced the gender gap, support for postmaterialist values should be closely associated with left-wing female voting patterns. In a related argument Conover (1988) argues that the American gender gap is due to mobilization by the women's movement around issues of gender equality and the growth of feminist identity (see, however, Cook and Wilcox 1991). Lastly some suggest that women give greater support to a range of left-wing issues, not just 'feminist' ones, such as government spending on the welfare state and public services, environmental protection, and pacifism in the use of force (Page and Shapiro 1992; Rinehart 1992; Seltzer *et al.* 1997).

We can therefore examine demographic, structural and cultural factors. The logistic regression models used here adopt the classic 'funnel of causality' heuristic, developed by Campbell *et al.* (1960), to order the variables conceptually. In this funnel the most stable characteristics of voters are seen as most distant from voting choice. Demographic characteristics like gender and birth cohort fall into this category and are therefore regarded as exogenous to the voting model.[2] These are givens in the sense that, for example, gender or age can influence income, but income cannot influence age or gender. After these, social structural variables like class, education and religion tend to be the next most stable characteristics. While not frozen in time, these characteristics are often acquired in early youth and then persist throughout a person's lifetime. Lastly cultural values like support for feminism are assumed to be less stable than structural variables, although also located closest to voting choice. Since the aim of this chapter is to explain long-term patterns of voting behaviour, not election results in specific years, we exclude from the model even more proximate and short-term variables which can be expected to fluctuate according to particular elections, such as party image, leadership preferences or economic evaluations.

Given the complexities of the causal mechanisms at work here many of the variables may plausibly interact, for example cultural values can determine what careers people choose or where they live, and hence structural characteristics. Nevertheless given our limited knowledge about reciprocal effects for the sake of parsimony the analysis assumes one-way causation between blocks of variables from demography through structure to culture. On this basis, gender can be understood to have a direct effect on voting choice, and also an indirect effect through the mediating influence of age, structural and cultural characteristics. These hypothetical relationships are tested by examining the direct effect of gender on the probability of voting Conservative or Labour, using logistic regression models, then entering the variables in blocks, examining the change in the relationship between gender and the Conservative–Labour vote.

Analysis of Results

Generational Effects

The results of analysing the gender gap by age group are shown in Table 8.3. In successive elections from 1964 to 1997 the modern gender gap has been evident in the youngest cohort, with younger women consistently more Labour-leaning than men. At the same time, the traditional gap has persisted among the older generation, with women usually more Conservative than men. Therefore in Britain the gender gap does reverse direction with age. This pattern was maintained in the 1997 election: among the under 25-year-olds over half of the women (55%) voted Labour compared with only 44% of men. In contrast, among the older generation, 39% of women voted Conservative compared with 31% of men. In the 1997 election the gender gap among the young generation was therefore 14.2 points, with women more left wing than men, while among the older generation it was 13.4 points, with women more right wing than men.

The long-term secular dealignment of the gender gap in postwar Britain, and its realignment in other advanced industrialized countries, may therefore be the product of generational turnover as older voters gradually die out and younger voters replace them. Cohort analysis allows us to explore this further. The combined BES data set 1964–92 was divided

TABLE 8.3   *Gender gap by age group, 1964–97*

Year	Under 25	Aged 25–44	Aged 45–65	Aged 65+
1964	26	–3	–11	0
1966	23	–14	–8	–5
1970	–6	–7	–5	–30
1974 (F)	–5	–7	7	–10
1974 (O)	–17	–3	–10	–2
1979	22	–6	–1	–11
1983	2	1	–2	–4
1987	6	–3	1	3
1992	23	–3	–5	–19
1997	14	5	–12	–13

Note: The gender gap in the two-party vote lead is calculated as the percentage Con–Lab lead among women minus the percentage Con–Lab lead among men for each age group. A negative gap indicates that women are more Conservative than men.
Source: BES, 1964–97.

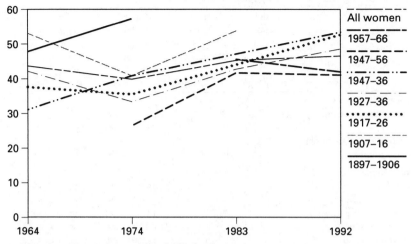

FIGURE 8.2   *Women Conservatives by birth cohort (%)*

into seven cohorts based on the decade of birth. The proportion of women voting Conservative was compared at roughly ten-year intervals (1964, 1974, 1983 and 1992). The results of the analysis in Figure 8.2 confirm that the least Conservative group were the younger cohort of women born in 1947–56, who grew up during the second-wave women's movement of the 1970s and the social revolution associated with the convergence of sex roles. In contrast the most Conservative group proved to be the oldest cohort of women, who came to political consciousness just after the female franchise was granted and during the interwar years of Conservative predominance.

Yet why should gender realignment be evident among younger voters? To explore this pattern in more depth in the 1997 election we can use logistic regression models controlling for a range of structural and cultural variables discussed earlier. In these models the vote for the major parties was turned into an indicator (dummy) variable where a positive coefficient indicates the propensity to vote Conservative (Conservative vote = 1, Labour vote = 0). Variables are entered in blocks reflecting the assumed stability of demographic, structural and cultural characteristics. Model 1 includes the direct effects of gender on voting choice without any controls. Model 2 adds age and then an interaction term for the effects of gender (where 1 = female and 0 = male) and age (in years). The interaction term therefore represents the effects of older women while the remaining gender variable represents the effects of younger women. Model 3 enters the structural controls already discussed, including the respondent's occupational (Goldthorpe–Heath) five-fold class classification. In all the models the working class are the base or referent category. Model 3 also enters employment status, union membership, educational qualifications, marital status and religiosity (see the Appendix to this chapter for the

TABLE 8.4   *Logistic regression models of the Conservative vote,* 1997

	Model 1 (gender only)		Model 2 (gender + age + interaction)		Model 3 (gender + social structure)		Model 4 (gender + social structure + culture)	
	R	Sig.	R	Sig.	R	Sig.	R	Sig.
Demographic factors								
Gender (younger women)	.00		–.03	*	–.04	*	ns	
Age			.01		.05	**	.05	**
Interaction (Age*Gender)				'				
(older women)			.05	**	.05	**	.05	**
Social structure								
Class: salariat					.15	**	.14	**
Class: routine non–manual					.11	**	.10	**
Class: petty bourgeoisie					.14	**	.13	**
Class: supervisors					ns		.03	*
Employment status					ns		ns	
Education					.06	**	.05	**
Union member					–.12	**	–.10	**
Marital status					.04	*	.05	*
Religiosity					ns		ns	
Cultural values								
Women's rights							–.03	*
Postmaterialism							–.13	**
Jobs v. prices							.09	**
Taxation v. spending							.15	**
Nationalization							.16	**
n	1,897		1,897		1,897		1,897	
Constant	–.69		–1.00		–2.74		–5.6	
Chi Sq	1.0		35.8		265		538	
Degrees of freedom	1		3		12		18	
Per cent correct	65.4		65.7		70.6		76.6	
–2 log likelihood	2,445		2,410		2,180		1,908	
Nagelkerke R^2	.001		.019		.131		.25	

Note: Logistic regression analysis models with the vote coded Conservative (1) Labour (0) as the dependent variable. Ns = not significant ** = p >.01; * = p >.05. See Appendix A for measures and coding.

Source: BES, 1997, cross-section weighted by Wtfactor.

specific items and coding of all variables). The aim of the design is to examine how far gender, or the interaction of age and gender, remains significantly associated with voting choice after controlling for structural differences in the lives of women and men. Lastly, model 4 adds the effects of cultural attitudes, including support for gender equality, postmaterialist values and three scale indicators of traditional left-right attitudes in British politics (measuring attitudes towards privatization v. nationalization, jobs v. prices and taxes v. spending).

Table 8.4 presents the logistic regression models of the probability of voting Conservative in the 1997 British general election. The results of model 1 confirm that the *direct* effect of gender on voting choice was insignificant in the 1997 election, supporting the argument for gender dealignment among all age groups. Nevertheless the results in model 2 confirm an important interaction between the effects of gender and age. In the 1997 election *younger women were more likely to vote Labour than younger men*, by a small but significant margin, while *older women were more likely to vote Conservative than older men*.

Moreover these gender gaps are not simply the product of socioeconomic differences in men and women's lives, since they persisted even after we added controls for blocks of structural variables. Model 3 shows a familiar profile of British voting behaviour: Conservative support was higher among middle-class than working-class voters, as well as among the well-educated and those who were married, while Labour support was stronger among trade union members. As expected, model 3 progressively improved the goodness of fit and the percentage of correctly predicted voters. But, most importantly, even after entering the full battery of structural factors, the gender gap among younger women continued to prove significant.

Lastly, model 4 added controls for cultural attitudes. Again the pattern proved familiar, with all the coefficients pointing in the predicted direction and another modest improvement in the overall goodness of fit of the model when predicting Conservative support. After including the full range of structural and cultural controls, two findings are important. First, *the traditional gender gap continued to prove significant among the older generation*. What this suggests is that the greater Conservatism of older women cannot be explained away as the by-product of structural or cultural differences between women and men, as some argue (Hayes 1997). Secondly, after including the cultural controls, *the modern gender gap becomes insignificant*. This suggests that the younger generation of women have shifted left due to the changing values of women and men in modern society. Younger women are more left wing than men on many traditional issues, such as prioritizing public spending over tax cuts, as well as supporting postmaterialist values. In this age group, cultural attitudes and values mediate the relationship between gender and party support in Britain, as in other advanced industrialized societies (Inglehart and Norris 1998).

To examine these differences further we can run the final combined model for women and men subdivided by the prewar and postwar generation. This allows us to explore differences in the relative weight given to different structural and cultural factors in voting choice in the 1997 election. Since employment status, marital status and religiosity proved weak or insignificant indicators in previous models these were dropped from the analysis. The comparison in Tables 8.5 highlights some important contrasts between the age groups. Among the prewar generation the analysis confirms that age remains far more significant as a predictor of voting Conservative for women than for men. The influence of the other structural and cultural variables operates in the same direction for older

TABLE 8.5 *Logistic regression models of Con–Lab vote by generation and gender, 1997*

Prewar generation	Older men		Older women	
	R	Sig.	R	Sig.
Demographic factors				
Age	.07	**	.14	**
Social structure				
Class: salariat	.17	**	.19	**
Class: routine non-manual	ns	**	.18	**
Class: petty bourgeoisie	.16	**	.16	**
Class: supervisors	ns		ns	
Education	ns		ns	
Union member	ns	**	−.10	**
Cultural values				
Women's rights	ns		ns	
Postmaterialism	−.07	**	−.06	*
Jobs v. prices	.14	**	.05	*
Taxation v. spending	.13	**	.12	**
Nationalization	.21	**	.13	**
n	678		598	
Per cent correct	79.9		74.5	
−2 log likelihood	559		729	
Nagelkerke R^2	.41		.32	

Postwar generation	Younger men		Younger women	
	R	Sig.	R	Sig.
Demographic factors				
Age	ns		ns	
Social structure				
Class: salariat	.10	*	ns	
Class: routine non-manual	ns		ns	
Class: petty bourgeoisie	ns		ns	
Class: supervisors	ns		.10	**
Education	ns		ns	
Union member	−.07	*	−.13	**
Cultural values				
Women's rights	−.11	**	ns	
Postmaterialism	−.16	**	−.13	**
Jobs v. prices	.14	**	ns	
Taxation v. spending	.11	**	.17	**
Nationalization	.13	**	.08	*
n	282		342	
Per cent correct	76.9		78.4	
−2 log likelihood	263		315	
Nagelkerke R^2	.38		.29	

Note: Logistic regression analysis models with the vote coded Conservative (1) Labour (0) as the dependent variable. Ns = not significant ** = $p > .01$; * = $p > .05$. See Appendix A for measures and coding.

Source: BES, 1997, cross-section weighted by Wtfactor.

women and men, although economic left-right attitudes proved slightly stronger for men than women. Among the older group, class proved a strong predictor of Conservative support.

In contrast among the postwar generation age differences proved insignificant predictors of voting behaviour, and the influence of social class also usually proved far weaker or insignificant. In terms of attitudes, one of the most striking findings was that traditional views about gender roles proved a strong predictor of Conservative support among younger men but insignificant among younger women. This suggests that the modern gender gap may perhaps be influenced by a male backlash against changing sex roles as much as by the positive link between feminist attitudes among women and support for parties of the left, although further exploration of this relationship is necessary to support this proposition. The issue of jobs v. prices also proved significant for men but not for women but other cultural items were fairly similar in their influence on the sexes. We can conclude that the gender gap reverses among the prewar and postwar generations, a phenomenon with important consequences for the long-term pattern of British party politics.

Conclusions and Discussion

Ever since women were enfranchised the Conservative Party has attempted to mobilize female support, incorporating women as the backbone of the grassroots organization (Lovenduski *et al.* 1994). The Tories maintained a slight edge among women voters during the 1950s and 1960s. Labour has recently intensified its efforts to reverse this pattern. During the last decade Labour has tried to expand its constituency by appealing strategically to women, most notably by selecting far more women parliamentary candidates, as well as by crafting its programmatic appeal and marketing strategy. Since 1987, Labour has slightly strengthened its policy commitments on issues such as more generous provision of nursery places, revised sex equality legislation and the introduction of a minimum wage, although these promises can hardly be regarded as adopting a radical feminist agenda (see Chapter 1). The changes in women's parliamentary representation which occurred in 1997 will probably have the most lasting consequences. Labour has now abandoned the use of compulsory all-women shortlists but the incumbency status of many younger women MPs in safe seats means that the 1997 election produced a dramatic stepped shift in women's representation, or a punctuated equilibrium model at élite level, which is unlikely to be sharply reversed.

The issue this chapter has addressed has been whether there is evidence for a dealignment or realignment in gender politics in Britain. We found that during the last decade among all age groups gender has faded as a significant electoral cleavage in British politics. Despite the transformation of Labour's parliamentary face, from 1992 to 1997 the pro-Labour vote swing was of a similar magnitude for both women and men.

Yet this was partly because older women proved more right wing than men while younger women proved more left wing than men, in effect 'cancelling' out the effects of gender. Age proved to be an important factor mediating the relationship between gender and the vote. The traditional gender gap persisted among the prewar generation but among the postwar generation the modern gender gap has emerged, with younger women leaning towards Labour. The most plausible reason for this, we can suggest, is that the younger generation of women spent their formative years during the height of the second-wave women's movement, the social revolution in sex roles which occurred in the 1960s, and the changes in cultural values associated with feminism. This pattern can best be understood as a cohort effect which implies that in the long term we can expect a gradual *secular* realignment in gender politics, as older voters progressively die out and younger voters eventually take their place. As our study of the 1992 election concluded:

> The implications of this analysis are that in the short-term it is probably extremely difficult for the Labour party to mobilise more female support in the next campaign. The party may give greater emphasis to issues such as strengthening the legislation on equal pay, creating a Ministry for Women, and improving the visibility of women within its ranks. Such measures seem likely to prove popular among Labour women activists. But there is little evidence that these sorts of proposals will change the well-established patterns of voting behaviour . . .
>
> In the longer term, however, the implications . . . may prove more positive for Labour. As the older generation of Conservative women is gradually replaced by population change we can expect the proportion of women voting Conservative to slowly decrease. Given the gradual shrinkage of the old working class base . . . the growth of new support among women may be vital to the future of the Labour party. This change is unlikely to produce a sudden change in party fortunes, but in the long-term this seems likely to have significant consequences (Norris 1993).

The results of the 1997 election confirm these predictions. It did not prove, as some hoped and others feared, a critical election in terms of gender realignment. But secular trends of generational turnover seem likely to produce a long-term shift of women towards the left in future decades.

Acknowledgement

I would like to thank Anna Greenberg and Mark Franklin for helpful comments on an earlier draft of this chapter.

Notes

1. See, for example, Greg Cook, 'Whither the gender gap?' *Polling and Electoral Bulletin* 18, 10 October 1996 (the Labour Party, unpublished paper).
2. It should be noted that ethnicity is also relevant as another demographic characteristic but this variable is excluded here due to the small number of cases in the analysis prior to the 1997 BES.

Appendix: Measures and Coding

Measure	Coding
Vote	VOTE Conservative (1) Labour (0)
Demographic factors	
Gender	RSEX Women (1) Men (0)
Age	RAGE (Years)
Interaction	Gender*Age (Women+years)
Structural factors	
Class	RGHGRP (1) Salariat (2) Routine NM (3) Petty Bourgeoisie (4) Manual supervisor compared against Working Class as the base group.
Education	HEDQUAL Highest Educational Qualification; scaled from None (1) to Degree (7)
Employment status	CSES full or part-time paid employment
Union member	UNIONSA2 recoded into Trade Union or Staff Association (1), Not (0)
Marital status	MSTATUS recoded into Married (1) Other (0)
Religiosity	RELIGIUS religiosity on a four-point scale
Cultural values	All issues scaled 1 = 11
Women's rights	Q.424 Recently there has been a lot of discussion about women's rights. Some people feel that women should have an equal role with men in running business, industry and government. These people would put themselves in Box A (coded 11). Other people feel that a woman's place is in the home. These people would put themselves in Box K. (coded 1) And other people have views somewhere in-between. Please tick whichever box comes closest to your own views about this issue. Low=traditional
Jobs v. prices	Q.341
Taxation v. spending	Q.359
Nationalization scale	Q.377
Postmaterialist values	Desire1+Desire2 recoded into three-point scale from Materialist (1), Mixed (2) to Postmaterialist (3)

Source: BES, 1997 (see Table 8.3).

9   New Sources of Abstention?

Anthony Heath and Bridget Taylor

Critical elections may produce an abrupt shift in party competition through two primary mechanisms: mass conversion of one group of party supporters into another camp, or alternatively the mobilization (or demobilization) of voters into the electorate. Hence, the enfranchisement of the working class in 1918 is often held to have been a decisive factor in the critical realignment of 1924 and the rise of the Labour Party, while the Labour landslide of 1945 has also been attributed to the entry of new generations of voters (Franklin and Ladner 1995). Secular realignments over successive elections can also be influenced by trends in turnout, for example if certain social groups gradually become demobilized over time. Lastly, deviating elections are characterized by more sudden but temporary shifts in participation, caused by particular circumstances, which are unlikely to persist over the longer term. Within this context the aim of this chapter is to explore the pattern of turnout in British elections since 1945, focusing in particular on understanding the causes and consequences of the sharp fall in participation in 1997.

Theoretical Context

Much of the literature on electoral turnout is concerned with differences between countries (Powell 1986; Jackman 1987), with differences between individuals within a country (Merriam and Gosnell 1924; Piven and Cloward 1988) or with comparisons between national elections and second-order elections such as European or local elections (Reif and Schmitt 1980). In this chapter our concern is with over-time variation, and in particular with the low turnout in the 1997 election. The factors which help to explain these different types of variation are not necessarily the same. As we shall see, a factor that can explain a great deal of individual variation may not give any purchase on changes over time.

In explaining the low turnout in 1997 one obvious possibility is that Conservative voters were disillusioned with the government, could not bring themselves to vote for any of the Opposition parties and therefore simply stayed at home. There is good evidence that this had happened at the mid-term elections in 1994 (Heath *et al.* 1995).

Another possibility is that, as New Labour under Tony Blair moved towards the centre-ground of British politics, so traditional working-class supporters became disillusioned and decided not to vote rather than to support a party that no longer represented their interests. There is some evidence from America that, as the Democrats moved towards the centre of the political spectrum, class differences in turnout increased (Weakliem and Heath forthcoming). There is some suggestion that this may have happened in 1997 in Britain too. Curtice and Steed (1997) have drawn attention to the fact that safe Labour seats had some of the lowest partic- ipation of all, contrasted with Labour's previous landslide of 1945 when safe Labour seats had some of the highest turnouts (see also Denver and Hands 1997).

A third possibility that has been widely discussed is the growing cynicism of the electorate about politics generally and Parliament in particular (Curtice and Jowell 1995). This cynicism had probably been greatly encouraged by the 'sleaze' of the 1992–97 Parliament and on the face of it this could account for a decline in turnout.

A fourth kind of explanation for the low turnout generally in 1997, and for that in safe Labour seats in particular, focuses on the structure of party competition. On standard rational choice theory, there is less incentive to turn out and vote if the result is a foregone conclusion (Aldrich 1993). Previous research has suggested that turnout is higher in marginal seats (Denver and Hands 1974, 1985). Few people doubted that Labour would win in 1997 and, given that the swing was clearly going to be from Conservative to Labour, people in safe Labour seats had least incentive of all to turn out and vote. The low turnout may not therefore represent

TABLE 9.1   Turnout, 1945–97

	% of the electorate	% of the voting-age population	Difference
1945	72.6	70.1	2.5
1950	83.6	81.6	2.0
1951	81.9	81.4	0.5
1955	76.8	75.7	1.1
1959	78.7	77.5	1.2
1964	77.2	75.1	2.1
1966	76.0	73.8	2.2
1970	72.2	71.2	1.0
1974 Feb	79.1	78.4	0.7
1974 Oct	73.0	71.8	1.2
1979	76.2	75.9	0.3
1983	72.7	72.4	0.3
1987	75.6	74.7	0.9
1992	77.9	75.3	2.6
1997	71.6	69.2	2.4

Source: Column 1: 1945–70 figures for the UK from IDEA (1997) and for 1974–97 for Great Britain from Denver and Hands (1997a); column 2: 1945–70 figures for the UK from IDEA (1997), and for 1974–97 for Great Britain calculated by the authors.

a 'crisis for democracy' but rather a realistic adaptation to the particular nature of the party competition in 1997.

Turnout in British General Elections, 1945–97

Table 9.1 shows the official turnout figures from 1945 to 1997. Turnout has ranged from a high point of 83.6% (in the UK) in 1950 to 71.6% in 1997, a range of 12 points (Figure 9.1). Turnout in 1997 was thus the lowest in the postwar period, although it was slightly higher than in 1935, when turnout fell to its lowest-ever level (since full adult franchise) of 71.2%. For the 1970 election the franchise was extended from age 21 and over to age 18 and over. Since younger people are in general less likely to vote, we would expect turnout to be lower from 1970 onwards than before. Since 1970 turnout has ranged from a low of 71.6% (in Great Britain) in 1997 to a high of 79.1% in February 1974. However, it was also low in 1970, when turnout was only 72.0% (in Great Britain), and was relatively high in 1992, when it reached 77.9%.

Neither the long-term figures, nor the shorter-term series from 1970, therefore suggest any major *secular* decline in turnout, unlike the situation in the USA (see Teixeira 1992). The most striking feature of the 1970–97 period in Britain is the large election-to-election fluctuation, and it is on this, rather than the secular trend, that we concentrate in this chapter.

In accounting for the sharp drop in 1997 we need to remember the possible impact of the poll tax (community charge) on electoral registration in 1992 (Smith and McLean 1994). It is quite likely that some people decided not to register in 1992 in view of the risk that the registers might be used in the collection of the poll tax. If such people had a

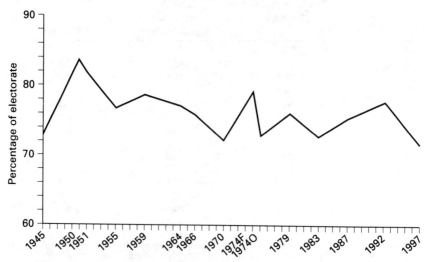

FIGURE 9.1   *Turnout, 1945–97*
Source: Table 9.1

relatively low propensity to turn out, then this could account for the apparently higher turnout in 1992 and, assuming that many had returned to the registers in 1997 after the abolition of the poll tax, it could also account for the lower turnout in 1997. We cannot definitively check this explanation, but we can calculate turnout not on the basis of the electoral registers but on the basis of the population of voting age. This is also useful because, quite aside from the issue of the poll tax, there has been some concern that the electoral registers may have been becoming increasingly inaccurate in recent years.

Figures for turnout as a proportion of the adult population since 1945 are shown in the second column of Table 9.1. As we can see, these are generally lower than the figures based on the electoral registers, but the election-to-election variations are of similar magnitude. In particular, column one shows a drop of 6.3 points between 1992 and 1997, whereas column two shows an only slightly smaller drop of 6.1 points.

Official Turnout and BES Figures

We shall be basing the analysis that follows on the reports of respondents to the British Election Surveys rather than on the official figures. One standard problem with survey reports is that they give much higher apparent levels of turnout than do the official figures. It is important, therefore, to be sure that the surveys give us a sound basis for analysing variations in turnout. There are several possible reasons for the discrepancy:

1) *Survey response bias*: those who turn out and vote are more likely to participate in an election survey, and *vice versa*: they are likely to be better educated, more interested in politics, easier to locate and interview; in particular movers are both less likely to vote and are particularly difficult to track down to interview. (But note below that neither the level of reported turnout in BES, nor the difference between the survey measure of turnout and the official turnout appear to be directly related to the survey response rate over the series of ten election studies.)

2) *Bias in survey report of turnout*: respondents have a tendency to over-report turnout – perhaps as a result of misremembering, acquiescence bias or pressures for social conformity (particularly in the context of an interview about politics).

3) *Redundancy in the register*: not everyone on the register is actually able to vote; for example, dual registration, carry-over and of course deaths or migration inflate the denominator, thus reducing the official turnout rate.

Evidence from the 1987 BES turnout validation study, the first such validation study linked to the BES, which was repeated in 1992 and 1997, showed a gap between the 86% of survey respondents who reported in the post-election interview that they had voted, and the 81% of respondents who actually voted according to the official records (Swaddle and Heath 1989). This discrepancy of five points was probably due to misremembering, acquiescence bias and so on.

The validated turnout for the survey sample of 81% was also higher than the official national rate of 75.6% in 1987, and this discrepancy should be attributed partly to response bias and partly to redundancies in the register. Discrepancies between reported and validated turnout rates of similar magnitude have been identified in the 1992 and 1997 BES.

Table 9.2 compares the official and the BES turnout figures for the period covered by the election studies, and also explores some methodological factors which might relate to the differences between the two. The discrepancy in the two rates ranges from 7.5 points in 1966 to 12.2 points in 1974, averaging 9.7 points. So it is fairly consistent over the run of election studies, which is the first reassuring point. The pattern of variation in turnout over time in the survey data is not identical to the official figures but is largely similar, mirroring the high turnouts in February 1974, 1992 and 1964, and low turnouts in 1997 and 1970, which again is reassuring.

The size of deviations between the BES and the official turnout rates does not appear to be related to variations in the BES response rate.[1] This again should reassure us about the representativeness of the BES data, since we might have expected that a lower survey response rate would lead to higher survey turnout and a larger discrepancy. Note in particular that despite the fall in response rate from 1992 to 1997, the survey data still reflected the real fall in turnout.

The largest discrepancies between the official and survey turnouts correspond to the elections held on the oldest registers (1964 and October 1974), and the smallest differences to the youngest registers (1966 and

TABLE 9.2 *Official and reported turnout, 1964–97*

	GB official turnout (%)	BES reported turnout (%)	Difference official/ BES turnout	BES response rate (%)	Age of register (days)
1964	77.2	88.8	11.6	68.3	241
1966	76.1	83.6	7.5	69.9	43
1970	72.0	81.5	9.5	69.7	122
1974 Feb	79.1	87.8	8.7	75.8	12
1974 Oct	73.0	85.2	12.2	73.7	236
1979	76.2	85.6	9.4	60.9	76
1983	72.7	83.3	10.6	72.4	113
1987	75.6	86.1	10.5	70.0	115
1992	77.9	87.5	9.6	72.6	83
1997	71.6	81.3	9.7	62.2	74

Source: Column 1: Denver and Hands (1997a) (unadjusted); column 2: BES (excludes 'Not answered').

February 1974). Increasing age of the register entails processes some of which contribute to an apparent reduction in the turnout rate (increasing redundancy of the register as names of people who can no longer vote, or who find it difficult to vote continue to appear on the register), and some of which contribute to an apparent increase in the turnout rate (for example as people reach the age of eligibility to vote, or move to an area and become eligible to vote there but do not appear on the register; other non-registration; late claims do not appear on the published register).

While in a sense, then, the survey measures are biased because of misremembering and response bias, the surveys do seem to mirror the real changes in turnout (in so far as we can be sure what the real changes were) and would seem to provide an acceptable basis for exploring the decline in turnout in 1997. We should also note that Swaddle and Heath's analysis suggested that respondents' reports and the validated measures of turnout told very similar stories about the factors that influence turnout. In this chapter we use respondents' reports, since validated measures are available only back to 1987, but we have checked our main results against the validated measures.

Differential Conservative Abstention?

One explanation for the low turnout which we need to dispose of straight away is that it was a consequence of disillusioned Conservative supporters staying at home. Ever since Black Wednesday on 16 September 1992, when sterling had been unceremoniously ejected from the Exchange Rate Mechanism, the Conservative government had been deeply unpopular. It was quite clear that, at the mid-term elections in 1994 for example, many disillusioned Conservatives had stayed at home and that the Conservative losses in the European and local elections could in large part be explained by differential abstention (Heath *et al.* 1995). It is therefore of considerable interest to discover whether differential abstention also played a part in the 1997 general election. In theory, abstention looks to be a plausible explanation both for Conservative losses and for the low turnout; moving from a particular party to abstention is a smaller psychological step than is moving from one party to another, and previous research has shown that there is indeed a high level of fluidity in and out of abstention (Heath *et al.* 1992).

We begin our analysis, then, by looking at the flow of the vote from 1992 to 1997. Was there a particularly high flow from Conservative voting in 1992 to abstention in 1997? Two sources can be used for constructing the 1992–97 flow-of-the vote matrix. The 1997 BES contains people's reports in 1997 of how they voted in 1992; or we can use the 1992–97 British Election Panel Study, which contains people's reports from 1992 of how they voted at that election. Both sources have their drawbacks: the panel study suffers from differential attrition, whereas people's memories of how they voted five years earlier are notoriously subject to bias. In Table 9.3 we use both measures. The first of each pair of rows is based on the panel, and the second of each pair is based on recall measures from the 1997 BES.

One problem that is immediately apparent from Table 9.3 is that the panel study is particularly low on 1997 non-voters. The bottom two rows of the table show that, overall, only 12% of the panel members said that they did not vote in 1997, compared with 22% of the members of the 1997 BES. We can also see that relatively few members of the 1997 BES reported that they had voted Liberal Democrat in 1992. Both these biases are well known from the previous literature.

However, it is the internal structure of the table that is crucial, not the marginals. When we turn to the internal structure of the table, we find some slightly contradictory patterns. The panel data suggest that people who had voted Conservative in 1992 were slightly more likely to abstain in 1997 than were 1992 Labour or Liberal Democrat voters. Thus 11% of Conservatives abstained compared with 9% and 8% for the other two parties respectively. The 1997 cross-section survey, however, tells the opposite story: people who recalled voting Conservative at the 1992 election were slightly less likely to abstain in 1997 than were people who recalled a Labour or Liberal Democrat vote, although the differences were again very small. Thus in the cross-section 12% of recalled Conservatives abstained compared with 13% of Labour and 13% of Liberal Democrats.

A priori we have no compelling grounds for preferring the story told by the panel over that told by the recall measures from the cross-section. Moreover, these differences are all rather small, and in fact none of them reaches statistical significance. The contradictory pattern is thus likely to be a result simply of sampling error. Analyses of aggregate data (Curtice and Steed 1997; Denver and Hands 1997a) have also failed to find good grounds for supposing that the Conservatives were harmed by differential

TABLE 9.3 *Flow of the vote, 1992–97*

| | | \multicolumn{6}{c}{Vote in 1997 (%)} | | | | | |
		Con	Lab	LD	Other	DNV	n
	Con	59	13	12	4	11	633
		58	15	11	4	12	1,151
	Lab	2	83	4	2	9	473
Vote		2	78	6	2	13	1,112
in	LD	6	31	50	6	8	267
1992		4	27	51	5	13	354
	Other	0	39	11	42	9	39
		0	13	4	73	10	41
	DNV	19	27	10	2	42	121
		9	20	8	2	61	587
	All	28	40	16	5	12	1,533
		23	39	13	4	22	3,467

Note: DNV = Did not vote.
Sources: Upper rows – BEPS, 1992–97; lower rows = BES, 1997.

abstention. We are inclined therefore to reject the hypothesis that the low turnout in 1997 can be explained by disillusioned Conservatives staying at home. At most, it can be only a tiny part of the story.

In this respect the 1997 general election was certainly quite different from the 1994 mid-term elections. In these elections differential abstention reached 13 points in the European elections and 16 in the local elections. Thus in the Euro-elections 50% of former Conservatives abstained compared with only 37% of former Labour voters (Heath *et al.* 1995). We can be fairly sure then that differential abstention was a much less important factor in 1997 than it had been at mid-term.

Working-Class Abstention?

Demographic factors such as social class, housing tenure, age, gender and education have been found to have modest associations with turnout in Britain (Swaddle and Heath 1989; Pattie and Johnston 1998), although a very significant effect elsewhere (Verba *et al.* 1972). In general people in more advantaged circumstances tend to have a higher propensity to turn out than do the disadvantaged. Since over time the electorate is gradually becoming more educated and more middle class we might, other things being equal, expect to find political participation increasing. One of the paradoxes of the long-term trends in turnout is why this increase has failed to materialize. Demographic factors do not therefore look to be a plausible source for explaining the fall in turnout in 1997. In any event, as Ivor Crewe has rightly argued, social change is likely to take on a 'glacial' character and is unlikely to explain the sharp decline in turnout that was evident in 1997.

We need to distinguish, however, between what might be termed 'compositional' changes and 'interactive' changes. *Compositional* changes are those where a particular group such as the middle class changes in size while continuing to participate in the same way as before. Thus if middle-class people have a higher propensity to turn out and vote, and have also been growing as a proportion of the electorate, then we might expect, *ceteris paribus*, that turnout would rise. Hence the paradox.

Interactive changes on the other hand are those where a particular group, perhaps in response to a changed political context, alters its propensity to vote. For example, working-class voters may feel that the Labour Party no longer represents their interests as much as it did in the past, and they may therefore be less inclined to participate than they were formerly. What we might expect to see in this case is a weakened association between class and vote. In technical terms there is an interaction between class, vote and election.

We do indeed have some evidence that the working class were less likely to believe that Labour represented their interests in 1997 than they had done previously (Heath and Curtice 1998). Thus in 1987, 47% of voters said that they thought Labour looked after working-class interests very closely, but in 1997 this had fallen to 34%. Moreover members of the working class took much the same view as the rest of the population about the changes in New Labour. This might in principle account for the decline in turnout in safe Labour seats noted by Curtice and Steed, since safe Labour seats are more likely to be working class in composition (Denver and Hands 1997).

As we can see from Table 9.4, there was a modest class gradient in turnout in both 1992 and in 1997 with the salariat generally showing a higher propensity to vote. This is in line with previous research (Swaddle and Heath 1989). Comparing the two elections, however, we find a small increase of 3.7 percentage points in non-voting among the salariat, whereas the absolute increase in the working class was much larger (at 7.1 points).

We have to treat these figures with some care, however. It is not self-evident that they reflect working-class disillusion with Labour. With a highly skewed variable such as turnout, there are likely to be 'floor' and 'ceiling' effects. Since the salariat is much closer to the floor, we would not expect such a large absolute increase in abstention as we would among the working class, which is further from the floor. Odds ratios take account of these floor and ceiling effects; what we find is that the salariat:working class odds ratio in 1992 was 1.80:1 rising only slightly to 1.95:1 in 1997. Testing for the significance of this change, we cannot reject the hypothesis that the odds ratio remained constant (chi square = 3.02 for 4 df; p = .553).

However, it could be argued that the hypothesized impact of disillusion with Labour would have occurred only among previous Labour voters. After all, a change in Labour's appeal is unlikely to have disillusioned people who had voted for some other party, or who had not voted at all, at the previous election. We therefore need to restrict our analysis to respondents who reported having voted Labour at the previous election, and this is done in the third and fourth columns of Table 9.4.

TABLE 9.4   *Class and turnout, 1992–97*

| | % who did not vote | | | |
| | All respondents | | Respondents who voted Labour at the previous election | |
	1992	1997	1992	1997
Salariat	9.1	12.8	5.8	7.2
Routine non-manual	11.4	17.9	7.8	8.4
Petty bourgeoisie	10.8	21.4	15.0	17.0
Foremen, etc	8.3	18.0	4.0	7.8
Working class	15.3	22.4	7.7	13.8
All	12.0	18.1	7.3	10.9

Source: BES, 1992, 1997.

There are two striking features of these columns. First, abstention was rarer among former Labour voters than it was in the electorate as a whole (see also Table 9.3). Secondly, there was only a small increase in abstention among previous Labour voters in the salariat (1.4 points) but a much larger one among the working class of 6.1 points. There is accordingly a much bigger change in the odds ratios than we saw when we looked at the electorate as a whole. Thus among previous Labour voters, the salariat:working class odds ratio rises from 1.36 to 2.07 between 1992 and 1997. To be sure, the numbers involved are rather small, but this does point in the direction of Labour disillusion in the working class. There could be an element of complacency as well, as working-class former Labour voters are more likely to be in safe Labour seats than are other electors.

The survey evidence on group representation also suggests that New Labour was not felt to represent trade unionists or the unemployed as much as before. Thus there was a decline from 42% to 28% in the proportion who felt that Labour looked very closely after the interests of the unemployed and an even bigger decline from 67% to 31% in the proportion who felt that Labour looked very closely after the interests of trades unions. Tables 9.5 and 9.6 therefore carry out the same analyses for trade union members and the unemployed that we conducted in Table 9.4 for the working class.

Table 9.5 looks at the unemployed. Again as previous research has shown, the unemployed have a lower propensity to turn out, due perhaps to their lack of social connectedness. This is a common feature in both 1992 and 1997. And while the absolute decline in turnout is much greater among the unemployed, the odds ratios stay more or less constant. In the case of the electorate as a whole the employed:unemployed odds ratio moves from 2.1:1 in 1992 to 2.0:1 in 1997, while among previous Labour voters it moves from 1.9:1 to 2.1:1.

However, it is the change in the extent to which New Labour represents trade union interests that is most striking and perhaps provides the key test of the disillusion thesis. The results are in Table 9.6 which shows that, in general, trade union members have higher levels of turnout than does the electorate as a whole. This is in line with the theory of social connectedness (Teixeira 1992). However, we can also see that the decline in turnout was greater among the union members than it was for the electorate as a whole; thus there was a change of 6.6 points among non-members but a change of 9.2 points among members. This is not what we would have expected on the basis of floor and ceiling effects, and accordingly we find that the superiority of the union members, as measured by odds ratios, declines from 1.91:1 in 1992 to 1.34:1 in 1997 (although again the change is not significant with chi square of 2.46 for 1 df; $p = .117$). If we focus just on previous Labour voters the decline is slightly larger, the odds ratio falling from 2.55 in 1992 to 1.23 in 1997.

These results are not conclusive, given the small numbers on which they are based. But they do point in the direction of increased working-class

TABLE 9.5   *Economic activity and turnout, 1992–97*

| | % who did not vote | | | |
| | All respondents | | Respondents who voted Labour at the previous election | |
	1992	1997	1992	1997
Employed	11.3	19.5	5.4	11.5
Unemployed	21.4	32.7	9.7	21.6
Retired	8.8	12.7	5.7	8.2
Looking after home	14.2	17.4	11.8	9.7
Full-time education	21.9	30.0	—	—
Other activity	21.5	17.3	19.3	12.7
All	12.5	18.7	7.7	11.1

Source: BES, 1992, 1997.

TABLE 9.6   *Trade union membership and turnout, 1992–97*

| | % who did not vote | | | |
| | All respondents | | Respondents who voted Labour at the previous election | |
	1992	1997	1992	1997
Not a TU member	13.6	21.2	8.0	13.1
TU member	7.6	16.8	3.3	10.9
All	12.0	20.1	6.0	12.2

Source: BES, 1992, 1997, economically inactive respondents excluded.

and trade union apathy, particularly among previous Labour voters. We should not however overestimate the significance of these results: first, while there were big declines in the proportions who felt that Labour looked 'very closely' after the interests of the working class and so on, this was balanced by increases in the proportions who felt that Labour looked after their interests 'fairly closely'. This cannot really be regarded as disillusion with Labour; rather it should be interpreted as lack of enthusiasm. It is not as though working-class voters felt that New Labour was uninterested in their interests. It follows that we would not expect very large changes in turnout.

Secondly, this increased working-class apathy, if true, cannot be the whole explanation for the decline of turnout between 1992 and 1997. As we saw from Tables 9.4–9.6, there was some decline in turnout 'across-the-board' among the middle class, non-union members and the employed as well as among the working class, trade unionists and the unemployed. We therefore need to look for some more general explanations of the decline in turnout.

Trust, Involvement and Efficacy

In the explanation of individual differences in turnout, scholars have largely focused on socio-psychological factors rather than on demographic ones (Sabucedo and Cramer 1991; Pattie and Johnston 1998). Thus, it has been argued, people fail to vote because of a feeling of political ineffec- tiveness (Schaffer 1981), or they lack a sense of civic obligation (Verba and Nie 1972), or they feel little partisan attachment (Campbell *et al.* 1960), or they lack political interest and involvement (Teixeira 1992).

As well as explaining individual differences, we might also expect some of these sociopsychological factors to respond to the political context and thus to explain short-term variations in turnout. In particular, there was a great deal of discussion in the 1990s about declining trust in MPs and in the political system (Curtice and Jowell 1995). This decline in trust could be seen in large part as a response to the long period of Conservative rule and to the increasing reputation of the governing party for 'sleaze'.

There is a limited number of socio-psychological variables, relevant to turnout, which have been included over the long series of election studies and which might in principle explain the over-time changes. However, there are a few promising candidates. Respondents have regularly been asked whether or not they cared a good deal who won the election. Strength of party identification has also been included throughout the series. Measures of trust and efficacy have not been included consistently over time, but a number of relevant items were included in 1997: on trust we use the item *How much do you trust British governments of any party to place the needs of the nation above the interests of their own political party?* On personal efficacy we use the item *people like me have no say in what the government does.*

We begin by including these items in a logistic regression of turnout in 1997. That is, we use them to explain individual differences in turnout. The results are given in Table 9.7. For 1997 we find that much the most powerful effect comes from the variable 'cared who won', which has a highly significant association with turnout. Strength of party identification

TABLE 9.7   *Logistic regression of turnout on socio-psychological variables,* 1997

	Parameter estimate	se
CAREWON	1.29	(.13)
Strength of party ID		
very strong	-0.99	(.23)
fairly strong	-1.15	(.19)
not very strong	-0.53	(.17)
none (reference)		
GOVNOSAY	-0.05	(.06)
GOVTRUST	0.26	(.09)
n	2,772	
Model improvement	251.04	(6 df)

Source: BES, 1997.

also has a significant association: as we can see, there is no difference between very strong and fairly strong identifiers in their propensity to turn out and vote, but there are quite marked differences between these strong identifiers, the weaker identifiers and people with no party identity. Our measures of trust and efficacy, however, have much weaker associations with turnout, and in the case of personal efficacy the relationship is not significant. Experiments with alternative measures did not change the picture.

However, to explain changes over time it is not sufficient for the variable to explain individual differences; we also need to see whether the marginal distributions have changed. Thus the variable 'cared who won' can explain the drop in turnout in 1997 only if there was a substantial decline in the overall proportions who cared about the election result. If the overall proportions have stayed the same, then the variable will not explain the over-time change, however successful it is at explaining individual differences (assuming that the relationship has stayed constant, which in fact it has). Table 9.8 looks at the changing distributions over time.

Here we see that the proportion who 'cared who won' has changed very little over time and for example shows no marked 'dip' in the years of low turnout such as 1970, 1983 or 1997. Despite the fact that it is a strong predictor of individual turnout, therefore, it cannot be expected to explain the variations over time.

In contrast, the percentage with no party identification does show a marked increase over time (as discussed in Chapter 4 by Crewe and Thomson). The pattern of election-to-election change in party identification does not, however, correspond all that well with the pattern of turnout. The results are rather ambiguous and we cannot be sure of the link between the two.

We can be sure, however, that declining political trust fails to explain the drop in turnout. As we can see, there was no change in the overall levels of political trust between 1992 and 1997. The decline in political

TABLE 9.8 *Changes in distribution of socio-psychological factors, 1964–97*

	Reported turnout %	Cared a good deal %	Trust in government %	No party identification %
1964	88.8	69.1	—	7.1
1966	83.6	70.9	—	8.6
1970	81.5	69.1	—	9.4
1974 Feb	87.8	68.2	39	10.4
1974 Oct	85.2	68.4	—	10.0
1979	85.6	—	—	12.8
1983	83.3	74.5	—	14.3
1987	86.1	76.9	38	14.3
1992	87.5	76.4	33	11.5
1997	81.3	75.6	34	12.4

Source: BES, 1964–97; column 3: Curtice and Jowell (1995).

trust seems to have been largely a phenomenon associated with the poor reputation of the governing party in the mid-1990s and it clearly recovered (albeit not to a very high level) in 1997. The alleged 'crisis of democracy' was probably much exaggerated, and in retrospect looks more like a 'crisis' for the Conservative Party.

The Changing Political Context

Finally, we turn to a consideration of the changing political context. Rather than focusing on the characteristics of the individual voters, we turn to the nature of the political options that confront the voter.

One of the most consistent findings in British turnout studies based on aggregate data is the relationship between turnout and the marginality of the seat. As Pattie and Johnston (1998) point out, this can be interpreted in rational choice terms: the closer the contest is expected to be, the more likely it is that an individual's vote will make a difference, and hence the greater incentive there is for the individual to turn out and vote. From the aggregate data it appears that the overall association between marginality and turnout had been declining at recent elections, although Denver and Hands (1997a) show that it increased once again in 1997. However, Pattie and Johnston's most recent work combining aggregate and individual-level data suggests that the association between marginality and turnout was no longer significant once individual characteristics, such as the socio-psychological ones described in the previous section, have been controlled for.

While there have been some changes over time in the number of seats that are marginal, the factor that is more likely to affect over-time changes in turnout is the overall closeness of the *national* election result. Indeed, on rational choice grounds, it could be argued that there is little incentive to turn out and vote, even in a marginal seat, if the overall result is a foregone conclusion. In Table 9.9 we explore the over-time relationship between turnout and the closeness of the national result.

There are several possible measures of overall closeness that we can use. We can look at the actual election result, both the shares of the vote won by the parties and their shares of the seats in the House of Commons. And we can also look at the 'expected' outcome as measured by the pre-election opinion polls. All three will tend to be closely related, although from a theoretical point of view it is better to use a prior measure, such as the pre-election polls, rather than a measure such as seats won which could in principle be affected by people's decisions whether to turn out or not.

In Table 9.9 all three measures indicate that the low election turnouts in 1997 and 1983 both correspond to substantial differences in the party shares, while high turnouts in 1964 and February 1974 correspond to close election results. If we take the time series further back, we also find that the very low turnout in 1935 corresponded with a huge difference in party shares, while the high turnout in 1950 corresponded with a very close race. There

TABLE 9.9 *The changing electoral context, 1964–97*

	GB official turnout (%)	% perceiving a good deal of difference between the parties	Final opinion polls. Mean Conservative/ Labour difference*	Election result Conservative/ Labour vote share difference GB (percentage points)	Conservative/ Labour seats difference GB
1945	72.8	–	6.0	13.1	204
1950	84.1	–	0.6	3.8	27
1951	82.6	–	4.5	1.6	17
1955	76.9	–	3.7	1.9	58
1959	79.0	–	2.8	4.2	95
1964	77.2	46.3	1.9	1.9	25
1966	76.1	42.4	10.4	7.4	122
1970	72.0	32.3	3.1	2.2	34
1974 Feb	79.1	33.1	3.6	–0.7	4
1974 Oct	73.0	39.0	8.9	3.3	42
1979	76.2	46.4	5.3	7.1	70
1983	72.7	82.2	19.8	15.2	188
1987	75.6	83.6	8.0	11.7	147
1992	77.9	55.0	0.4	7.6	65
1997	71.6	32.9	16.0	12.9	253

Notes: *These figures are the mean of the Conservative/Labour difference in the final opinion polls published before each general election. Note that the number of polls and the polling companies vary from election to election. For fuller information about the polls, see Butler and Butler (1994) and, for 1997, Butler and Kavanagh (1997). Note also that in 1997 in particular, the methodology used differed between polling companies.
Source: Column 1: Denver and Hands (1997); column 2: BES; column 3: Butler and Butler (1994), Butler and Kavanagh (1997); columns 4 and 5: Craig (1989) for 1945–87, Butler and Kavanagh (1992, 1997) thereafter.

are still a few exceptions, such as 1970 and 1992 although it will be remembered that these are two elections where the pre-elections polls were notoriously inaccurate and may have given the voters a misleading impression of the likely state of the parties. Certainly, the pre-election polls in 1992 indicated a very close race and this expectation could well have accounted for the unusually high turnout that year. The year 1970, however, remains an anomaly since the pre-election polls indicated a fairly close race (but note that this was the first election after the franchise was extended).

Table 9.9 also includes the changing distributions of respondents who perceived a good deal of difference between the parties. On rational choice grounds, if there is a great deal of difference between the parties, then the outcome is likely to make more difference to the country's political future and hence there is more reason to turn out and vote. Conversely, if there is little difference between the parties, then the election result will not make much difference either. We would, therefore, expect to see the highest turnouts when the parties are furthest apart ideologically from each other. Strictly speaking, the standard rational choice model of turnout is a multiplicative one, and we would expect to see the highest turnout when there was both a large difference between the parties and a close race. Conversely, low turnout would be expected when there was either little difference between the parties or the result was a foregone conclusion.

Table 9.9 shows that few people perceived much difference between the parties in 1970, when the percentage fell to its lowest level of 32.3. This could help to account for the low turnout in that year. Again, the small perceived difference between the parties in 1997 would tend to reinforce the pressure, already present from the one-sided nature of the race, towards low turnout.

To be sure, large perceived differences between the parties in 1983 and 1987 were not associated with high turnout, but this makes good sense in a multiplicative model: in the absence of a close race, large ideological differences between the parties may count for little in the voter's decision. However, it is notable that some of the highest turnouts did occur, as in 1950, 1951 and 1992 when there were both large differences between the parties and close races. (On ideological differences before 1964, see Budge's Chapter 1 in this volume.)

Of all the evidence we have reviewed, then, the perceived closeness of the election, in conjuction with the perceived ideological difference between the parties, seems to offer the most convincing source of the election-to-election differences in turnout. Given the small number of elections available to us for study, it would be wise to be cautious, and we cannot be sure whether a multiplicative model that incorporates both closeness of the race and ideological difference between the parties is to be preferred to the simpler model that focuses only on the national race. On theoretical grounds, however, we should keep the implications of the multiplicative model in mind.

Conclusions and Implications

The theory of secular realignments suggests that there are long-term cumulative changes in the electorate which contribute towards major shifts in the system of party competition, for example if certain social groups gradually become demobilized over a succession of elections. The evidence which we have reviewed of trends in turnout since 1945 shows an overall pattern of trendless fluctuations rather than a major secular decline over time. The fall in turnout from 1992 to 1997 does show a fairly sharp break, however, reaching in 1997 its lowest level for 60 years.

The evidence which we have presented suggests that differential Conservative abstention had, if anything, only a tiny effect on turnout. In this regard 1997 was unlike the situation in 1994. We considered the evidence for differential working-class Labour abstention and found some suggestion of a modest effect over time, consistent with the work of Denver and Hands (1997a). But based on the evidence we cannot explain whether this was due to a deeper disillusion with politics or to complacency. Moreover the likely effect was tiny and it can do little to explain the overall fall in turnout from 1992 to 1997. We also considered the role of political trust and cynicism, but found that this could explain neither the over-time trends in turnout nor the decline in 1997.

We therefore conclude that the overall closeness of the race, perhaps in conjuction with the ideological difference between the parties, seems the most convincing explanation for variations in turnout from one election to the next. The state of the national contest is important with high turnout found in close races and low turnout characteristic of landslide elections. As such, the fall in turnout in 1997 can most plausibly be attributed to the way that the opinion polls, mid-term elections and political commentators all predicted a safe Labour victory so that few could doubt the outcome of the contest. The particular circumstances therefore encouraged Labour voters to stay home, particularly in safe Labour seats, confident in their calculations that one vote more or less would not affect the outcome in a Liverpool Walton, Glasgow Maryhill or Pontypridd.

The broader implications of this analysis are that if Labour continues to command substantial leads in the opinion polls, we might well find that turnout in the next general election remains relatively low. On the other hand if the Conservatives and Liberal Democrats gradually recover support, as we might expect, so that subsequent general elections are regarded as far closer contests, we would expect turnout to increase. In this regard the pattern of participation in 1997 more accurately reflects a 'deviating' election, representing a model of trendless fluctuations, rather than either a secular or critical realignment. However, there is also the possibility that the ideological difference between the parties plays a role in voters' decisions to turn out and vote: if New Labour remains close to the centre of the political spectrum, as seems likely, and the Conservatives also move back towards the centre-ground, as seems possible, we may enter a new political phase with little difference between the parties and continuing low turnout.

Of course, by the time of the next general election, the Scottish Parliament and Welsh Assembly (and the Northern Ireland Assembly) will be up and running, and elections to those bodies (with their proportional voting systems) could be, or become, the first-order elections for those nations. And by the time of the following general election, the UK itself may have a reformed electoral system. In other words, the whole game may be about to change fundamentally.

Note

1. It should be noted that since different survey and sample designs have been used in the BES over the years, the response rates are not exactly comparable.

PART III

NEW ISSUE ALIGNMENTS?

10 The Impact of Left–Right Ideology

David Sanders

For much of the twentieth century, the left–right ideological cleavage has played an important role in the electoral politics of most democratic countries. The precise meanings of 'left' and 'right' have obviously varied both over time and with geographical context. At their root, however, is the notion that the left favours collectivist solutions to the problem of economic distribution whereas the right favours a more individualistic approach. In Britain, at least until recently, the Labour Party was traditionally regarded, by its members and by voters, as the main bastion of the collectivist approach to public policy. It advocated an active role for the state in production, distribution and exchange. It favoured a system of progressive taxation that raised sufficient government revenues to provide a 'cradle to the grave' welfare state. And it was generally supportive of working-class trade unionism and suspicious of the aims and activities of big business. The Conservative Party, in contrast, represented the interests of 'business', of private enterprise and of fiscal rectitude. It was, for the most part, antipathetic to nationalized industries and distrustful of the growth of the welfare state – even if pragmatic considerations obliged it for much of the postwar period to accept them both.

For many observers, the ideological basis of British politics began to change during the 1980s (Butler and Kavanagh 1992; Crewe 1992). Thatcherism represented a conscious attempt by Conservatives to 'roll back the frontiers of the state'. By reducing state involvement in industry and commerce, and by cutting back on welfare recipients' reliance on state benefits, private enterprise would be reinvigorated and the long-term fortunes of the British economy (and, by implication, polity) would be restored. The electoral success of Thatcherism between 1979 and 1987 – achieved against the backdrop of Labour's contrapuntally radical 1983 manifesto – profoundly affected both Labour's definition of itself and the policy stances that it subsequently took (Shaw 1994; Blair 1995; Gamble 1996; Wickham-Jones 1996; Butler and Kavanagh 1997; Seyd 1997). The

1989 Policy Review accelerated the process of moderation that had begun after the debacle of 1983. As Ian Budge demonstrated in Chapter 1, Labour's 1997 manifesto represented a marked policy shift to the right. Privatization was embraced. The virtues of private enterprise and the dangers of welfare dependency were fully recognized. And the principle of fiscal rectitude was so firmly entrenched in Labour's thinking that the party promised to keep public spending within the targets set by the Conservatives for at least two years after the election. Outside the economic sphere, Labour would retain Britain's independent nuclear deterrent and be as vigorous in its pursuit of criminals and criminality as any Conservative Home Secretary addressing the Conservative Party conference.

All these changes in Labour policy – with the 1997 Labour leadership, apparently, accepting much of the policy agenda advocated for the previous two decades by the Conservatives – were bound to lead to speculation that ideological concerns would no longer be so important in the electoral calculations of British voters. The end of the Cold War, and the attendant collapse of communism in eastern Europe, had robbed socialists worldwide of a viable working model of collectivism in action. For some observers on the left, Labour's shift to the right denied British voters a real ideological choice. The end of ideology which Daniel Bell had anticipated in the 1960s (Bell 1962) and which Francis Fukuyama had announced in 1990 (Fukuyama 1992) had, perhaps, finally arrived.

As discussed in this book's Introduction, a key feature of a critical election is that it involves a significant ideological dealignment or realignment of the electorate. This chapter explores the extent to which ideological considerations continued – or failed – to motivate the electoral choices of British voters in 1997. *It considers the potentially 'critical' nature of the 1997 election in terms of whether it witnessed a marked change in the role of ideological considerations in the decision calculi of individual voters*. This represents a more subtle – and more important – question than whether or not Labour's move to the centre enabled it to garner additional votes in 1997. The answer to that question is prosaic: of course it did, but not hugely. Table 10.1 shows how voters in the ideological centre-ground[1] voted in the 1992 and 1997 elections. Although Labour certainly did better among 'centre' voters in 1997 than in 1992, as the table shows it also drew substantially more support from *non*-centre voters as well. Simple calculations based on the table suggest that Labour's rightward shift added roughly four percentage points to its share of the popular vote.[2] That Labour's move to the right worked to its electoral advantage is undeniable, even if the magnitude of the effect might itself be disputed. What is far less clear is whether or not 1997 marked a watershed in the extent to which ideology affected voters' electoral choices. It is this, much more fundamental, question that is addressed here.

The first part of the chapter outlines the general model specification that is employed in order to assess the extent to which ideological factors

TABLE 10.1   *Distribution of the ideological 'centre-ground' vote by party, 1992–97*

	1992		1997	
	Not centre	Centre	Not centre	Centre
Con (%)	47	40	32	22
Lab (%)	36	32	47	49
Lib Dem (%)	10	19	11	19
n	505	905	964	1,689
Row % total	36	64	36	64

Notes: Figures given are column percentages, except where stated. The 1992 and 1997 BES surveys ask respondents to describe their own position (and that of the major parties) on four 11-point scale ideology items: prioritizing unemployment v. inflation; increasing taxes and spending more on services v. reducing taxes and spending less; nationalization v. privatization; and equalizing v. not equalizing incomes. The responses were recoded so that a score of 11 indicated an extreme right-wing response and 1 an extreme left-wing response. The scores on each of the four items were summed (giving a scale running from 4 to 44) and for each year, the 'centre-ground' was defined to encompass all respondents whose composite scores were within one standard deviation of the the the mean composite score.
Source: BES, 1964–97.

exerted an influence on individual voters' party preferences. The second part presents a set of empirical results which compare the effects of ideology in 1997 with those observed over the 1964–92 and 1979–92 periods. The final part makes a more detailed comparison of the effects of ideology in the 1992 and 1997 elections. The balance of evidence suggests that in ideological terms 1997 was *not* a 'critical election'. There were certainly some significant changes in the relationship between vote and ideology in 1997. For the most part, however, these changes were merely the continuation of a process of weakening ideological effects that had been evident over several previous elections. The analysis throughout focuses primarily on the Conservative and Labour parties. This is not to imply that Liberal Democrat or nationalist voting is unimportant in British general elections. It merely reflects the fact that it is Conservative and Labour support patterns that have historically been most closely associated with British voters' ideological positions. Centre party voting, for the most part, has been uncorrelated with voters' ideological stances.[3]

Specifying a Model of the Effects of Ideology on Vote

The notion of ideology has been employed in a variety of different contexts and with a number of different meanings. These range from Marx's use of the term 'ruling ideology' to connote the entire ideational apparatus that underpins capitalism (Marx 1961) to Rokeach's rather more restrictive usage of ideology as a 'value orientation' that both crystallizes and represents the individual's core beliefs about freedom and equality (Rokeach 1973). The usage of the term employed here corresponds far more closely to Rokeach than to Marx. I follow Heath *et al.*

(1994: 115) in regarding an ideology as a 'fundamental and enduring [set of] attitudes towards general moral and political principles ... [which] ... can account for the individual's attitudes towards the more transient political issues of the day'. More specifically, I focus on *left–right* ideology, or as Heath *et al.* (1994: 117) describe it, the *socialist/laissez-faire* ideological domain. There are clearly other potentially important dimensions of voter ideology in the UK, involving voters' positions on a libertarian/authoritarian axis (Evans and Heath 1995) and their orientations towards nationalism versus internationalism (Heath *et al.* 1999). However, these ancillary dimensions have never featured as prominently as left–right ideology either in explanations of the evolution of postwar British politics or in statistical models of the effects of ideology on voting patterns (Butler and Stokes 1974; Särlvik and Crewe 1983; Heath *et al.* 1985, 1991, 1994). Moreover, the lack of suitable over-time data prevents the effects of these other ideological dimensions from being properly considered in the 1964–97 time-frame that is addressed in this book.

In any event, it has frequently been recognized that left–right ideological considerations have played both a direct and an indirect role in British electoral politics (Särlvik and Crewe 1983; Scarbrough 1984; Heath *et al.* 1985; Evans *et al.* 1996a; Bartle 1997). The direct role has been fairly straightforward: left-wingers have tended to support Labour and right-wingers to support the Conservatives. The indirect effects of ideology have been rather more complicated, involving a nexus of class identities, partisan identifications, ideological positions and voting preferences. At the risk of oversimplification, this nexus can be summarized as follows:

1) For most of the postwar period, Labour advocated 'left-wing' policies – progressive taxation, a strong welfare state and state intervention in the economy – which favoured the interests of the working class and trade unionists. The Conservatives, in contrast, advocated 'right-wing' policies – low taxation, minimalist welfare provision and the facilitation of private enterprise – which favoured the interests of the middle and business classes.

2) Voters who thought of themselves as working class or who prioritized the interests of the working class above those of the middle class tended to identify with and to vote for the party which represented the interests of the working class – Labour. Voters who thought of themselves as middle class or who prioritized business interests and private enterprise tended to identify with and to vote for the party which best represented those interests – the Conservatives.

There is a considerable amount of evidence (admittedly, some of it contentious) to suggest that, over the last three decades, Britain has witnessed significant declines in both class-based voting and the extent of partisan identification (Crewe 1986, 1992; Heath *et al.* 1995). There are two, very different, sets of implications which might be expected to follow from these long-term declines. First, the declines could have produced a concomitant reduction in the importance of ideology in voting. In terms of the nexus described above, if fewer people vote according to their class position and fewer people 'identify' to a significant degree with either of the major parties, then voters may be less likely to view party politics in ideological terms – implying a *reduced* role for ideology in the formation of voting preferences.

A second, contrasting, possibility is that weakening class and party alignments could create space for an *increase* in the importance of ideology. Inglehart (1990), Franklin (1985), and Sanders (1997) have argued that class and partisan dealignment imply a stronger role in voters' decision calculations, respectively, for postmaterialist values, issue preferences and economic perceptions; the same argument could also apply, in principle, to ideological considerations.

Beyond these two general sets of expectations there is a third possibility, linked more directly to Labour's transformation under Tony Blair. The changes in Labour's policy platform which moved the party to the centre-right imply that left–right ideology should not have acted as such a strong cue for Labour voters in 1997 as it did in previous elections. By the same token, given that the Conservative Party did *not* shift its overall policy stance towards the centre in 1997, the impact of ideology on Conservative voting in 1997 should not have changed noticeably from the previously observed pattern. The Conservatives' relative constancy in the face of Labour's calculated rightward shift, therefore, implies a third hypothesis: that the effects of left–right ideology on Labour voting weakened significantly in 1997 while its effects on Conservative voting remained unaltered.

A key problem confronting any attempt to investigate the impact of ideology on voting, of course, is how ideology should be measured (Evans and Heath 1995; Evans *et al.* 1996a). Broadly, there are two alternatives available: either to ask respondents directly where they position themselves on a single left–right dimension; or to ask them indirect (and ideally, unobtrusive) questions which allow the analyst to infer the respondent's ideological stance. In the analysis conducted here, only indirect measures are employed – for two reasons. First, the more direct measures of left–right ideological position presuppose a degree of political understanding on the part of respondents that may not in fact be warranted (Klingemann 1979). Indirect measures, in contrast, simply require respondents to take a position in relation to a series of clearly specified issues. Secondly, given that direct measures of left–right position are simply not available for most BES surveys prior to the 1980s, indirect measures are the only ones that can be employed across the entire 1964–97 period. In the first set of models examined here, I use four indirect measures of left–right ideological position, all of which have previously been shown to be associated with voting preferences (Heath *et al.* 1991). It is assumed that responses which indicate that an individual is *opposed to nationalization, pro-privatization, supportive of big business* or *opposed to trade union power* connote a right-wing stance; and that their opposites connote a left-wing stance.[4] These particular indicators of ideology are used because they are the only ones that are available for (almost) every election since 1964.

The first two columns of Table 10.2 summarize the bivariate relationship between Conservative versus Labour voting and four measures of left–right ideological position, in 1964 and 1992. The import of these simple findings is clear. The relationship between voting preferences and voters' attitudes towards 'big business' and trade unions (as indicated by the size and significance of the lambda coefficients) only weakened marginally between 1964 and 1992; and the relationship between preferences and attitudes towards nationalization and privatization changed hardly at all. While these are clearly not the only dimensions of ideology that could be explored, they none the less represent important aspects of ideology that were very much at the centre of political debate throughout the 1964–92 period. In short, although the results shown in Table 10.2 are limited, they provide *prima facie* evidence that in the early 1990s, notwithstanding the long-term processes of class and partisan dealignment that had affected British politics since at least the 1960s, ideological concerns apparently continued to relate quite strongly to patterns of partisan preference.

The question that arises from this observation is whether or not the

TABLE 10.2   *Attitudes towards nationalization, privatization, big business and trades union power, 1964, 1992 and 1997*

	1964		1992		1997	
Nationalization						
	Does not	Favours more	Does not	Favours more	Does not	Favours more
Con	63	8	66	16	44	10
Lab	37	92	34	84	56	90
Lambda	.39***		.35***		.00	
Denationalization/privatization						
	Does not	Favours more	Does not	Favours more	Does not	Favours more
Con	40	82	43	90	29	73
Lab	60	18	57	10	71	27
Lambda	.23***		.23***		.19***	
Big business						
	Does not	Favours	Does not	Favours	Does not	Favours
Con	38	71	47	76	29	56
Lab	62	29	53	24	71	44
Lambda	.25***		.10**		.07**	
Trades union power						
	Does not	Opposes	Does not	Opposes	Does not	Opposes
Con	28	64	45	75	29	55
Lab	72	36	55	25	71	45
Lambda	.22***		.16***		.06*	
n	1,366		2,303		2,102	

Note: Figures reported are column percentages: *** indicates a coefficient is significant at .001; ** at .01; * at .05.
Source: BES, 1964–97.

1997 general election represented a 'critical' departure from the previous long-term pattern of ideological effects. There is certainly good reason to suppose that 1997 might have been 'critically' different from previous elections. The very policies that Labour adopted under Blair in order to make itself more attractive to the electorate meant that there was less ideological differentiation between Labour and the Conservatives. As noted above, Labour's platform in 1997 embraced many of the key policy positions – on taxation, private enterprise, the need to reform the welfare state – that had previously been associated with the Conservatives. Labour even undertook not to repeal the 'anti-trade union' Employment Acts passed by the Conservatives in 1982 and 1984. And, if there was less ideological differentiation between the Labour and Conservative *Parties* in 1997, it would be expected that *voters* would be less likely to make their electoral choices on the basis of ideological considerations.

Comparison between columns 2 and 3 of Table 10.2 shows that there were indeed some interesting changes in the bivariate ideology–vote relationship between 1992 and 1997. In 1997, Labour's relative position improved noticeably among those opposed to more nationalization (56% Labour support compared with 34% in 1992); among anti-trade unionists (45% Labour support in 1997 compared with 25% in 1992); and among those who were not supporters of big business (up from 24% in 1992 to 44% in 1997). In other words, in 1997 Labour picked up considerably *more* support among groups that displayed what have traditionally been regarded as right-wing attitudes – suggesting that ideological position was significantly less important as an influence on Labour voting than it had been in 1992 (or, for that matter, in 1964).

However, before we leap to the conclusion that 1997 was therefore a 'critical' election in terms of the reduced importance of ideology, we need to put the raw statistics presented in Table 10.2 in context. There are two other major sets of factors that need to be considered. First, it is necessary to examine the extent to which the changes in the ideology–vote relationship observed between 1992 and 1997 compare with any changes that occurred between other pairs of adjacent elections for which data are available. Secondly, in order to obtain proper estimates of the effects of ideology on vote we need to apply statistical controls for other theoretically relevant variables that are known to influence voting preferences. All the relationships involved, moreover, need to be examined in a comparable way over as long a timescale as possible. Although BES data go back to 1964, the core of questions which have been asked in every wave of the survey is relatively small. The analysis here is accordingly constrained to using measures that are available throughout the 1964–97 period. This obviously limits the empirical scope of the inquiry – particularly in terms of the measurement of ideology. However, it does not prevent us from examining a series of clearly specified (and, as it turns out, well determined) models that allow for the rigorous testing of the proposition that 'critical' changes in the ideology–vote relationship occurred in 1997.

The core model specification that I employ is as follows:

Vote preference for Conservative/not or for Labour/not =
  f (ideological position
  + parental vote preference
  + objective and subjective class position
  + perceptions of differences between the main parties
  + whether respondent cares about the outcome of the election
  + sociodemographic characteristics)   [1]

where ideological position is measured by responses to the four ideology-related questions that were asked in every BES survey between 1964 and 1997 – those concerned with respondents' attitudes to nationalization, denationalization/privatization, trades unions and big business.[5]

As intimated above, the selection of variables owes much to the constraints of data availability and comparability across the 1964–97 period. This said, the set of exogenous variables identified in [1] includes most of the major factors that previous BES-based research has found to exert an effect on vote (Butler and Stokes 1974; Särlvik and Crewe 1983; Heath *et al.* 1985, 1991). Apart from ideology, the list includes both long-term influences on vote (parental vote, objective class position and other sociodemographic characteristics) as well as shorter-term attitudinal effects (subjective class, party difference perceptions and caring about the election outcome). The specific measures used to operationalize each of these variables are outlined in the Appendix to this chapter. The only notable omission from the list that is made on grounds other than lack of data availability is party identification. This variable is excluded because of serious doubts about the way in which party identification has been measured in successive BES surveys. Recent evidence suggests that measures of party identification in the British context are not independent of voting preference (Brynin and Sanders 1997). Indeed, to employ party identification as a predictor of vote would be to engage in a tautology that would lead to the underestimation of the effects on vote of the other exogenous variables in the model; it is accordingly excluded from the specification.

The empirical analysis conducted here divides conveniently into two parts. The first part involves estimating parameters for the specification described in [1] for each of the general elections between 1964 and 1997 inclusive. The estimates for the different elections can then be compared and, in particular, the size of the coefficients on the ideology measures can be examined to see if the pattern of effect in 1997 is significantly different from the pattern observed in earlier years. If it is, then we can regard the 1997 election as 'critical' in terms of the changing effect of left–right ideology on vote; if it is not, then the critical nature of the 1997 election can reasonably be questioned. Model [1] is initially estimated in three distinct, if complementary, ways:

1) Estimate [1] for each election (1964 1966 . . . 1997) separately in order

to observe the way in which different variables – including ideology – influence voting preferences over time.

2) Estimate [1] as a pooled cross-section for the entire 1964–97 period, allowing the parameters on the ideological variables to vary for 1997. This approach allows for a formal test of the hypothesis that the effects of ideology were significantly different in 1997 from the general pattern of effect between 1964 and 1992.

3) Estimate [1] as a pooled cross-section for the period 1979–97, allowing the parameters on the ideological variables to vary for 1997. This approach allows for a formal test of the hypothesis that the effects of ideology in 1997 marked a distinct break with the pattern that had obtained during the period of Conservative electoral hegemony between 1979 and 1992.

The second part of the empirical analysis uses the same set of control variables as identified in model [1], but it takes advantage of the fact that recent BES surveys have collected far more detailed measures of respondents' ideological positions and perceptions than their earlier counterparts. This analysis uses both 1) more extensive measures of ideology and 2) measures of voters' perceptions of the differences between their own ideological positions and those of the parties to establish if the typical ideological calculus in 1997 was noticeably different from that in 1992. The initial approach is to estimate [1] for 1992 and for 1997 using four, more detailed, measures of voters' ideological positions that were available for those two elections: on employment versus inflation, taxation versus public spending, privatization versus nationalization, and degree of concern for income equality.[6] The empirical question that is tested is straightforward: were the effects on vote of these ideology variables in 1997 sufficiently different from those observed in 1992 to suggest that ideological considerations played a 'critically' different role in 1997?

The final part of the empirical analysis involves ascertaining which party each respondent positions him or herself closest to on each of the four dimensions identified immediately above. These proximity measures are then substituted into [1] to estimate the effects of the respondent's ideological proximity to each of the major parties. The hypothesis tested is that respondents who perceive themselves to be closer to a particular party on a given ideological dimension will be more likely to vote for that party. If 1997 was a critical election in ideological terms, in the sense that ideology was substantially less important to voters' electoral choices in 1997 than in 1992, then we would expect to observe that the ideological proximity measures are less significant in 1997 than in 1992.

Empirical Evidence on the Ideology–Vote Relationship, 1964–97

Table 10.3 describes the marginal distributions for the core variables in model [1] drawn from successive BES surveys since 1964. A blank entry means that the question concerned was not asked in the year indicated. Several features of the table are worth highlighting. First, the Labour and Conservative support figures (which include non-voters in the percentage base) oscillate predictably over time, with the Conservatives recording their worst performance (and Labour its strongest performance since 1966) in 1997. Secondly, the pro-nationalization and pro-privatization marginals in the 1990s are not noticeably different from the levels recorded in the 1960s – though in the 'Thatcher elections' (1979–87) nationalization was clearly less popular and privatization clearly more popular. Thirdly, although there was a rise in anti-trade union sentiment in the 1970s and early 1980s, by the 1990s anti-trade unionism was substantially lower than it had been in the 1960s. Fourthly, sympathy towards 'big business' did not change substantially between 1964 and 1979 – though it gradually declined thereafter, falling below 20% in 1997. Fifthly, in spite of the steady increase in owner-occupation up to 1987 and the progressive decline in the size of the manual class, the proportion of respondents who regarded themselves as middle class did not change noticeably between 1964 and 1997. Sixthly, the proportion of respondents who identified their fathers as consistent Conservative voters remained more or less constant throughout the 1964–97 period. What all these marginals suggest is that there was nothing decidedly distinctive about the distribution of attitudinal predispositions among the electorate in 1997. To be sure, there was some evidence of a leftward shift between 1992 and 1997 (the percentage of anti-trade unionists fell from 30.5% to 21.8%, and the percentage of privatization supporters fell from 21 to 13). Yet these changes apart, there is little in the contents of Table 10.3 to suggest that 1997 was noticeably different from previous elections.

Marginal distributions, however, reveal almost nothing about the decision calculus of the individual voter – and it is precisely that calculus which we need to consider in order to evaluate claims about the critical nature of the 1997 general election. Tables 10.4 and 10.5 report the effects of estimating model [1] for each of the elections between 1964 and 1997 for the Conservative and Labour Parties, respectively. Note that the precise magnitudes of the coefficients are less important than their signs, significance levels and relative magnitudes over time. The dependent variable in each case is whether or not the respondent voted for the specified party. Estimation is by logistic regression.

Consider, first, the results shown in Table 10.4. The models reported are theoretically plausible and well determined. The sociodemographic and other background variables are generally highly significant and correctly signed. The probability of Conservative voting increases with age (after

TABLE 10.3 Marginal distributions of the core analytic variables, 1964–97

	1964	1966	1970	Feb 1974	Oct 1974	1979	1983	1987	1992	1997
Conservative	36.7	32.2	36.0	32.0	39.8	38.7	36.2	36.7	35.5	20.3
Labour	40.5	42.8	35.9	34.2	35.1	31.0	23.7	26.1	29.6	37.8
Support more nationalization	25.3	25.3		24.2	28.8	15.6	15.7	16.2	22.9	26.8
Support more privatization	18.4	19.4		21.2	19.5	37.0	37.5	30.3	21.0	13.2
Pro big business	29.0	32.3	38.7		35.1	35.4	27.6		22.8	19.3
Anti trades union power	54.1	63.9	65.0		77.5	77.5	70.1		30.5	21.8
Care about election outcome	68.9	70.6	68.4	67.6	68.3		74.3	76.8	75.0	74.5
Lot of difference between parties	45.4	41.5	32.0	32.8	38.9	45.9	82.2	83.5	54.5	32.5
Subjective middle class	28.2		31.8	33.5	33.1	32.0	33.8	33.4	32.1	34.5
Father was Conservative	26.7	24.2	27.0	27.2	27.4	27.6	24.7	26.0	25.0	24.9
Owner-occupier	46.0		48.0	52.8	53.5	55.8	65.6	70.8	69.1	66.8
Trades union member	23.6		24.0	24.0	25.2	28.8	25.0	19.9	17.6	21.5

Note: Figures are the percentage of respondents in the specified category. For variable definitions, see the Appendix to this chapter. A blank entry means the relevant question was not asked in the year shown.
Source: BES, 1964–97.

1966), home-ownership, middle-class identity and parental Conservatism; it falls with manual occupation and trade union membership. The coefficients of most interest for our purposes, however, are those which relate to the four measures of ideological position. Here, again, the results are theoretically plausible: a preference for more nationalization consistently reduces the probability that a respondent will vote Conservative; a preference for more privatization, a liking for big business and a dislike of trade union power all increase that probability.

The central issue with regard to these coefficients, however, is the manner in which they change over time. What is immediately noticeable about all the ideology coefficients in Table 10.4 is how little systematic variation there is across elections. There is certainly a tendency for the magnitudes of the coefficients to change during the middle of the period. For example, the anti-trades union coefficients are larger between October 1974 and 1983 – the peak period of the trades unions' general unpopularity among voters. Similarly, the pro-privatization effect is stronger and the (negative) pro-nationalization effect weaker during the 1979–87 period – at precisely the time when Thatcherism is alleged to have turned the ideological agenda decisively in its favour. However, if we are seeking to determine the extent to which the findings reported in Table 10.4 support the notion of 1997 as a 'critical' election in ideological terms, the most germane comparison we can make is between the ideology coefficients in 1997 and those in 1992. And here, the picture looks decidedly non-critical: the pro-nationalization coefficient falls from –1.34 to –1.13; the pro-privatization coefficient from .94 to .92; the pro-big business coefficient from .86 to .73; and the anti-trades union power coefficient rises from .92 to .94. On the face of it, and in comparison with the changes that occurred from election to election in earlier years, these do not appear to be major changes. In essence they suggest that, in so far as ideological considerations underpinned Conservative voting in 1997, the decision calculus of the typical voter was no different from that which obtained in 1992. As we saw in Table 10.3, there may have been marginally fewer anti-trades unionists and big business supporters around in 1997 (in comparison with 1992), but the *effect* on Conservative support of being pro-big business or of being opposed to trades union power remained broadly the same.

But if the basis of Conservative support in 1997, as shown in Table 10.4, did not appear to be particularly distinctive in ideological terms, the same is not true for Labour support. Table 10.5 shows the equivalent set of findings about the sources of Labour support over the 1964–97 period.[7] The coefficients on the four ideology terms give the first intimation that 1997 may have been qualitatively different from previous elections in terms of ideological effects. The pro-nationalization coefficient for 1997 ($b = .44$) is the smallest observed over the entire 1964–97 period and represents more than a halving of the effect shown for 1992 ($b = 1.12$). A similar pattern, though not quite so pronounced, is also evident for the

TABLE 10.4 The effects of ideology on Conservative voting, 1964–97

Independent variable	1964	1966	1970	Feb 1974	Oct 1974	1979	1983	1987	1992	1997
Supports more nationalization	-2.09***	-1.88***		-1.60***	-1.96***	-0.93***	-0.26*	-0.79***	-1.34***	-1.13***
Supports more privatization	0.26	0.62***		0.66***	0.41**	1.04***	0.91***	1.58***	0.94***	0.92***
Pro big business	0.54***	0.93***	0.72***		0.66***	0.61***	0.56***		0.86***	0.73***
Anti trade union power	0.72***	0.92***	0.81***		1.60***	1.25***	1.31***		0.92***	0.94***
Care about election outcome	0.59***	0.38**	0.87***	0.80***	0.71***		1.19***	1.09***	1.15***	0.32**
Perceive difference between parties	0.33***	0.27	0.39***	0.14	0.23	0.16	0.39***	-0.04	0.25**	-0.44***
subjectively Middle class	0.72***		0.64***	0.45***	0.32**	0.36**	0.26**	0.30***	0.28**	0.65***
Father was Conservative	0.92***	1.27***	1.06***	1.00***	0.72***	0.78***	0.73***	0.77***	1.00***	0.89***
Manual working class	-0.71***	-0.82***	-0.50***	-0.66***	-0.61***	-0.23	-0.29***	-0.19*	-0.29***	-0.54***
Owner-occupier	0.54***		0.32**	0.72***	0.65***	0.54***	0.43***	0.56***	0.83***	0.84***
Trades unionist	-0.39*		-0.34*	-0.46***	-0.45***	-0.23	-0.21*	-0.51***	-0.28*	-0.39***
Constant	-1.91***	-2.50***	-3.12***	-2.89***	-4.13***	-3.08***	-3.93***	-2.50***	-3.09***	-3.46***
n	1,159	1,282	1,308	2,095	2,038	1,440	3,752	3,635	3,399	3,433
% correct	77.7	78.6	75.1	77.2	79.2	75.6	76.4	76.9	78.7	83.0

Note: Logistic regression models. Dependent variable is whether or not the respondent voted Conservative. Statistical controls applied for region and gender (results not reported: available from the author on request). *** indicates that a coefficient is significant at .001; ** at .01; * at .05. A blank entry means that the relevant question was not asked in year shown.

Source: BES, 1964–97.

TABLE 10.5　The effects of ideology on Labour voting, 1964–97

Independent variable	1964	1966	1970	Feb 1974	Oct 1974	1979	1983	1987	1992	1997
Supports more nationalization	1.80***	1.10***		1.14***	1.17***	0.54**	0.83***	0.99***	1.12***	0.44
Supports more privatization	−0.92***	−1.02***		−0.94***	−1.24***	−1.31***	−1.13***	−1.87***	−1.08***	−0.74***
Pro big business	−0.66***	−0.77***	−0.92***		−0.40***	−0.44**	−0.65***		−0.53***	−0.36***
Anti trade union power	−0.78***	−0.72***	−0.28*		−1.25***	−0.92***	−1.21***		−0.80***	−0.58***
Constant	−0.64	−0.54	−0.05	−0.99***	−0.51*	−0.34	−0.61**	−1.06***	−0.87***	−1.46***
n	1,159	1,282	1,308	2,095	2,038	1,440	3,752	3,635	3,399	3,433
% correct	80.2	71.4	68.8	75.7	78.5	77.0	82.2	79.6	76.7	71.2

Note: Logistic regression models. Dependent variable is whether or not the respondent voted Labour. Statistical controls applied for respondent's attitudinal and sociodemographic characteristics, as in Table 10.4, and for region (results not reported: available from the author in request). *** indicates that a coefficient is significant at .001; ** at .01; * at .05.

Source: BES, 1964–97.

TABLE 10.6 *The effects of ideology on Conservative and Labour voting, 1964–97*

Independent variable	Conservative support/not		Labour support/not	
	Coefficient	Standard error	Coefficient	Standard error
Supports more nationalization	−1.24***	0.04	+1.06***	0.06
Nationalization 1997 interaction	+0.01	0.17	−0.59***	0.09
Supports more privatization	+0.93***	0.06	−1.34***	0.04
Privatization 1997 interaction	−0.06	0.13	+0.65***	0.15
Pro big business	+0.56***	0.04	−0.36***	0.05
Big business 1997 interaction	+0.19	0.12	+0.00	0.16
Anti trades union power	+0.52***	0.04	−0.44***	0.04
Trades union 1997 interaction	+0.38***	0.11	−0.12	0.10
1997/not dummy	−0.84***	0.08	+0.55***	0.07
n	23,541		23,541	

Note: Pooled cross-section logistic regression models allowing the coefficients for 1997 to vary. Interaction terms defined by multiplying the election year dummy (1 for 1997, zero otherwise) by the specified 'parent' variable. Statistical controls applied for respondent's attitudinal and sociodemographic characteristics, as in Table 10.4, and for region (results not reported: available from the author on request). *** indicates that a coefficient is significant at .001.
Source: BES, 1964–97.

coefficients for pro-privatization (down from −1.08 to −.74), for pro-big business (from −.53 to −.36) and for anti-trades union power (from .80 to .58). The fact that all these effects declined so clearly between 1992 and 1997 – after a 30-year period in which they had fluctuated around means similar to the values observed in 1992[8] – suggests that *ideological considerations exerted less of a constraining influence on voters' decisions to vote Labour in 1997 than in any previous election since 1964*. Table 10.5, in short, provides partial evidence for the notion that 1997 may indeed have been a critical election in ideological terms – at least as far as Labour voting was concerned.

These conclusions – that the role of ideology changed critically in 1997 for Labour but not for the Conservatives – are tested out more explicitly in Table 10.6. The table estimates model [1] as a pooled cross-section for the 1964–97 period, with interaction terms for 1997 on each of the four ideology measures (plus a dummy variable term for 1997 itself). Estimation is again by logistic regression. The 'ordinary' coefficients reported in the table show the average effects on vote of each of the predictor variables over the whole period. As we noted in relation to Tables 10.4 and 10.5, they are plausible and correctly signed. The interaction terms show the extent to which the effects of ideology in 1997 deviated from the general pattern between 1964 and 1992. The significance levels attached to the interaction terms broadly confirm the conclusions that were drawn from Tables 10.4 and 10.5. In the Conservative equation, none of the ideology interactions is significant, suggesting that ideological calculations were no more nor less important as determinants of Conservative support in 1997 than they were in previous elections. In the Labour equation, however, although the big business and trade union power interactions are non-significant, the nationalization and privatization interactions are highly significant. The nationalization coefficient is negative, indicating that voters' positions on nationalization were less important in 1997 than in previous elections (b for 1997 = +1.06 −.59 = +.47). The privatization coefficient is positive, with a similar implication (b for 1997 = −1.34 + .65 = −.69). What all this suggests, in short, is that in 1997 pro-nationalization sentiments failed to mobilize Labour support and pro-privatization sentiments failed to inhibit Labour support to a degree hitherto unprecedented in postwar British politics. Here, in limited measure, is evidence that 1997 was, in ideological terms at least, a distinctive election – even if its 'critical' status as an ideologically

Table 10.7   *The effects of ideology on Conservative and Labour voting,* 1979–97

Independent variable	Conservative support/not		Labour support/not	
	Coefficient	Standard error	Coefficient	Standard error
Supports more nationalization	−0.82***	0.04	+0.95***	0.06
Nationalization 1997 interaction	−0.40**	0.17	−0.47***	0.10
Supports more privatization	+1.16***	0.06	−1.44***	0.07
Privatization 1997 interaction	-0.24	0.13	+0.77***	0.16
Pro big business	+0.51***	0.06	−0.30***	0.07
Big business 1997 interaction	+0.25*	0.12	−0.07	0.16
Anti trades union power	+0.54***	0.05	−0.53***	0.05
Trades union 1997 interaction	+0.34**	0.12	−0.06	0.11
1997/not dummy	−0.75***	0.08	+0.50***	0.07
n	15,659		15,659	

Note: Pooled cross-section logistic regression models allowing the coefficients for 1997 to vary. Interaction terms defined by multiplying the election year dummy (1 for 1997, zero otherwise) by the specified 'parent' variable. Statistical controls applied for respondent's attitudinal and sociodemographic characteristics, as in Table 10.4, and for region (results not reported: available from the author on request). *** indicates that a coefficient is significant at .001; ** at .01; * at .05.
Source: BES, 1964–97.

dealigning or realigning election remains unclear.

This relatively straightforward picture is clouded a little by the results shown in Table 10.7. The rationale underpinning the findings reported is the same as with Table 10.6. In Table 10.7, however, it is assumed that the 'critical' nature of the 1997 election needs to assessed against the baseline of the 1979–97 period of Conservative hegemony rather than against the entire 1964–97 period. The results of the Labour equation are similar to those shown in Table 10.6 (the coefficients on the pro-nationalization and pro-privatization terms both indicate an attenuated effect in 1997). The Conservative equation, however, now produces three significant inter-action terms – for pro-nationalization (a further negative effect for 1997), for pro-privatization and for anti-trade union power (both further positive effects for 1997). Each of these interaction terms, in short, suggests ideological considerations exerted a *greater effect* on Conservative voting in 1997 than during the 1979–92 period – in contrast to the Labour position, where the ideological effects were smaller in 1997. The probable explanation for this apparent anomaly is simple: the Conservatives were so unpopular in 1997 that their support base was reduced to its right-wing ideological core; ideology mattered more to potential Conservatives in 1997 – but, for other reasons, there were simply fewer of them around.

What all this suggests is that, in comparison with previous elections, ideological considerations did play a distinctive role in 1997. Although the connections between ideology and Conservative voting were stronger in 1997 than between 1979 and 1992, this effect was probably an artefact of the 'condensing' of the Conservative support base. For Labour, in contrast, 1997 represented a significant departure in comparison with both 1964–92 and 1979–92. Labour's policy shift towards the ideological centre-ground was clearly not lost on voters. The relationship between Labour voting and ideology was significantly weakened in 1997 – though whether this weakening was sufficient to regard the election as 'critical' remains to be seen.

The Impact of Respondent–Party Ideological Distance on Vote, 1992–97

The models considered so far have all estimated the direct effects of voters' ideological positions on the probability that they will (or will not) support a particular party. In this section, I consider a series of slightly more complex models which consider the impact of the *distance* between the voter's assessment of his or her own ideological position and that of each of the major parties. The core theoretical assumption that underpins these models is that, *ceteris paribus*, voters will support the party that they perceive to be closest to them in ideological terms (Alvarez and Nagler 1995). Because of a lack of suitable data for other years, the analysis is restricted to a comparison between 1992 and 1997.

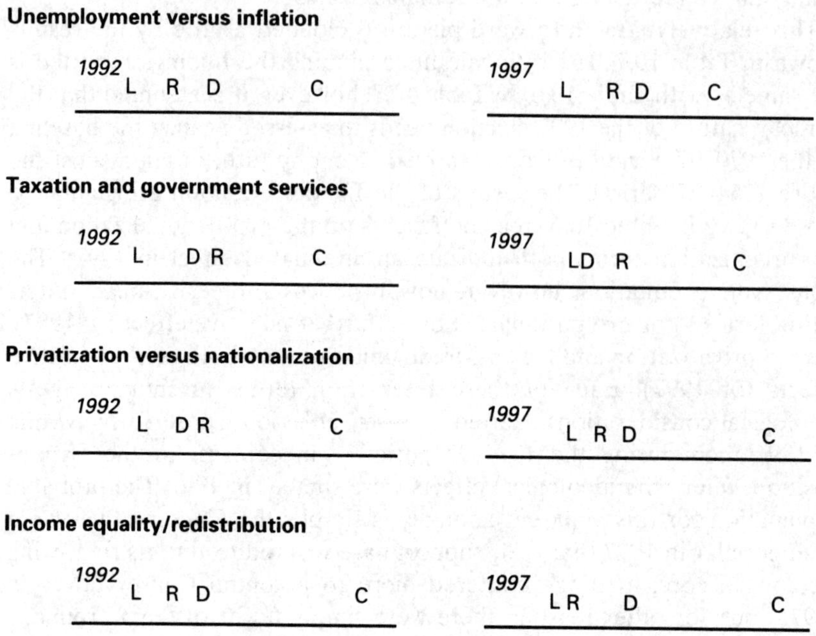

Unemployment versus inflation

1992

    L R D   C

1997

    L R D   C

Taxation and government services

1992

    L   D R   C

1997

    LD R   C

Privatization versus nationalization

1992

    L   D R   C

1997

    L R D   C

Income equality/redistribution

1992

    L R D   C

1997

    LR   D   C

Note: R denotes the position of the average respondent; C denotes average Conservative position; L average Labour position; D average Liberal Democrat position. The range on each scale is 1–11

FIGURE 10.1   *Voters' position and perception of the major parties on ideological scales, 1992 and 1997*

TABLE 10.8   *Distance of the average respondent from the major parties, 1992 and 1997*

	Conservative		Labour		Liberal Democrat	
	1992	1997	1992	1997	1992	1997
Unemployment versus Inflation	−2.98	−2.58	+1.48	+0.48	+0.70	−0.55
More tax and services versus less tax and services	−2.94	−3.29	+1.29	+0.47	−0.16	−0.12
Privatization versus nationalization	−2.98	−2.74	+2.06	+0.09	−0.26	−0.17
More versus less concern from income equality	−3.40	−4.08	+1.42	+0.60	+0.12	−0.47
Average distance	−3.07	−3.17	+1.31	+0.30	+0.10	−0.33

Note: All (11-point) scales were coded so that a high score denoted a right-wing position. A positive score in the table indicates that the average respondent was to the right of the average perceived position of the party in question; a negative score that the average respondent was to the left of the party.
Source: BES, 1964–97.

Figure 10.1 describes the average positions of respondents, as well as the average positions ascribed to each of the three major parties, on four measures of ideological position in 1992 and 1997.[9] Table 10.8 shows the *distances* between the average respondent's position and his or her estimate of the parties' positions. A positive number in the table indicates that the mean respondent placed him or herself to the right of the party in question; a negative number that he or she placed him or herself to the left. Two features of the figure and table are immediately noticeable. First, on each dimension, the mean respondent's position in both 1992 and 1997 was closer to Labour than to the Conservatives (and, in 1992, the mean respondent was closest of all to the Liberal Democrats). Secondly, as the bottom row of Table 10.8 indicates, whereas the gap between the average respondent's mean position and that of the party widened marginally on the four dimensions both for the Conservatives (from –3.07 to –3.17) and for the Liberal Democrats (from +.01 to –.33), for Labour it closed significantly (from +1.31 to +.30).

Although it seems likely that these aggregate movements assisted Labour's cause to some extent in 1997, the crucial question is whether, at the individual level, ideological proximity to a particular party had less of an effect on vote in 1997 than it had in 1992. In order to investigate this question, a set of 'distance/proximity' dummy variables was created which identified whether the respondent was closer to Labour or to the Conservatives on each of the ideological issue dimensions shown in Figure 10.1. If the respondent was closer to the Conservatives on a particular dimension then, for that dimension, he or she was coded as 1; if the respondent was equidistant between Labour and Conservative or closer to Labour, he or she was coded as zero.[10] These distance measures were then employed as the ideological component in model [1]. The results are shown in Table 10.9 (model A). The signs and significance levels of the coefficients conform entirely to theoretical expectations. Across all the dimensions and in both elections, being closer to the Conservatives increases the probability that a respondent will vote Conservative and reduces the probability that he or she will vote Labour. The magnitudes of the coefficients in the two election years also support the conclusions about ideological effects that were drawn earlier. In the Conservative support models, there is little change in the sizes of the coefficients between 1992 and 1997, and one of the coefficients (for the equality dimension) increases quite markedly (from +1.11 to + 1.53). In the Labour models, however, three of the four 1997 coefficients are noticeably smaller than their 1992 equivalents.

Model B in Table 10.9 seeks to simplify the analysis even further. The composite ideology variable used records the number of issue dimensions (0–4) on which the respondent was closer to the Conservatives than to Labour.[11] The coefficients for this composite variable in the Conservative equations are almost identical in both 1992 (+1.21) and 1997 (+1.22); in the Labour equation, the coefficient is smaller in 1997 (–.93) than in 1992

TABLE 10.9 *The effects on Conservative and Labour voting of respondents' ideological closeness to the Conservative Party, 1992–97*

	Conservative Vote/Not		Labour Vote/Not	
	1992	1997	1992	1997
Model A				
Respondent is closer to Conservatives than to Labour on the unemployment versus inflation scale	+0.95***	+0.82***	–0.61***	–0.91***
Respondent is closer to Conservatives than to Labour on more tax and services versus less tax and services	+1.55***	+1.24***	–1.08***	–0.62***
Respondent is closer to Conservatives than to Labour on privatization versus nationalization	+1.19***	+1.23***	–1.39***	–0.87***
Respondent is closer to Conservatives than to Labour on more versus less concern for income equality	+1.11***	+1.53***	–1.59***	–1.27***
Model B				
Respondent is closer to Conservatives than to Labour on composite scale based on all four items above	+1.21***	+1.22***	–1.18***	–0.93***
n	1,340	2,511	1,340	2,511

Note: Logistic regression models on four measures of ideological position. Attitudinal, sociodemographic and regional controls included in the estimation but not reported. Details, including standard errors, available from the author on request: *** indicates that a coefficient is significant at .001.
Source: BES, 1964–97.

(–1.18), again implying a weaker ideological effect. This pattern reinforces the notion alluded to earlier: that while ideology in 1997 remained just as powerful a source of Conservative voting as it did in 1992 (and before), Labour support in 1997 owed rather less to ideological calculation than it had in previous elections.

Summary and Conclusions

Labour's decision to move its core policy stances to the political centre during the 1992 Parliament – and its subsequent claims to be pursuing a 'third way' based on community, opportunity and responsibility – represented a self-conscious attempt to move the party away from its traditional ideological roots. It is hardly surprising in these circumstances that political observers should have speculated – sometimes quite wildly – about the impact of these changes on voters. There is no doubt, as the evidence presented in Figure 10.1 showed, that voters on average perceived that Labour in 1997 was closer to them in ideological terms than it had been in 1992. But the anomaly here is that, even in 1992, voters believed that Labour was on average closer to their own positions than the Conservatives were. Indeed, if average ideological position had been the decisive factor in voters' calculations in 1992, the Liberal Democrats – the party closest by far to the mean voter position on the ideological dimensions measured here – would easily have won the election. There is clearly much more to voting decisions than the ideological closeness of the average voter to a particular political party. And, in any case, aggregate patterns can often hide a great deal more than they reveal about the electoral calculations that individual voters make.

The empirical analysis conducted in this chapter has shown that, since at least 1964, voters' party preferences have been related to their ideological perceptions in theoretically predictable ways. The core question that has been addressed is the extent to which the 1997 election was 'critical' in ideological terms. It is indubitably true that Labour's shift to the centre, and its efforts to deideologize British party politics more generally, attracted more voters to its cause in 1997.[12] But this tells us nothing about the impact (or lack of it) of ideology on the voting decision.

The logic underpinning the analysis conducted here has been to examine the historical record – such as it is – in order to see if the impact of ideological factors on vote in 1997 differed markedly from the pattern that was evident in earlier elections. The inquiry has obviously been restricted by the lack of comparable over-time data. This said, the balance of evidence reported does not point overwhelmingly to the conclusion that the 1997 election was ideologically critical. To be sure, the effects of ideology on *Labour* support were weaker in 1997 than in any previous election for which BES data are available. However, the decline in effect magnitudes in 1997 was not especially pronounced in comparison with earlier changes – and the effects of ideology on *Conservative* support in 1997 were just as strong as (if not stronger than) they had been in previous years. These effect patterns appeared to hold, moreover, irrespective of whether the respondent's ideological position or the ideological closeness of the respondent to one party rather than another were being considered.

These findings fail to support the hypothesis that, as a result of progressive class and partisan dealignment, ideological voting has *declined* noticeably since the 1960s. Equally, they also fail to support the notion that dealignment has been associated with a secular *increase* in ideological voting. Critically, however, Labour's decisive move to the right does appear to have weakened the importance of ideology as a cue to Labour voting in 1997. This finding, moreover, is rendered all the more significant by the contrasting position of the Conservatives: their continued right-wing stance in 1997 did *not* reduce the impact of ideological factors on Conservative voting.

The central question this chapter has sought to address is whether or not 1997 can be characterized as an ideologically critical election, that is, whether it witnessed a significant *ideological dealignment or realignment*. The wisest answer to this question is that it is still too early to tell. We need to know the outcome of at least one more election before we can make a definitive judgement about the ideological mould-breaking capacity of 1997. On the information that is currently available, it would be premature to conclude that 1997 had witnessed a decisive ideological realignment in British politics. Changes in the ideology–vote relationship undoubtedly occurred, but they were fundamentally modest in their scope and implications. Labour's shift to the right – documented in earlier chapters – undoubtedly meant that ideology was not as important in 1997 as it had been between 1964 and 1992. However, internal policy developments within either of the major parties in the years ahead could easily produce a return to the status quo ante as far as the impact of ideology on voting is concerned. A definitive assessment must await further – future – evidence.

Notes

1. I opt for a statistical definition of centre-ground that is described in the note to Table 10.1. Experimentation with other operational definitions produces results very similar to those shown in the table.
2. In 1992, 32% of centre voters supported Labour compared with 36% of non-centre voters – a centre 'deficit' for Labour of 32% – 36% = 4%. The equivalent figures for 1997 were 49% (centre) and 47% (non-centre) – a centre 'surplus' of 2%. These figures imply that Labour's shift to the right in advance of the 1997 election increased its share of the centre-ground vote by roughly six percentage points. Since, on the definition employed here, just under two-thirds of voters were in the centre-ground, this suggests that Labour's rightward shift added in the region of four percentage points to its aggregate vote share.
3. There have certainly been occasions in the post-1964 period when Liberal (including Alliance/Liberal Democrat) voting has been associated with ideological position. In the 1980s, for example, Liberal voting correlated with opposition to both privatization and 'big business'. However, the sort of robust, long-term relationship between ideological position and party preference characteristic of Conservative and Labour voting has never consistently applied to the Liberals. As Table 10A.2 in the Appendix to this chapter shows, using a model specification that is developed in detail later in this chapter, the relationship between ideological position and Liberal voting is far weaker and less consistent than the equivalent relationships for Labour and the Conservatives that are shown in Tables 10.5–10.8.
4. The question wording relating to these four items varied slightly over the 1964–97 period. For variations in the wording of the nationalization and privatization items, see Crewe *et al.* (1998: 490–1); for variations in trade union power wordings, see pages 499–500; and for business power variations, see page 485.
5. The four indicators are used separately in the analysis that follows rather than combined into a single index (though the use of a single additive index

produces exactly the same substantive results as those reported below). The rationale underlying this usage is that, although the intercorrelations among the four items are fairly constant over time, the overall level of intercorrelation (in the region of $r = .2$) is not sufficiently high to justify their incorporation into a single left–right scale measure. Indeed, scale reliability tests yield a Cronbach's alpha well below the 0.6 threshold usually employed to justify the construction of a single index. In essence, the four items are included separately because they all measure different, if related, aspects of left–right ideology.

6. These measures have been used in previous BES research. See, for example, Heath *et al.* (1994).

7. Although the coefficients on the control variables are not reported, as with the results in Table 10.4, they are all theoretically plausible and correctly signed. Details are available on request from the author.

8. The mean effect for the MORENAT variable is +1.09; for MOREPRIV it is –1.19; for PROBB –.62; and for ANTITU +.85.

9. Table 10A.1 in the Appendix to this chapter estimates model [1] using the ideological measures shown in Figure 10.1 rather than the ideological measures used in earlier tables. Table 10A.1 also shows the consequences of using a left–right ideological index measure which additively combines respondents' scores on the four individual dimensions shown. The results shown in the table are broadly consistent with the results reported earlier using the simpler ideological measures. The coefficients in the Conservative support models change very little between 1992 and 1997. Two of the coefficients in the Labour models, however, decline quite markedly: the size of the privatization/nationalization effect halves (from –.16 to –.08) and the taxation/services effect falls from –.18 to –.05. Note also that, in line with previous research suggesting the non-ideological basis of Liberal Democrat support, only one coefficient (for taxation/services) is significant in the Liberal Democrat equations.

10. Several alternative codings were explored. These included 1) combining equidistants with Conservative rather than Labour voters and 2) coding Conservatives as +1, equidistants as 0 and Labour supporters as –1. These alternative codings produced substantively the same results as those reported below.

11. Scale reliability tests for the four items yield a Cronbach's alpha of 0.60.

12. The mean scores (higher score means more right wing) on respondents' positions were:

	1992	1997
Unemployment v. inflation	3.46	3.58
Taxation and services	4.12	3.65
Private/nationalization	5.65	5.26
Income equality	4.50	4.09
Composite index	4.44	4.15

This generally leftward shift in the electorate's positions between 1992 and 1997 is consistent with panel data from the British Household Panel Survey. See Sanders and Brynin (1999).

Appendix

Independent variables used in the analysis

1) *Measures of ideological position*

MORENAT	Respondent favours further nationalization/not
MOREPRIV	Respondent favours denationalization or (post 1979) further privatization/not
PROBB	Respondent supports big business/not
ANTITU	Respondent opposes or believes there is too much trades union power/not

2) *Attitudinal controls*

CARELOT	Respondent cares a lot about the election outcome/not
DIFFLOT	Respondent believes there are significant differences between the major parties/not
MCLASSID	Respondent regards self as middle class/not
DADCON	Respondent's father was Conservative voter/not

3) *Sociodemographic controls*

AGE	Respondent's age in years
GENDER	Respondent is male/not
MANUAL	Respondent is manual worker/not
OWNER	Respondent is from owner-occupied household/not
UNION	Respondent belongs to a trades union/not
MIDLANDS	Respondent lives in Midlands/not
NORTH	Respondent lives in north/not
SWEST	Respondent lives in south west/not
SCOT	Respondent lives in Scotland/not
WALES	Respondent lives in Wales/not

TABLE 10A.1   *Effects of position on ideology scales on voting, 1992 and 1997*

	Conservative/not		Labour/not		Liberal Democrat/not	
	1992	1997	1992	1997	1992	1997
Unemployment versus inflation	+0.02	+0.04*	–0.02	–0.05**	–0.00	+0.03
More tax and services versus less tax and services	+0.22***	+0.15***	+0.18***	–0.05***	–0.09*	–0.13***
Privatization versus nationalization	+0.17***	+0.11***	–0.16***	–0.08***	+0.02	+0.01
More versus less concern for income equality	+0.17***	+0.18***	–0.17***	–0.15***	–0.03	–0.02
Combined left–right index[1]	+0.56***	+0.49***	–0.54***	–0.34***	–0.08*	–0.07*
n	1,397	2,595	1,397	2,595	1,397	2,595

Notes: 1) Index is constructed by summing scores on the four items above. The table describes the results of estimating two distinct models: one containing the four 11-point ideology scales but not the summary index measure; and one containing the summary index measure only. Estimation is by logistic regression. Attitudinal, sociodemographic and regional controls included in the estimation but not reported. Standard errors available from the author on request: *** indicates that a coefficient is significant at .001; ** at .01; * at .05.

Source: BES, 1964–97.

TABLE 10A.2 *The effects of ideology on Liberal (Democrat) voting, 1964–97*

Independent variable	1964	1966	1970	Feb 1974	Oct 1974	1979	1983	1987	1992	1997
Supports more nationalization	−0.45	−0.15	0.13	−0.27	−0.21	−0.67*	−0.83***	−0.65**	−0.29*	0.05
Supports more privatization	−0.00	−0.06	−0.63*	−0.08	−0.01	−0.13	−0.58***	−1.00***	−0.85***	−0.69**
Pro big business	−0.25	−0.37	−0.88****	−0.38**	−0.43***	−0.27	−0.24**	−0.08	−0.51***	−0.48***
Anti trades union power	0.15	0.27	−0.55	−0.21	0.68***	0.19	0.11	0.37***	0.14	−0.36***
n	1,159	1,282	1,308	2,095	2,038	1,440	3,752	3,635	3,399	3,433

Note: Logistic regression models. Dependent variable is whether or not the respondent voted Liberal (Democrat). Statistical controls applied for respondents' attitudes, sociodemographics and region (results not reported). *** indicates that a coefficient is significant at .001; ** at .01; * at .05.
Source: BES, 1964–97.

11 Europe: A New Electoral Cleavage?

Geoffrey Evans

A fundamental characteristic of a critical election is the occurrence of a change in the basis of party support and, by implication, party competition. Two conditions need to be present for the emergence of such a new dimension to electoral politics. First, new issues need to emerge that political entrepreneurs might seize on to help boost an electorally threatened position. These issues should be highly salient 'hot button' issues at the top of the political agenda which divide the public in fundamental ways and which polarize parties. In other words they should meet the requirements of Butler and Stokes' (1974) classic specification of the requirements for issue voting, *viz.* an issue has to be salient, divisive and party polarized. To produce a decisive change in party support, however, these issues need also to fulfil the second condition: they should produce ideological cleavages that cut across traditional bases of party support. They should conflict with other ideological positions held by a party and those who vote for it and through this they should restructure the social bases of partisanship.

As we have seen elsewhere in this book, the traditional axis of division in postwar British politics has been between the adherents of more or less interventionist, redistributive versus *laissez-faire*, free market policy regimes. The electoral basis of support for the two main parties has been understood in ideological terms as reflecting voters' relative positions on a set of inter-related issues that can be characterized as a left–right dimension (see Sanders' Chapter 10 in this volume; Heath *et al.* 1994; Evans *et al.* 1996a). If 1997 is to be seen as in some way critical in the terms elaborated in the introductory chapter, or even in the less demanding sense of being in some way different from previous elections, we should expect to see new issues and by implication possibly new social groupings providing a basis for major party support that cross-cuts and weakens these traditional cleavages. New issues, or old issues that have become newly salient, should display signs of the potential not merely to augment left–right divisions, but to supplant them as the basis of vote choice, at least in part. This chapter examines whether Britain's relationship with the European Union, arguably currently the most significant single public policy issue facing the country, has become such an electorally consequential issue.

Traditionally European integration has been an issue with low political salience, only occasionally emerging as a topic that moves British public opinion (Janssen 1991; Evans 1995; Rasmussen 1997).[1] In recent years, however, the increasing prominence and proximity of integration could be expected to have promoted Europe to a more central political position. Since the period of the Maastricht Treaty, European electorates have become increasingly aware of – and sceptical about – the integration agenda (Niedermayer 1995; Franklin and Wlezien 1997). The initial failure of the Danish electorate to endorse the ratification of the Maastricht Treaty and the extremely narrow pro-Maastricht result in the French referendum are but two particularly significant examples of a widespread disquiet over European economic union since 1991 (Franklin *et al.* 1994). Unsurprisingly, integration has also affected British electoral politics. Its most obvious manifestations have been the splits within the Conservative administrations which formed the key axis of division in the party's leadership elections in 1990, 1995 and 1997, while the ERM crisis of autumn 1992 appears to have been the single event that most undermined the last government's standing in the opinion polls.[2] The emergence of the Referendum Party during the 1997 general election campaign served further to highlight the controversies surrounding integration which show no sign of disappearing as the process of monetary union moves onward.[3] It seems reasonable to suppose, therefore, that Europe has become a more salient issue for the public over recent years, with a consequent increase in its relevance to political competition.

These changes are consistent with evidence of the increasing public awareness of the issues posed by integration presented in Evans (1998a), who found that the internal consistency of attitudes towards various aspects of integration increased substantially in the space of a few years as the public related their views on issues that had been seen as hitherto disparate – EMU and the increasingly centralized influence of various areas of policy-making – to their support for integration in principle. By 1997 the issue of European integration was more firmly based on an awareness of what it might involve and, in consequence, markedly less positive, than it had been only three or four years earlier. These changes are what would be expected of an issue that has become increasingly salient and meaningful to the electorate.[4]

However, if Europe is to form a second dimension of political competition rather than simply augmenting pre-existing polarization over left–right issues, it also has to cross-cut these older issues and their accompanying bases of party support. That it is likely to do so is a basic premise accepted by theorists of new political cleavages, for whom the creation of supranational organizations in general, and the European Union in particular, forms a significant facet of the 'new politics' (Dalton 1996). Many advocates of the new politics theory of realignment take their lead from Inglehart's thesis that the growth of postmaterial values has resulted in the emergence of new political cleavages that cross-cut the old left–right, class-based divisions (see, for example, Inglehart 1997: 237).[5]

The axis of political competition has thus shifted, with left-wing parties emphasizing 'new-left' policies as well as, or instead of, their more familiar concern with redistribution and state intervention in the economy. European integration is a key element of such a new left policy agenda.

A key element of new politics arguments is the idea that this 'new left' has different bases of support in terms of both political values and social groups than has the 'old left'. This bifurcation of the left in turn reduces divisions rooted in traditional left–right conflicts and their primary social bases. Lipset (1981: 509–10) elaborates the implications of such changes for patterns of class voting:

> There are now two lefts, the materialist and the post-materialist, which are rooted in different classes ... The reform elements concerned with postmaterialist or social issues largely derive their strength not from the workers or the less privileged, the social base of the left in industrial society, but from affluent segments of the well-educated, students, academics journalists, professionals and civil servants ... Most workers on the other hand, remain concerned with material questions. Less educated, less cosmopolitan, less affluent, less secure, they are also more traditional, discernibly more conservative in their social views ... Some workers move to the right as a result, to more conservative groupings ... The left, however, picks up support from the growing ranks of the intelligentsia. Thus the correlations between class and party voting have been reduced.

In Britain, however, Labour's traditionally anti-European position has fitted rather well with the 'old left' and Eurosceptic character of its working-class support base. The cross-cutting impact of new issues referred to by Inglehart, Lipset and others would therefore not apply (for evidence, see Heath *et al.* 1990; Studlar and McAllister 1992). But during the 1980s this state of affairs began to change and a cross-cutting effect did become more likely. This change was facilitated by the about-turn in Labour's position on Europe leading up to, and incorporated into, the 1989 policy review. Remarkably, Labour shifted from advocating complete withdrawal from the EC in 1983 to ardent support by 1989 (see George and Rosamund 1992). The Conservative Party, in contrast, although pro-European in the 1970s became openly less Europhile over time and also experienced public splits over the issue (Baker *et al.* 1993; Sowemimo 1995; Evans 1998b). Thus the change of policy in 1989 is likely to have splintered Labour support in the way predicted by theorists of new politics, creating potentially the two types of Labour supporter identified, although somewhat prematurely in the British case, in the above quotation from Lipset. The move towards an anti-integration position by the Conservatives should have likewise consolidated Europe's cross-cutting impact.

The question then is whether the political character of European integration has changed since the original debates in the 1960s and whether it in fact now cross-cuts the more traditional bases of partisanship. We would only expect to see such cross-cutting effects reducing class voting/left–right voting *after* Labour's policy review in 1989 – only then would the new politics argument apply. They would only apply also if people vote, at least to some degree, on the basis of the issues rather than getting their opinions on issues from the parties they support, which is the model of voting behaviour that might be thought, at least until recently, to be particularly applicable to the relatively weakly established issue of European integration.[6] On questions concerning the European Union voters have been characterized as acquiescent rather than directive and a prominent role has been attributed to party leadership as an influence on the public's attitudes (see Flickinger 1994). If this were to be the case, Labour's policy review and the Tories' increasing Euroscepticism should make no difference to the basis of party support – the party faithful would simply shift their views to coincide with their party's change of position. As mentioned above, however, in recent decades the signals sent to the party faithful on the merits of European integration have gone through a state of flux. The significance of cues from parties to voters is likely to have declined as the parties themselves have changed the messages sent to their supporters, which increases the possibility that voters themselves will instead send 'messages' to parties – through opinion polls and their electoral behaviour.

If this is the case there are likely to be implications for party strategy. In particular, Europe could provide a route through which the currently hard-pressed Conservatives might steal votes from Labour. For this to occur, Conservatives would need to be in a better position *vis-à-vis* the opinions of the electorate than Labour – and there is some evidence that they are (Evans 1998b) – and the issue would have to be seen as relevant to partisanship. Whether this latter condition holds is still uncertain – although again, there is some supportive evidence (Evans 1998b) – but it could well have been facilitated by Labour's move to the centre on the traditional left–right dimension (see Budge's Chapter 1 in this volume) thus reducing the differentiation between them and the Conservative Party. Any reduction in the relevance of the left–right dimension to vote choice should provide room for manoeuvre on another dimension. The axis of competition might thus be shifted. If this were to be the case, it would in turn carry implications for the social bases of party support. Although it is generally considered that those Labours voters who are most anti-integration – i.e. the traditional working class – are those for whom left–right issues tend to be more central (see Heath and Evans 1988), if there is no longer much perceived difference between the main parties on such economic and redistributive issues they might find the Conservatives' Euroscepticism a distinctive and congenial option.

Analysis

Attitudes towards Europe in Long-Term Perspective

First, what has happened to attitudes towards Britain's involvement in the European Community (since 1991, the European Union) since the 1960s?

Figure 11.1 shows the distributions on the question on EC/EU membership that has been asked in most of the BES surveys stretching back to 1964. It also includes a shorter, more recent but denser time series taken from the BSA surveys.

Inevitably, direct comparison of distributions over time cannot tell us much about attitude change over the long haul as the phrasing of questions on this issue has changed as Britain's relationship with the European Community has changed.[7] The shorter-term trends are more amenable to comparison, however. Consistent with other recent evidence, both the BES and the BSA surveys show a decline in endorsement of EU membership since 1992. There was also a increase – to the highest levels since the 1960s – in the proportion of the public who didn't know whether they thought continued membership was a good thing or not. Polling data on the evolution of attitudes towards the European Union also suggest that there was a steady increase in British acceptance of EC membership up until 1991 (Niedermayer 1995). After the Maastricht Treaty in December of that year, and in the context of difficulties such as the ERM crisis, support for closer links with Europe dropped markedly and has shown little subsequent sign of recovery.

The start of the decade may therefore have been the high-water mark of British public support for European integration. As the implications of economic and political union became increasingly well known, the prevalence of Lindberg and Scheingold's (1970) notion of 'permissive consensus' – the general affirmation of a somewhat hazily understood

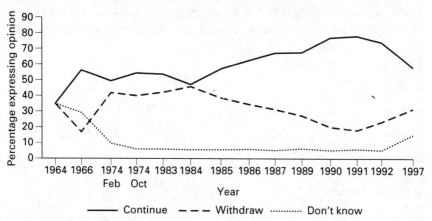

Question wording
1964, 1966: If the question of Britain going into the Common Market comes up again, do you think that Britain should go in or stay out?
October 1974: Should Britain stay in the EEC on present terms/stay but try to change/change or leave/get out?
1987, 1992, 1997 and BSA series: Do you think Britain should continue to be a member of the European Community/Union or should it withdraw?

FIGURE 11.1 *Attitudes towards membership of the European Union, 1964–97*
Source: BES Cross-section Surveys, 1964–74; 1987; 1992; 1997. BSA series, 1983–86; 1989–91.

European project by an uninvolved public – seems to have declined (see Evans 1998a for further evidence). This in turn alters the strategic benefits for the main parties of adopting pro- or anti-integration policies. Europe is now more likely to have an impact on vote choice than it was in less contentious periods.

The Changing Partisan Character of Attitudes towards Europe

Despite changes in the question format, the *relative* positions of groups within the electorate can be compared over the full period with some confidence. What we see in Figure 11.2, which shows the gap between pro- and anti-EU attitudes for the supporters of each of the main parties, is long-term continuity in the partisan character of attitudes to Europe from 1964 to 1987. Conservative supporters were a little more supportive in the 1960s and become more clearly so by 1974 when membership of the European Community was a topical issue. After 1987, though, party differences started to switch around: by 1992 they were fairly evenly balanced and by 1997 they were fully reversed. Labour supporters are now pro-Europe and Conservatives are sceptical.

Moreover, this switch round in the partisan character of the European question is not minor: in 1987 no less than 40% of Labour voters wanted to leave the European Union compared with only 23% of Conservatives; by 1997 this figure had dropped to 25% among Labour voters and jumped to 37% among Conservatives. For Labour, this change took place very clearly between 1987 and 1992 – by which time only 24% wanted to leave the EU, effectively the same as in 1997. For the Conservatives, however,

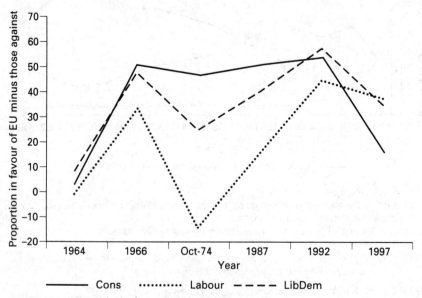

FIGURE 11.2   *EU attitudes by vote, 1964–97*

the proportion wanting to leave the EU in 1992 (21%) was still as low as in 1987; the change in attitudes occurred only after that election, when at least some of the Conservative Party expressed their Euroscepticism with increasing fervour (Sowemimo 1995; Berrington and Hague 1998). That the electorate picked up on this shift can be seen from answers to a question asked in the British Election Panel Study in both 1992 and 1997 which inquires about respondents' views on where the parties stand on Europe. In 1992 only 36% saw the Conservatives as being anti-integration. By 1997 this figure had risen to 53%. In contrast, both Labour and the Liberal Democrats were perceived to have become more pro-integration over the same period. Despite the evident splits in the Conservative Party during this period the general impression was of an increasingly anti-European party and their supporters also became accordingly more Eurosceptic.

Changes in the Social and Ideological Bases of Attitudes towards Europe?

The partisan nature of attitudes towards the European Union appears to have switched after the parties changed their relative positions on integration. However, the explanation of this change is less clear-cut. It could have occurred for two rather different reasons: either because their supporters switch their views to be consistent with the party, or because the parties attracted different sorts of voters as a result of their recently reversed positions on Europe.

If the former were to be the case we would expect a change in the social and ideological bases of support for European integration. As the parties changed their position on Europe so would the types of people who supported them. So we might expect the core social groups who provide the parties with their most solid support to have followed suit and have changed their opinions to be like their party's. We would thus find evidence for a 'top-down' model of voters' preference formation. A useful way of assessing the plausibility of this explanation of the changing partisan nature of attitudes towards Europe is to examine the class basis of such attitudes over time. After all, Labour's strongest support lies in the working class – a sector of the electorate usually considered to be among the least cosmopolitan in its attitudes (Lipset 1959; Heath and Evans 1988). If the Labour Party had simply pulled its support base along with it to a new more positive position on Europe, then a corresponding change should be observed in the attitudes of the working-class heartland of Labour support. Conversely, we might also expect to see the class heartland of Conservative support shifting to a relatively more Eurosceptic position as the party became more overtly sceptical in recent years. Do classes change their relative positions on Europe in line with switches in party policies and attitudes between 1987 and 1997? Figure 11.3 shows the gap between pro- and anti-European Union opinions in four class groupings – the professional and managerial middle class

(Classes I and II), routine non-manual workers (Class III), the self-employed (Class IV) and a 'working class' of foremen and technicians, and skilled, semi- and unskilled manual workers (Classes V, VI, and VII) – across the BES series.[8]

We can see that class differences in attitudes to Europe are extremely stable: the only move in the relative positions of the classes shown in Figure 11.3 occurred in the 1970s, and this involved the smallest class category – class IV – for whom estimates are likely to be less reliable; and it had reverted back to the picture observed in the 1960s by the time of the 1987 election. After that point there was no change: Labour's traditional working-class support base was and is consistently more Eurosceptic even in the era of 'new Labour'. The Conservatives' middle-class support base is staunchly more Europhile even though the party is not. The changing positions of the parties do not seem to have affected the relative appeal of European integration to different social groups, which suggests that orientations to Europe are not merely partisan reflections of party positions.[9]

The social basis of attitudes towards Europe is stable over time, but what of their ideological basis? If attitudes towards Europe are derived from party positions we would expect a change in their relations with core political values associated with partisanship. Prior to the late 1980s voters on the left should be anti-Europe, while after that period they should be pro-Europe. To explore this issue we examined the relationships between a series of attitude questions that have been consistently in the BES since

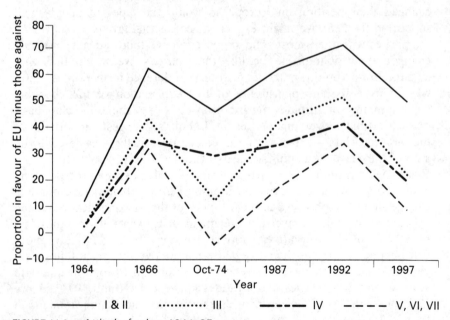

FIGURE 11.3   *Attitudes by class, 1964–97*

1974. Most of these questions concern issues identified as traditional left–right in character. They concern the reduction of inequality through government intervention in the workings of the market; the perceived trade-off between unemployment v. inflation; the long-running disputes over nationalization v. privatization; and the reduction of levels of taxation v. the provision of services. There is also a question which concerns attitudes towards a rather different issue: support for overseas aid. This latter item can be thought to tap into, if only imperfectly, a more or less cosmopolitan orientation among the electorate.

Table 11.1 shows that the patterns of correlations between attitudes display considerable continuity. This continuity is in the form of the relative orthogonality of attitudes towards EU membership/integration and the left–right issues. In other words, across all the elections examined there are only weak and inconsistent correlations between attitudes towards the EU and those towards left–right issues. The most noticeable sign of change is a decline from the 1970s in the correlation between attitudes to the EU and the question asking explicitly about attitudes towards redistribution, so that by 1997 these are effectively orthogonal. A similar increase can be observed with respect to the correlation between attitudes towards the EU and attitudes towards overseas aid, so that by 1997 opinions on these issues are more closely related to each other and less so to the other issues measured. In other words, Europe is distinct from left–right issues; which means that it can cross-cut those issues. It can therefore provide a basis for cross-cutting patterns of voting that are

TABLE 11.1 *Correlations between attitudes towards the European Union and other issues,* 1974–97

	Oct 1974	1987	1992	1997
Wealth	–.19	–.14	–.08	–.05
Poverty	–.07	–.07	–.02ns	.01^{ns}
Workers	–.07	–.06	.01^{ns}	.03^{ns}
NHS	–.02^{ns}	–.10	–.05	.03^{ns}
Overseas aid	.05	.16	.21	.24
$n =$	(2,154)	(3,638)	(2,657)	(2,406)

Note: All correlations are significant at $p < 0.05$ except where indicated; ns = not significant.

Question wording: Should the government spend more money to get rid of poverty? Should the government put more money into the *National Health Service*? Should the government give more *aid to poor countries* in Africa and Asia? Government should give *workers more say* in running the places where they work? Responses on a five-point scale: very important/fairly important/doesn't matter/fairly important not done/very important not done. (Response codes were definitely/probably instead of very/fairly in 1987, 1992, 1997.) *Wealth*: October 1974, 1979: What is your view about redistributing income and wealth in favour of ordinary working people? (Very important etc.); 1987–97: Income and wealth should be redistributed towards ordinary working people (five-point 'agree/disagree' scale).

Source: BES cross-section surveys.

distinct from the usual pattern of left–right divisions.[10]

A Cross-Cutting Issue Cleavage?

To examine the possibility that the question of European integration cross-cuts more established bases of voting preferences we need to model the effect of attitudes towards the EU on vote in a multivariate context. Attitudes towards the EU are clearly associated with partisanship, but so are many other issues and it may be these issues that account for party preferences. Attitudes towards the EU might make no significant *extra* contribution to voting to that derived from other traditional 'bread and butter' issues of British politics. We need therefore to control for the effects of these other attitudes. For this purpose we can use the BES questions shown above concerning the traditional 'left–right' conflicts over the relative 'slice-of-the-cake' received by different sections of society. This allows an examination of the pattern of issue effects on voting from the October 1974 election onwards.

The analysis is conducted using logistic regression, which is the most suitable technique for modelling the prediction of non-ordered or dichotomous choices of this sort. To interpret the models in Table 11.2 it need only be remembered that the coefficients are the log-odds of voting for a given party and that a positive coefficient indicates an increased likelihood of voting for the Labour Party rather than the Conservative Party.

These analyses show that voting is predictably influenced by attitudes towards issues concerning the redistribution of wealth, the NHS, workers' rights, the amelioration of poverty and also by attitudes towards support for overseas aid. They also show, however, that attitudes towards the European Union *continue to predict voting intention even when these other core issues are included in the analysis*. Attitudes towards the European Union are also the only attitudes that change the direction of their effects

TABLE 11.2   *The effects of attitudes on Labour–Conservative voting, 1974–97*

	Oct 1974	1987	1992	1997
Poverty	.07^{ns}	.52	.35	.40
Workers	.32	.13	.22	.23
NHS	.23	.92	1.17	.47
Wealth	.82	.92	.83	.74
Overseas aid	.04^{ns}	.18	.10^{ns}	.13
Withdraw from EU	1.34	.62	−.01^{ns}	−.75
Don't know on EU	.61	.96	1.01	.00^{ns}
Model chi^2	586.0	1,027.5	735.7	513.8
n	(1,471)	(2,374)	(2,270)	(2,055)

Notes: All parameters are significant at $p < 0.05$ except where indicated. Positive coefficients indicate a greater propensity to vote for Labour rather than the Conservatives. With the exception of the EU question, all responses to attitude questions are coded so that a high score indicates a 'left-wing' position; ^{ns} = not significant.
Source: BES cross-section surveys.

after 1987. Up until that point Euroscepticism was associated with Labour voting; in 1992 there was no effect of having an anti-EU attitude, only the 'don't knows' were clearly more likely to be Labour voters – perhaps because the parties' change of position on the EU was not yet fully consolidated in some voters' minds – and by 1997 the reversal was complete.

But how important is this cross-cutting effect in terms of party support? Can we assume, for example, that at least some of the jump in Labour support in recent years has come from voters who are pro-EU? Using the BES cross-section, we find that in 1997 people who had voted Conservative in 1992 and who had shifted to Labour were a little more pro-European (6%) than those who remained Conservative. This is a weak effect and one on which the inevitable problems of recall bias from questions asked five years after the event cast further doubt. A better test can be obtained by using the British Election Panel Study (BEPS). The BEPS consists of stratified random sample surveys with repeated interviews of the same set of respondents over a five-year period starting with the cross-section election survey in 1992.[11] We can therefore control for prior partisanship – i.e. whether respondents had voted for Labour in 1992 – and see if attitudes towards the EU still predict a move to voting Labour in 1997. We can also control for the other main ideological bases of party preference more effectively than in the over-time comparisons shown above by including the left–right (or socialist/*laissez-faire*) and libertarian-authoritarian scales in our model.[12] We can also measure attitudes towards the EU somewhat more fully by forming a composite scale of responses to three questions on slightly different aspects of integration that were asked in the BEPS.[13]

Table 11.3 presents three sets of logistic regressions, the first of which examines the decision to vote for Labour or the Conservatives while the second contrasts Labour voters with Liberal Democrats, and the third Conservatives with Liberal Democrats. In addition to the log-odds coefficients, the table presents effect size indicators in parentheses. The latter enable the magnitude of effects for the scales to be compared.

The first of these analyses shows that attitudes towards the EU predict Labour voting in 1997 even when prior partisanship and the two core values underlying voting preferences are controlled. What is more, these effects are of a somewhat greater magnitude than are those obtained with the libertarian–authoritarian scale. This again suggests that their impact is not just a reflection of partisan allegiances but that they are an independent influence on vote choice. The second analysis shows that EU attitudes have no impact on the decision to vote for Labour rather than the Liberal Democrats. The similarity of the two parties' positions on Europe – Labour were perceived as being pro-integration by 66% and the Liberal Democrats by 58% of respondents – renders this issue irrelevant. The third model shows, in contrast and predictably, that EU

TABLE 11.3 *Logistic regressions of 1997 vote on left–right, libertarian-authoritarian and EU attitudes, controlling for 1992 vote*

	Labour (1)/ Conservative(0)		Labour (1)/ Liberal Democrat (0)		Conservative (1)/Liberal Democrat (0)
Socialist–*Laissez-faire* scale	.53**	*(.50)*	.14**	*(–.08)*	–.30** *(–.33)*
Libertarian– authoritarian scale	.15**	*(.12)*	–.04		–.09* *(–.08)*
Attitudes towards the EU	1.05**	*(.19)*	–.18		–1.07** *(–.19)*
Vote in 1992	3.85**		2.92**		2.26
Model improvement in chi²	837.28**		282.80		352.20
	4 df		4 df		4 df
n	(1,068)		(899)		(663)

Note: ** Significant at *p*< .01; * significant at *p* < .05. High scores on the scales indicate left-wing, libertarian, pro-EU positions.
Figures in parentheses are effect size coefficient (*R*) for significant parameters. Vote in 1992 is Labour for models 1 and 2 and Conservative for model 3.
Source: BES cross-section surveys.

attitudes strongly divide Conservatives from Liberal Democrats – again to a greater degree than the libertarian–authoritarian scale. In other words, Europe divides the centre left – Labour and the Liberal Democrats – from the 'right', the Conservatives, further testifying to the shared ideological position of new Labour and the Liberal Democrats.

Has Europe Changed the Social Basis of Voting?

It would now appear that the parties have realigned their positions in a way that is conducive to attitudes towards the EU having a cross-cutting impact on traditional cleavages. In particular, by 1997 the ideological character of attitudes to Europe is such that they could be expected to cross-cut the class basis of left–right politics. The working class remain relatively Eurosceptic, but Labour are now somewhat more pro-integration – especially when compared with the Conservatives. If Europe does have a cross-cutting impact we should see that including attitudes towards the EU in models of voting actually *increases* some class divisions after 1989, while at the same time reducing them in previous years when party policy on the EU was more consistent with their traditional bases of support. In other words, the partisan nature and social distribution of these attitudes should now serve to suppress the extent of the class cleavage.

This effect is likely to be rather specific, however: the one area of class divisions that the party realignment on Europe is most likely to have affected is that between the pro-EU professional and managerial middle classes (the 'salariat') and the anti-EU working class. Routine non-manual workers and the self-employed have never been particularly pro-EU – their views are closer to the working class than the salariat – so that the changes since the late 1980s in party positions on Europe are unlikely to be consequential for differences in voting between these classes and the working class.

Empirical support for these arguments is provided in Table 11.4, which presents the parameters for the log-odds of voting Labour rather than Conservative for the salariat relative to the working class from 1974 onwards, with and without controlling for attitudes towards the EU and other issues. To maintain clarity of presentation, other class effects and the effects of issues on vote are not shown (they can be obtained from the author).

Table 11.4 shows that attitudes towards the EU do cross-cut and vitiate the class basis of voting. This can be seen by comparing the class parameter before and after controlling for attitudes towards the EU (columns 1 and 2, respectively). Once attitudes towards the EU are entered into the model all the decline in the salariat versus working-class parameter over the period from 1974 to 1997 is removed. Even when the effects of other attitudes in explaining class differences are taken into account, EU attitudes have almost as large an impact (compare columns 3 and 4).

From being an issue that helped to account for differences between the salariat and the working class in 1974 – as shown by the reduction of that parameter when EU attitudes are entered into the models presented in Table 11.3 – the EU has become an issue that accounts for the weakened strength of such divisions in 1997. This change took place primarily after 1992 and is indicated by the relative increase in the class vote coefficient in 1997 after controlling for attitudes towards the EU compared with the reduction in the parameter which occurs in the analyses which do not include attitude towards the EU.

The decline in the strength of the class voting parameters observed in 1997 compared with 1992 shown in Chapter 5 is thus interpretable as, at least in part, a consequence of party realignment on Europe. This is

TABLE 11.4   *The impact of party realignment on Europe on levels of class voting, 1974–97*

| | Salariat v. working-class parameters for Labour v. Conservative voting | | | |
	Class only	Class + EU attitudes	Class + left–right attitudes	Class + left–right + EU attitudes
October 1974	1.83 (.15)	1.63 (.16)	1.61 (.18)	1.43 (.19)
1987	1.64 (.12)	1.51 (.12)	1.08 (.14)	0.99 (.15)
1992	1.63 (.13)	1.59 (.13)	1.14 (.15)	1.12 (.16)
1997	1.42 (.14)	1.62 (.15)	1.06 (.16)	1.29 (.16)
Change 1974–97	–0.41	–0.01	–0.55	–0.14
Change 1992–97	–0.21	+0.03	–0.08	+0.17

Note: A positive coefficient indicates a propensity to vote Conservative rather than Labour. Standard errors in parentheses. All parameters are significant at $p < .01$.
Source: BES cross-section surveys.

perhaps not surprising: support for European integration has its strongest base in the educated middle classes – the very group with which Blair's new Labour supposedly has most affinity, while opposition continues to reside in 'old' Labour's working-class support base.

Conclusions

European integration became a salient feature of the political landscape in the 1990s. With the realignment in the positions of the Labour and Conservative Parties on the EU from the late 1980s onwards it also became an issue that had the potential to cross-cut and restructure partisan divisions in the British electorate. In other words, it became exactly the sort of issue that might facilitate a significant and possibly durable realignment of the sort identified in characterizations of critical elections.

And this appears to have been exactly what happened: the partisan character of attitudes towards the EU were relatively ill-defined in the 1960s and then became associated with Conservative voting during the 1970s and 1980s. In the 1990s all this changed and Labour supporters became clearly more pro-EU than were Conservatives, with the effect of EU attitudes on voting remaining robust even when controlling for core traditional issues accounting for party preference. During this same period, however, the social and ideological basis of EU attitudes remained relatively fixed. Its ideological position changed if anything only to make it more clearly orthogonal to the traditional left–right dimension of British electoral politics. The upshot of these developments is that Europe now cross-cuts the left–right basis of voting and because of party realignment on the issue now serves to reduce the effect of class on vote. The remodelling of new Labour and its centrist strategy – one which brings its views on the EU more in line with the middle classes it has gained support within – and the Conservatives' move to a more Eurosceptic position (even if this position is rather confused by their splits on the issue) have helped to make the 1997 election distinct from any that went before.

But of course, realignment on one issue does not make for a critical change of the sort we are concerned with in this book unless it has a substantial impact on electoral realignment. Whether Europe has a *causal* impact still remains uncertain – as is the case for most issue attitudes – but our panel-based analysis indicates that the net impact was of rather small magnitude.

So we can conclude that 1997 was distinct from any previous contest with respect to Europe and its effect on electoral cleavages. But at present this impact remains small. Yet it may become more important as integration proceeds and new and possibly more contentious questions than even monetary union arrive inescapably on the political agenda. In that case, 1997 could be taken as heralding a new era of British politics in which Britain's relationship with the rest of the EU forms a new significant and realigning influence.

Notes

1. Rasmussen (1997) shows that even in the late 1980s when the Conservative government was giving voters clear messages – in the form of Mrs Thatcher's personal Euroscepticism – it appears to have had little impact on the electorate's attitudes.
2. See Sanders (1996) for an aggregate-level analysis of polling data and Evans (1999b) for an individual-level analysis of panel data on this issue.
3. Norris (1997) shows, for example, that Europe dominated certain later parts of the 1997 campaign in the media far more than in previous elections.
4. Some evidence of the increasing awareness of the issues posed by integration is presented in Evans (1998a) who finds that the internal consistency of attitudes towards various aspects of integration increased substantially in the space of a few years as the public related their views on issues that had been seen as hitherto disparate – EMU, increasingly centralized influence various areas of policy-making – to their support for integration in principle. By 1997 the issue of European integration was both more firmly based on an awareness of what it might involve and in consequence markedly less positive than it had been only three of four years earlier. These changes are what would be expected of an issue that has become increasingly salient and meaningful to the electorate.
5. Inglehart (1977: Chap. 12; Inglehart *et al.* 1991) argues explicitly that the move towards the development of supranational bodies such as the European Union is a reflection of the increasing cosmopolitanism associated with such 'postmaterial', or to use his more recent (Inglehart 1997) term, 'postmodern' values.
6. This view of the voter's relationship to party positions has been advocated most influentially in the party identity theory electoral behaviour expounded by Campbell *et al.* (1960). Although it is not assumed that all voters' opinions are moulded by parties, this 'top-down' process is seen as especially likely to occur on issues that are not centrally important to voters' everyday concerns and on which they are not well informed.
7. Although it should be noted that the use of any one particular item to assess trends in attitudes towards Europe is not without its interpretative problems (Evans, 1995: 121, 1998a).
8. For more information on these social classes and the Goldthorpe class schema, see Chapter 5.
9. Further analysis indicates that other social groupings show similar levels of over-time stability in their relative positioning on the question of EU membership (details available from the author).
10. In addition to the correlations presented in Table 11.4 a series of principal components analyses were undertaken. These confirm the general picture of a two-dimensional structure to the responses to the six questions. This was found in all four surveys, but was particularly clearly structured in the 1990s. An analysis which looked at the structure of a fuller range of issues in 1992 and 1997 also showed that attitudes towards Europe cluster with a 'national' dimension, including other foreign policy issues and devolution and do not form part of a left–right dimension.

11. The respondents in the first wave of the BEPS were those obtained for the 1992 British Election Study cross-section survey, the *n* for which (after reweighting for a Scottish oversample) was 2,855. By the 1997 wave of the survey the number of respondents had dropped to 1,667. To correct for differential panel attrition, responses in all waves of the BEPS are weighted by the distribution of votes in the 1992 sample.
12. For details of these scales, see the Technical Appendix.
13. This scale included the question about whether respondents wanted to 'remain in the EU' used in the rest of this chapter and the following items:

> *Do you think Britain's long-term policy should be to*: leave the EU; stay in the EU and try to reduce EU powers; leave things as they are; stay in EU and try to increase EU powers; work for the formation of a single European government? *Which comes closest to your view*: replace the pound by a single currency; use both the pound and a new European currency in Britain; keep the pound as the only currency for Britain?
>
> Responses to these three items displayed reasonably high levels of internal consistency (alpha = .67).

12 Scotland: Constitutional Preferences and Voting Behaviour

Paula Surridge, Alice Brown, David McCrone and Lindsay Paterson

This book has examined the 1997 general election in Britain to assess whether or not the contest can be described as a critical election. One of the most important characteristics of realignment theory, as V.O. Key (1955) emphasizes, is that elections may have differing characters in different regions. In this context we suggest that, in Scotland, 1997 was not a 'critical' election. Despite the dramatic outcome in Scotland, voter–party alignments were largely similar to those at the 1992 election (Brown *et al.* 1998), and as such 1997 could be described as a maintaining election. In contrast, we argue that in Scotland the election of October 1974 proved to be the last critical election as it produced a major realignment of the electorate that has proved to be enduring and to have radically altered the nature of party competition in Scotland.

The Theory of Critical Elections

The classic definition of a critical election, given by Key (1955), is an election in which 'the depth and intensity of electoral involvement are high, in which more or less profound readjustments occur in the relations of power within the community and in which new and durable electoral groupings are formed'. Such elections represent a radical realignment of the electorate around new issues and social cleavages. In Britain the situation is complicated by the existence of substates which have seen their party systems diverge over the last three decades. Since the mid-1970s Scotland has experienced four main parties competing for the support of the electorate at general elections, whereas in England there have only been three.[1] The very presence of the SNP, gaining a significant share of the vote in Scotland, suggests that alignments of social groups with political parties are likely to differ between Scotland and England. If these alignments do indeed vary then it also seems unlikely that any 'profound readjustments' that occur will occur in the same manner or at the same time in these two differing party systems. In this chapter we assess, first, whether new alignments have been forged in Scotland along new cleavages; secondly, the extent to which alignments between political parties and social groups are the same in Scotland and England; and, finally, whether there is evidence to suggest that any recent election in Scotland can be described as 'critical'.

Social Cleavages and Partisan Alignment

To assess the basis of political alignments in Scotland and England we turn to the theory of social cleavages put forward by Lipset and Rokkan (1967a). In their classic work on the determinants of partisan alignment Lipset and Rokkan identified three cleavages which divide western societies and may produce alignments of social groups with political parties. These are divisions

- between the core and periphery;
- due to religion; and
- due to social class.

Scotland provides an excellent test-bed for these cleavages as all three of these have existed within the appeals parties have made to the electorate and have at varying times and with varying degrees of success shaped party competition. In the immediate postwar period religion had a strong influence on party politics especially in the west of Scotland which had a large immigrant Irish community. This led large proportions of working-class Protestants in these areas to vote for the Conservative Party, against their class allegiances (Seawright and Curtice 1995). Later, as the Labour Party become more influential in Scotland the class cleavage appeared to become more important, with the SNP in more recent years adopting an explicitly left-wing policy programme in the hope of capturing this working-class vote. Finally, in the last two decades appeals from the parties have increasingly been made around issues of national identity, linked to the over-riding issue of constitutional change.[2] Many commentators have seen the two issues as inextricably linked; that a desire for constitutional change is simply an expression of a desire for every nation's right. Later in the chapter, these issues are considered in more detail but it is clear that the situation in Scotland is more complicated. National identity and constitutional reform are linked but not in a simple deterministic manner (Brown *et al.* 1998).

The key question, therefore, is which of these cleavages, if any, was the most important at the 1997 general election? Did the electorate largely follow traditional class-based loyalties or was support shaped by one of the other cleavages, such as national identity, or perhaps the electorate were largely 'dealigned', casting their votes on the basis of issue positions rather than durable alignments?

Historical Background

It is often suggested that the distinctiveness of Scottish politics, when compared with England, is the presence of the SNP. Although, as we will argue later, this is the key factor in explaining recent divergence, from the very beginnings of modern party politics Scotland was distinctive. During the nineteenth century, when party competition was between the Liberals and the Conservative Party, the Scotland–England difference in voting patterns was larger than any differences we have seen in recent decades (Field 1997). The Liberal Party's position in Scotland was much stronger than its position in England, never dropping below 50% and regularly topping 80% of the vote. It is only when we consider more recent electoral history that divergence between Scotland and England appears as something new.

Political commentators during the 1950s and 1960s pointed to the homogeneity of the British system; this position was the norm in British politics until the early 1980s. The position was based on the concept of uniform swing across the system as expressed by Crewe (1985: 101–3):

> In every election but one (1959) at least three-quarters of the constituency swings were within two per cent of the national median and only a handful of seats bucked the national trend. To know the swing in Cornwall was to know within a percentage or two the swing in the Highlands.

It was also based on the fact that the same parties contested the elections across the whole of Britain. Even after the emergence of the SNP as an electoral force in Scotland many continued to assert that the system in Scotland continued to be British as the majority of votes were cast for 'British' parties (McAllister and Rose 1984). To express this in terms of Lipset and Rokkan's cleavage politics, there was not a division in the electorate around a core–periphery cleavage. Moreover, there were no parties attempting to mobilize support around such a cleavage.

To understand the basis of the electoral divergence between Scotland and England in the last two decades, it is necessary to understand the rise of support for the SNP. Support for the SNP and its electoral successes not only placed the question of Scotland's constitutional position firmly on the political agenda but also changed the shape of party competition in Scotland. The SNP was officially formed in 1934, the product of a merger between the National Party of Scotland and the Scottish Party. The party did not immediately achieve electoral success, as Figure 12.1 shows. The party contested just eight seats in 1945 and won only 30,000 votes. The first breakthroughs for the party came in by-elections, where although they did not win seats (except in the unusual circumstances of the wartime Motherwell by-election in 1945) the SNP managed to gain a respectable share of the vote. The turning point came in 1967, with Winnie Ewing winning the Hamilton by-election. At the 1970 general election the party won the seat of the Western Isles (its first victory at a general

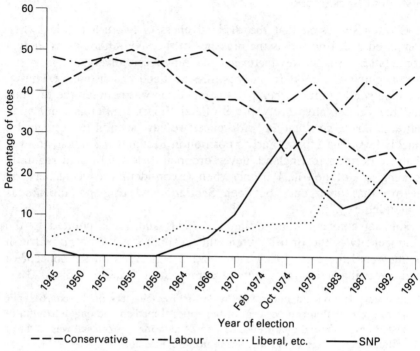

FIGURE 12.1   *Party shares of the vote in Scotland, 1945–97*

election). At that election the SNP won 11% of the vote (some 300,000 votes) and finally placed itself firmly on the popular political agenda. The peak of electoral support for the party came at the October 1974 election where they managed to secure a little over 30% of the popular vote. Although this support fell dramatically at the start of the 1980s the party has rebuilt its base of support and has consistently polled around a quarter of the Scottish vote in elections in the 1990s.

The legacy of the initial rise of the SNP remains. The interpretation placed on the support for the SNP in the beginning was that it was an expression of discontent with the current system (McLean 1970). It was not, initially, seen as a direct call for independence but rather as a call against the status quo. This prompted responses from the other parties in Scotland, most notably from the Labour government who set up a Royal Commission to look into the government of Scotland. When the commission reported in 1973, it recommended a form of Scottish Assembly, with powers covering a wide range of policy issues. The Labour government, acting on the proposals of the Royal Commission, put legislation before Parliament but was forced, by strong opposition both from outside and inside its own party, to concede both many of the parliament's powers and the ruling that, in a referendum, 40% of the total electorate must vote in favour of the parliament. The referendum was held on the 1

March 1979 and although an overall majority of votes cast were in favour of the parliament (52%), with turnout of 64% this was not enough to secure the 40% of the electorate required for the legislation to proceed. At the general election a few months later the SNP's support fell dramatically and the election of the Conservative government saw all hope for immediate constitutional reform dashed.

The importance of the SNP in placing constitutional change on the agenda and in the minds of the Scottish electorate cannot be overstated. Their electoral success in the late 1960s and early 1970s forced the other parties to respond and shaped Scottish politics into the situation of the 1997 campaign. The Conservative Party throughout the 1980s and 1990s campaigned in Scotland on a strong Unionist platform – to their cost. Labour and the Liberal Democrats (and their predecessors) have followed a campaign for home rule. In the run-up to 1997, as in 1992, the 'constitution card' was played by all the parties and was seen as central to the campaign north of the border.

Thus, in terms of the debate over critical elections, it would appear that a new cleavage emerged in Scottish politics with the rise of the SNP. Whereas it was traditionally expected that votes would be cast along a class cleavage, with some legacy of a religious divide remaining (Curtice and Seawright 1995), the rise of the SNP led parties to base their appeals to voters along lines of national identity. In Scotland throughout the era of modern politics parties have attempted to be seen as 'Scottish' and in the 1990s only those parties who do this successfully can survive.

Earlier work on the nature of support for the SNP (Brand *et al.* 1994) characterized their vote as one based on rational choices of an electorate who felt deprived relative to other parts of the same polity and who believed that independence would make Scotland better off. Our own study of the 1997 referendum in Scotland (Surridge *et al.* 1997) suggests that decisions on how to vote in the referendum were not simply an expression of national sentiment. Instead they were based around expectations of what the parliament would deliver in Scotland, in terms of improvements in welfare and the economy, regardless of expectations of higher taxation. Nevertheless it is clear that support for constitutional change and national identity are closely linked, as shown in Table 12.1.

The table shows the very clear relationship between national identity[3] and constitutional preference but as already suggested the relationship is far from deterministic. Among those who felt 'Scottish and not British' almost as many respondents favoured home rule as favoured independence. As we move through the scale of national identity towards those who felt at least equally Scottish and British the proportion supporting the status quo increases, although in no group is there a majority support for the status quo. This suggests that any relationship between national

TABLE 12.1 *National identity[1] and constitutional preferences[2] in Scotland, 1997*

	Scottish not British	Scottish more than British	Scottish equal to British	British more than Scottish	British not Scottish
No change	9	11	31	29	25
Home rule	42	60	54	65	62
Independence	48	28	15	6	12
Unweighted *n* (= 100%)*	179	315	217	34	31

* In this and other tables in this chapter, those who answered 'Don't know' or who did not answer the question are not included.

Notes:
1) Which, if any, of the following best describes how you see yourself?
2) An issue in Scotland is the question of an elected parliament – a special parliament for Scotland dealing with Scottish affairs. Which of these statements comes closest to your view?'

   1. Scotland should become independent, separate from the UK and the European Union.
   2. Scotland should become independent, separate from the UK but part of the European Union.
   3. Scotland should remain part of the UK, with its own elected assembly which has *some* taxation powers.
   4. Scotland should remain part of the UK, with its own elected assembly which has *no* taxation powers.
   5. Scotland should remain part of the UK *without* an elected assembly.

   For the purposes of this (and other) tables these responses are collapsed into independence (responses 1 and 2), home rule (responses 3 and 4) and no change (response 5).

identity and constitutional preference is complex, not merely an expression of a desire for a national right, but also not unrelated to it.[4]

Understanding Support for Constitutional Change

To what extent does support for constitutional reform and national identity form one or more new cleavages in Scottish politics? In trying to answer this question it is crucial to understand the basis of support for constitutional reform. Is support for reform an expression of class or religion-based loyalties or is it distinct from these already existing cleavages?

Table 12.2 shows how levels of support for various measures of constitutional change have varied over the last 25 years. As the table demonstrates, there has been a clear decline in support for the status quo. By the 1997 election, less than 20% of the Scottish electorate were in favour of no change. Support for complete independence has risen slightly over the period, but with a large drop in 1979 (the survey being conducted only a few months after the referendum). Similarly support for home rule has increased, so that in 1997 a majority of the Scottish electorate favoured this option.

TABLE 12.2   *Constitutional preferences in Scotland, 1974–97*

	1974[1]	1979[2]	1992[3]	1997[4]
No change	34	30	25	18
Home rule	44	62	51	54
Independence	21	8	24	27
Unweighted *n* (= 100%)	944	633	924	803

Notes:

Question wordings and coding:

1) There has been a lot of discussion recently about giving more power to Scotland. Which of the statements comes closest to what you yourself feel?
   1. Keep the governing of Scotland much as it is now   (No change).
   2. Make sure the needs of Scotland are better understood by the Government in London   (No change)
   3. Allow more decisions to be made in Scotland   (Home rule)
   4. Scotland should completely run its own affairs   (Independence)

2) Here are a number of suggestions which have been made about different ways of governing Scotland. Can you tell me which one comes closest to your own *view?*
   1. No devolution or Scottish Assembly of any sort   (No change)
   2. Have Scottish Committees of the House of Commons come up to Scotland for their meetings   (No change)
   3. An elected Scottish Assembly which would handle some Scottish Affairs and would be responsible to Parliament at Westminster   (Home rule)
   4. A Scottish Parliament which would handle most Scottish affairs, including many economic affairs, leaving the Westminster Parliament responsible only for defence, foreign policy and international economic policy (Home rule)
   5. A completely independent Scotland with a Scottish Parliament   (Independence)

3) An issue in Scotland is the question of an elected parliament – a special parliament for Scotland dealing with Scottish affairs. Which of these statements comes closest to your view?
   1. Scotland should become independent, separate from the UK and the European Union   (Independence)
   2. Scotland should become independent, separate from the UK but part of the European Union   (Independence)
   3. Scotland should remain part of the UK but with its own elected assembly that has some taxation and spending powers   (Home rule)
   4. There should be no change from the present system   (No change)

4) See notes to Table 12.1.

Source: Scottish Election Studies, 1974, 1979, 1992, 1997.

Despite the positions taken by the electorate on this issue, previous work on issue voting has shown that simply holding a position on an issue need not in itself have an impact on voting behaviour. For the issue to have an impact on voting decisions certain conditions must be satisfied (Butler and Stokes 1974). First the individual voter must not only be aware of the issue but must also hold a 'genuine attitude' towards the issue. To put this another way the issue must be salient to the voter. Secondly, the individual must be able to link the parties to clear and differing positions towards the issue. No matter how salient an issue to a voter if he or she

TABLE 12.3   *Perceived positions of parties on constitutional reform*[1]

	Conservative	Labour	Liberal Democrat	SNP
No change	77	11	20	2
Home rule	19	78	72	10
Independence	4	11	8	88
Unweighted *n* (= 100%)	742	726	548	746

Notes:
1) Which of these statements comes closest to the view of the (party name) Party?
   1. Scotland should become independent, separate from the UK and the European Union.
   2. Scotland should become independent, separate from the UK but part of the European Union.
   3. Scotland should remain part of the UK, with its own elected assembly which has *some* taxation powers.
   4. Scotland should remain part of the UK, with its own elected assembly which has *no* taxation powers.
   5. Scotland should remain part of the UK *without* an elected assembly.

Source: Scottish Election Study, 1997.

believes all the parties to have the same position on the issue it cannot form the basis of a voting decision.

Thus, to test the significance of constitutional reform in Scotland for the outcome of the 1997 election, it is not enough to show that the electorate held opinions; the salience of issues must also be demonstrated. The 1997 Scottish Election Survey asked respondents to indicate how important the issue of a Scottish parliament had been in their decision to vote as they did. The Scottish electorate seemed divided on the importance of this issue. Only 18% said that the issue was very important, whilst a further 33% said it was fairly important. On the other hand almost 50% said the issue was either not very or not at all important in making up their minds how to vote. The second step in the issue-voting model requires that the voters perceive the parties as having different positions on the issue. Table 12.3 shows the positions on constitutional reform that the Scottish electorate assigned to parties in 1997.

As Table 12.3 shows, although by no means all the electorate correctly identified the positions of the parties on this issue, the majority were able to place the parties. In addition there were clear differences between the positions given to the parties, suggesting that the second condition for issue voting was satisfied on this issue. Voters were able to distinguish between parties on this issue and as such could use it as the basis for voting decisions. Table 12.4 provides further evidence for this as it shows the relationship between constitutional preference and voting behaviour at each election since 1974.

It would seem, looking at Table 12.4, that whatever voters say about the importance of constitutional change to voting decisions there is a very strong relationship between party choice and constitutional preference. The relationship is weakest in 1974, which is unsurprising given that this

TABLE 12.4 *Constitutional preferences*[1] *by vote, 1974–97*

	1974			1979			1992			1997		
	No change	Home rule	Independence	No change	Home rule	Independence	No change	Home rule	Independence	No change	Home rule	Independence
Conservative	34	28	7	51	31	16	61	20	5	46	8	4
Labour	46	36	29	32	44	20	24	47	32	34	62	46
Liberal, etc.	10	10	4	11	9	9	12	14	5	15	18	6
SNP	9	26	60	6	16	56	4	18	58	5	12	44
Unweighted *n* (=100%)	270	358	177	155	350	45	190	399	186	153	435	215

Note:

1) Question wordings and codings as for Table 12.2.

Source: Scottish Election Studies, 1974, 1979, 1992, 1997.

was the first election where such issues were firmly on the agenda. At each of the four elections, covered by separate Scottish surveys, SNP support is strongest amongst those who favoured independence, whilst Conservative support is strongest amongst those favouring the status quo.

In order to claim that this relationship between constitutional preference and voting behaviour represents a new cleavage in Scottish politics, it is necessary to examine the relationship between this and other cleavages. It is also necessary to understand where support for constitutional change comes from. Is it simply another expression of an old cleavage – for example religion – or is it a new cross-cutting cleavage unrelated to the traditional predictors of party support?

In order to try to capture some of the complexities of the relationship between constitutional preference and other cleavages, two logistic regression models were fitted to the 1997 data.[5] The first takes as its dependent variable support for independence v. all other options; the second looks at support for change v. support for no change. The results of these models are presented in Table 12.5.

The models include measures of the other cleavages in Scottish politics, namely class-based divisions and those based on religion and national identity.[6] As Table 12.5 shows when looking at support for independence, the dimension of social class (as measured by occupation, housing tenure, attitudes on a left-right scale) is not significant, although holding a working-class self-identity is. Further evidence that constitutional preference is only weakly related to the class cleavage is provided by the fact that the positions of individuals on a left-right attitudinal scale are not a significant predictor of constitutional preference.[7]

The other two cleavages are more complicated. Religion remains a significant predictor of (or lack of) support for independence, with Catholic respondents significantly less likely to be in favour. Linked to this dimension, those who have more authoritarian positions (on a libertarian–authoritarian value scale) are also less likely to favour independence. National identity proves to be a strong predictor of support for independence, with those who claim to be 'Scottish and not British' the most in favour.[8]

Comparing the model of support for independence with that of support for change, there are two key differences. First, religion is no longer a significant predictor, suggesting that the religious divide is around independence and not constitutional change *per se*. Secondly, in the model of support for change, position on a left-right scale is a significant predictor. One possible explanation for this is that it is the left-of-centre parties in Scotland that have promoted constitutional change (Paterson 1998). Thus, in the popular media and the rhetoric of the parties, positions of nationalism and socialism have been linked.

These models suggest that constitutional preference and national identity may form a new issue cleavage in Scottish politics. Constitutional preference is strongly linked to national identity and to attitudes towards

Table 12.5   *Logistic regression models of support for independence and change in the constitution*

	Independence	Change
Constant	–1.44	4.01
Class cleavage		
Social class (salariat):		
Routine non-manual	–0.31	–0.35
Petty bourgeoisie	–0.63	0.73
Manual foremen	–0.85	–0.19
Working class	0.32	0.22
Housing tenure (owner-occupier):		
Rents: local authority	0.42	0.06
Rents: private	–0.49	0.31
Other tenure	–0.32	1.49
Working-class identity	0.56*	0.65*
Socialist–*laissez-faire* scale	–0.04	–0.20**
Religious cleavage		
Religion (Protestant):		
Catholic	–1.15**	0.33
Other	0.29	–0.11
Libertarian–authoritarian scale	0.07*	–0.10*
National cleavage		
National identity (equally Scottish and British):		
Scottish not British	1.47**	0.79*
Scottish more than British	0.78**	1.20**
British more than Scottish	–0.78	0.23
British not Scottish	0.30	0.55
British national sentiment scale	0.14**	0.14**
Other variables		
Gender (female)	0.18	0.27
Age (in years)	–0.02**	–0.01

Note: * indicates coefficient significant at 0.05; ** indicates coefficient significant at 0.01. For details of methods used and measurement of the variables see the Appendix to this chapter.
Source: Scottish Election Study, 1997.

British national pride. It is not, however, strongly linked with either of the other two classic cleavages. In this sense, it would appear that the 'national dimension' is a cross-cutting cleavage and as such has the potential to be a realigning force in Scottish politics.

The National Dimension and Voting Behaviour

To assess if realignment around this issue has occurred, it is necessary to consider the relationship between these cleavages and voting behaviour. To test the extent to which these alignments differ between Scotland and England we present the results of the same models of voting behaviour for each country. Table 12.6 shows the results of these models.

TABLE 12.6   Logistic regression models of vote at 1997 general election

	Conservative		Labour		Liberal Democrat		SNP
	Scotland	England	Scotland	England	Scotland	England	
Constant	-5.08	-6.53	2.09	2.71	-4.66	-1.03	-5.96
Class cleavage							
Social class (salariat):							
Routine non-manual	-0.23	-0.26	0.38	0.05	-0.47	-0.08	0.31
Petty bourgeoisie	-0.39	0.17	0.16	-0.36	-1.01	-0.13	-0.07
Manual foremen	0.78	-0.46	0.33	0.41	-1.34	-0.16	-0.04
Working class	-0.61	-0.47**	0.36	0.17	-0.51	-0.11	0.09
Housing tenure (owner-occupier):							
Rents: local authority	-1.45*	-1.04**	0.44*	0.20	-1.02*	-0.66*	0.45
Rents: other	-0.86	-0.25	0.26	-0.25	-0.60	-0.34	0.04
Working-class identity	-0.83*	-0.65**	0.44	0.56**	-0.45	-0.33*	0.09
Socialist–*laissez-faire* scale	0.27**	0.31**	-0.18**	-0.22**	-0.02	-0.03	0.04
Religious cleavage							
Religion (Protestant)							
Catholic	-0.85	-0.53*	0.67*	0.47**	-1.50*	0.14	-0.58
Other	0.21	-0.30	0.00	0.48*	0.80*	-0.12	-0.30
Libertarian–authoritarian scale	0.09	0.15**	0.00	-0.07**	0.04	-0.05*	-0.01
National cleavage							
National identity (equally Scottish/English and British):							
Scottish/English not British	-0.01	0.00	0.22	-0.18	-0.51	0.55*	0.14
Scottish/English more than British	-0.27	0.16	-0.11	-0.12	0.09	0.25	0.49
British more than Scottish/English	-0.03	0.19	-0.02	-0.20	-0.09	0.04	0.21
British not Scottish/English	0.62	-0.30	0.03	-0.15	0.23	0.31	-0.15
Constitutional preference for Scotland (no change)							
Independence	-1.14*	-0.46	-0.77*	0.47*	-0.91	-0.40	3.14**
Home rule	-1.45**	-0.01	0.38	0.22	0.04	0.08	1.28*
British national sentiment scale	-0.12	-0.14**	-0.01	0.03	0.15**	0.07**	0.06
Other variables							
Gender (female)	0.13	0.51**	-0.14	-0.09	0.48	-0.03	0.03
Age (in years)	0.01	0.00	-0.01	0.01**	0.01	0.00	0.02*

Notes: * indicates coefficient significant at 0.05; ** indicates coefficient significant at 0.01.
Source: British/Scottish Election Study, 1997.

The first point to note from these models is that the class cleavage, as measured by occupational class group, appears no longer to have a significant impact on voting behaviour in either Scotland or England. Nevertheless, other indicators of social class are important. Of these, it is worth noting that the position on the attitudinal scale measuring socialist–*laissez-faire* (or left-right) attitudes is strongly related to occupational class (Brown *et al.* 1998). Thus, whilst there no longer appears to be a direct effect of occupational class on voting there remains a strong indirect effect. Within the 'class cleavage', housing tenure has a significant impact on voting behaviour, with those living in local authority rented accommodation being less likely to vote Conservative or Liberal Democrat in both Scotland and England and more likely to vote Labour in Scotland. The evidence, then, on the presence of the class cleavage is mixed. This may be a function of a shifting meaning of class (Saunders 1990; Lee and Turner 1996) or it may be related to the lack of class-based appeals made by the parties (see Chapter 5). Perhaps surprisingly, there is evidence that a religious cleavage still exists in British politics, with the Labour Party picking up votes among Catholics in both Scotland and England.

The key dimension of interest, though, is that of nationality and constitutional reform. The models show that once constitutional preference is taken into account, national identity is not significant in predicting voting behaviour. This seems a little paradoxical in the Scottish case but may be explained in part by the very skewed distribution of this measure, leaving us with very few respondents in those categories which hold Britishness higher than Scottishness. Attitudes towards constitutional reform are, as we would expect, very strongly related to voting behaviour in Scotland, although show only a slight impact (on Labour voting only) in England. In addition, the measure of British national sentiment is not related to voting behaviour in Scotland (with the exception of votes cast for the Liberal Democrats). This suggests that it is issues of 'Scottishness' and the Scottish constitution which are the more salient in Scotland.

A final key feature of these models is the support for the SNP. Of all the dimensions included in the model only constitutional preference and age are significant predictors of SNP support, confirming earlier findings (Brand *et al.* 1994) that the party does not have a socially distinct base of support. Such findings point to support for the SNP being centred around a single issue (constitutional reform) and yet the standing of the SNP in opinion polls in the run-up to the Scottish Parliament elections suggests otherwise. It remains an interesting question as to whether support for the SNP will hold out in the long term if the setting up of the Scottish Parliament allows issues of constitutional reform to slip further down the political agenda.

Do these findings suggest that there is a new electoral cleavage in Scotland? On the face of it there seems little evidence to suggest there is. National identity is not significantly related to voting behaviour once the effects of constitutional preferences have been taken into account. The difficulty is that it is unclear at the moment how this will be affected by the setting up of the Scottish Parliament. If the issue is seen as settled it is possible that national identity could become more prominent in determining voting behaviour or it is equally possible that national identity could become depoliticized. To add to these difficulties there is also the problem we highlighted earlier: national identity and the issue of constitutional reform are linked in complex ways, such that it is difficult to separate their effects and problematic to treat them separately.

Despite these difficulties, a further way to test these theories is to look at party support in Scotland after the referendum result. Using the Scottish Referendum Study, party identity was modelled using (where possible) the same measures as in Table 12.6. The only measure which was

TABLE 12.7   *Logistic regression models of party identity, autumn 1997*

	Conservative	Labour	Liberal Democrat	SNP
Constant	–11.01	2.53	–0.68	–1.50
Class cleavage				
Social class (salariat):				
Routine non-manual	–1.19*	0.71**	–0.06	–0.39
Petty bourgeoisie	–0.56	–0.12	0.44	0.22
Manual foremen	–0.82	0.62	0.03	–0.30
Working class	–0.87*	0.85**	–1.06	–0.12
Housing tenure (owner-occupier)				
Rents: local authority	–0.21	0.04	0.32	0.03
Rents: other	0.05	–0.28	0.39	–0.26
Working-class identity	–0.35	0.25	–0.75	0.19
Socialist–*laissez-faire* scale	0.39**	–0.14**	–0.07	–0.01
Religious cleavage				
Religion (Protestant)				
Catholic	–1.25*	1.64**	–2.63	–1.43**
Other	–0.47	0.27	0.26	–0.45
Libertarian–authoritarian scale	0.20**	–0.05	–0.04	–0.00
National cleavage				
National identity (equally Scottish and British)				
Scottish not British	–1.07**	–0.09	–2.63*	1.21**
Scottish more than British	–0.78*	0.14	0.36	0.34
British more than Scottish	0.89	–0.29	–0.25	–0.50
British not Scottish	1.02	–1.89**	2.03**	–5.93
Supports independence	–0.94*	–0.36	–1.01*	1.71**
Other variables				
Gender (female)	0.97**	–0.22	–0.08	–0.08
Age (in years)	0.00	0.00	0.01	–0.02*

Notes: * indicates coefficient significant at 0.05; ** indicates coefficient significant at 0.01. For details of methods used and measurement of the variables see the Appendix to this chapter.
Source: Scottish Referendum Study, 1997.

not available on the referendum study was the scale of British national sentiment; however this variable was not a significant predictor of support in Scotland at the 1997 general election and so its omission from these models should make only a marginal difference to the findings. In addition we have included only one dummy variable for constitutional preference, independence v. all others as it is assumed that this will be the main line of debate once the parliament has had its first elections. The results of these models are shown in Table 12.7

The models presented in Table 12.7 suggest that it would be wrong to write off allegiances based on national identity. In each of the models, national identity is a significant predictor of support. The rest of the coefficients in the models are very similar to those for vote in the 1997 general election. This suggests that there may well be a new cleavage in Scottish politics around issues of national identity. It also suggests that should this dimension remain strong, the parties may need to find new ways to assert their 'Scottishness' to the electorate.[9]

Conclusions: A Critical Election?

Where, then, does this leave the theory of critical elections? We have already argued that we do not believe that the 1997 election in Scotland was critical in the way implied by the theory. Elsewhere we have shown that voters largely voted in the same way as they did in 1992; the issues and campaigns of the parties were also similar to 1992 (Brown *et al.* 1998: Chap. 3). There were no new issues or alignments: a large majority of the electorate voted (or refrained from voting) in the same way at both elections. The dramatic nature of the results, which saw the Conservative Party left with no Scottish representatives in Westminster, was due to the workings of the electoral system and not to a sudden realignment of the electorate.

Returning to the party fortunes shown in Figure 12.1, in Scotland if any election since 1945 has been critical it must be that of October 1974. It was this contest which changed the shape of party competition in Scotland. The emergence of the SNP as a strong electoral presence altered alignments on a durable basis. In addition, the October 1974 election placed the issue of constitutional reform on the electoral agenda. As we have shown in Table 12.6 in the 1997 general election this issue continued to be a strong predictor of support for the parties in Scotland but not in England. This suggests that these parts of the British state realigned in different ways and at different times. Furthermore, the analysis presented in Table 12.7 suggests that the realignment that occurred around issues of constitutional reform and national identity is enduring, even beyond the issue that first triggered it. The one thing we can be sure of is that elections will continue to be played out on a political stage that is influenced by both old and new social cleavages. It will be the party that manages to appeal to the electorate along a mix of those cleavages that will be successful.

Notes

1. For the purposes of this chapter Wales is excluded from analysis. Although it too has had four parties competing at general elections and provides an important comparison with Scotland the number of Welsh cases in the BES sample is too small to allow comparisons to be made.
2. Here and elsewhere constitutional change refers to the issue of the government of Scotland and not to other wider constitutional changes. It is this issue which is salient for Scottish politics and the 1997 election.
3. Here we are using a measure of dual-nationality developed by Luis Moreno in 1986.
4. All survey data are problematic in understanding complex patterns of personal identity. In this case it is further complicated as we cannot be sure which is the prior variable. Here we treat constitutional preference as the dependent variable, and similarly later we treat vote as dependent on constitutional preference. In order to disentangle these issues panel data would be required but even given panel data in the absence of either a very large sample size or a large proportion of respondents who changed one or more of the identities or preferences it would be almost impossible to analyse these issues statistically.
5. Similar models were also run for the earlier years. These showed broadly similar patterns to those reported in Table 12.5 although direct comparisons are not possible due to the unavailability of measures of national identity in the earlier surveys.
6. For details of the operationalization and measurement of these variables, see the Appendix to this chapter.
7. See Brown *et al.* (1998: Chap. 4) for a discussion of how a position on the attitude scales relates to measures of social location in Scotland.
8. The lack of significant coefficients for those who felt British more than Scottish or British not Scottish is likely to be explained by the very small numbers in those groups.
9. For further analysis of this data and a discussion of the likely direction politics in Scotland may take, see Brown *et al.* (1998: Chap. 7).

Appendix

The models presented in Tables 12.5, 12.6 and 12.7 are based on logistic regression analysis. This technique is appropriate when the outcome (dependent) variable is a binary measure; for example, voted Conservative v. did not vote Conservative.

The value scales used in the models were each constructed from six questionnaire items. The socialist–*laissez-faire* and libertarian–authoritarian scales are described in the Technical Appendix. The British national sentiment scale was constructed as follows:

British national sentiment
1) Britain has a lot to learn from other countries in running its affairs.
2) I would rather be a citizen of Britain than any other country in the world.
3) There are some things about Britain today that make me ashamed to be British.
4) People in Britain are too ready to criticize their country.
5) The government of Britain should do everything it can to keep all parts of Britain together in a single state.
6) Britain should co-operate with other countries, even if it means giving up some independence.

In each case the possible responses were 'strongly agree, agree, neither, disagree, strongly disagree'. The items have been recoded so that they are in the same direction (for example, so that liberal responses all correspond to the 'agree' end of the responses), and then added together to produce two scales with a range of 6–30. Low values on the scales represent the socialist, liberal and 'nationalist' positions respectively.

The value scales are treated in the models as continuous independent variables. For each of the categorical variables used, dummy variables were entered for each category except the reference category which is shown in brackets within the tables. Working-class identity and gender are binary variables.

13 Dynamic Representation in Britain

Mark Franklin and Christina Hughes

Was the election of 1997 a critical election? The size of the Labour landslide was certainly surprising, but surprise has to do with poor prediction, not with underlying changes in the basis of voting choice. If there has been a critical election in Britain since 1945 we suggest that it was the election of October 1974, not that of 1997.

Yet the major change that has occurred in British politics in recent years is very hard to date because processes of change took several elections to work themselves out. From one perspective, the change can be dated to as early as 1970, the first general election in which class voting broke down to any substantial degree, yielding a great many Conservative votes from individuals who would in previous elections have voted Labour and (more importantly) many Labour votes from those who previously would have voted Tory (Crewe *et al.* 1977; Franklin 1982). From a different perspective the change can be dated to as late as 1983, the first general election to show that the postwar party system itself was at risk. We choose to focus on October 1974 as the critical election in this sequence partly because that was the first one in which the new issue basis of voting choice manifested itself in an election outcome that was clearly different from what would have been possible in what Samuel Beer once called the 'collectivist age' (Beer 1965). We want to argue that the general election of October 1974 marked the start of a new age in British electoral politics, whereas that of May 1997 was just a milestone to mark its progress.

In this chapter we are going to do more than just defend the contention that the decline of class voting in Britain was the critical development leading eventually to the results of the 1997 British general election (Franklin 1985). That would be merely to go over old ground. Instead we are going to paint a picture of evolving British politics in elections starting with that of 1974 that, we will argue, is a picture of dynamic adaptation of parties to voters' issue concerns, and of voters to parties' issue stances – a picture quite different in important respects from any that could have been painted during the collectivist age. We will also suggest that, within a broader perspective, the collectivist age itself can be viewed as an episode in what, in the American context, Stimson *et al.* (1995) have called 'dynamic representation'. What happened with the decline of class voting was that previous limits on the scope of British politics were removed, allowing the issue basis of electoral choice to expand from a single dimension into more than one dimension so that dynamic representation became possible on a more general basis than before. The removal of these temporary limits also permitted party support to vary more greatly than it could have done before, laying the basis for upset elections of every kind – including the landslide of 1997.

The Responsive Public

One seldom-noted requirement for the proper functioning of democratic institutions is public responsiveness to policy. There is, after all, little reason to expect politicians to pay attention to what the public wants if the public does not pay attention to what politicians do. A responsive public would adjust its preference for 'more' or 'less' policy in reaction to policy itself, much like a thermostat (Wlezien 1995). This argument has been made most forcibly in relation to particular policy domains such as defence spending in the USA (Wlezien 1996) and integration policies in the countries of the European Union (Franklin and Wlezien 1997). In the context of this chapter, however, we want to take a broader perspective, more along the lines of Stimson's *Public Opinion in America* (1991) in which public opinion was characterized as exhibiting broad swings in mood over periods measured in decades. Later on, this insight was linked to Wlezien's concept of thermostatic control, regarding the changes in mood as manifesting a feedback mechanism by which voters react to the changing policy environment (Stimson *et al.* 1995).

To put it simply, in this account voters have policy demands that are catered to by parties and candidates. Parties win office to meet those demands. If the demands are satisfied then voters do not necessarily want more of the same; and if more of the same is rammed down their throats they can react quite dramatically against those who do the ramming. We feel that the outcome of the British general election of 1997 is best understood in such terms. By continuing to produce Thatcherite policy long after Thatcher had been replaced as leader, the Conservative Party was unresponsive to the changing mood of the British electorate and the public reacted by throwing them out. Pippa Norris has shown how attitudes to privatization, trade union reform and moral traditionalism – attitudes that had became dramatically supportive of Mrs Thatcher's policies during the late 1970s – had swung back again by 1992 to resemble those of the 1960s (Norris 1997: 165–9; cf. Crewe and Searing 1988). Party control of government eventually followed suit.

Much of British electoral history can be understood in similar terms. The decline of class voting can be seen, as one of the present authors argued in 1985, as a consequence of the delayed realization that the socialist project in Britain had essentially been completed by 1950 and that subsequent Labour governments had nothing substantial to add that would bring about a 'socialist Britain' (Franklin 1985: 174). The earlier rise of the Labour Party can do doubt be seen in terms of a reaction against the limitations of nineteenth-century Liberalism. One could continue to trace the swing of the political pendulum backwards in time indefinitely in such terms.

Still, there is an important difference between the swings prior to what Särlvik and Crewe (1983) called the 'decade of dealignment' and those that followed. Before 1970, swings that occurred from one election to the next were limited because established voters were 'immunized' against change (Butler and Stokes 1974). In those days, large changes in the fortunes of political parties had to await the slow emergence of new generations of voters. Small changes from one election to the next could be accomplished by those who were not yet party loyalists, but landslides were possible only in elections that saw the entry of large numbers of new voters (see Franklin and Ladner 1995 for an analysis of the Labour victory of 1945 in these terms). After 1974, however, increasingly larger swings became possible because increasingly fewer voters were immunized against change (Franklin 1985). Moreover, in 1974, the terms of political discourse started to show their liberation from class concerns, so that not only could the swing of the pendulum become more dramatic in extent, it could also respond to dramatically new issues. The first politician to benefit from this enlargement of the issue space was the leader of the previously tiny Liberal Party, Mr Thorpe, in 1974. The first change of government resulting from the enlargement happened with Mrs Thatcher's victory in 1979. But what goes around comes around, and every swing of the political pendulum presages an eventual opposite swing. Except for the fact that the left vote in Britain became split after 1982, the pendulum might well have swung back in 1987 (or most certainly in 1992). By 1997 such a swing was long overdue. So the size of the 1997 swing can perhaps be explained as the result of two developments: 1) the removal of a straitjacket that previously would have inhibited the extent of any swing; and 2) the accumulated demand for change whose realization had been blocked by the split on the centre-left.

This story is not one amenable to empirical testing on the basis of data collected in the British Election Studies. However, in the remainder of this chapter we will show that the impact of class and issues on party choice in the years leading up to 1997 is consistent with the general picture given above.

The Evolving Issue Space of British Politics

In characterizing the years after the Second World War as the 'collectivist age' in Britain, Samuel Beer (1965) had in mind a political discourse in which other axes (particularly the libertarian–authoritarian axis) had been squeezed out by the dominance of class–orientated concerns. Both the major parties competed along a dimension that assumed a high level of government involvement in social and economic life, differing only in terms of who should be the major beneficiaries of government largesse. With the decline of class voting, this dominance of class–orientated concerns started to erode and new issues sprang up to compete for voter support. In particular, concern for the rights of minorities and women, and devolution of government powers of all kinds, started to distinguish a 'new left' electorate from an 'old left' more concerned with traditional issues of pensions, job protection, poverty and the like (Graham and Clarke 1986: xii). On the right of the political spectrum, a new concern for school choice and privatization of all kinds started to distinguish a 'new right' electorate from an 'old right' which retained traditional concerns about law and order, defence spending and overly generous handouts to the poor (cf. Jenkins 1987: 375; Norris 1997: 154–6). In other work, one of the present authors (Franklin 1988) has shown how these new issues can be seen to have moved progressively between 1974 and 1983 to distinguish themselves on a dimension at right angles to the traditional left–right dimension. Figure 13.1 shows the resulting issue space in 1983, defined by factor analysis of 39 issues about which respondents were asked in the

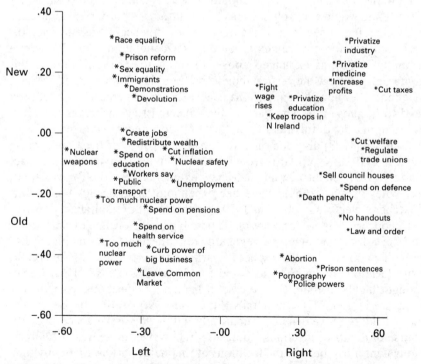

FIGURE 13.1   *The issue space of the British electorate in 1983, represented in two dimensions defined by factor loadings*

British Election Study of that year (see Franklin 1988 for details of how the analysis was performed).[2]

The way to think of this illustration is as depicting issues in proximity to each other when the positions concerned tended to be held by the same people (respondents to the 1983 British Election Study survey), and at a distance from each other when the positions concerned tended to be held by different people. Thus race equality is depicted about as far as it possibly could be from prison sentencing, because those who want tougher prison sentences are not at all the same people who are concerned that society should treat different races more equally. On the other hand, such concerns tend to be held by very much the same people who believe that prisons should be reformed – and so those two variables are depicted quite close to each other. The orientation of the variables on the basis of factor analysis is entirely arbitrary. However we have manually rotated the space until the lower half of the horizontal dimension resembles the familiar left–right spectrum contrasting those who would tax and spend on services with those who would not, those who support big business with those who support trade union power, those who support more income equality with those who do not and so on. Other issues then take up the positions they need to take up in order to retain the proximities discovered by factor analysis.

How the vertical dimension should be characterized is not completely clear. Some would certainly see it as a 'libertarian/authoritarian' dimension but we prefer to see it in terms of the re-emergence of debate over the desirability of non-governmental solutions to economic and social problems (Franklin 1988), as explained above. In order to forestall unproductive argument as to how the vertical dimension should be characterized, we have labelled it the 'new/old' dimension because the issues in the lower quadrants tend to be those that date back to the collectivist age, whereas the issues in the upper quadrants tend to be those of more recent vintage.

Franklin (1988) also demonstrated that new votes for the Conservative Party in 1979 came primarily from the new right quadrant of the issue space (though also from the new left, to a lesser extent). Indeed, the Tories actually *lost* votes in what should have been their old right stronghold. So Mrs Thatcher's electoral victory in 1979 was the result of capitalizing on new issue concerns – issue concerns made possible by the decline of class voting and the consequential loss of hegemony for collectivist notions. Figure 13.2 shows locations in the issue space of parties and party leaders, based on the issue locations of voters who voted for them (in the case of parties) or thought highly of them (in the case of leaders), in elections from 1974 to 1983 (see Franklin 1988 for details of these analyses). As can be seen, major party leaders moved quite dramatically within this issue space over the course of the three elections. Interestingly, however, there was virtually no equivalent movement in the locations of the major parties. Evidently their locations are determined by *what sort of people* vote for them rather than *how many people* vote for them, and their support can ebb and flow without

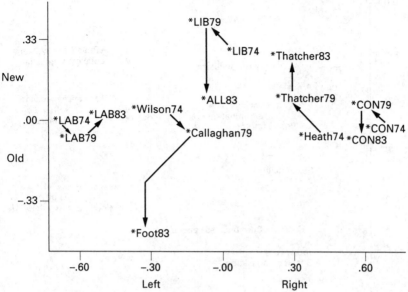

Notes:
1) Liberal /Alliance leaders suppressed to simplify presentation.
2) See Franklin (1988) for details of the analysis.

FIGURE 13.2   *Movement of the supporters of various parties (upper case) and leaders (lower case)* [1]*within the issue space, 1974–83*[2]

much affecting their locations in the issue space. However, if we want to understand why their support ebbs and flows we can perhaps get some clues by looking at movement in the location of party leaders. Such movements can be inferred from plots such as this one because if there are changes in the locations of respondents who think highly of someone, this is very likely because of movements in the locations of those who are being judged – or more properly in their *perceived* locations.

The plot shows clearly the changing perceptions of where the leaders stood in the two-dimensional issue space, with the Liberal Party being the first beneficiary of 'new' issue concerns, though its position was rapidly taken by Mrs Thatcher who, by 1983, had moved to dominate the upper half of the issue space. In this context, the fact that most new votes for Mrs Thatcher came from the upper quadrants is easily explicable in Downsian terms.

How can the events of the following 15 years be understood in similar terms? The first thing we need to establish is whether the issue space developed further after 1983, or whether it remained essentially unchanged. Figure 13.3 shows the locations of issues in 1997, on the same basis as they were shown for 1983 in Figure 13.1, by locating them according to their proximity with each other in two dimensions determined by factor analysis of the answers given by respondents to issue questions asked in the British

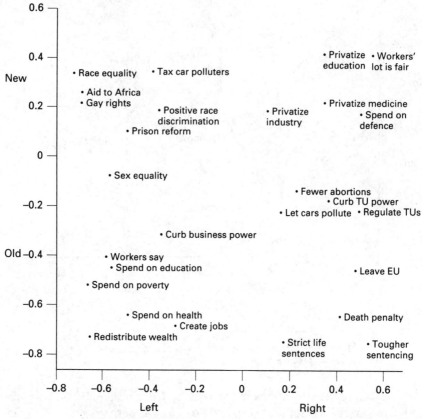

FIGURE 13.3 *The issue space of the British electorate in 1997, represented in two dimensions defined by factor loadings*

Election Study of that year. It shows what appears to be precisely the same issue space, with many variables occupying almost precisely the same locations, to within sampling error. On the left, race equality, spend on poverty and spend on health are unmoved, as are privatize medicine, regulate trade unions and tougher prison sentencing on the right. Other variables appear to have moved in understandable – even predictable – ways. Those who want to leave the Common Market have become those who want to leave the European Union and have moved from the far left to the far right of the lower half of the issue space (consistent with arguments made elsewhere in this volume). Some issues that were central to the left as a whole in 1983 (the idea that government should create jobs, for instance) had moved far down into the old left quadrant by 1997. At the same time, some issues that were well up in the new left quadrant (sex equality) or well down in the old left quadrant (curb business power) have moved to occupy the middle ground in left-wing opinion. Similar changes have occurred on the right, where privatization and anti-abortion sentiments have moved towards the middle ground.

But the most important way in which the issue space in 1997 differs from that in 1983 is that the vertical dimension has continued the trend established before 1983 (Franklin 1988) of expanding relative to the horizontal dimension. In 1983 the vertical dimension spanned a range of about –0.5 to +0.3 in standard deviation units, while in 1997 it spanned a range from almost –0.8 to +0.4 – a 50% increase in its total span. The range encompassed by the horizontal dimension, meanwhile, remained about constant at –0.6 to +0.6 (see Appendix to this chapter for details of the factor and regression analyses conducted for this chapter).[3]

Accounting for Voting Choice

How can issues help to account for party choice? One way to answer this question is to place the parties and candidates within an issue space defined for the years 1987–97, as was done in Figure 13.2 for the years 1974–83. We did this for the later period by running a new set of factor analyses in which the variables employed were restricted to those that all three surveys had in common, and obtaining the correlation with each factor of support for particular parties and preferences for particular candidates.[4] These correlations were then used as x–y co-ordinates to plot the positions of the parties and candidates just as we had earlier plotted the positions of variables. As in years leading up to 1983 (Figure 13.2), the movement of parties is not as interesting as the movement of leaders, and in this case the parties occupy locations that overlap with the locations of leaders so that party locations have been suppressed in the interests of clarity. The resulting plot, shown in Figure 13.4, displays a number of contrasts with the picture, shown in Figure 13.2, for 1974–83.

In the first place, despite the continued expansion of the vertical dimension of the issue space over the period, most of the movement of parties (not shown) and candidates was horizontal, in contrast to the movement that occurred between 1974 and 1983 which was almost entirely in the vertical dimension. It is as though the period between 1983 and 1987 saw the acceptance by all party leaders of the new basis for competition between the parties, allowing them to present themselves in very similar terms on this dimension. By 1987, the Labour leader (now Neil

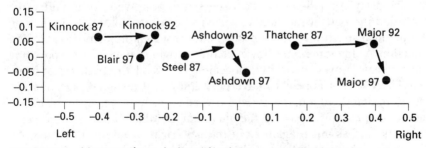

FIGURE 13.4   *Movement of party leaders within the issue space, 1987–97*

Kinnock) had repudiated the old left stance associated with Michael Foot in 1983 (see Figure 13.2), and was placed even slightly above Mrs Thatcher (who had herself somewhat moderated her stance) on this dimension.

In the second place, the movement by all party leaders was not only horizontal, but also largely towards the right. This had the effect of moving Labour towards the centre-ground, and of moving the Conservatives away from it. Noteworthy, however, is that between 1992 and 1997 there was much less movement in this direction by the leader of any party. Instead, all three party leaders moved slightly downwards, towards a more collectivist orientation to political concerns.

The net result of all these perceived movements was to leave the Labour leader centrally placed on the new/old dimension, and much closer to the middle than was the Conservative leader on the left/right dimension, while the Conservative leader seems to have been viewed as moving deep into the old right quadrant. This is more or less what commentators suggested was happening, though the movement towards the centre associated with Blair's new leadership appears to have been uniquely on the new/old dimension. If these movements are thought of along the same lines as Mrs Thatcher's perceived changes of location in 1974–83, we can view Tony Blair as having taken up a strategic position that would make him the natural standard-bearer for both new and old left voters, whereas we could view John Major's retreat as being intended to defend the traditional bastions of Tory orthodoxy.

In contrast to the earlier period, however, the outcome (in terms of where votes for the two main parties came from in the issue space) appears to have been somewhat different from what would have happened had all these strategies been successful. Table 13.1 divides the issue space into four quadrants, and shows the extent to which parties gained or lost votes in each quadrant between 1992 and 1997.[5] It shows that the Labour Party gained votes almost equally from the new and old left quadrants, in line with Blair's location midway between the two. This shift seems consistent with the changes in patterns of party competition observed earlier in the book. Chapter 1 found that Labour Party manifestos moved decisively towards social conservatism from 1992 to 1997 while Chapter 2 confirmed a similar shift in the attitudes and values of Labour politicians. Apparently some voters, who previously had thought the Labour Party too far away from them in the issue space, perceived these shifts and rewarded the party with their votes. With regard to voters on the left of the political spectrum, all these independent indicators point in a similar direction. At the same time, however, on the right of the political spectrum the strategic moves made by Mr Major to defend the bastions of Tory orthodoxy do not appear to have paid equivalent dividends. Despite his moves in that direction, the Tories suffered a haemorrhage of votes in the old right quadrant which is the quadrant in which Labour won most converts: half as much again as in the new right quadrant. It is possible that New Labour's rhetoric ('Tough on Crime, Tough on the Causes of

TABLE 13.1 *Changes in the percentage of voters in each quadrant, 1992–97*

		Left			Right	
New	Con	−9.9		Con	−14.9	
	Lib	−3.2		Lib	+2.3	
	Lab	+16.3		Lab	+13.6	
Old	Con	−10.0		Con	−24.6	
	Lib	−1.0		Lib	+6.1	
	Lab	+17.2		Lab	+20.6	

Source: BES, 1992–97

Crime') had particular appeal to this quadrant; but we still must ask ourselves how the Conservative Party came to lose so much credibility in its heartland that even well directed appeals by an Opposition party could have had so much effect.

Accounting for Party Choice in 1997

The pattern of shifting loyalties shown in Table 13.1 cannot be used to validate our assumption that dynamic representation is occurring in Britain. That would take quite different data. We do not have measures of how satisfied voters were with the responsiveness of their government from election to election. Nor do we have measures of voters' reactions to policy outputs except in a few idiosyncratic policy areas. Nevertheless, the pattern we see is consistent with the story told at the start of this chapter, and even fleshes out that story in some respects. The strategic moves made by Tony Blair to position himself at the centre of the left-hand side of the issue space, and much closer to the centre of the left/right spectrum than John Major, would probably have guaranteed a Labour victory. Voters who positioned themselves to his left had nowhere else to go and those who were to his right, but closer to his new position than they were to Mr Major, could have been expected (according to Downsian logic) to defect to Labour in some numbers. What made the resulting victory into a rout for the Tories was the fact that millions of Tory voters who located themselves in the heartland of old Tory orthodoxy also defected, despite the fact that John Major was positioned much closer to them in the issue space than was Tony Blair. This aspect of the outcome is hard to understand in conventional Downsian terms of voters supporting candidates who are closest to them ideologically. According to Downsian logic, Labour's greatest gains should have come from the New Right quadrant, which Major had abandoned in his downward policy shift and many of whose voters would consequently have found themselves much closer to Blair.

It is hard to make sense of the vote–switching we observe in the right-hand quadrants except in terms of massive disillusionment on the part of traditional Tories with the 'new' Conservative policies once championed by Mrs Thatcher and left as a legacy to her party. The Tories lost almost twice as many votes in their traditional heartland as they did in Mrs

Thatcher's territory, the New Right quadrant.

Nevertheless, there is another possible conventional explanation for the pattern of switching that we observe, which would be that many working-class voters who had been wooed by Thatcher waited until 1997 to return to the Labour Party fold. Class voting did increase after 1987. Does this account for the movements we observe? To address this question we ran a series of regression analyses to predict Conservative voting in elections from 1987 to 1997. In order to assure comparability between the years, only those variables were employed which had been asked in similar terms in all three election studies (the same variables as were used in the factor analyses reported earlier). The findings reported in Table 13.2 are suggestive. There the EU issue has been abstracted from the rest and placed in a separate column. Class effects are the sum of the effects of parents' class, education, occupation and union membership. Issue effects are the sum of the effects of 23 issue variables available in all three studies in similar terms, and already employed in the factor analysis whose results are detailed in the Appendix to this chapter (excluding attitude to the European Union). In the 'total' column the European Union issue is added to the rest (see the Appendix for details).

Clearly evident in Table 13.2 is the fact that class effects more than doubled between 1987 and 1992, dropping only somewhat in 1997, though it should be borne in mind that all these effects are very low compared to class effects measured in the 1960s (Franklin 1985: 145n). Issue effects remained high throughout the period (much higher than in the 1970s) but with a notable drop of 19% between 1992 and 1997 (a drop which amounted to a quarter of the earlier year's value). This drop is quite anomalous, because when voters change their party allegiance it is logical to expect them to do so as a result of issue preferences. So issue voting is generally stronger among switchers than among non-switchers (Franklin 1985: 136). The only other reason that conventional wisdom provides for a change of allegiance is a return to deep-rooted party preferences after an earlier defection. But deep-rooted party preferences in Britain are expected to be class based, and class voting saw no increase between 1992 and 1997 – indeed, if anything, the class column in Table 13.2 shows the reverse. So analysis of issue voting reinforces our findings based on issue locations. From both perspectives conventional explanations of party choice would leave us scrambling to account for voters' decisions in 1997. To explain what happened we need to introduce a consideration new to British voting

Table 13.2 *Total effects of class and issues on Conservative voting, 1987–97*

Year	R^2	Class	Non–EU issues	EU issue	Total issues
1987	0.496	0.117	0.634	0.023	0.657
1992	0.498	0.276	0.737	0.030	0.767
1997	0.328	0.237	0.566	0.005	0.571

Source: BES, 1987–97

studies, a sort of *deus ex machina*, to account for behaviour that would otherwise be anomalous. We have already indicated the nature of the explanation that we think is needed.

The Dynamics of Representation in Britain

The British general election of 1997 was not the first to occasion surprise. Commentators were also surprised by the outcome of the 1992 election. In 1992 they were surprised by the small magnitude of the swing against the Tories. In 1997 they were surprised by the extent of the swing. If we do not regard the 1997 election outcome as a stand-alone result, but instead view it in the light of the result in 1992, we can envision an explanation that goes something as follows. By 1992 the British electorate, which had never given Mrs Thatcher's party an outright majority, were tired of Thatcherite policies. They would not necessarily undo her reforms, but they wanted no more of them. Opinion polls presaged a Tory defeat in 1992. Voters confidently expected that if they retained their current preferences the Tories would indeed be defeated.

But the polls were wrong. The Tories were not defeated in 1992. Frustrated voters who might have changed long-standing party allegiances, had they realized that this would be necessary in order to throw the rascals out, geared themselves up to do exactly that in 1997. And in 1997 many of them did not believe the opinion polls. They wanted to make sure that this time there was no mistake. So long-standing Tory voters abandoned their party in large numbers in 1997, even though opinion polls had made it clear that such large-scale defections were not needed.

Such a picture cannot be verified with the data to hand. It views voters as interacting in a sophisticated fashion with policy outputs and predicted election outcomes – showing, indeed, more sophistication than generally expected by those who design election studies. To verify the picture's accuracy we would need richer data in which elections are not seen in isolation from each other, or from the nature of the policy outputs that accumulate over time when one party dominates the political agenda of a nation.[6] So the picture may be wrong. But the picture is above all consistent with the view that since 1974 voters have no longer been tied down by allegiance to social groups, and that in their new-found freedom they behave quite differently than they used to behave before the decline of class voting (or, more generally, before the decline of cleavage politics – see Franklin *et al.* 1992).

The main reason why many commentators believed that the election of 1997 was a realigning election was because of the size of the vote swing and seat turnover that occurred in that year. When change in political allegiances could arise only from the enlargement or replacement of large portions of the electorate, large swings really meant something. Now large swings can occur for no better reason than that many voters become fed up with the status quo. The size of the swing is no longer any guarantee of its durability. Indeed the very fact that the swing occurs makes it likely that there will be a swing back again. We have already referred to the well established tendency for erstwhile defectors to return to the fold at a later election. New voters do not do that. They have no prior allegiance to return to. But new voters are no longer the only ones responsible for electoral change. So the message of this chapter is that there is today much more to voting than class and issues, and the election of 1997 brings us face to face with this fact. Ironically, however, election studies as currently conducted are not well suited to studying the dynamics of representation in the postcollectivist age.

Notes

1   The contention has been disputed by Heath *et al.* (1985, 1990) on the basis of several different arguments which in turn were disputed by Crewe (1986) giving rise to a response by Heath *et al.* (1987). Franklin (1988) has pointed out that there is no disagreement about the fact that there was lower class voting after 1970 than before; merely about whether this drop should be characterized as a 'decline'.

2.   The issue space is presented in two dimensions mainly for heuristic reasons: that is the largest number of dimensions that can conveniently be displayed on the (two-dimensional) page of a book. But exploratory analysis has shown us that if we had pulled out another dimension it would have consisted uniquely of the European question. With only one issue defining the dimension, it would be impossible to tell whether any movements observed were due to changes in the definition of the issue or changes in the positions of parties and candidates. By embedding the European issue in a two-dimensional space we can see how far that issue has moved in relation to other issues.

3.   Of course this new dominance of new–old issues could be partly the result of changes in the questions asked, but if those who planned the 1997 election study asked more questions that distinguished voters on new–old terms, this was presumably because those questions were judged to be the more important ones.

4.   The party support variables were dummy variables derived from questions that asked respondents which party they had voted for. The candidate preference variables were derived from questions that asked respondents whether each candidate would make a good prime minister. Correlations with particular factors are precisely what was used to place the issues within the spaces depicted in Figures 13.1 and 13.3, so the locations of parties and candidates shown in Figures 13.2 and 13.4 are consistent with those depictions.

5.   It does this by counting the proportion of Labour, Conservative and Liberal Democrat voters in each quadrant (Alliance voters in 1987), and subtracting the proportions found voting for each party in 1997 from the proportions found voting for the same party in 1992.

6.   Some questions asked in the British Election Study of 1997 do have an appropriate format. Questions asking whether reforms had 'gone too far . . .' applied to government policies at the centre of the Thatcherite revolution would have enabled us to gauge the extent of disillusion. Taken in conjunction with suitable questions about the expected outcome of the

election, such questions would have enabled us to ascertain whether voters who switched other than in accord with Downsian logic were those who 1) felt the Thatcher revolution had gone too far and who 2) nevertheless feared that the Tories might win. Unfortunately, the question format 'gone too far ...' was used only in regard to certain policies and above all not to policies regarding privatization and trade union power.

Appendix

Factor Analysis

The factor scores used to create the issue space for Figure 13.3 were obtained by running principal axis factor analysis on 27 issue variables. The factor scores after varimax rotation (but prior to manual rotation) are listed below.

To create the issue space for Figure 13.4 only issue variables that were present for all of the years 1987, 1992 and 1997 were used. There were 24 of these. The factor scores were obtained by the principal axis factor method, and the rotated factor scores were obtained by using varimax rotation. The loadings for the rotated factor scores (prior to manual rotation) and the eigenvalues are listed below for each year separately.

The vote variables were plotted into the factor space by first creating dummy variables for each of the party votes, coded 1 for those who supported the party and 0 for others. These variables were created separately for each year. Correlations were then run between the vote variables and the factor scores for each year. These correlations were then used to plot the vote variables in the issue space. The candidate variables are dummy variables created from the survey question *Who would make the best Prime Minister?* Correlations were then ran between the candidate dummy variables and the factor scores for each year and used as x–y co-ordinates to plot the candidate variables. It is important to note that these variables are located in relation to the variables that define the issue space. Had they been plotted on the same page their proximity to specific issues would have been manifest.

Regression Analysis

A separate regression analysis was run for each year. The class variables used in the regression were dummy variables created for parent's class, education, occupation and union. In each case the variables were coded 1 to represent the class characteristics associated with left voting (see Franklin, 1985 for discussion of these variables). The class variables were then entered into the regression equation along with all the issue variables that were used in the factor analysis. Only variables that were present in all years were used in the analysis. The European Union variable was presented separately due to the fact that the original factor analysis demonstrated that the EU variable could reasonably be represented as occupying a dimension of its own. The regressions are presented below for each year separately.

Rotated factor matrix for all issues

1997

Variables	factor 1	factor 2
REDUCE ABORTIONS	−0.02388	0.150579
LEAVE EU	0.46194	−0.44438
PRIVATIZE EDUCATION	0.49951	0.4078
SPEND ON POVERTY	−0.6577	−0.51714
PRIVATIZE MEDICINE	0.346867	0.18493
SPEND ON HEALTH	−0.49214	−0.63751
SPEND ON EDUCATION	−0.55614	−0.44472
AID TO AFRICA	−0.6825	0.2548
SPEND ON DEFENCE	0.4846	0.1662
PRIVATIZE INDUSTRY	0.26299	0.1768
REGULATE TUS	0.4949	−0.2269
WORKERS SAY	−0.5753	−0.4052
REDISTRIBUTE WEALTH	−0.65073	−0.73041
TOUGHER SENTENCES	−0.5382	0.7605
LET CARS POLLUTE	0.39894	−0.22859
TAX CAR POLLUTERS	−0.37592	0.335681
PRISON REFORM	−0.04846	0.099
STRICT LIFE SENTENCES	−0.4629	0.7483
POSITIVE RACE DISCRIMINATION	−0.64791	0.178639
GAY RIGHTS	−0.6827	0.2148
RACE EQUALITY	−0.7116	0.3355
SEX EQUALITY	−0.5634	−0.0805
CURB TU POWER	0.37066	−0.18676
CURB BUSINESS POWER	−0.33991	−0.31381
WORKERS' LOT IS FAIR	0.5671	0.4006
CREATE JOBS	−0.2843	−0.6818
DEATH PENALTY	0.68039	−0.65492
Eigenvalues	3.53	2.25

Note: Factor 1 explains 13.09% of the variance. Factor 2 explains 8.35% of the variance. Together the two factors explain 21.44% of the variance.

1987: rotated factor matrix for issues common to all years

Variables	factor 1	factor 2
ABORTION	−0.00442	0.17217
CURB BUSINESS POWER	0.274726	−0.12566
CENSORSHIP	−0.0659	0.346926
GAY RIGHTS	−0.16574	0.454126
RACE EQUALITY	−0.19165	0.519265
SEX EQUALTIY	−0.21573	0.312567
DEATH PENALTY	−0.07042	0.664734
DEFENCE SPENDING	0.430628	−0.24127
LEAVE EU	−0.2281	−0.27088
WORKERS' LOT FAIR	0.651877	0.041888
AID TO AFRICA	0.170497	−0.48018
SPEND ON EDUCATION	0.436053	−0.13883
CREATE JOBS	0.610107	−0.0502
SPEND ON HEALTH	0.559144	−0.04519
HANDOUTS	−0.38842	0.463064
PRIVATIZE MEDICINE	−0.4547	0.153716
PRIVATIZE INDUSTRY	0.577354	−0.16558

PRIVATIZE EDUCATION	0.59999	−0.0803
REDISTRIBUTE WEALTH	0.652945	−0.01087
SPEND ON POVERTY	0.514639	−0.10017
TOUGHER SENTENCING	−0.01841	0.633063
REGULATE TUS	0.465369	−0.17725
CURB TU POWER	−0.47938	0.31704
WORKRS SAY	0.323534	−0.05591
Eignevalues	4.7	1.7

Note: Factor 1 explains 19.78% of the variance. Factor 2 explains 7.07% of the variance. Together the two factors explain 27% of the variance.

1992: rotated factor matrix for issues common to all years

Variables	factor 1	factor 2
ABORTION	0.00	0.138594
CURB BUSINESS POWER	0.363783	−0.00498
GAY RIGHTS	−0.088	0.461905
RACIAL EQUALITY	−0.10035	0.557411
SEX EQUALITY	−0.20987	0.332386
DEATH PENALTY	−0.01655	0.633484
DEFENCE SPENDING	0.250786	−0.28514
LEAVE EU	−0.08023	−0.34562
FAIRSHARE	0.481988	−0.03546
AID TO AFRICA	0.113176	−0.48245
SPEND ON EDUCATION	0.503205	−0.13322
SPEND ON HEALTH	0.624104	0.013123
CREATE JOBS	0.592743	0.019623
HANDOUTS	−0.3203	0.48386
PRIVATIZE MEDICINE	−0.36875	0.161329
CENSORSHIP	0.080822	0.23849
PRIVATIZE INDUSTRY	0.531536	−0.03835
PRIVATIZE EDUCATION	0.459166	−0.10522
REDISTRIBUTE WEALTH	0.642597	−0.01773
SPEND ON POVERTY	0.580333	−0.06194
TOUGHER SENTENCING	0.014527	0.583354
CURB TU POWER	−0.1402	0.299245
REGULATE TUS	−0.23815	0.398019
WORKERS SAY	0.337447	−0.07602
Eigenvalues	3.7	1.92

Note: Factor 1 explains 15.40% of the variance. Factor 2 explains 8.00% of the variance. Together the factors explain 23% of the variance.

1997: rotated factor matrix for issues common to all years

Variables	factor 1	factor 2
ABORTION	0.049245	0.232816
CURB BUSINESS POWER	0.295628	0.04692
CENSORSHIP	0.028709	0.294812
GAY RIGHTS	0.21783	0.49888
MINORITY EQUALITY	0.218808	0.513678
SEX EQUALITY	0.315133	0.248265
DEATH PENALTY	0.007879	0.634055
SPEND ON DEFENCE	−0.3392	−0.15672
LEAVE EU	−0.00447	−0.46121
FAIRSHARE	0.453557	0.113407

AID TO AFRICA	−0.22278	−0.44613
SPEND ON EDUCATION	0.544467	0.039299
SPEND ON HEALTH	0.601846	−0.07472
CREATE JOBS	0.475804	−0.18155
PRIVATIZE MEDICINE	−0.26933	−0.14035
PRIVATIZE INDUSTRY	−0.187	−0.05972
PRIVATIZE EDUCATION	−0.424	−0.12961
SPEND ON POVERTY	0.603695	0.063197
TOUGHER SENTENCING	−0.1205	0.608399
REGULATE TUS	0.109883	0.408843
CURB TU POWER	−0.07168	−0.2958
WORKERS SAY	0.429358	0.124648
Eigenvalues	2.98	1.73

Note: Factor 1 explains 13.53% of the variance. Factor 2 explains 7.84% of the variance. Together the two factors explain 22% of the variance.

1987: Regression analysis for common variables

	Unstandardized coefficient		Standardized Coefficient
	B	*Std. Error*	*beta*
(Constant)	0.12042	0.169506	
REDUCE ABORTIONS	−0.02086	0.013839	−0.03167
CURB BUSINESS POWER	−0.00921	0.014234	−0.01398
CENSORSHIP	−0.01507	0.010719	−0.0306
GAY RIGHTS	−0.01528	0.012532	−0.02792
RACE EQUALITY	−0.00934	0.012857	−0.01753
SEX EQUALITY	0.019227	0.014237	0.030151
DADCLASS	0.000725	0.025256	0.000627
DEATH PENALTY	−0.02586 **	0.009865	−0.06292
SPEND ON DEFENCE	0.040186***	0.007929	0.115331
LEAVE EU	−0.00156	0.023682	−0.00142
WORKERS' LOT IS FAIR	0.07962	0.012193	0.164176
AID TO AFRICA	0.002232	0.010284	0.005119
SPEND ON EDUCATION	−0.00679***	0.013547	−0.01198
CREATE JOBS	−0.06244***	0.013235	−0.11483
SPEND ON HEALTH	−0.05926***	0.015145	−0.1002
PRIVATIZE MEDICINE	0.037713***	0.009078	0.09803
PRIVATIZE INDUSTRY	0.086031***	0.014233	0.150934
OCCUPATION	0.021326	0.024213	0.019943
PRIVATIZE EDUCATION	0.039158***	0.01008	0.09663
SOCIAL CLASS	−0.03466	0.024626	−0.03088
REGULATE TUS	−0.01592	0.015481	−0.02586
CURB TU POWER	0.089186***	0.014112	0.162448
UNION MEMBER	−0.00887	0.022538	−0.00827
WORKS SAY	0.000435	0.010429	0.000894
YEARS OF EDUCATION	−0.05126*	0.026114	−0.04608

Dependent variable: VOTECON
R square = .496; *n* = 1276

Note: *** = sig. .000; ** sig. .01; * = sig. .05 (1992).

1992: Regression analysis for common variables

	Unstandardized coefficient		Standardized Coefficient
	B	Std. Error	beta
(Constant)	0.175826	0.255889	
REDUCE ABORTIONS	0.033927	0.017686	0.04893
YEARS OF EDUCATION	0.038164	0.030818	0.036073
CURB BUSINESS POWER	−0.04709	0.02897	−0.0425
CENSORSHIP	−0.01634	0.011602	−0.03648
GAY RIGHTS	−0.02113	0.014927	−0.04005
RACE EQUALITY	0.008861	0.015877	0.016555
SEX EQUALITY	−0.00276	0.018835	−0.004
DADS CLASS	−0.09819***	0.027915	−0.09519
DEATH PENALTY	−0.01433	0.010165	−0.04068
SPEND ON DEFENCE	0.033028***	0.00931	0.09287
LEAVE EU	0.049943	0.030766	0.0421
WORKERS' LOT IS FAIR	0.044903***	0.012017	0.105153
AID TO AFRICA	−0.00616	0.012703	−0.01407
SPEND ON EDUCATION	−0.00496	0.021135	−0.00717
SPEND ON HEALTH	−0.07512***	0.022145	−0.10982
CREATE JOBS	0.068721***	0.016826	0.116903
PRIVATIZE MEDICINE	0.017566	0.010976	0.045183
PRIVATIZE INDUSTRY	0.112183***	0.016701	0.195536
OCCUPATION	−0.07624**	0.028291	−0.07488
PRIVATIZE EDUCATION	0.084474***	0.011255	0.201777
SOCIAL CLASS	−0.05704*	0.027074	−0.05635
REGULATE TUS	−0.0497***	0.012187	−0.12407
CURB TU POWER	0.059768*	0.030651	0.05534
UNION MEMBER	−0.00656	0.027558	−0.00604
WORKS SAY	−0.03576**	0.012608	−0.07064

Dependent variable: VOTECON
R square = .498; n = 917***

Note: *** = sig. .000; ** = sig. .01; * = sig. .05 (1997).

1997: Regression analysis for common variables

	Unstandardized coefficient		Standardized Coefficient
	B	Std. Error	beta
(Constant)	0.756574	0.236965	
REDUCE ABORTIONS	−0.00678	0.015398	−0.01203
YEARS OF EDUCATION	−0.03445	0.029251	−0.03504
CURB BUSINESS POWER	−0.04905	0.02936	−0.04669
CENSORSHIP	−0.02721**	0.00991	−0.07314
GAY RIGHTS	−0.03523**	0.012936	−0.0827
RACE EQUALITY	−0.0068	0.014842	−0.01425
SEX EQUALITY	−0.01437	0.016902	−0.02428
DADS CLASS	−0.01104	0.025949	−0.01207
DEATH PENALTY	−0.00183	0.009497	−0.00596
SPEND ON DEFENCE	0.020692*	0.009234	0.061396
LEAVE EU	0.004744	0.026294	0.005164
WORKERS' LOT IS FAIR	−0.08648***	0.013272	−0.1908
AID TO AFRICA	0.010616	0.011441	0.027772
SPEND ON EDUCATION	−0.04865*	0.020101	−0.0827

CREATE JOBS	0.005272*	0.021589	0.008478
SPEND ON HEATLH	−0.02359	0.012024	−0.05677
PRIVATIZE MEDICINE	0.024433*	0.009565	0.071381
PRIVATIZE INDUSTRY	0.012303	0.013023	0.02504
OCCUPATION	−0.09945***	0.026177	−0.11227
PRIVATIZE EDUCATION	0.059595***	0.010513	0.165628
SOCIAL CLASS	−0.03921	0.024692	−0.04445
CURB TU POWER	−0.02868**	0.009964	−0.08521
REGULATE TUS	0.095328**	0.029761	0.090616
UNION MEMBER	−0.05255*	0.026051	−0.05415
WORKS SAY	−0.00902	0.01129	−0.02316

Dependent variable: VOTECON
R square = .328; n = 1029

Note: *** = sig. .000; ** = sig. .01; * = sig. .05.

14 Conclusion: Was 1997 a Critical Election?

Pippa Norris and Geoffrey Evans

In the immediate aftermath of Labour's victory many commentators claimed that British party politics before and after the 1997 election could legitimately be regarded as distinct eras. In this perspective, 1997 represented a watershed, or critical election, producing a major long-term shift in the familiar pattern of party competition. After the initial furore ebbed, however, more sceptical voices were heard. Some believed that Labour's victory was due to mounting disgust and anger with the Conservative government over sleaze, perceptions of economic mismanagement and cabinet divisions and splits over Europe, but that there was little evidence of a durable surge in new Labour loyalists or a change in the social character of such supporters. Once memories of sleaze faded, it was argued, then the sharp swing towards Labour could be replaced by an equally sharp swing away from them. Others claimed that although there had been a decisive change of government, after 18 years of the Conservatives in power, this was not due to a single election *per se* but rather to a series of incremental steps which allowed Labour gradually to recover from the nadir which they faced in 1983. In this view secular realignment over successive elections provides a more convincing account of electoral change than a dramatic and abrupt stepped shift in one contest.

This final chapter aims to draw together the evidence within this book to give our overall interpretation of the 1997 election. The core argument we will present is that there is plausible evidence that in 1997 the party order at Westminster did indeed differ significantly from the past, notably with Labour's leapfrogging over the Liberal Democrats to become the party in the middle of the ideological spectrum. The move towards abandoning socialism, embracing private enterprise, as well as adopting social conservatism on issues like law and order, represents the most centrist strategy which Labour has ever adopted in the postwar period. Most importantly, revisions to official Labour Party policy were not just on paper since the move towards the centre-ground was reflected in the political culture of the Parliamentary Labour Party and, to a lesser extent, in the attitudes of party members. To this extent, the 1997 election did represent an important break with the past pattern of party competition.

Coupled with the new Blair government after almost two decades of Tory predominance, and the change in the public policy agenda as the issue of constitutional reform dominated centre-stage at Westminster, the outcome of the election could legitimately be regarded as providing a critical watershed in British *parliamentary* politics.

Nevertheless we argue that many popular accounts of the 1997 election did exaggerate the degree to which a new dawn had broken as Blair took to the stage on the South Bank on 2 May. Labour's landslide of seats was largely the product of the exaggerative qualities of the electoral system, rather than a landslide of votes. After summarizing the evidence presented in this book we conclude that the changes at élite level could increase the possibility of realignment among the electorate in future contests, especially under the new 'rules of the game' established by constitutional modernization. In particular if electoral reform is implemented for Westminster, with the introduction of an alternative vote system with top-up regional party lists, this could transform the basis of party competition. Nevertheless, irrespective of future developments, in our judgement the 1997 election itself cannot be classified as a critical realignment in the electorate. The marked character of change at the élite level is not matched by the same extent of electoral repositioning. If we compare party–voter alignments in 1964 and in 1997 a wide range of trajectories can be observed – certain elements of continuity, some robust evidence of dealignment, and some indicators of actual or potential realignment. Some of these patterns can be understood in the light of party strategy, but no simple picture can be affirmed.

The Evidence for a Critical Election

Historically we can identify at least two decisive twentieth-century British watersheds – in 1924 and 1945 – which are widely acknowledged to represent critical turning points in the long-term party order (Norris 1997). Are there plausible grounds to believe that the 1997 general election, like those in 1924 and 1945, represents a parallel reordering of the party system? For many reasons it remains too early to tell with certainty, as even with a thorough examination of the available evidence we can only be confident about interpretations of the 1997 election after patterns of voting behaviour become consolidated over subsequent contests. We can, however, assess how far 1997 breaks with previous elections with respect to many relevant characteristics and thereby judge its likely implications for future contests.

As noted in the Introduction, Blair's landslide of seats provides the most immediate evidence of radical discontinuity. The numbers bear repeating. From April 1992 to May 1997 Labour surged from 271 MPs to 419, the party's highest ever number and more than could be comfortably accommodated on the government benches. During the same period the Liberal

Democrats more than doubled their number of MPs from 20 to 46. And of course the Conservative Parliamentary Party shrank from 336 to 165. As the electoral guillotine proceeded, the heads of 33 ministers (a third of the government) joined the 93 defeated Conservative backbenchers, along with the 72 retiring Tory members who would shortly be able to spend more time with their families. Moreover the sheer size of the vote swing from 1992 to 1997, at 10.3%, was by far the largest on record since 1935–45 (see the 'Butler swing' in Table 14.1). Nor was this simply the product of the measure used, since the Pedersen index which provides an alternative measure of volatility was at 12.3, the third highest figure in the postwar era. The opinion polls, by-elections and local elections had consistently suggested an upheaval was on the cards ever since Black Wednesday in September 1992 but nevertheless the size of the political earthquake in 1997 surprised nearly all (for the unhappy record of the pundits see, for example, Worcester 1998).

Table 14.1 *Indicators of net electoral volatility*

	Butler swing	Pedersen index
1935–45	11.8	13.7
1945–50	2.9	3.8
1950–51	0.9	7.3
1951–55	2.0	2.1
1955–59	1.0	3.2
1959–64	3.0	5.9
1964–66	2.7	4.3
1966–70	4.7	6.0
1970–F74	1.3	13.3
F74–O74	2.1	3.1
O74–79	5.2	8.2
1979–83	4.1	11.9
1983–87	1.7	3.2
1987–92	2.1	5.6
1992–97	*10.3*	*12.3*

Source: Updated from Norris (1997).

The continued popularity of the new Blair government in the early stages, well after most honeymoons had faded, reinforced the notion of a watershed in British politics. As shown in Figure 14.1, if we compare the Gallup series of monthly polls, all governments tend to experience a short-lived honeymoon when first returned before 'the mid-term blues' set in. In the late 1960s Wilson suffered a bad case of the blues, as did Callaghan in the late 1970s. But under John Major the government broke new post-war records in terms of the depth of their position in the polls. In contrast, during their first 18 months in office Labour averaged 55% in monthly Gallup polls, over double the level of support for the Conservatives who lagged on 26%, remaining below their share at the general election. Similar lop-sided ratings were evident for the leaders, with over two-thirds of all voters satisfied with Mr Blair's performance as Prime Minister while only 28% approved of Mr Hague's leadership. At

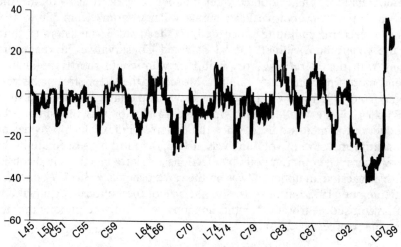

FIGURE 14.1   *Government (Con–Lab) lead: monthly Gallup polls, 1945–99*
Source: Gallup polls

this stage in Parliament the Opposition normally picks up support but, despite the depths plumbed by the Conservatives in the general election, the opinion polls suggest that they continued to have difficulties in regaining their footing. Nevertheless, based on past patterns of recovery, as Rose (1997) has argued, we would expect Labour's popularity to be eroded as the mid-term approaches.

Any analysis of the critical elections thesis needs, however, to be based on more than the mere ephemera of current opinion polls. More weighty evidence for our interpretation comes from the analysis of party competition in parliamentary politics. Chapter 1 by Ian Budge documented the content of British election manifestos since the war. The evidence demonstrates that the familiar order of the major British parties along the left–right spectrum did ratchet in a different direction.   Labour's long movement into power in the last four elections was not a steady and consistent glide towards the right; instead, the manifesto data summarizing the position of British parties on the overall left-right scale - show their leftist stance in 1983 on unilateralism, public ownership and trade union rights. Labour moved towards the centre under Kinnock in 1987 but again turned left in 1992, especially on welfare spending. By 1997 official Labour policy had been transformed under Blair in certain highly distinctive ways. First, by 1997 Labour was located in the centre of party competition, only the second time this has happened in the entire postwar era (the other, perhaps not coincidentally, was in 1964). *By 1997 Blair was flanked to the right by Major and to the left by Ashdown.* This turns established notions of left and right in the British political order on their heads. For the first time ever the balance of Labour Party policy was on the right of the spectrum. Moreover, the shift to the right was not just evident with Labour's acceptance of the market economy and public spending discipline, but also on the agenda of social conservatism. For all these reasons, in terms of official policy 1997 was remarkable, and could be regarded legitimately as an abrupt and decisive break with the postwar party order. If Thatcherism forged a new consensus about the value of markets and the limited role of the state in the economy, then under Blair's leadership New Labour can be regarded as its heir and beneficiary. The public philosophy of the Blair project continues to evolve, whether characterized as 'communitarianism', 'the stakeholder society' or 'the third way'. It is clearer what it is not (postwar socialism) than what it is. But the most accurate way to understand New Labour is perhaps as the inheritor of social liberalism, in the tradition from Gladstone through Lloyd George to Joe Grimond, emphasizing market incentives, opportunities and civic responsibilities within a devolved state.

Yet sceptics could well argue, and we would accept, that the evidence from manifestos is far from sufficient to prove a persistent and deep-rooted alteration in party competition. Official Labour Party policies could well represent a shift of packaging and presentation, controlled by the ruthless leadership determined on electoral success at any price, imposed on the party and sold to the public by 'Mandelsonian' marketing. Although picked up by the chattering classes, manifestos are rarely read by the mass public and may serve the function of a glossy company report, providing window-dressing to show Labour in the best possible light but not binding on government. Moreover, as Ian Budge notes, past shifts towards the left or right have usually been followed by an erratic countermove in subsequent elections, like a drunken walk with one step forward and one step back, rather than a steady march in a straight line. As a result, based solely on party policy, we might expect Labour gradually to drift leftwards in subsequent elections.

Such an argument, however, would need to take account of the other evidence about changes in the culture of the Labour Party, at parliamentary and grassroots levels. Chapter 2 demonstrates that New Labour policies were not imposed on recalcitrant backbenchers; instead the shift towards the centre-ground of British politics reflected fairly accurately the attitudes of Labour politicians. By 1997 Labour politicians had abandoned, or at least diluted, many of the classic touchstones of socialist faith on issues like public ownership, Keynsian demand management and public spending. By the last election the attitudes and values of Labour politicians were closely in tune, not only with their own voters, but also with the position of the British public. One important reason why the Conservatives failed to appreciate how far apart they were on basic economic issues from the median British voter, and even from their own core voters, lies in their perception of public opinion. All politicians assumed that the public was more right wing on the economy than was actually the case, and this perceptual error was particularly marked among Tory politicians. This may well have led the Conservative Party to advocate more right-wing policies than the public could stomach.

The Parliamentary Labour Party could, of course, also shift back towards the social democratic left in subsequent elections. As memories of Thatcherism gradually fade, along with their hard years on the Opposition benches, Labour politicians might feel confident enough to reassert a more traditional set of social democratic priorities concerning public spending and the welfare state. But the analysis of politicians in Chapter 2 also revealed one important clue about the durability of cultural change. The evidence showed that the shift towards the right was particularly prevalent among the younger generations of politicians, who came to political maturity with memories of the affluent 1980s rather than 1950s collectivism. In the long term we would expect that as younger politicians gradually replace older members this may consolidate and reinforce Labour's move towards the centre.

Still sceptics could press us further, and argue that Labour politicians remain accountable to the grassroots party organization. If the 'electoralist' party composed of careerist Labour MPs has moved towards the catch-all centre-ground, this does not demonstrate that change has penetrated any deeper into the joints and sinews of the party. After all, conflict between left-wing constituency activists and more centrist MPs was an enduring feature of Labour Party politics in the 1960s, 1970s and early 1980s. Chapter 3 therefore set out to explore attitudes among party members. The evidence presented by Webb and Farrell confirms the picture we have uncovered so far: the changes in official party policy and among the Parliamentary Labour Party were also reflected in the attitudes and ideology of grassroots members. Where we have indicators of left-right attitudes over time, such as support for nationalization, the redistribution of wealth and socialist values, Labour Party members were found to have moved significantly centre right.

The case for a critical election so far therefore rests on the argument that the 1997 election saw the emergence of a new pattern of party competition – evident in separate studies of official party policy and in the attitudes of politicians and party members – with Labour moving to occupy the centre-ground of British politics while the Conservatives remain stranded and beached in lonely isolation on the far right, away from their own supporters let alone mainstream public opinion. Yet there is far more room for debate about whether these important developments have affected the long-term ideological and social basis of the vote. Labour's landslide of seats involved an abrupt and dramatic tipping in the balance of parliamentary power, but it may well rest, like a delicate fulcrum, on more modest and subtle shifts among the mass electorate.

Social Dealignment or Realignment?

One of the most important indicators of electoral dealignment or realignment comes from measures of party identification provided in the BES series since 1964. The evidence presented in Chapter 4 shows that in 1997 the redistribution of party identification was easily the most dramatic of any election since the BES series began. But since changes in party identification in Europe tend to travel in tandem with the swing of the vote, we cannot automatically assume that this indicates a persistent and durable alteration in the loyalties people feel towards Labour and the Conservatives. The BES data reveal that the strength of party identification has weakened over successive elections during the last three decades, a process of dealignment that continued in 1997. We cannot therefore conclude that 1997 saw a positive surge of new loyalists towards Labour. Yet Crewe and Thomson argue that New Labour have the opportunity to harden the overwhelming but soft Labour partisanship of young voters into a New Labour generation, although these same voters are open to conversion to another party if the government is perceived to fail.

If there has been a sea-change in the party order, we would also expect to see a decline in the long-term, traditional party–voter alignments, notably those based on the traditional bedrock of class and left-right ideology, and the emergence of 'new' social cleavages in the electorate. The question of whether the traditional class cleavage has weakened in Britain has proved a controversial area. The evidence presented in Chapter 5 demonstrates that the alignment between class and party has not followed a smooth path of secular decline. Nevertheless there has been a general weakening in levels of class voting in Britain since 1964, and this relationship eroded even further in 1992–97. The main reason for this, Chapter 5 suggests, is the change in Labour Party strategy and ideology, and Blair's shift towards the centre-ground noted earlier. The strength of the link between class and party now appears to be more sensitive to changes in party image and policy programmes than it was in the 1960s. Evidence, then, that party shifts can translate into dealignment (or realignment) in the class basis of voting.

This pattern does not apply to all social cleavages, however. In many other European countries, such as France, Italy and Germany, race and ethnicity have proved the potent spark which have ignited strong anti-immigrant parties of the far right. Yet after the brief heyday of the British National Front in the 1970s the issue of race has proved the dog which did not bark in British elections. The growth of the ethnic minorities in Britain since the 1950s is an important source of support for Labour, as Britain has moved towards a multicultural electorate. As Chapter 6 demonstrates the best estimates of ethnic minority support for the major parties show a fairly stable pattern since the early 1970s, with overwhelming majorities (84%) of Asian and black voters supporting the Labour Party in the 1997 election. Saggar and Heath conclude that there was considerable stability in minority voting patterns in the last election with black voters strongly aligned with Labour.

Polarizing regional cleavages have also emerged in other societies which have disrupted and fragmented traditional patterns of party support, notably in Canada, Belgium and Italy. Chapter 7 examines the regional patterns of voting behaviour in Britain. Curtice and Park found that the geography of voting behaviour changed in two major ways in 1997, with significant consequences for the outcome of the election. First, there was further closure of the north–south divide as Labour made inroads into southern England, picking up Tory bastions in places such as Enfield Southgate, Hastings, Hove, Finchley and Golders Green, all with swings of more than 15%. This dealignment in the north–south divide has proceeded apace since it reached its peak in 1987 indicating a pattern of change in the strength of north–south divisions that has closely reflected party polarization – a pattern not dissimilar to that observed for social class. Moreover anti-Conservative 'tactical voting' increased, allowing voters to switch to whichever Labour or Liberal Democrat candidate was best positioned to get rid of the Conservative incumbent. Curtice and Park estimate that about 5% of voters switched tactically in this way in 1997 compared with 3–3.5% who made the same move in the previous three general elections. The most convincing reason for both patterns is party strategy, and in particular voters' perceptions of the Labour Party. Labour's modernization project moved its perceived policy position closer to the average southern voter and also facilitated the switch between the Opposition parties. The chapter concludes that these changes represent the success of Labour party strategy at widening its electoral appeal. If Labour continues to maintain this strategy then we can anticipate that the electoral geography of 1997 will continue to be evident or that north–south divisions will attenuate even further. But on the other hand if the Conservatives can regroup and remobilize their southern supporters, and if policy differences between the Liberal Democrats and Labour widen, then the geography of voting behaviour may well change again.

The gender cleavage in British politics has long been assumed to be fairly stable, with women favouring the Conservatives while men lean towards Labour. The gender gap in the 1960s confirmed this pattern; since patterns of longevity and turnout meant that there are more women in the electorate this usually gave a marginal edge to the Conservatives. In the 1997 election Labour, recognizing the shrinking size of their traditional electoral base among the old working class, trade unionists and council tenants, actively sought to widen their appeal by attracting more female support. The most visible aspect of this strategy included selecting far more female candidates for winnable parliamentary seats. This policy proved effective in altering the parliamentary face of the Labour Party, with the election of record numbers of women to the Commons. But despite this Labour failed to gain an edge among all age groups of women voters. Yet Chapter 8 concludes that although 1997 did not produce a critical and sudden break in the pattern of gender voting, if we analyse the pattern of voting by gender and age cohort there is evidence of a gradual and more incremental secular realignment underway in British politics. In recent elections older generations of women continue to prove more Conservative than older men, in the traditional pattern, but among the younger generation women are more Labour-leaning than men. Given the long-term process of generational replacement we can expect that women will gradually move towards the left in Britain, with the emergence of the modern gender gap, just as they have in many other postindustrial democracies such as the USA.

Electoral politics does not only hinge upon the distribution of votes cast between parties, but also the extent of abstention. The pattern of turnout in 1997 was different from previous years; indeed it reached the lowest level since 1935. Many speculated that this could have been due to the demobilization of Conservative voters, who were turned off by the sleaze and disunity afflicting their party, or by Labour voters who stayed at home disproportionately because disillusioned by Blair's abandonment of traditional socialist values. Chapter 9, based on the analysis of non-voting since 1964, concludes that the overall closeness of the race was the most important factor contributing to over-time variations in turnout. Lower voting participation in 1997 can therefore most plausibly be attributed to the way that so many indicators had pointed for a long time to a comfortable Labour victory. The particular circumstances of the general election encouraged Labour voters to stay home because one more vote would be unlikely to make the difference. On this basis we must conclude that if there appears to be a tighter contest in subsequent elections then turnout levels should rebound back to higher levels. But it also indicates that levels of turnout are not intimately related to whether an election is 'critical', in the way defined in classic formulations of the notion, but primarily to how close an election is expected to be – a very different question. More consistent with the implications of a critical election was the evidence presented in this chapter on the possible change in the social basis of abstention, which suggests that in 1997 there was a small move to increased abstention from the left – in particular among trade union members and the working class who had previously been Labour voters. This may reflect a natural reaction to Labour's centre shift, but it is also possible that it reflects confidence that turnout is not so necessary in core Labour seats.

Ideological Dealignment or Realignment?

What of the ideological divisions in British politics? We might expect that the 'end of ideology' produced by Labour's move to the middle of the party spectrum would reduce the salience of the old economic divisions of left and right for Labour voting in the last election. At the same time for realignment to occur we would seek evidence of the emergence of new polarizing and conflictual issues which cross-cut established patterns of party politics, whether those like race in the USA or environmental concerns in Germany. In Britain, the most plausible candidates for such issues in the last election are Europe, which split the Conservative Party into two irreconcilable factions which continue to war in public well after the event, and devolution in Scotland and Wales. Both these issues can be seen to be tapping into cleavages of national identity, dividing those who believe in the virtues of a strong and sovereign nation-state from those who advocate a more limited nation-state where powers are devolved downwards towards local communities and upwards towards international bodies.

During the postwar era the left–right ideological cleavage dominated British politics based on the virtues of free enterprise and a minimal state v. public ownership and Keynsian economic management. For many commentators this cleavage started to change in the mid-1980s with the rise of Thatcherism. As Chapter 10 documented, the 1997 election saw Labour shift to become the centre of the ideological spectrum, adopting a 'third way' between socialism and free enterprise. The core issue is whether the electorate responded to these changes in the 1997 election and whether there was a marked change in the role of ideological consid-erations in voting decisions. Chapter 10 concludes that Labour's move to the centre proved electorally popular in 1997 and it also weakened the importance of ideology as a cue to Labour voting. In this sense there was ideological dealignment along the traditional economic cleavage. But in contrast the continued right-wing stance of the Major government did not reduce the impact of ideological factions on Conservative voting. Sanders concludes that we need to await the outcome of at least one more election before we can make a clear evaluation of the ideological mould-breaking capacity of 1997. We may be entering the era of the 'end of ideology' in voting behaviour, but it remains too early to tell.

Europe is one, if not *the*, major policy issue which has the potential to produce new cross-cutting cleavages in British politics. Europe is tradi-tionally a low salience topic, similar to other issues of foreign affairs where there is a 'permissive consensus' among the public. Since Maastricht, however, the expansion in the powers and scope of the European Union has produced stronger rumblings of disquiet among European publics, a process that has perhaps gone further in Britain than elsewhere. Europe is also an issue where the major parties in Britain have done a remarkable waltz during the last decade. The Conservatives, the most pro-European under the leadership of Harold Macmillan and Edward Heath, steadily drifted into a Eurosceptic camp under Thatcher and now Hague. In contrast Labour, who were most critical of Britain's original application for membership, and who advocated a complete withdrawal from the EC in 1983, have swung round towards becoming solid if not ardent Europhiles, advocating signature of the 'Social Chapter'. One question from this remarkable development is whether the partisan nature of views on Europe has switched to coincide with the changes in party positions. Chapter 11 indicates that, strikingly, the pattern of party voting associated with Europe has reversed during the space of a decade: in 1974

Conservative voters were more supportive of Europe than Labour, by 1987 this division had weakened somewhat, by 1992 they were evenly balanced, and by 1997 they were fully reversed. Today Labour voters are now the most pro-Europe while Conservatives are most sceptical. Evidence on the continued stability of the social and ideological basis of attitudes towards Europe, as well as their impact on vote switching, indicates moreover that this change was not simply the party faithful switching their views to coincide with those of their party. One consequence of these changes is that attitudes towards Europe now cross-cut the class basis of voting, helping to explain the class dealignment examined in Chapter 5. To this extent Britain's position within the European Union does represent a new issue which may help to break up the older pattern of voter alignments and may help reorder party competition.

A second theme of the 1997 election, that of nationalism and constitutional reform, also provides one of the chief issues which could have caused realignment in British electoral politics. The outcome of the contest proved dramatic for the party order in Scotland, with all Conservative and Unionist MPs losing their seats, even the Cabinet ministers Malcolm Forsyth in Stirling, Ian Lang in Galloway and Upper Nithsdale, and Malcolm Rifkind in Edinburgh Pentlands. As a result the Conservatives were wiped out, without a single MP, MEP or control of a local authority in Scotland. Yet as Chapter 12 argues at the level of the electorate in Scotland the 1997 election proved to be one which maintained the pattern of voting and party competition which had been evident over successive elections in recent years, not a radical break with the past. The critical realignment in Scotland occurred in the early 1970s, with the rise of the SNP peaking with 30% of the vote in October 1974. Even though support for the SNP subsequently subsided, nevertheless all contests in Scotland since then have been based on a four-party system. The chapter demonstrates that constitutional preferences and national identities form the basis of a new cross-cutting issue cleavage in Scottish politics, one which is not linked to the old classic cleavages of class and religion, and which seems likely to endure. It remains to be seen how party fortunes are shaped by the introduction of the new Scottish Parliament elected under the AMS system but this promises to have major consequences for all parties in Scotland.

Lastly, Chapter 13 by Franklin and Hughes examines the overall ideological map of voting behaviour in the early 1980s and in the 1990s. Unlike many of the others, this chapter emphasizes the negative reaction against the Conservatives rather than Labour's move to the centre as a crucial factor explaining the difference between 1997 and previous elections. None the less, the analysis suggests that the issue space of British politics has evolved in important ways during recent decades, moving from an ideological cleavage based primarily on the old class-orientated concern with traditional issues like pensions, poverty and job creation towards what these authors term the 'new' political agenda. In 1997 Blair gained votes almost equally from the 'new' and 'old' left, in line with Blair's location between the two. But in contrast Labour made most converts in the 'old right' category, the ideological dimension most closely associated with issues such as tougher law and order and stricter sentencing. It appears that the move towards social conservatism, noted by Budge and Norris in earlier chapters, may have paid electoral dividends.

With Skill, Luck and Will

The overall picture presented in this book suggests that the most convincing evidence for a new party order in the 1997 election occurred at the level of Westminster politics. Labour's move to abandon its historic position on the left and to become the middle way in British politics was a bold and radical step which has had reverberations for all parties. There have been major consequences in terms of the break-up and reconsolidation of the constitutional settlement in Scotland, Wales and England. The Pandora's box opened with devolution, gathered momentum with Northern Ireland and seems destined, with some steps forwards and some steps back, to remake the British constitution. Many issues here remain to be resolved and some of the more radical proposals for reform of the House of Lords and the electoral system may ultimately be tempered, or even abandoned, before implementation. Labour MPs favour many aspects of constitutional modernization but the Parliamentary Labour Party remains evenly split on electoral reform for Westminster (Norris 1998). Nevertheless despite set-backs, constitutional reform, while only a minor feature in the 1997 election, may become the defining project of the Blair administration, functioning in the same way as the issue of privatization for Mrs Thatcher, and causing as much upheaval in the political system as Thatcherism caused in the public sector. In this sense the outcome of the election may prove historic for the politics of the centre left, drawing the Liberal Democrats and Labour closer together ideologically, changing the predominant policy agenda and permanently altering the rules of the British Constitution. How this process, in turn, ultimately affects the fortunes of all the parties remains to be seen. It may produce, as Tony Blair and Paddy Ashdown suggest, a new coalition on the centre left: 'the ascendancy of progressive politics in Britain, against a Conservative Party which seems determined to travel further and further to the Right . . . to continue the reshaping of British politics for the next century' (Tony Blair and Paddy Ashdown, 11 November 1998). Or the unintended consequences of constitutional reform may produce a very different outcome and Lib–Lab co-operation may change under different leaders.

But did the 1997 election produce radical discontinuity at the level of the electorate? Here we must be far more sceptical. Many of the popular accounts have exaggerated how far the Labour victory signified a new era of political behaviour among voters. The most consistent evidence suggests a pattern of continuing secular dealignment in the British electorate due to political changes in party competition. In particular, in response to Labour's centre shift, class voting reached its lowest level since the BES series began in the early 1960s. Regional cleavages also weakened, with the further closure of the north–south divide. And strong partisan loyalties, already eroded in a series of elections during the 1970s, fell further. The 'old' politics of ideological divisions over the virtues of the market v. public ownership declined in importance for Labour voting, while the 'new' issues of Europe increasingly cross-cut these patterns of voting behaviour. This analysis suggests that Labour's impressive majority obtained in 1997 will ultimately prove vulnerable to disillusion or attack. The weakening of partisan identities and the increased instrumentality of voting characteristic of late twentieth-century electorates make all electoral groups more open to competitive appeals. The dealignment perspective suggests that the substantial swing to Labour will prove less durable than many have assumed and the Conservatives can be expected eventually to restore their support, if not in one election then, like Labour in 1983, in a series of subsequent contests.

Yet not all indicators pointed in a consistent direction and there are also some faint indicators of at least potential realignment among certain groups in the electorate. In particular, the largest shift in party identification from the Conservatives to Labour occurred among the youngest age group, which may indicate that new voters are moving into the Labour camp. There was also gradual movement towards the Labour Party among younger generations of women, a development which may have significant consequences for gender politics in future. If changes at party level precede, and may thereby shape, social and ideological divisions within the electorate, we may expect greater realignment among voters in future contests. If Blair succeeds in consolidating Labour's position, with 'skill, luck and will', if Labour–Liberal Democrat co-operation strengthens and persists, and if Europe continues deeply to divide the Conservatives, then the changes in party politics may well prove more enduring.

Technical Appendix

Bridget Taylor and Katarina Thomson

Introduction

The British General Election Surveys (BES) constitute the longest series of academic surveys in Britain. They have taken place immediately after every general election since 1964, giving a total of 11 to date. In addition to these post-election cross-section surveys, panel surveys (in which respondents to the previous election survey were reinterviewed at the subsequent election) have been conducted between every pair of elections except 1979 and 1983. The 1992–97 Parliament was covered by the first British Election Panel Study (BEPS) in which the panel was interviewed on eight occasions starting as the 1992 BES post-election cross-section survey and concluding with a wave following the 1997 general election. A second British Election Panel Study follows from the 1997 post-election cross-section survey and the panel is planned to be interviewed on approximately eight occasions, again with the concluding wave immediately following the next general election. There have also been two non-election year surveys (in 1963 and 1969); a postal referendum study in 1975; additional or booster Scottish studies in 1974, 1979, 1992 and 1997; an additional Welsh study in 1979; a Northern Ireland election study in 1992; campaign studies in Britain in 1987, 1992 and 1996–97; a booster sample of ethnic minority members in 1997; a qualitative study in 1997; Scottish (two) and Welsh referendum studies in 1997; and a Northern Ireland referendum and election study in 1998.

The data sets arising from these surveys, together with questionnaires and technical documentation, have been deposited at the ESRC Data Archive at the University of Essex. Summary information about the 1963–87 surveys, and further references, are provided in an Appendix to *Understanding Political Change* (Heath *et al.* 1991), and for the 1992 surveys in the Appendix to *Labour's Last Chance?* (Heath *et al.* 1994b).

The series was originated by David Butler (Nuffield College Oxford) and Donald Stokes (University of Michigan) in 1963, who also conducted the 1964, 1966 and 1970 surveys. The series then passed to Bo Särlvik and Ivor Crewe (University of Essex) who conducted the February and October 1974 surveys, joined by David Robertson for the 1979 survey. The

1983, 1987, 1992 and 1997 surveys have been directed by Anthony Heath (Jesus then Nuffield College Oxford), Roger Jowell (Social and Community Planning Research – SCPR – London) and John Curtice (University of Liverpool then Strathclyde); in 1997 these directors were joined by Pippa Norris (Harvard University). The associated 1997 Scottish Election Study was conducted in collaboration with David McCrone (University of Edinburgh) and colleagues, and the 1997 Ethnic Minority Survey with Shamit Saggar (Queen Mary and Westfield College, London) – see below. The British Election Panel Studies and the 1997–98 Scottish, Welsh and Northern Ireland surveys were conducted by the Centre for Research into Elections and Social Trends (CREST), a research centre funded by the Economic and Social Research Council (ESRC) and based jointly at SCPR and Nuffield College Oxford, directed by Anthony Heath and Roger Jowell, with John Curtice.

The principal component of the British Election Study time series of surveys is the post-election cross-section survey. All the BES surveys have been based on probability samples representative of the electorate (in 1997, the resident adult population) of Great Britain (south of the Caledonian Canal, except in 1992 and 1997). Northern Ireland has always been excluded from the British Election Study. All the post-election cross-section surveys have been conducted by face-to-face interview. They have been noted for the high quality of their fieldwork and the richness of their data, especially that on the respondents' social and occupational characteristics.

The 1997 British Election Study Cross-section Survey

The 1997 British Post-election Cross-section survey was funded by the Economic and Social Research Council (ESRC) (grant no. H552/255/003) and the Gatsby Charitable Foundation, one of the Sainsbury Family Charitable Trusts, which again allowed its core funding of SCPR's British Social Attitudes survey series to be devoted to the BES series in election year. This Appendix also provides information about the Scottish Election Study (SES) and Ethnic Minority Study (EMS), additional components of the 1997 cross-section survey (see below). More detailed information about the cross-section survey design and fieldwork, including the SES and EMS, is presented in *The 1997 British Election Studies: Technical Report* (Thomson *et al.* 1998); both the full questionnaires and a comprehensive codebook are available from the ESRC Data Archive at the University of Essex, as are the data files. Information is also available at http://www.strath.ac.uk/Other/CREST.

The BES survey was designed to yield a representative sample of the population resident in private households in Britain aged 18 or over. Previous election studies have used the electoral register as the sampling frame. Evidence suggests that the coverage of the electoral register has declined over the last decade or so, and consequently the chances of bias in its coverage have increased. Concern about these inadequacies as well as substantive interest in the characteristics of people who are not registered but would be eligible to vote if they were registered, lead to the decision to change the sampling frame. The sample of addresses was drawn from the Postcode Address File (Lynn and Taylor 1995). In order to maintain the comparability of the BES time series, the presence or absence of each respondent on the electoral register was subsequently checked (see below).

Sampling from the Postcode Address File involves a multi-stage design. First, any postal sectors with fewer than 500 delivery points (DPs) were grouped with another. The list of (grouped) sectors was then stratified on the basis of subregion (32 for England/Wales and five for Scotland), population density and SEG profile (percentage of household heads who are employer/managers). Some 218 postal sectors were selected with probability proportional to DP count: 164 in England and Wales, 54 in Scotland. Thirty DPs were sampled systematically from throughout each sector, giving 6,540 issued addresses: 4,920 in England and Wales and 1,620 in Scotland.

At each issued address, the interviewer established the number of occupied dwelling units (DUs) and, where there were several, selected one DU at random for interview (using a Kish grid and random numbers generated separately for each serial number). At each (selected) DU the interviewer established the number of adults aged 18+ normally resident there, and selected one adult at random (using the same procedure as for selecting a DU). The unequal selection probabilities arising from these procedures, and the oversampling of Scotland, are taken into account by the weighting (see below).

Two small-scale pretests of questions were carried out in October and December 1996. The pilot interviewers were personally debriefed by the research team.

The survey, conducted by SCPR interviewers, consisted of a face-to-face interview and a self-completion supplement. The face-to-face interview was administered in 1997 for the first time using a lap-top computer. The use of computer-assisted personal interviewing or CAPI was introduced following methodological work by SCPR which established that the change should not introduce significant mode effects (Martin *et al.* 1993). This enabled the use of more complex filtering and question selection routines in 1997 than had hitherto usually been used. The face-to-face interview lasted on average 62 minutes (66 minutes in Scotland). The self-completion supplement, either collected by the interviewer or returned by post, was completed by 86% of respondents. The self-completion supplement was first introduced on the 1987 election study, and has been used at each study since then; it substantially increases the number of questions which can be asked.

All interviewers working on the main fieldwork phase were personally briefed by members of the SCPR BES research team. In all, 222 interviewers worked on the survey (170 in England and Wales, and 52 in Scotland). Fieldwork for the survey began on 2 May; 74% was complete by the end of May, and 96% by the end of June; the remainder was completed by 1 August – mainly recalls on respondents who were unable or unwilling to be interviewed earlier.

The names of some potential respondents who had been difficult to find at home, or had moved, or had refused, or had broken appointments, were reissued to interviewers (in most cases interviewers who had not made the initial calls) during the later phase of fieldwork.

The Scottish Election Study

The linked Scottish Election Study (SES) was funded by a separate ESRC grant (no. H552/255/004) to David McCrone, Alice Brown (University of Edinburgh), Paula Surridge (University of Aberdeen) and Katarina Thomson (SCPR). The SES consisted of, first, an over-sample in Scotland

TABLE A.1   BES *response rate*

	England and Wales		Scotland		Total	
	n	%	*n*	%	*n*	%
Address issued	4,920		1,620		6,540	
Address out of scope (Empty, demolished, no trace, no private dwellings, etc.)	561		165		726	
Total in scope	4,359	100	1,455	100	5,814	100
Interview obtained – of which:	2,733	63	882	61	3,615	62
With self-completion	2,337	54	756	52	3,093	53
Without self-completion	396	9	126	9	522	9
Interview not obtained – of which:	1,626	37	573	39	2,199	38
Refusal by selected person/ broken appointment	831		260		1,091	
Refusal on behalf of selected person (proxy refusal)	92		44		136	
Refusal prior to selection	150		37		187	
Refusal to office	133		37		170	
No contact: selected person	66		42		108	
No contact: prior to selection	130		62		192	
Senile/incapacitated	56		34		90	
Away or in hospital	43		17		60	
Ill at home	37		14		51	
Inadequate English	58		3		61	
Other unproductive	30		23		53	

on the BES post-election cross-section survey in order to enable more detailed investigation of voting behaviour in Scotland, including analyses comparing subgroups within Scotland; and, secondly, approximately 40 extra questions with special reference to Scotland asked only of Scottish respondents.

With the booster sample, 882 productive interviews were achieved in Scotland, instead of the 270 or so Scottish interviews we would expect without sampling extra addresses. Thus whereas Scotland represents approximately 9% of the population of Great Britain, Scottish respondents make up 24% of the sample. The weighting scheme (see below) down-weights the Scottish over-sample to form a representative British sample.

The Ethnic Minority Study

The BES Ethnic Minority Study was conducted by CREST in collaboration with Shamit Saggar (Queen Mary and Westfield College, London). The ethnic minority extension was funded by the ESRC (grant no. R000/222/123) and the Commission for Racial Equality. The study consisted of a booster sample of ethnic minority members and approximately 40 extra questions as part of the face-to-face interview asked only of ethnic minority respondents (respondents who were part of the samples generated from the screening exercises – see below – were correspondingly given a shortened version of the self-completion questionnaire, omitting the CSES questions – see below). This was the first ethnic minority booster sample to the BES series, its purpose being to enable more detailed investigation of voting behaviour and political attitudes among ethnic minority members. The ethnic minority sample covered England and Wales only. The survey definition for eligible ethnic minority members was 'black or of Indian, Pakistani or Bangladeshi origin'. Other ethnic minorities were excluded from the booster sample as there would be insufficient numbers for separate analysis.

The sample was generated from three sources:

- Ethnic minority respondents who happened to be generated by the main BES sample (106 cases).
- A large-scale screening exercise in areas of high ethnic minority concentration (430 cases).
- Next-door screening at some sample points with high ethnic minority concentrations. (The screening was carried out at the two addresses immediately to the left and the two addresses immediately to the right of the original household.) (194 cases).

The unequal selection probabilities arising from the three sample types are taken into account in the weighting. Table A.2 (below) shows the response rate of the two screening exercises.

TABLE A.2 *Ethnic minority study screening: response*

	Large-scale screening		Door-to door screening		Total	
	n	%	*n*	%	*n*	%
Address issued	3,425		504		—[1]	
Address out of scope[1] (Empty, demolished, no trace, no private dwellings, no ethnic minority persons, etc.)	2,495		74		—	
Total in scope	930	100	430	100	1,360	100
Interview obtained – of which:	405	44	194	45	599	44
With self-completion	322	35	128	30	450	33
Without self-completion	83	9	66	15	149	11
Interview not obtained – of which:	525	56	236	55	761	56
Refusal by selected person/ broken appointment	144		61		205	
Refusal on behalf of selected person (proxy)	11		12		23	
Refusal prior to selection	35		16		51	
Refusal to office	7		0		7	
No contact: selected person	57		11		68	
No contact: prior to selection	94		24		118	
Senile/incapacitated	8		0		8	
Away or in hospital	16		8		24	
Ill at home	6		1		7	
Inadequate English	139		82		221	
Other unproductive	8		21		29	

Note: 1) Because of the different methodologies used in the two screening surveys, the out-of-scope figures are not comparable.
The weighted and unweighted sample sizes (on the preliminary datafile used in this book) are given in Table A.4.

Questionnaire Design

For the first time on the BES, the research team engaged in a formal consultation exercise with members of the BES user community – an extension of the customary informal consultation procedure. This was conducted in conjunction with the Election Studies Management and Advisory Committee (ESMAC) set up by the series' principal funder, the ESRC. Members of the research team distinguished 'core' from 'non-core' survey items. BES users were invited to submit a case for the inclusion of questions or groups of questions, and these were evaluated by subject working groups comprising both members of the research team and members of the user community. A conference of invited users was held under the auspices of ESMAC on 4 June 1996, and the draft questionnaire was discussed at a session of the 1996 annual conference of the Elections,

Public Opinion and Parties (EPOP) subgroup of the Political Studies Association (held in Sheffield 13–15 September 1996).

The survey carried a split-half experiment on the administration of the customary question about respondents' income. This question is conventionally asked in the BES using a show card on which appear income bands each denoted by a letter, and the respondent is asked to tell the interviewer the letter corresponding to his or her income. Refusal to answer the income question in the 1992 BES survey was found to be a strong predictor of drop-out from the British Election Panel Study (Taylor *et al.* 1996). In order to investigate the effect on response and subsequent panel attrition of different methods of administering the income question, a random half of the sample was administered the question in the conventional way; the other half was given a ballot form, asked to indicate their income band then to put the form in an envelope, seal it and return it to the interviewer. Variables are included on the data set for each version of the question separately and for the combined data.

The self-completion questionnaire included a module of around 30 questions on the subject of attitudes towards democratic institutions and processes (see the documentation of the questionnaires) administered as part of the Comparative Study of Electoral Systems (CSES) programme. Around 30 countries are to administer a similar module on their respective national election study between 1996 and 1999, to enable cross-national comparisons to be made.

Validation of Turnout and Registration

As in 1987 and 1992, respondents' reports of turnout at the 1997 election were checked against the official records (Swaddle and Heath 1989). The marked-up Electoral Register held at the Lord Chancellor's Office for a year after the general election shows which electors voted, or were issued with postal votes, and is available for public inspection. Corresponding information for respondents in Scotland was obtained from the Sherriffs' Clerks. Supplementary checks of registration (but not turnout) were carried out on ordinary (that is, not marked-up) registers at the Office of National Statistics offices in Titchfield in July 1998.

Because the 1997 BES used the PAF as its sampling frame, rather than the Electoral Register as in previous surveys in the series, the full sample includes some people who were not on the electoral register and thus not entitled to vote. In order to make the 1997 BES fully comparable to earlier surveys, a check was carried out against the Electoral Register on whether the respondent was on the register or not.[1] For comparability with earlier BES surveys, the 1997 data can be weighted to exclude non-registered respondents. Analyses reported in this volume were carried out on data weighted in this way. Figures reported on in this volume use data based on the initial validation study; results from the supplementary registration study are included in the final data file.

Weighting

A weighting scheme has been devised to take account of differential selection probabilities (see Table A.3). In particular, the weights take account of two factors: 1) the Scottish over-sample and 2) unequal selection probabilities at the household level. (In brief, the PAF sample generated addresses with equal probability. However, since only one person was interviewed at each address, people in small households had a larger selection probability than people in large households.) The weights also use information about non-responding addresses to counterbalance the effect of non-response biases. The weights have been scaled to reflect the downweighting on the Scottish boost (hence the weighted sample size is radically smaller than the unweighted sample size). A separate file with Scottish cases only is also provided.

Additional weights take account of the outcome of the Electoral Register checks to generate a sample of registered electors.

Some members of the 1997 BES sample of course happen to be members of ethnic minorities; these cases are integral to the British cross-section survey. A separate ethnic minority file includes both these ethnic minority respondents from the cross-section sample and those sampled through the additional screening exercises. The ethnic minority file has its own weights which additionally take account of the differing selection probabilities of respondents from the different sample types (see Table A.4).

Geographic information

The addresses of all respondents to the 1997 survey have been post-coded. Certain geographic information has been added to the survey data, such as constituency and ward name and number, and local authority identifiers.

TABLE A.3   BES *survey weighting*

	England and Wales	Scotland[1]	Total
Unweighted (whole sample)	2,733	882	3,615
Weighted (whole sample)	2,643	882[1]	2,906
Weighted (electors only)	2,477	851[1]	2,731

Note: 1) Using the separate Scottish file.

TABLE A.4   *Ethnic minority survey weighting*

	Main sample	Large-scale screening	Door-to-door screening	Total
Unweighted (whole sample)	106	405	194	705
Weighted (whole sample)	161	313	231	705
Weighted (electors only)	146	271	219	636

The British Representation Study 1997

The linked British Representation Study 1997 (BRS-97) involved a national survey of prospective parliamentary candidates and MPs from all major parties standing in the 1997 British general election. This is the second survey, following a similar study in 1992 (Norris and Lovenduski 1995). A battery of attitudinal items on the BRS was designed to be identical to those in the BES facilitating mass–élite comparisons.

The research project was conducted under the direction of Pippa Norris (Harvard University) in collaboration with Joni Lovenduski (Southampton University), Anthony Heath (Nuffield College/CREST), Roger Jowell (Social and Community Planning Research/CREST) and John Curtice (Strathclyde University/CREST). The research was distributed and administered from the School of Economic and Social Studies at the University of East Anglia and funded by the Nuffield Foundation.

The mail survey was sent to all parliamentary candidates selected by the main British parties (Conservative, Labour, Liberal Democrat, SNP, Plaid Cymru, and Green) by 1 June 1996. The Labour and Conservative parties had chosen about 600 candidates at this stage, although other parties had selected fewer. The first wave of the survey was sent out, with an official covering letter from each party, from 18 June to 3 July 1996. A post-card reminder was sent out two weeks later, followed by a third wave with a complete questionnaire and reminder letter in mid to late July. In total 1,628 questionnaires were sent out and we received 999 replies, representing a response rate of 61.4%. The survey includes 178 incumbent British MPs and 821 other parliamentary candidates. In addition, we received 122 refusals (7.5%), usually from MPs who noted that as a matter of policy they never responded to any surveys. The response rate was evenly balanced between parties so that the survey reflects the composition of the 1997 House of Commons (see Table A.5). For more details see: http://www.ksg.harvard.edu/people/pnorris/data.htm

Value and Issue Scales

Many chapters use value scales designed to measure socialist–*laissez-faire* and libertarian–authoritarian values (see, for example, Tables 2.1 and 2.3), and also responses to six issue questions measured on 11-point scales.

The *socialist–laissez-faire value scale* included the following six items with a 5-point agree/disagree response scale:

- Ordinary people get their fair share of the nation's wealth.
- There is one law for the rich and one for the poor.
- There is no need for strong trade unions to protect employees' working conditions and wages.
- It is government's responsibility to provide a job for everyone who wants one.

TABLE A.5 BRS *sample of British MPs and parliamentary candidates*

	Survey (n)	Survey (%)	1997 (n)	1997 (%)	Average/ error
MPs					
Con	60	21.7	165	25.8	−4.1
Lab	180	64.9	418	65.4	−.5
LDem	32	11.5	46	7.2	4.3
Nat	5	1.8	10	1.6	.2
ALL	277	100.0	639	100.0	2.3
Parliamentary candidates					
Con	295	30.2	648	31.7	−1.5
Lab	333	34.1	640	31.4	2.7
LDem	285	29.2	639	31.3	−2.1
Nat	63	6.4	112	5.4	1.0
ALL	976	100.0	2,039	100.0	1.8

Source: British Representation Study, 1997.

- Private enterprise is the best way to solve Britain's economic problems.
- Major public services and industries ought to be in state ownership.

The *libertarian–authoritarian value scale* included the following six agree/disagree items:

- Young people today don't have enough respect for traditional British values.
- Censorship of films and magazines is necessary to uphold moral standards.
- People in Britain should be more tolerant of those who lead unconventional lives.
- Homosexual relations are always wrong.
- People should be allowed to organize public meetings to protest against the government.
- Even political parties which wish to overthrow democracy should not be banned.

These items were also used in the 1992 British Candidate Study and the 1997 British Representation Study.

The following six issue questions were asked about with an 11-point response scale, on which respondents were asked to place themselves and then each of the parties in turn (including in Scotland, the SNP).

Jobs v. Prices Scale

Some people feel that getting people back to work should be the government's top priority. These people would put themselves in box 1. Other people feel that keeping prices down should be the government's top priority. These people would put themselves in box 11. Other people have views in-between: 'Using the following scales . . . where would you place your view?'

Taxation and Spending Scale

Some people feel that government should put up taxes a lot and spend much more on health and social services (1). These people would put themselves in box 1. Other people feel that government should cut taxes a lot and spend much less on health and social services. These people would put themselves in box 11. Other people have views in-between: Using the following scale . . . Where would you place your view?

Privatization and Nationalization Scale

Some people feel that government should nationalize many more private companies. These people would put themselves in box 1. Other people feel that government should sell off many more nationalized industries. These people would put themselves in box 11. Other people have views somewhere in-between: Using the following scale ... Where would you place your view?

Redistribution Scale

Some people feel that government should make much greater efforts to make people's incomes more equal. These people would put themselves in Box A. Other people feel that government should be much less concerned about how equal people's incomes are. These people would put themselves in Box K. And other people have views somewhere in-between. Using the following scale . . . Where would you place your view?

EU Scale

Some people feel Britain should do all it can to unite fully with the European Union. These people would put themselves in box 1. Other people feel that Britain should do all it can to protect its independence from the European Union. These people would put themselves in box 11. Other people have views somewhere in-between: Using the following scale . . . Where would you place your view?

Women's Rights Scale

Recently there has been discussion about women's rights. Some people feel that women should have an equal role with men in running business, industry and government. These people would put themselves in box 1. Other people feel that a woman's role is in the home. These people would put themselves in box 11. Other people have views somewhere in-between. Using the following scale ... Where would you place your view?

In addition, the survey included the 11-point left–right scale, on which respondents were asked to place themselves and then each of the parties in turn (including in Scotland, the SNP, and in Wales, Plaid Cymru).

Left–Right Scale

In politics people sometimes talk of left and right: Using the following scale, where 1 means left and 11 means right, where would you place yourself . . .?

Note

1. In order to make the check as complete as possible, the survey collected not only the 'issued address', but also asked the respondent 1) whether there was another address where he or she thought he or she was on the register and 2) where he or she had been living in October 1996 (the qualifying date for the 1997 registers). Thus in some cases up to three addresses were checked.

References

Alderman, Geoffrey. 1983. *The Jewish Community in British Politics*. Oxford: Clarendon Press.

Aldrich, John H. 1993. 'Rational choice and turnout.' *American Journal of Political Science* 37: 246–78.

Aldrich, John H. 1995. *Why Parties?* Chicago, IL: University of Chicago Press.

Alford, Robert. 1963. *Party and Society: The Anglo–American Democracies*. Westport, CT: Greenwood Press.

Ali, A. and G. Percival. 1993. *Race and Representation: Ethnic Minorities and the 1992 Elections*. London: Commission for Racial Equality.

Alvarez, R.M. and J. Nagler. 1995. 'Voter choice in 1992: economics, issues and anger.' *American Journal of Political Science*, 39: 714–44.

Andersen, Kristi. 1979. *The Creation of a Democratic Majority, 1928–36*. Chicago, IL: University of Chicago, Press.

Andersen, Kristi. 1996. *After Suffrage*. Chicago, IL: University of Chicago Press.

Anderson, Paul and Nyta Mann. 1997. *Safety First: The Making of New Labour*. London: Granta Books.

Anwar, Mohammed. 1996. *Race and Elections*. London: Routledge.

Atkinson, Simon and Roger Mortimore. 1997. 'Blair – one year on' (http://www.mori.com/pubinfo/blairone.htm).

Baker, David, Andrew Gamble and Steven Ludlam. 1993. 'Conservative splits and European integration.' *Political Quarterly*, 62: 420–35.

Bald, Suresh. 1989. 'The south Asian presence in British electoral politics.' *New Community*, 15 (4): 537–48.

Ballard, R. and Ballard C. 1977. 'The Sikhs: the development of south Asian settlements in Britain.' In *Between Two Cultures: Migrants and Minorities in Britain*, ed. J. L. Watson. Oxford: Blackwell.

Bartels, Larry M. 1998. 'Electoral continuity and change, 1868–1996.' *Electoral Studies*, 17(3): 301–326.

Bartle, John. 1997. 'Political awareness and heterogeneity in models of voting: some evidence from the British election studies.' In *British Elections and Parties Yearbook, 1997*, ed. David Denver. London: Frank Cass.

Bartolini, Stefano and Peter Mair. 1990. *Identity, Competition and Electoral Availability 1885–1985*. Cambridge: Cambridge University Press.

Beck, Paul Allen. 1979. 'The electoral cycle in American politics.' *British Journal of Political Science*, 9: 129–56.

Behrens, R. and J. Emonds. 1981. 'Kippers, kittens and kipper boxes: Conservative populists and race relations.' *Political Quarterly*, 52: 342–7.

Bell, Daniel. 1962. *The End of Ideology: On the Exhaustion of Political Ideas in the Fifties*. New York: Free Press.

Berrington, Hugh and Rod Hague. 1998. 'Europe, Thatcherism and traditionalism: opinion, rebellion and the Maastricht Treaty in the backbench Conservative Party, 1992–94.' In *Britain in the Nineties: The Politics of Paradox*, ed. Hugh Berrington. London: Frank Cass.

Blair, Tony. 1995. *Let Us Face the Future*. London: Fabian Society.

Blondel, Jean. 1970. *Voters, Parties and Leaders*. London: Penguin.

Brand Jack, James Mitchell and Paula Surridge. 1994. 'Social constituency and ideological profile: Scottish nationalism in the 1990s.' *Political Studies*, 42: 616–29.

Brown Alice, David McCrone, Lindsay Paterson and Paula Surridge. 1998. *The Scottish Electorate*. London: Macmillan

Brynin, Malcolm and David Sanders. 1997. 'Party identification, political preferences and material conditions: evidence from the British Household Panel Survey, 1991–92.' *Party Politics*, 3: 53–77.

Budge, Ian. 1994. 'A new spatial theory of party competition.' *British Journal of Political Science*, 24: 443–67.

Budge, Ian, Ivor Crewe and Dennis Farlie. Eds. 1976. *Party Identification and Beyond*. New York: Wiley.

Budge, Ian and Dennis Farlie. 1977. *Voting and Party Competition*. London: Wiley.

Budge, Ian, David Robertson and Derek Hearl. Eds. 1987. *Ideology, Strategy and Party Change: Spatial Analyses of Post–War Election Programmes in 19 Democracies*. Cambridge: Cambridge University Press.

Burnham, Walter Dean. 1970. *Critical Elections and the Mainspring of American Politics*. New York: Transaction Books.

Burnham, Walter Dean. 1975. 'American politics in the 1970s: beyond party?'. In *The Future of Political Parties*, eds. Louis Maisel and Paul M. Sacks. Beverly Hills, CA: Sage.

Butler, David. 1951. *The Electoral System in Britain*. Oxford: Clarendon Press.

Butler, David and Denis Kavanagh. 1992. *The British General Election of 1992*. Basingstoke: Macmillan.

Butler, David and Dennis Kavanagh. 1997. *The British General Election of 1997*. Basingstoke: Macmillan.

Butler, David and Anthony King. 1965. *The British General Election of 1964*. London: Macmillan.

Butler, David and Richard Rose. 1960. *The British General Election of 1959*. London: Macmillan.

Butler, David and Donald E. Stokes. 1974. *Political Change in Britain: the Evolution of Electoral Choice*. 2nd edn. London: Macmillan.

Campbell, Angus, Philip Converse, Warren E. Miller and Donald E. Stokes. 1960. *The American Voter*. New York: Wiley.

Campbell, Angus, Philip Converse, Warren Miller and Donald Stokes. 1966. *Elections and the Political Order*. New York: Wiley

Carmines, Edwards G. and James A. Stimson. 1989. *Issue Evolution: Race and the Transformation of American Politics*. Princeton, NJ: Princeton University Press.

Cathcart, Brian. 1997. *Were You Still Up for Portillo?* London: Penguin.

CAWP. http://www.rci.rutgers.edu/~cawp/ggap.html

Christie, Carol. 1987. *Sex Differences in Political Participation* New York: Praeger.

Clarke, Peter. 1996. *Hope and Glory: Britain 1900–1990*. London: Allen Lane/The Penguin Press.

Clubb, Jerome and Howard Allen. Eds. 1971. *Electoral Change and Stability in American Political History*. New York: Free Press.

Clubb, Jerome M., William H. Flanigan and Nancy H. Zingale. 1990. *Partisan Realignment: Voters, Parties, and Government in American History*. Boulder, CO: Westview Press.

Conover, Pamela Johnston. 1994. 'Feminists and the gender gap.' In *Different Roles, Different Voices: Women and Politics in the United States and Europe*, eds. Marianne Githens, Pippa Norris and Joni Lovenduski. New York: HarperCollins.

Conservative Party. 1997. *Fresh Future*. London: Conservative Party.

Cook, Chris. 1975. *The Age of Alignment: Electoral Politics in Britain 1922–1929*. London: Macmillan.

Cook, Chris. 1993. *A Short History of the Liberal Party, 1900–92*. London: Macmillan.

Cook, Elizabeth A. and Clyde Wilcox. 1991. 'Feminism and the gender gap: a second look.' *Journal of Politics*, 53: 1111–22.

Cowley, Philip and Philip Norton. 1996. 'Blair's bastards: discontent within the parliamentary Labour Party.' *Centre for Legislative Studies*.

Cowling, David. 1998. 'And this is how it's been for us'. *New Statesman*, 1 May: 25.

CRC. 1975. *Participation of Ethnic Minorities in the General Election of October 1974*. London: Community Relations Commission.

CRE. 1980. *Votes and Policies*. London: Commission for Racial Equality.

CRE. 1984. *Ethnic Minorities and the 1983 General Election*. London: Commission for Racial Equality.

Crewe, Ivor. 1981. 'Why the Conservatives won.' In *Britain at the Polls 1979*, ed. Howard Penniman. Washington, DC: American Enterprise Institute.

Crewe, Ivor. 1983. 'Representation and ethnic minorities in Britain'. In *Ethnic Pluralism and Public Policy*, eds. Ken Young and Nathan Glazer. London: Heinemann.

Crewe, Ivor. 1985. 'Great Britain.' In *Electoral Change in Western Democracies*, eds. Ivor Crewe and David Denver. London: Croom Helm.

Crewe, Ivor. 1986. 'On the death and resurrection of class voting: some comments on how Britain votes.' *Political Studies*, 35: 620–38.

Crewe, Ivor. 1987. 'A new class of politics?' *Guardian*, 15 June.

Crewe, Ivor. 1992. 'Changing votes and unchanging voters.' *Electoral Studies*, 11: 335–45.

Crewe, Ivor. 1996. '1979–1997'. In *How Tory Governments Fall*, ed. Anthony Seldon. London: HarperCollins.

Crewe, Ivor. 1997. 'By–elections since 1983: did they matter?' In *By–elections in British Politics*, eds. Chris Cook and John Ramsden. London: UCL Press.

Crewe, Ivor, Tony Fox and James Alt. 1977a. 'Non–voting in British general elections.' In *British Political Sociology Yearbook 3*, ed. Colin Crouch. London: Croom Helm.

Crewe, Ivor, Anthony Fox and Neil Day. 1995. *The British Electorate, 1963–1992*. (2nd edn. Cambridge: Cambridge University Press.

Crewe, Ivor, Brian Gosschalk and John Bartle. Eds. 1998. *Political Communications: Why Labour Won the General Election of 1997*. London: Frank Cass.

Crewe, Ivor and Anthony King. 1995. SDP: *The Birth, Life and Death of the Social Democratic Party*. Oxford: Oxford University Press.

Crewe, Ivor, Bo Särlvik and James Alt. 1977b. 'Partisan dealignment in Britain 1964–74.' *British Journal of Political Science*, 7: 129–90.

Crewe, Ivor and Donald Searing. 1988. 'Ideological change in the British Conservative Party.' *American Political Science Review*, 82(2): 361–84.

Crewe, Ivor and Donald Searing. 1988. 'Mrs Thatcher's crusade: conservatism in Britain, 1972–1986.' In *The Resurgence of Conservatism in Anglo–American Democracies*, eds. B. Cooper, A. Kornberg and W. Mishler. Durham, NC: Duke University Press.

Curtice, John. 1988. 'One nation?' In *British Social Attitudes: The 5th Report*, eds. Roger Jowell, Sharon Witherspoon and Lindsay Brook. Aldershot: Gower.

Curtice, John. 1996. 'One nation again?' In *British Social Attitudes; the 13th Report*, eds. Roger Jowell, John Curtice, Alison Park, Lindsay Brook and Katarina Thomson. Aldershot: Dartmouth.

Curtice, John. 1997. 'Anatomy of a non–landslide.' *Politics Review*, 7(1): 2–8.

Curtice, John and Roger Jowell. 1995. 'The sceptical electorate.' In *British Social Attitudes, the 12th Report*, eds. Roger Jowell *et al.* Aldershot: Dartmouth.

Curtice, John and Roger Jowell. 1997. 'Trust in the political system.' In *British Social Attitudes: the 14th Report*, eds. Roger Jowell *et al.* Aldershot: Ashgate.

Curtice, John and Michael Steed. 1982. 'Electoral choice and the production of government: the changing operation of the electoral system in the United Kingdom since 1955.' *British Journal of Political Science*, 12(3): 249–98.

Curtice, John and Michael Steed. 1986. 'Proportionality and exaggeration in the British electoral system.' *Electoral Studies*, 5(3): 209–28.

Curtice, John and Michael Steed. 1992. 'Appendix 2: the results analysed.' In *The British General Election of 1992*, David Butler and Dennis Kavanagh. London: Macmillan

Curtice, John and Michael Steed. 1997. 'Appendix 2: the results analysed.' In *The British General Election of 1997*, David Butler and Dennis Kavanagh. Basingstoke: Macmillan.

Curtice, John and Michael Steed. 1998. 'Neither Representative Nor Accountable: First Past the Post in Britain.' Paper presented at the Annual Workshops of the European Consortium for Political Research, University of Warwick.

Dahya, B. 1974. 'The nature of Pakistani ethnicity in industrial cities in Britain.' In *Urban Ethnicity*, ed. A. Cohen. London: Tavistock.

Dalton, Russell. 1994. *The Green Rainbow*. New Haven, CT: Yale University Press.

Dalton, Russell. 1996. *Citizen Politics: Public Opinion and Political Parties in Advanced Industrial Democracies.* 2nd edn. Chatham, NJ: Chatham House Publishers.

Dangerfield, George. 1935. *The Strange Death of Liberal England*. New York: H. Smith & R. Hass.

Denver, David and Gordon Hands. 1974. 'Marginality and turnout in British general elections.' *British Journal of Political Science*, 4: 17–35.

Denver, David and Gordon Hands. 1985. 'Marginality and turnout in British general elections in the 1970s.' *British Journal of Political Science*, 15: 381–8.

Denver, David and Gordon Hands. 1992. 'Constituency campaigning.' *Parliamentary Affairs*, 45: 528–44.

Denver, David and Gordon Hands. 1997a. 'Turnout.' In *Britain Votes, 1997*, eds. Pippa Norris and Neil Gavin. Oxford: Oxford University Press.

Denver, David and Gordon Hands. 1997b. *Modern Constituency Electioneering*. London: Frank Cass.

De Vaus, David and Ian McAllister. 1989. 'The changing politics of women: gender and political alignments in 11 nations.' *European Journal of Political Research*, 17: 241–62.

Donoughue, Bernard. 1987. *Prime Minister: The Conduct of Policy under Harold Wilson and James Callaghan*. London: Jonathan Cape.

Drucker, Henry M. 1989. *Multi–Party Britain*. London: Macmillan.

Dunleavy, Patrick and Christopher Husband. 1985. *British Democracy at the Crossroads*. London: Allen & Unwin.

Dunleavy, Patrick and Helen Margetts. 1997. 'The electoral system.' In *Britain Votes 1997*, eds. Pippa Norris and Neil Gavin. Oxford: Oxford University Press.

Durant, Henry W. 1949. *Political Opinion*. London.

Durant, Henry. 1969. 'Voting behaviour in Britain 1945–1966.' In *Studies in British Politics*, ed. Richard Rose. London: Macmillan.

Duverger, Maurice. 1954. *Political Parties*. Paris: Colin.

Duverger, Maurice. 1955. *The Political Role of Women*. Paris: UNESCO.

Eagle, Maria and Joni Lovenduski. 1998. *High Time or High Tide for Labour Women?* Fabian Pamphlet 585. London: Fabian Society.

Eichenberg, Richard and Russell Dalton. 1993. 'Europeans and the European Community: the dynamics of public support for European integration.'

International Organization, 47: 507–34.

Emler, Nick and Liz Frazer. Forthcoming. 'The education effect.' *Oxford Review of Education.*

Epstein, Leon. 1967. *Political Parties in Western Democracies.* New Brunswick, NJ: Transaction Books.

Erikson, Robert and John H. Goldthorpe. 1992. 'Individual or family? Results from two approaches to class assignments.' *Acta Sociologica,* 35: 95–106.

Evans, Brendan and Andrew Taylor. 1996. *From Salisbury to Major.* Manchester: Manchester University Press.

Evans, Geoffrey. 1994. 'Tactical voting and Labour's prospects.' In *Labour's Last Chance? The 1992 Election and Beyond,* eds. Anthony Heath, Roger Jowell and John Curtice with Bridget Taylor. Aldershot: Dartmouth.

Evans, Geoffrey. 1995. 'The state of The Union: attitudes towards Europe.' In *British Social Attitudes: the 12th Report,* eds. Roger Jowell, John Curtice, Alison Park and Lindsay Brook. Aldershot: Dartmouth.

Evans, Geoffrey. 1998a. 'How Britain views the EU.' In *British – and European – Social Attitudes, the 15th Report,* eds. Roger Jowell, John Curtice, Alison Park, Lindsay Brook, Katarina Thomson and Caroline Bryson. Aldershot: Ashgate.

Evans, Geoffrey. 1998b. 'Euroscepticism and Conservative electoral support: how an asset became a liability.' *British Journal of Political Science,* 28: 573–90.

Evans, Geoffrey. Ed. 1999a. *The End of Class Politics? Class Voting in Comparative Context.* Oxford: Oxford University Press.

Evans, Geoffrey. 1999b. 'Economics and politics revisited: explaining the decline in Conservative support, 1992–95.' *Political Studies* 47 (1): 139–51.

Evans, Geoffrey, John Curtice and Pippa Norris. 1998. 'New Labour, new tactical voting?' In *British Elections and Parties Review* 8, eds. David Denver, Justin Fisher, Phillip Cowley and Charles Pattie. London: Frank Cass.

Evans, Geoffrey and Anthony Heath. 1995. 'The measurement of left–right and libertarian–authoritarian values: comparing balanced and unbalanced scales.' *Quality and Quantity,* 29: 19–206.

Evans, Geoffrey, Anthony Heath and Mansur Lalljee. 1996a. 'Measuring left–right and libertarian–authoritarian values in the British electorate.' *British Journal of Sociology,* 47: 93–112.

Evans, Geoffrey, Anthony Heath and Clive Payne. 1991. 'Modelling the class/party relationship 1964–87', *Electoral Studies,* 10: 99–117.

Evans, Geoffrey, Anthony Heath and Clive Payne. 1996b. 'Class and party revisited: a new model for estimating changes in levels of class voting.' In *British Elections and Parties Yearbook, 1995,* eds. Colin Rallings, David Farrell, David Denver and David Broughton. London: Frank Cass.

Farrell, David M. 1996. 'Campaign strategies and tactics'. In *Comparing Democracies: Elections and Voting in Global Perspective,* eds. Lawrence LeDuc, Richard G. Niemi and Pippa Norris. Thousand Oaks, CA: Sage.

Field, William. 1997. *Regional Dynamics: The Basis of Electoral Support in Britain.* London: Frank Cass.

Finkelstein, Danny. 1998. 'Why the Conservatives lost.' In *Political Communications: Why Labour Won the General Election of 1997,* eds. Ivor Crewe, Brian Gosschalk and John Bartle. London: Frank Cass.

Firth, David. 1998. 'LLAMA: an object–oriented system for log multiplicative models.' In *COMPSTAT 98, Proceedings in Computational Statistics,* eds. Roger Payne and Peter Green. Heidelberg: Physica-Verlag.

Flickinger, Richard. 1994. 'British political parties and public attitudes towards the European Community: leading, following or getting out of the way?' In *British Elections and Parties Yearbook 1994,* eds. David Broughton, David Farrell, David Denver and Colin Rallings. London: Frank Cass.

Franklin, Mark. 1985. *The Decline of Class Voting in Britain: Changes in the Basis of Electoral Choice, 1964–1983.* Oxford: Clarendon Press.

Franklin, Mark and Matthew Ladner. 1995. 'The undoing of Winston Churchill: mobilization and conversion in the 1945 realignment of British voters.' *British Journal of Political Science*, 25(4): 429–52.

Franklin, Mark, Tom Mackie, Henri Valen, *et al.* 1992. *Electoral Change: Responses to Evolving Social and Attitudinal Structures in Western Countries.* Cambridge: Cambridge University Press.

Franklin, Mark, Michael Marsh and Lauren McLaren. 1994. 'Uncorking the bottle: popular opposition to European unification in the wake of Maastricht.' *Journal of Common Market Studies*, 32: 455–72.

Franklin, Mark and Christopher Wlezien. 1997. 'The responsive public: issue salience, policy change, and preferences for European unification.' *Journal of Theoretical Politics*, 9: 347–63.

Fukuyama, Francis. 1992. *The End of History and the Last Man.* Harmondsworth: Penguin.

Gamble, Andrew. 1988. *The Free Economy and the Strong State.* Basingstoke: Macmillan Education.

Gamble, Andrew. 1996. 'The legacy of Thatcherism.' In *The Blair Agenda*, ed. M. Perryman. London: Lawrence & Wishart.

Garner, Robert and Richard Kelly. 1993. *British Political Parties Today.* Manchester: Manchester University Press.

Geddes, Andrew and Jonathan Tonge. Eds. 1997. *Labour's Landslide.* Manchester: University of Manchester Press.

George, Stephen and Ben Rosamund. 1992. 'The European Community.' In *The Changing Labour Party*, eds. Michael Smith and Jim Spear. London: Routledge.

Giddens, Anthony. 1998. *The Third Way.* Oxford: Polity.

Goldstein, H. 1995. *Multilevel Statistical Models.* London: Edward Arnold.

Goldthorpe, John. 1996. 'Class and politics in advanced industrial societies.' In *Conflicts about Class: Debating Inequality in Late Industrialism*, eds. David Lee and Bryan Turner. London: Longman.

Goldthorpe, John. 1999. 'Modelling the pattern of class voting in British elections, 1964–92.' In *The End of Class Politics? Class Voting in Comparative Context*, ed. Geoffrey Evans. Oxford: Oxford University Press.

Goldthorpe, John and Anthony Heath. 1992. *Revised Class Schema 1992'.* JUSST Working Paper No. 13. Oxford: Nuffield College and SCPR.

Goldthorpe, John, David Lockwood, Frank Bechhoffer and Jennifer Platt. 1968. *The Affluent Worker: Political Attitudes and Behaviour.* Cambridge: Cambridge University Press.

Goot, Murray and Elizabeth Reid. 1984. 'Women: if not apolitical, then Conservative.' In *Women and the Public Sphere*, eds. Janet Siltanen and Michelle Stanworth. London: Hutchinson.

Graham, David and Peter Clarke. 1986. *The New Enlightenment: The Rebirth of Liberalism.* London: Macmillan.

Guardian, The. 1996. 'The campaign will urge black people to use their vote.' 2 December.

Gudgin, Graham and Peter Taylor. 1979. *Seats, Votes and the Spatial Organisation of Elections.* London: Pion.

Hanham, H.J. 1959. *Elections and Party Management: Politics in the Time of Disraeli and Gladstone.* London: Longman.

Harrop, Martin and Andrew Shaw. 1989. *Can Labour Win?* London: Unwin Hyman.

Hayes, Bernadette C. 1997. 'Gender, feminism and electoral behaviour in Britain.' *Electoral Studies*, 16(2): 203–16.

Hayes, Bernadette C. and Ian McAllister. 1997. 'Gender, party leaders and election outcomes in Australia, Britain and the United States.' *Comparative Political*

Studies, 30: 3–26.

Heath, Anthony and John Curtice. 1998. 'New Labour, New Voters?' Paper presented at the annual conference of the PSA, April.

Heath, Anthony and Geoffrey Evans. 1988. 'Working class conservatives and middle class socialists.' In *British Social Attitudes: The 1988 Report*, eds. Roger Jowell, Sharon Witherspoon and Lindsay Brook. Aldershot: Gower.

Heath, Anthony, Geoffrey Evans and Jean Martin. 1994a. 'The measurement of core beliefs and values: the development of balanced socialist/laissez faire and libertarian/authoritarian scales.' *British Journal of Political Science*, 24: 115–31.

Heath, Anthony, Geoffrey Evans, and Clive Payne. 1995a. 'Modelling the class–party relationship in Britain, 1964–92'. *Journal of the Royal Statistical Society*, Series A, 158: 563–74.

Heath, Anthony and Roger Jowell. 1994. 'The impact of Labour's policy review.' In *Labour's Last Chance? The 1992 Election and Beyond*, eds. Anthony Heath, Roger Jowell and John Curtice with Bridget Taylor. Aldershot: Dartmouth.

Heath, Anthony, Roger Jowell and John Curtice. 1985. *How Britain Votes*. Oxford: Pergamon Press.

Heath, Anthony, Roger Jowell, John Curtice and Geoffrey Evans. 1990. 'The rise of a new political agenda?' *European Sociological Review*, 6: 31–49.

Heath, Anthony, Roger Jowell, John Curtice, Geoffrey Evans, Julia Field and Sharon Witherspoon. 1991. *Understanding Political Change: The British Voter 1964–1987*. Oxford: Pergamon.

Heath, Anthony, Roger Jowell and John Curtice with Bridget Taylor. Eds. 1994b. *Labour's Last Chance? The 1992 Election and Beyond*. Aldershot: Dartmouth.

Heath, Anthony, Roger Jowell, John Curtice and Bridget Taylor. 1995b. 'The 1994 European and Local Elections: Abstention, Protest and Conversion.' Paper presented at the annual conference of the PSA, April.

Heath, Anthony and S.-K. McDonald. 1988. 'The demise of party identification theory.' *Electoral Studies* 7: 95–107.

Heath, Anthony and Dorren McMahon. 1992. 'Changes in values.' In *British Social Attitudes: The 9th Report*, eds. Roger Jowell, Lindsay Brook and Bridget Taylor. Aldershot: Dartmouth/SCPR.

Heath, Anthony and Dorren McMahon. 1997. 'Education and occupational attainments: the impact of ethnic origins.' In *Ethnicity in the 1991 Census, Volume 4*, ed. Valerie Karn. London: HMSO.

Heath, Anthony and Roy Pierce. 1992. 'It was party identification all along: question order effects on reports of party identification in Britain.' *Electoral Studies*, 11: 93–105.

Heath, Anthony, Bridget Taylor, Lindsay Brook and Alison Park. 1999. 'British national sentiment.' *British Journal of Political Science*, 29: 155–75.

Heath, Anthony, *et al.* Forthcoming. *New Labour and the Future of the Left*. Oxford: Oxford University Press.

Heffernan, Richard and Mike Marqusee. 1992. *Defeat From the Jaws of Victory*. London: Verso.

Hewitt, Patricia and Deborah Mattinson. 1987. *Women's Votes: The Keys to Winning*. Fabian Pamphlet. London: Fabian Society.

Heywood, Paul. 1994. 'Britain's dominant–party system.' In *Britain's Changing Party System*, eds. Lynton Robbins, Hilary Blackmore and Robert Pyper. Leicester: Leicester University Press.

Holmberg, Soren. 1994. 'Party identification compared across the Atlantic.' In *Elections at Home and Abroad: Essays in Honor of Warren E. Miller*, eds. M. Kent Jennings and Thomas E. Mann. Ann Arbor, MI: University of Michigan Press.

Hoover, Kenneth and Raymond Plant. 1989. *Conservative Capitalism*. London: Routledge.

Inglehart, Ronald. 1977. *The Silent Revolution: Changing Values and Political Styles Among Western Publics*. Princeton, NJ: Princeton University Press.

Inglehart, Ronald. 1990. *Culture Shift in Advanced Industrial Society*. Princeton, NJ: Princeton University Press.

Inglehart, Ronald. 1997a. *Modernization and Postmodernization: Cultural, Economic and Political Change in 43 Societies*. Princeton, NJ: Princeton University Press.

Inglehart, Ronald. 1997b. 'Changing Gender Gaps.' Paper presented at the conference on Representation and European Citizenship, Rome.

Inglehart, Ronald and Pippa Norris. 1998. 'The Global Gender–Generation Gap.' Paper for the American Political Science Association annual meeting, Boston, MA.

Inglehart, Ronald, Jean–Jacques Rabier and Karl–Heinz Reif. 1991. 'The evolution of public attitudes towards European integration: 1970–86.' In *Eurobarometer: The dynamics of European Public Opinion*, eds. Karl–Heinz Reif and Ronald Inglehart. London: Macmillan.

International Institute for Democracy and Electoral Assistance (IDEA). 1997. *Voter Turnout from 1945 to 1997: A Global Report*. Stockholm: International IDEA.

Jackman, Robert W. 1987. 'Political institutions and voter turnout in the industrial democracies.' *American Political Science Review*, 81: 405–23.

Janssen, Jos. 1991. 'Postmaterialism, cognitive mobilization and public support for European integration.' *British Journal of Political Science*, 21: 443–68.

Jelen, Ted G., Sue Thomas and Clyde Wilcox. 1994. 'The gender gap in comparative perspective.' *European Journal of Political Research*, 25: 171–86.

Jenkins of Hillhead, Lord. Chmn. 1998. *The Report of the Independent Commission on the Voting System*. London: The Stationery Office, Cm 4090.

Jenkins, Peter. 1987. *Mrs Thatcher's Revolution: The Ending of the Socialist Era*. London: Jonathan Cape.

Johnston, Ron and Charles Pattie. 1995. 'The impact of spending on party constituency campaigns at recent British general elections.' *Party Politics*, 1: 261–73.

Johnston, Ron and Charles J. Pattie. 1996. 'The strength of party identification among the British electorate: an exploration.' *Electoral Studies*, 15: 295–310.

Johnston, Ron J. and Charles J. Pattie. 1997a. 'Fluctuating party identification in Britain: patterns revealed by four years of longitudinal study'. *Politics*, 17: 67–77.

Johnston, Ron and Charles J. Pattie. 1997b. 'Anchors a-weigh: variations in strength of party identification and in socio–political attitudes among the British electorate, 1991–4.' In *British Elections and Parties Review*, ed. Charles Pattie, David Denver, Justin Fisher and Steven Ludlam. London: Frank Cass.

Johnston, Ron, Charles Pattie and J. Allsopp. 1988. *A Nation Dividing? The Electoral Map of Great Britain 1979–87*. Harlow: Longman.

Jones, Nicholas. 1997. *Campaign 1997: How the General Election Was Won and Lost*. London: Indigo.

Katz, Richard S. and Peter Mair. 1994. *How Parties Organize: Change and Adaptation in Party Organizations in Western Democracies*. London: Sage Publications.

Katz, Richard S. and Peter Mair. 1995. 'Changing models of party organisation and party democracy: the emergence of the cartel party.' *Party Politics*, 1: 5–28.

Katz, Richard S., Peter Mair *et al.* 1992. 'The membership of parties in European democracies, 1960–1990.' *European Journal of Political Research*, 22: 329–45.

Kavanagh, Dennis. 1997 'The Labour campaign.' In *Britain Votes 1997*, eds. Pippa Norris and Neil Gavin. Oxford: Oxford University Press.

Kavanagh, Dennis and Peter Morris. 1994. *Consensus Politics From Attlee to Major*.

Oxford: Blackwell.

Kavanagh, Dennis and Anthony Seldon. Eds. 1994. *The Major Effect.* London: Macmillan.

Kellner, Peter. 1997. 'Why the Tories were trounced.' In *Britain Votes* 1997, eds. Pippa Norris and Neil Gavin. Oxford: Oxford University Press.

Key, V.O. 1955. 'A theory of critical elections.' *The Journal of Politics,* 17: 3–18.

Key, V.O. 1959. 'Secular realignment and the party system.' *The Journal of Politics,* 21(2): 198–210.

Kiernan, Kathleen. 1992. 'Men and women at work and at home.' In *British Social Attitudes: The 9th Report,* eds. Roger Jowell *et al.* Aldershot: Dartmouth/SCPR.

King, Anthony. 1992. 'The implications of one party government.' In *Britain at the Polls, 1992,* ed. Anthony King. Chatham, NJ: Chatham House.

King, Anthony. 1997a. 'Why Labour won – at last.' In *New Labour Triumphs: Britain at the Polls,* ed. Anthony King. Chatham, NJ: Chatham House Publishers.

King, Anthony. Ed. 1997b. *New Labour Triumphs: Britain at the Polls.* Chatham, NJ: Chatham House.

Kinnear, Michael. 1973. *The Fall of Lloyd George: The Political Crisis of 1922.* London: Macmillan.

Kirchheimer, Otto. 1966. 'The transformation of the western European party systems.' In *Political Parties and Political Development,* eds. Joseph LaPalombara and Myron Weiner. Princeton, NJ: Princeton University Press.

Kitschelt, Herbert. 1994. *The Transformation of European Social Democracy.* New York: Cambridge University Press.

Kitschelt, Herbert. 1995. *The Radical Right in Western Europe.* Ann Arbor, MI: University of Michigan Press.

Klingemann, Hans–Dieter, Richard Hofferbert and Ian Budge. 1994. *Parties, Policies and Democracy.* Boulder, CO: Westview Press.

Koelble, Thomas. 1992. 'Recasting social democracy in Europe: A nested games explanation of strategic adjustment in political parties.' *Politics and Society, 20:* 51–70.

Kogan, Maurice and David Kogan. 1982. *The Battle for the Labour Party.* London: Kogan Page

Krasner, Stephen. 1993. 'Approaches to the state: alternative conceptions and historical dynamics.' *Comparative Politics,* 16(2): 223–46.

LaPalombara, Joseph and Myron Weiner. 1966: *Political Parties.* Princeton, NJ: Princeton University

Laver, Michael and Ian Budge. Eds. 1992. *Party Policy and Government Coalitions.* London: Macmillan.

Layton-Henry, Zig. 1978. 'Race, electoral strategy and the major parties.' *Parliamentary Affairs,* 21: 274–5.

Layton-Henry, Zig and Donley Studlar. 1985. 'The electoral participation of Black and Asian Britons.' *Parliamentary Affairs,* 38: 307–18.

Le Lohe, Michael. 1998. 'Ethnic minority participation and representation in the British electoral system.' In *Race and British Electoral Politics,* ed. Shamit Saggar. London: UCL Press.

Lee, D.J. and B.S. Turner. Eds. 1996. *Conflicts about Class: Debating Inequality in Late Industrialism. London: Longman.*

Leigh, David and Ed Vulliamy. 1997. *Sleaze: The Corruption of Parliament.* London: Fourth Estate.

Lindberg, Leon and Stuart Scheingold. 1970. *Europe's Would-be Polity: Patterns of Change in the European Community.* Englewood Cliffs, NJ: Prentice-Hall.

Lipset, Seymour M. 1960. *Political Man: The Social Bases of Politics.* Garden City, NY: Doubleday.

Lipset, Seymour Martin. 1981. *Political Man.* 2nd edn. Garden City, NY: Doubleday.

Lipset, Seymour Martin and Stein Rokkan. Eds. 1967a. *Party Systems and Voter Alignments: Cross-national Perspectives*. London: Collier-Macmillan.

Lipset, Seymour Martin and Stein Rokkan. 1967b. 'Cleavage systems, party systems and voter alignments: an introduction.' In *Party Systems and Voter Alignments*, eds. Seymour Martin Lipset and Stein Rokkan. New York: Free Press.

Lovenduski, Joni. 1997. 'Gender politics.' In *Britain Votes 1997*, eds. Pippa Norris and Neil Gavin. Oxford: Oxford University Press.

Lovenduski, Joni and Pippa Norris. Eds. 1993. *Gender and Party Politics*. London: Sage Publications.

Lovenduski, Joni and Pippa Norris. Eds. 1996. *Women in Politics*. Oxford: Oxford University Press.

Lovenduski, Joni, Pippa Norris and Catriona Burness. 1994. 'The party and women.' In *Conservative Century*, eds. Anthony Seldon and Stuart Ball. Oxford: Oxford University Press.

Lynn, Peter and Bridget Taylor. 1995. 'On the bias and variance of samples of individuals: a comparison of the electoral registers and postcode address file as sampling frames.' *The Statistician*, 44: 173–94.

MacAskill, Ewen. 1998. 'Stuff that envelope, say the activists.' *Guardian*, 23 June: 17.

Mair, Peter. 1997. *Party System Change*. Oxford: Oxford University Press.

Mandelson, Peter and Roger Liddle. 1996. *The Blair Revolution: Can New Labour Deliver?* London: Faber & Faber.

Manza, Jeff and Clem Brooks. 1998. 'The gender gap in US presidential elections: when? why? implications?' *American Journal of Sociology*, 103(5): 1235–66.

Manza, Jeff, Michael Hout and Clem Brooks. 1995. 'Class voting in capitalist democracies since WWII.' *Annual Review of Sociology*, 21: 137–63.

Margetts, Helen and Gareth Smyth. Eds. 1994. *Turning Japanese? Britain with a Permanent Party of Government*. London: Lawrence & Wishart.

Martin, Jean, Colm O'Muircheartaigh and John Curtice. 1993. 'The use of CAPI for attitude surveys: an experimental comparison with traditional methods.' *Journal of Official Statistics*, 9: 641–61.

Marx, Karl. 1961. *Capital*. Moscow: Foreign Language Publishing House.

May, John D. 1973. 'Opinion structure of political parties: the special law of curvi-linear disparity.' *Political Studies*, 21: 135–51.

McAllister, Ian and Martin Wattenberg. 1995. 'Measuring levels of party identification: does question order matter?' *Public Opinion Quarterly*, 59: 259–68.

McCallum, Ronald B. and Alison V. Readman. 1947. *The British General Election of 1945*. London: G. Cumberlege.

McKibbin, R. 1974. *The Evolution of the Labour Party 1910–1924*. Oxford: Oxford University Press.

McLean, Iain. 1970. 'The rise and fall of the Scottish National Party.' *Political Studies*, 18: 367–72

Merriam, C.E. and H.F. Gosnell. 1924. *Non-voting: Causes and Methods of Control*. Chicago, IL: University of Chicago Press.

Messina, Anthony. 1989. *Race and Party Competition*. Oxford: Clarendon Press.

Messina, Anthony. 1998. 'Ethnic minorities and the British party system in the 1990s and beyond.' In *Race and British Electoral Politics*, ed. Shamit Saggar. London: UCL Press.

Miller, Warren and Merrill Shanks. 1996. *The Changing American Voter*. Ann Arbor, MI: University of Michigan Press.

Miller, William L. 1977. *Electoral Dynamics in Britain Since 1918*. London: Macmillan.

Miller, William, Stephen Tagg and Keith Britto. 1986. 'Partisanship and party preference in government and opposition: the mid–term perspective.' *Electoral Studies*, 5: 31–46.

Mills, Colin. 1994. 'Who dominates whom?' *Sociological Review*, 42: 639–63.

Mitchell, Austin. 1995. *Election '45*. London: Fabian Society.

Morgan, Kenneth. 1979. *The Lloyd George Coalition Government 1918–22*. Oxford: Oxford University Press.

MORI. 1997. 'Asian voting: preliminary results.' (Unpublished briefing notes.)

MORI. 1998. *British Public Opinion*, XXI (March).

Mueller, Carol. Ed. 1988. ed. *The Politics of the Gender Gap*. London: Sage.

Nardulli, Peter F. 1995. 'The concept of critical realignment, electoral behavior, and political change.' *American Political Science Review*, 89(1): 10–22.

Narud, H.M. and H. Valens. (1996). 'Decline of electoral turnout: the case of Norway.' *European Journal of Political Research*, 29: 235–56.

Nie, Norman H., Sidney Verba and John R. Petrocik. 1976. *The Changing American Voter*. Cambridge, MA: Harvard University Press.

Niedermayer, Oskar. 1995. 'Trends and contrasts.' In *Public Opinion and Internationalized Governance*, eds. Oskar Niedermayer and Richard Sinnott. Oxford: Oxford University Press.

Norris, Pippa. 1985. 'The gender gap in America and Britain.' *Parliamentary Affairs*, 38: 192–201.

Norris, Pippa. 1986. 'Conservative attitudes in recent British elections: an emerging gender gap?' *Political Studies*, 34: 120–8.

Norris, Pippa. 1988. 'The gender gap: a cross national trend?' In *The Politics of the Gender Gap*, ed. Carol Mueller. Beverly Hills, CA: Sage.

Norris, Pippa. 1990. *British By–elections*. Oxford: Clarendon.

Norris, Pippa. 1993. 'The gender–generation gap in British Elections.' In *British Elections and Parties Yearbook 1993*, eds. David Denver, Pippa Norris, David Broughton, Colin Rallings. London: Harvester Wheatsheaf.

Norris, Pippa. 1994. 'Labour Party factionalism and extremism.' In *Labour's Last Chance?* eds. Anthony Heath, Roger Jowell and John Curtice. Aldershot: Dartmouth.

Norris, Pippa. 1995. 'May's law of curvilinear disparity revisited: leaders, officers, members and voters in British political parties.' *Party Politics*, 1: 29–47.

Norris, Pippa. 1996a. 'Gender realignment in comparative perspective.' In *The Paradox of Parties*, ed. Marian Simms. Melbourne: Allen & Unwin.

Norris, Pippa. 1996b. 'Mobilising the women's vote: the gender-generation gap in voting behaviour.' *Parliamentary Affairs*, 49(1): 333–42.

Norris, Pippa. 1996c. *Electoral Change Since 1945*. Oxford: Blackwell.

Norris, Pippa. 1997a. *Electoral Change in Britain Since 1945*. Oxford: Blackwell.

Norris, Pippa. 1997b. 'The battle for the campaign agenda.' In *New Labour Triumphs: Britain at the Polls*, ed. Anthony King. Chatham, NJ: Chatham House.

Norris, Pippa. 1997c. 'Anatomy of a Labour landslide.' In *Britain Votes, 1997*, eds. Pippa Norris and Neil Gavin. Oxford: Oxford University Press.

Norris, Pippa. 1998. 'Political elites and constitutional change: principles or interests?' In *Understanding Constitutional Change: Special Issue of Scottish Affairs*. Edinburgh: University of Edinburgh.

Norris, Pippa. 1999. *Critical Citizens: Global Support for Democratic Government*. Oxford: Oxford University Press.

Norris, Pippa, John Curtice, David Sanders, Maggie Scammell and Holli Semetko. 1999. *On Message: Communicating the Campaign*. London: Sage.

Norris, Pippa and Neil Gavin. 1997. *Britain Votes 1997*. Oxford: Oxford University Press.

Norris, Pippa and Joni Lovenduski. 1995. *Political Recruitment: Gender, Race and Class in the British Parliament*. Cambridge: Cambridge University Press.

Norton, Philip. 1997. 'The Conservative Party.' In *New Labour Triumphs: Britain at the Polls*, ed. Anthony King. Chatham, NJ: Chatham House.

Oskarson, Maria. 1995. 'Gender gaps in Nordic voting behaviour.' In *Women in*

Nordic Politics, eds. Lauri Karvonen and Per Selle. Aldershot: Dartmouth.

Owen, Charlie, Peter Mortimore and Ann Phoenix. 1997. 'Higher education qualifications.' In *Ethnicity in the 1991 Census, Volume 4*, ed. Valerie Karn. London: HMSO.

Page, B. I. and R. Y. Shapiro. 1992. *The Rational Public*. Chicago: University of Chicago Press.

Panebianco, Angelo. 1988. *Political Parties: Organization and Power*. Cambridge: Cambridge University Press.

Paterson, Lindsay. Ed. 1998. *A Diverse Assembly: The Debate on a Scottish Parliament*. Edinburgh: Edinburgh University Press.

Pattie, Charles and Ron Johnston. 1998. 'Voter turnout at the British general election of 1992: rational choice, social standing or political efficacy?' *European Journal of Political Research*, 33: 263–83.

Peake, Lucy. 1997. 'Women in the campaign and in the Commons.' In *Labour's Landslide*, eds. Andrew Geddes and Jonathan Tonge. Manchester: Manchester University Press.

Pelling, Henry. 1967. *Social Geography of British Elections, 1885–1910*. London: Macmillan.

Perrigo, Sarah. 1996. 'Women and change in the Labour Party 1979–1995.' In *Women in Politics*, eds. Joni Lovenduski and Pippa Norris. Oxford: Oxford University Press.

Pimlott, Ben. 1992. *Harold Wilson*. London: HarperCollins.

Pimlott, Ben. 1997. 'New Labour, new era?' *Political Quarterly*, 68(4): 325–34.

Pinto-Duschinsky, Michael. 1998. 'Conservative Party Membership.' Paper presented at the EPOP annual conference, University of Essex, 27 September.

Piven, Frances Fox and Richard A. Cloward. 1988. *Why Americans Don't Vote*. New York: Pantheon Books.

Plissner, Martin. 1983. 'The marriage gap?' *Public Opinion*, 6.

Powell, G. Bingham Jr. 1986. 'American voter turnout in comparative perspective.' *American Political Science Review* 80: 17–44.

Przeworski, Adam. 1985. *Capitalism and Social Democracy*. Cambridge: Cambridge University Press.

Przeworski, Adam and John Sprague. 1986. *Paper Stones: A History of Electoral Socialism*. Chicago, IL: University of Chicago Press.

Pulzer, Peter G.J. 1967. *Political Representation and Elections in Britain*. London: Allen & Unwin.

Radice, Giles. 1992. *Southern Discomfort*. Fabian Society Pamphlet 555. London: Fabian Society.

Rallings, Colin and Michael Thrasher. 1997. *Local Elections in Britain*. London: Routledge.

Rasmussen, Jorgen. 1997. 'What kind of vision is that? British public attitudes towards the European Community during the Thatcher era.' *British Journal of Political Science*, 27: 111–18.

Ratcliffe, Peter. 1997. 'Race, ethnicity and housing differentials in Britain.' In *Ethnicity in the 1991 Census, Volume 4*, ed. Valerie Karn. London: HMSO.

Reif, Karl-Heinz and Hermann Schmitt. 1980. 'Nine second–order national elections.' *European Journal of Political Research* 8: 3–45.

Rentoul, John. 1995. *Tony Blair*. London: Little Brown.

Rex, John and Robert Moore. 1967. *Race, Community and Conflict: A Study of Sparkbrook*. Oxford: Oxford University Press.

Rich, Paul. 1998. 'Ethnic politics and the Conservatives in the post-Thatcher era.' In *Race and British Electoral Politics*, ed. Shamit Saggar. London: UCL Press.

Ridley, Fred and Alan Doig. 1995. *Sleaze: Politicians, Private Interests and Public Reactions*. Oxford: Oxford University Press.

Rinehart, S. T. 1992. *Gender, Consciousness and Politics*. London: Routledge.

Robertson, David. 1976. *A Theory of Party Competition.* London: Wiley.

Robinson, Vaughan. 1988. 'The new Indian middle class in Britain.' *Ethnic and Racial Studies*, 11 (4): 456–73.

Robinson, Vaughan. 1990. 'Roots to mobility: the social mobility of Britain's black population 1971–87.' *Ethnic and Racial Studies*, 13: 274–86.

Rokeach, M. 1973. *The Nature of Human Values.* New York: Free Press.

Rokkan, Stein. 1970. *Citizens, Elections, Parties. Approaches to the Comparative Study of the Processes of Development.* Oslo: Universitetsforlaget.

Rose, Richard. 1974. *Electoral Behavior: A Comparative Handbook.* New York: Free Press.

Rose, Richard. 1997. 'The new Labour government: on the crest of a wave.' *Parliamentary Affairs*, 50(4).

Rose, Richard and Ian McAllister. 1986. *Voters Begin to Choose: From Closed Class to Open Elections in Britain.* London: Sage.

Rose, Richard and Ian McAllister. 1990. *The Loyalties of Voters.* London: Sage.

Ross, James F.S. 1955. *Elections and Electors: Studies in Democratic Representation.* London: Eyre & Spottiswoode.

Sabucedo, J.M. and D. Cramer. 1991. 'Sociological and psychological predictors of voting in Great Britain.' *Journal of Social Psychology*, 131: 647–54.

Saggar, Shamit. 1997a. 'Racial politics.' *Parliamentary Affairs*, 50: 693–707.

Saggar, Shamit. 1997b. 'The dog that did not bite.' In *Labour's Landslide*, eds. Andrew Geddes and John Tonge. Manchester: Manchester University Press.

Saggar, Shamit. 1998a. 'Race and voting: some conceptual and theoretical concerns.' In *Race and British Electoral Politics*, ed. Shamit Saggar. London: UCL Press.

Saggar, Shamit. 1998b. 'Piecing together the puzzle.' In *Race and British Electoral Politics*, ed. Shamit Saggar. London: UCL Press.

Saggar, Shamit. 1998c. 'A late, though not lost, opportunity: ethnic minority electors, party strategy and the Conservative Party.' *The Political Quarterly*, 69: 148–59.

Saggar, Shamit. Forthcoming. 'Smoking guns and magic bullets: The "race card" debate revisited in 1997.' *Immigrants and Minorities.*

Sanders, David. 1996. 'Economic performance, management competence and the outcome of the next general election.' *Political Studies*, 44: 203–31.

Sanders, David. 1997a. 'The new electoral battleground.' In *New Labour Triumphs: Britain at the Polls*, ed. Anthony King. London: Chatham House.

Sanders, David. 1997b. 'Voting and the electorate.' In *Developments in British Politics 5*, eds. Patrick Dunleavy, Andrew Gamble, Ian Holliday and Gillian Peele. London: Macmillan.

Sanders, David and Malcolm Brynin. 1999. 'The dynamics of party preference change in Britain, 1991–96.' *Political Studies*, forthcoming.

Särlvik, Bo and Ivor Crewe. 1983. *Decade of Dealignment: The Conservative Victory of 1979 and Electoral Trends in the 1970s.* London: Cambridge University Press.

Sartori, Giovanni. 1969. 'From the sociology of politics to political sociology.' In *Politics and the Social Sciences*, ed. Seymour Martin Lipset. Oxford: Oxford University Press.

Saunders, P. 1990. *A Nation of Home Owners?* London: Unwin Hyman.

Scammell, Margaret. 1995. *Designer Politics: How Elections are Won.* London: Macmillan.

Scarbrough, Elinor. 1984. *Ideology and Voting Behaviour: An Exploratory Study.* Oxford, Clarendon Press.

Scarrow, Susan. 1996. *Parties and their Members: Organizing for Victory in Britain and Germany.* Oxford: Oxford University Press.

Schaffer, Steven D. 1981. 'A multivariate explanation of decreasing turnout in presidential elections, 1960–1976.' *American Journal of Political Science*, 25:

68–95.

Schmitt, Hermann and Sören Holmberg. 1995. 'Political parties in decline?' In *Citizens and the State*, eds. Hans-Dieter Klingemann and Dieter Fuchs. Oxford: Oxford University Press.

Seawright, David and John Curtice. 1992. 'The decline of the Scottish Conservative and Unionist Party: religion, ideology or economics?' *Contemporary Record*, 9 (2): 319–42.

Seldon, Anthony and Stuart Ball. 1994. *Conservative Century: The Conservative Party Since 1900*. Oxford: Oxford University Press.

Seltzer, Richard A., Jody Newman and Melissa V. Leighton. 1997. *Sex as a Political Variable*. Boulder, CO: Lynne Reinner.

Seyd, Patrick. 1992. 'Labour: the great transformation.' In *Britain at the Polls 1992*, ed. Anthony King. Chatham, NJ: Chatham House Publishers.

Seyd, Patrick. 1997. 'Tony Blair and New Labour.' In *New Labour Triumphs: Britain at the Polls*, ed. Anthony King. Chatham, NJ: Chatham House.

Seyd, Patrick and Paul Whiteley. 1992. *Labour's Grassroots*. Oxford: Clarendon Paperbacks.

Shafer, Byron E. 1991. *The End of Realignment?: Interpreting American Electoral Eras*. Madison, WI: University of Wisconsin Press.

Shaw, Eric. 1994. *The Labour Party Since 1979: Crisis and Transformation*. London: Routledge.

Shaw, Eric. 1996. *The Labour Party Since 1945*. Oxford: Blackwell.

Short, Clare. 1996. 'Women and the Labour Party.' In *Women in Politics*, eds. Joni Lovenduski and Pippa Norris. Oxford: Oxford University Press.

Smith, Martin and Joanne Spear. Eds. 1992. *The Changing Labour Party*. London: Routledge.

Smyth, Gareth. 1991. *Can the Tories Lose?* London: Lawrence & Wishart.

Sopel, Jon. 1995. *Tony Blair: The Moderniser.* London: Bantam.

Sowemimo, Matthew. 1996. 'The Conservative Party and European integration 1989–95.' *Party Politics*, 2: 77–97.

Stannage, Tom. 1980. *Baldwin Thwarts the Opposition: The British General Election of 1935*. London: Croom Helm.

Stimson, James. 1991. *Public Opinion in America: Moods, Cycles and Swings*. Boulder CO: Westview.

Stimson, James, Michael MacKuen and Robert Erikson. 1995. 'Dynamic representation.' *American Political Science Review*, 89(3): 543–65.

Stokes, Donald. 1966. 'Spatial models of party competition.' In *Elections and the Political Order*, eds. Angus Campbell *et al.* New York: Wiley.

Stokes, Donald. 1968. 'Parties and the nationalization of electoral forces.' In *The American Party Systems*, eds. William Chambers and Walter Dean Burnham. New York: Oxford University Press.

Studlar, Donley. 1986. 'Non–white policy preferences, political participation and the political agenda in Britain.' In *Race, Government and Politics in Britain*, eds. Zig Layton–Henry and Paul Rich. London: Macmillan.

Studlar, Donley and Ian McAllister. 1992. 'A changing political agenda? The structure of political attitudes in Britain, 1974–87', *International Journal of Public Opinion Research*, 4: 148–76.

Studlar, Donley, Ian McAllister and Bernadette Hayes. 1998. 'Explaining the gender gap in voting: a cross–national analysis.' *Social Science Quarterly*, 79.

Sundquist, James L. 1973. *Dynamics of the Party System: Alignment and Realignment of Political Parties in the United States*. Washington, DC: The Brookings Institution.

Surridge, Paula, Lindsay Paterson, Alice Brown and David McCrone. 1998. 'The Scottish electorate and the Scottish Parliament.' In *Understanding Constitutional Change: Special Issue of Scottish Affairs*. Edinburgh: University of Edinburgh.

Swaddle, Kevin and Anthony Heath. 1989. 'Official and reported turnout in the British general election of 1987.' *British Journal of Political Science*, 19: 537–70.

Sykes, Alan. 1997. *The Rise and Fall of Liberalism, 1776–1988*. London: Longman.

Taylor, Bridget, Anthony Heath and Peter Lynn. 1996. 'The British Election Panel Study 1992–95: response characteristics and attrition.' *CREST Working Paper* 40.

Teixeira, Ruy A. 1992. *The Disappearing American Voter*. Washington, DC: The Brookings Institute.

Thomassen, Jacques. 1976. 'Party identification as a cross–national concept: its meaning in The Netherlands.' In *Party Identification and Beyond*, eds. Ian Budge *et al.* London: Wiley.

Thomsen, Soren. 1987. *Danish Elections 1920–79: A Logit Approach to Ecological Analysis and Inference*. Aarhus: Politica.

Thomson, Katarina. 1995. 'Working mothers: choice or circumstance?' In *British Social Attitudes: The 12th Report*, eds. Roger Jowell *et al.* Aldershot: Dartmouth/SCPR.

Thomson, Katarina *et al.* 1999. *British Election Studies 1997. Technical Report.* London: SCPR.

Thorpe, Andrew. 1991. *The British General Election of 1931*. Oxford: Oxford University Press.

Tingsten, Herbert L.G. 1937. *Political Behavior: Studies in Election Statistics.* London: P.S. King.

Topf, Richard. 1994. 'Party manifestos.' In *Labour's Last Chance? The 1992 Election and Beyond*, eds. Anthony Heath *et al.* Aldershot: Dartmouth.

Turner, John. 1992. *British Politics and the Great War: Coalition and Conflict 1915–1918.* New Haven, CT: Yale University Press.

van der Eijk, Cees and Mark Franklin. 1996. *Choosing Europe?: The European Electorate and National Politics in the Face of Union.* Ann Arbor, MI: University of Michigan Press.

Verba, Sidney and Norman H. Nie. 1972. *Participation in America.* New York: Harper & Row.

Vincent, John R. 1966. *The Formation of the Liberal Party 1857–1868.* London: Constable.

Wald, Kenneth D. 1983. *Crosses on the Ballot: Patterns of British Voter Alignment since 1885.* Princeton, NJ: Princeton University Press.

Ware, Alan. 1996. *Political Parties and Party Systems.* Oxford: Oxford University Press.

Wattenberg, Martin P. 1996. *The Decline of American Political Parties 1952–1994.* Cambridge, MA: Harvard University Press.

Weakliem, David. 1991. 'The two lefts? Occupation and party choice in France, Italy, and The Netherlands.' *American Journal of Sociology*, 96: 1327–61.

Weakliem, David and Anthony Heath. 1999. 'The secret life of class voting: Britain, France, and the United States since the 1930s.' In *The End of Class Politics? Class Voting in Comparative Context*, ed. Geoffrey Evans. Oxford: Oxford University Press.

Webb, Paul. 1994. 'Party organizational change in Britain: the iron law of centralization?' in R. S. Katz and P. Mair (eds.) *How Parties Organize*. London: Sage.

Welch, Susan and Donley Studlar. 1985. 'The impact of race on political behaviour in Britain.' *British Journal of Political Science*, 15.

Wellhofer, E. Spencer. 1979. 'Strategies for party organization and voter mobilization: Britain, Norway and Argentina.' *Comparative Political Studies*, 12: 169–204.

Werbner, Pnina and Mohammed Anwar. Eds. 1991. *Black and Ethnic Leaderships: The Cultural Dimensions of Political Action.* London: Routledge.

Whiteley, Paul and Patrick Seyd. 1998. 'New Labour – New Grass-Roots Party?' Paper presented at the PSA annual conference, University of Keele.

Whiteley, Paul, Patrick Seyd and Jeremy Richardson. 1994. *True Blues*. Oxford: Oxford University Press.

Whitten, Guy and Harvey Palmer. 1996. 'Heightening comparativists' concern for model choice – voting behaviour in Great Britain and The Netherlands.' *American Journal of Political Science*, 40: 231–60.

Wickham-Jones, Mark. 1995. 'Anticipating social democracy, pre-empting social democracy.' *Politics and Society*, 23: 465–94.

Widfeldt, Anders. 1995. 'Party membership and party representativeness.' In *Citizens and the State*, eds. Hans-Dieter Klingemann and Dieter Fuchs. Oxford: Oxford University Press.

Wieviorka, Michael. 1994. 'Racism in Europe: unity and diversity.' In *Racism, Modernity and Identity on the Western Front*, eds. Ali Rattansi and Sally Westwood. Oxford: Polity Press.

Williamson, Philip. 1992. *National Crisis and National Government: British Politics, the Economy and Empire 1926–1932*. Cambridge: Cambridge University Press.

Wlezien, Christopher. 1995. 'The public as thermostat.' *American Journal of Political Science*, 39(4): 981–1000.

Wlezien, Christopher. 1996. 'Dynamics of representation: the case of US spending on defence.' *British Journal of Political Science*, 26(1): 81–104.

Name Index

Subject Index